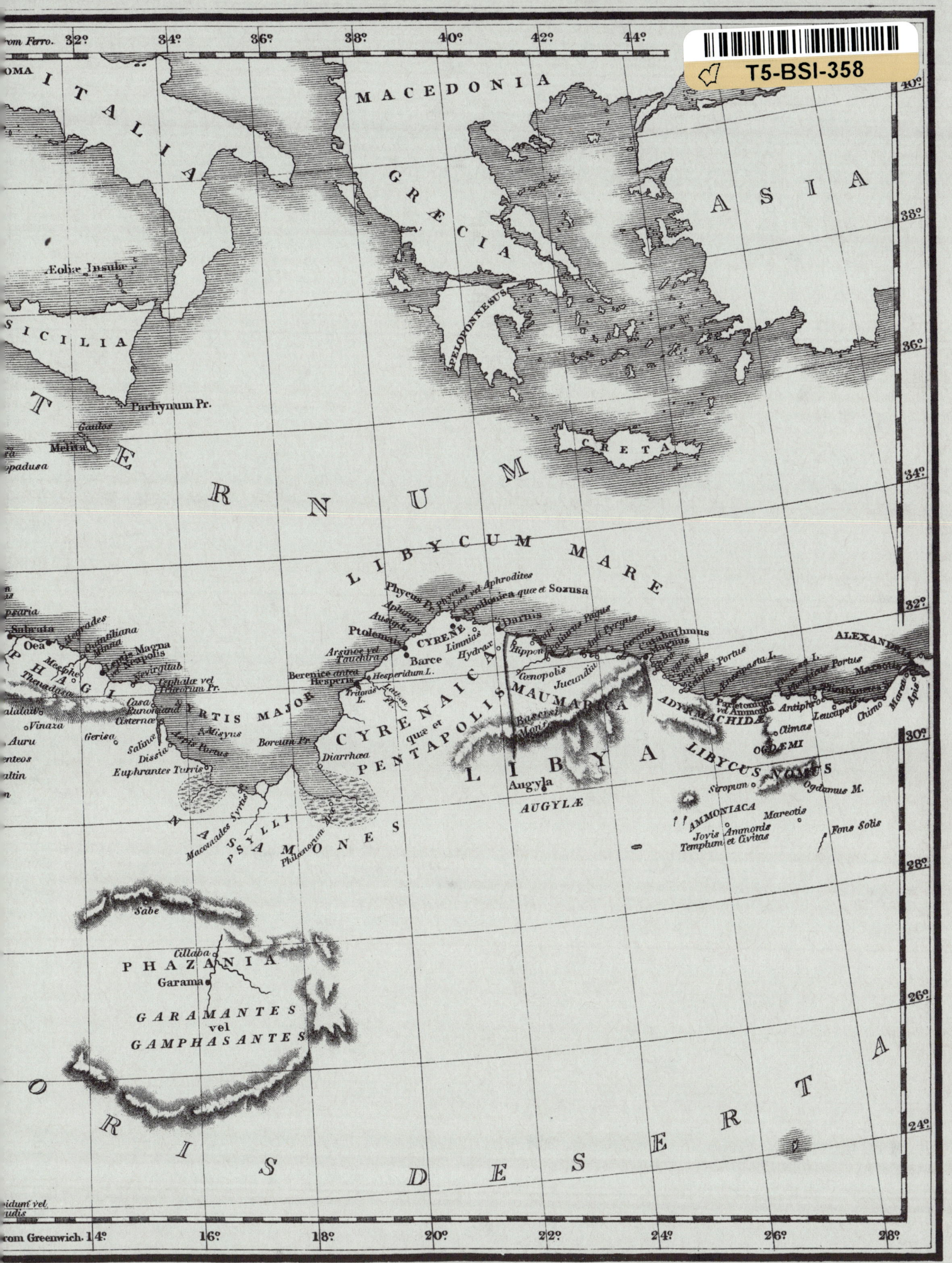

Part I: THE COINS FROM THE SANCTUARY OF DEMETER AND PERSEPHONE

Part II: ATTIC POTTERY FROM THE SANCTUARY OF DEMETER AND PERSEPHONE

University Museum Monograph 97

THE EXTRAMURAL SANCTUARY OF DEMETER AND PERSEPHONE AT CYRENE, LIBYA FINAL REPORTS

Donald White, Series Editor

Volume VI

Part I: THE COINS

T. V. Buttrey

Part II: ATTIC POTTERY

Ian McPhee

Published by

THE UNIVERSITY MUSEUM
University of Pennsylvania
Philadelphia
1997

Design, editing, production
  Publications Department
  The University Museum

Printing
  Science Press
  Ephrata, Pennsylvania

Library of Congress Cataloging-in-Publication Data
(Revised for vol.6)

The Extramural Sanctuary of Demeter and Persephone at
    Cyrene, Libya.

    (University Museum monograph: 52. 56. 67. 97)
    Arabic and English
    Spine title: Cyrene final reports
    Excavations conducted by the University of Pennsylvania, Philadelphia and the Department of Antiquities of the People's Socialist Libyan Arab Jamahiriya.
    Two folded plans in pocket, v. 1.
    Includes bibliographic references and indexes.
    Contents: v. 1. Background and introduction to the excavations / Donald White -- v. 2. The East Greek, island, and Laconian pottery / Gerald P. Schaus -- v. 3. The Site's architecture, its first six hundred years of development / Donald White -- v. 4. Excavations in the Extramural Sanctuary of Demeter and Persephone at Cyrene, Libya.
    1. Demeter (Greek deity)--Cult. 2. Persephone (Greek deity)--Cult. 3. Excavations (Archaeology)--Libya. 4. Sanctuary of Demeter and Persephone (Cyrene). 5. Cyrene (Ancient city). 6. Libya--Antiquities. I. White, Donald, 1935-   II. University of Pennsylvania. University Museum. III. Libya. Maslahat al-Athar. IV. Title. V. Title: Cyrene final reports. VI. Series. VII. Series: University Museum monograph ; 52, etc.
DT239.C9E98   1984   939'.75   83-19866
ISBN 0-934718-50-4 (set)
ISBN 0-934718-51-2 (v. 1)
ISBN 0-934718-55-5 (v. 2)
ISBN 0-934718-71-6 (v. 3)
ISBN 0-934718-50-4 (v. 4)
ISBN 0-924171-17-0 (v. 5)
ISBN 0-924171-48-0 (v. 6)

Copyright © 1998
The University Museum
University of Pennsylvania
Philadelphia
All rights reserved
Printed in the United States of America

Table of Contents

FIGURES viii
PLATES ix
TABLES AND CHARTS xi
MINOR ABBREVIATIONS xiii
BIBLIOGRAPHY xv
EDITOR'S PREFACE xix
PREFACE xxi

PART I: THE COINS FROM THE SANCTUARY OF DEMETER AND PERSEPHONE

I. INTRODUCTION 1
    Greek Coins of Cyrenaica 2
        Period I 3
        Periods II–III 5
        Period IV to Ptolemy Apion 5
    Other Greek Mints 6
    Roman Coinage of Cyrenaica 7
    Roman Empire 7

II. CATALOGUE OF COIN FINDS 9
    Introduction 9
    Catalogue 10
        Mint of Cyrene 10
            Period I ca. 510–475 B.C. 10
            Period II ca. 475–435 B.C. 14
            Period III ca. 435–308 B.C. 15
            Revolt, 313–312 B.C. 16
            Period IV, 308–ca. 250 B.C. 17
            Ptolemy I Soter, ca. 308–305 B.C. 17
            Revolt, ca. 305–300 B.C. 17
            Ptolemy I Soter, ca. 300–282 B.C. 17
            Magas in revolt, ca. 282–261 B.C. 18
            Magas reconciled, ca. 261–258 B.C. 18
            Ptolemy II Philadelphus, ca. 258–250 B.C. 19
            Koinon, ca. 250–246 B.C. 19
            Ptolemy III Euergetes, ca. 246–222 B.C. 19
            Ptolemy IV Philopater-Ptolemy VIII, 222–163 B.C. 20
            Ptolemy VIII Euergetes II as king in Cyrenaica, 163–145 B.C. 21
            Ptolemy VIII Euergetes II as king in Egypt, 145–116 B.C. 21
            Ptolemy IX Soter II, 115–104/1 B.C. 22
            Ptolemy VIII Euergetes II or Ptolemy IX Soter II 23

    Ptolemy Apion, 104/1–96 B.C. 24
    Ptolemy IX Soter II or Ptolemy Apion 25
    Late 2nd–early 1st century B.C. 26
   Mint of Barce 27
    Period II ca. 475–435 B.C. 27
    Period III ca. 435–308 B.C. 27
   Mint of Euesperides 27
    Period II ca. 475–435 B.C. 27
    Period III ca. 325–313 B.C. 27
    Ptolemy I Soter, ca. 300–282 B.C. 27
   Cyrenaica under the Romans 27
    Late 1st century B.C. 27
    1st century A.D. 28
    2nd century A.D. 28
   Greek Coins struck outside Cyrenaica 29
    Thessalonica 29
    Corcyra 29
    Achaean League, mint of Antigoneia 29
    Rhodes 29
    Judaea 29
    Egypt 29
    Uncertain mint 30
   Roman Republic 30
   Roman Empire 30
   Byzantine Empire 32
   Islamic 32
   Kingdom of Italy 32
   Illegible 33

III. THE BRONZE COINAGE OF CYRENAICA 35
  Introduction 35
  The Mint of Cyrene 35
  The Mint of Barce 52
  The Mint of Euesperides and Berenice 54
   Euesperides 54
   Berenice 55
  The Mint of Apollonia 57

APPENDIX. UNPUBLISHED FINDS FROM EUESPERIDES 59
  Introduction 59
  Catalogue 59
   Mint of Cyrene 59
   Mint of Barce 60
   Mint of Euesperides 61
   Cyrenaica under the Romans 61
   Greek Coins struck outside Cyrenaica 62
   Uncertain mint 62

CONCORDANCE OF INVENTORY AND CATALOG NUMBERS 63

PLATES ....follow p. 124

PART II: ATTIC POTTERY FROM THE SANCTUARY OF DEMETER AND PERSEPHONE

- I. INTRODUCTION 69
  - Attic Red-figure 71
    - Chronology 71
    - Shape 71
    - Style 73
    - Iconography 74
  - Attic White-ground 74
  - Attic Plastic Vases 75
  - Relief Ware 75
  - Uncertain Fabric 76
  - Conclusion 76

- II. CATALOGUE 79
  - Attic Red-figure (**1–129**) 79
    - Amphorai (**1–4**) 79
    - Pelikai (**5–14**) 80
    - Lebetes Gamikoi (**15–17**) 81
    - Column-kraters or Stamnoi (**18–30**) 82
    - Column-kraters (**31–36**) 84
    - Calyx-kraters (**37–41**) 85
    - Bell-kraters (**42–52**) 85
    - Kraters of Uncertain Shape (**53–60**) 87
    - Hydriai (**61–77**) 88
    - Oinochoai (**78–80**) 91
    - Lids (**81, 82**) 91
    - Skyphoi (**83–91**) 92
    - Cups (**92–106**) 94
    - Stemless Cup (**107**) 96
    - Cups or Stemless Cups (**108, 109**) 97
    - Plates (**110–112**) 97
    - "Closed" Shapes (**113–129**) 98
  - Attic Bilingual and Black-figure Epinetra (**130–132**) 100
  - Attic White-ground Alabastron (**133**) 101
  - Attic Plastic Vases (**134–136**) 101
  - Relief-vase (**137**) 102
  - Uncertain Fabric (**138**) 102

- INDEX OF FIND-SPOTS 103

- ARABIC SUMMARY OF PARTS I AND II *translated* by Jamal el Harami 111

- PLATES .... follow p. 124

Figures

Figure 1. Map 70
Figure 2. Profile of **41** 85

Plates

PART I: THE COINS FROM THE SANCTUARY OF DEMETER AND PERSEPHONE

Plate 1. Mint of Cyrene (**1–25**)
Plate 2. Mint of Cyrene (**26–56**)
Plate 3. Mint of Cyrene (**57–80**)
Plate 4. Mint of Cyrene (**81–108**)
Plate 5. Mint of Cyrene (**111–158**)
Plate 6. Mint of Cyrene (**166–216**)
Plate 7. Mint of Cyrene (**218–278**)
Plate 8. Mint of Cyrene (**281–410**)
Plate 9. Mint of Cyrene (**415–673**)
Plate 10. Mint of Barce (**726** and **727**), Euesperides (**728–736**), Cyrenaica Under the Romans (**737–759**)
Plate 11. Greek Coins Struck Outside Cyrenaica (**760A–773**), Roman Empire (**778–795**), Byzantine (**803**), Islamic (**805**)
Plate 12. Appendix: Unpublished Finds from Euesperides

PART II: ATTIC POTTERY FROM THE SANCTUARY OF DEMETER AND PERSEPHONE

Plate 13. Amphorai (**2–4**)
Plate 14. Pelikai (**5–9**)
Plate 15. Pelikai (**10–14**)
Plate 16. Lebetes Gamikoi (**15–17**)
Plate 17. Column-Kraters or Stamnoi (**18–20**)
Plate 18. Column-Kraters or Stamnoi (**21A–23**)
Plate 19. Column-Kraters or Stamnoi (**24–28**)
Plate 20. Column-Kraters or Stamnoi (**29–33**)
Plate 21. Column-Kraters (**34–36**)
Plate 22. Column-Kraters (**37–39**)
Plate 23. Bell-Kraters (**42–46**)
Plate 24. Bell-Kraters (**47A–E**)
Plate 25. Bell-Krater (**48A-G**)
Plate 26. Bell-Kraters (**49–52**)
Plate 27. Kraters (**53–58**)
Plate 28. Hydriai (**61–62**)
Plate 29. Hydriai (**63–65**)
Plate 30. Hydriai (**66–68**)
Plate 31. Hydriai (**69–73**)
Plate 32. Hydriai (**74–77**)
Plate 33. Oinochoai (**78–80**)
Plate 34. Lids (**81–82**)
Plate 35. Skyphoi (**83–86**)

Plate 36. Skyphos (**87A–M**)
Plate 37. Skyphos (**87N–T**)
Plate 38. Skyphoi (**88–91**)
Plate 39. Cups (**92–94**)
Plate 40. Cups (**95–103**)
Plate 41. Cups or Stemless Cups (**105–107**)
Plate 42. Cups or Stemless Cups, and Plates (**108–112**)
Plate 43. "Closed" Shapes (**113–116**)
Plate 44. "Closed" Shapes (**117–121**)
Plate 45. "Closed" Shapes (**122–124**)
Plate 46. "Closed" Shapes (**125–129**)
Plate 47. Epinetra (**130–132**)
Plate 48. Alabastron, Plastic and Relief Vases, and Uncertain Fabric (**133–138**)

Tables and Charts

PART I: THE COINS FROM THE SANCTUARY OF DEMETER AND PERSEPHONE

Table I ....foldout between 48 and 49
Table II 53
Table III ....foldout between 56 and 57
Table IV 58

PART II: ATTIC POTTERY FROM THE SANCTUARY OF DEMETER AND PERSEPHONE

Chart 1. Attic Red-Figure from the Sanctuary of Demeter and Kore at Cyrene 77
Chart 2. Attic Red-Figure from Cyrenaica 77

Minor Abbreviations

ANS	American Numismatic Society
diam.	diameter
H.	Height
W.	Width
Th.	Thickness
Max. dim.	Maximum dimension
est.	estimated
l.	left
obv.	obverse
Pl./pl.	Plate
Pt.	Ptolemy
r.	right
rev.	reverse

Bibliography

EXCAVATIONS AND FINDS

In this section are gathered all the publications of excavation and find coins from Cyrenaica.

John Boardman and John Hayes, *Excavations at Tocra 1963–1965* II. British School of Archaeology at Athens, supplementary vol. 10 ([London] 1973) 102, 123.

R. C. Bond and J. M. Swales, "Surface Finds of Coins from the City of Euesperides," *Libya Antiqua* 2 (1965) 91–101.

T. V. Buttrey, "The Coins," in *Apollonia, the Port of Cyrene: Excavations by The University of Michigan, 1965–67*, J. H. Humphrey ed. Supplements to Libya Antiqua 4 (Tripoli 1976) 335–360.

T.V. Buttrey, "The Norton Excavation Coins," in *Apollonia, the Port of Cyrene: Excavations by The University of Michigan, 1965–67*, J.H. Humphrey ed. Supplements to Libya Antiqua 4 (Tripoli 1976) 361–370. [The Norton coins included random purchases.]

L. Gasperini, in *L'Agorà di Cirene* I, by Sandro Stucchi (Rome 1964) 45–46. [On offerings found outside Oikos 2.]

John F. Healy, "The Coins," in *Cyrenaican Expeditions of the University of Manchester 1955–57*, Alan Rowe ed. (Manchester 1959) 29–32.

Carl H. Kraeling, *Ptolemais, City of the Libyan Pentapolis*, University of Chicago, Oriental Institute Publications 90 (Chicago 1962) 263–269.

R. Reece, "Coins," in *Excavations at Sidi Khrebish, Benghazi (Berenice)*, Supplements to Libya Antiqua 5 (Tripoli 1977) 229–232.

BIBLIOGRAPHIC ABBREVIATIONS

This series of reports adopts the standard abbreviations used by the *American Journal of Archaeology*.[1] The works listed below are supplementary.

Alfieri, *Spina*	N. Alfieri, *Spina, Museo archeologico nazionale di Ferrara* (Bologna 1979).
Apollonia	T. V. Buttrey, "The Coins," in *Apollonia, the Port of Cyrene*. See above.
Arias, Hirmer, Shefton	P. Arias, M. Hirmer, and B. Shefton, *A History of Greek Vase-painting* (London 1963).
Asyut	Martin Price and Nancy Waggoner, *Archaic Greek Silver Coinage, the "Asyut" Hoard* (London 1975).
Becker	R.-M. Becker, *Formen Attischer Peliken von der Pioniergruppe bis zum Beginn der Frühklassik* (Zurich 1977).
BMC	E.S.G. Robinson, *Catalogue of the Greek Coins of Cyrenaica* [in the British Museum] (London 1927).
BMCRE	Harold Mattingly et al., *Coins of the Roman Empire in the British Museum* (London 1923–).

---

1. The formula used for abbreviating the references to the *CVA* is as follows:
CVA Oxford 2 [9], pl. 53 [417], 3 = *Corpus Vasorum Antiquorum* Oxford, fascicule 2 [Great Britain fascicule 9], plate 53 [Great Britain plate 417], figure 3.

BMCCar	Barclay V. Head, *Catalogue of the Greek Coins of Caria, Cos, Rhodes, &c.* [in the British Museum] (London 1897).		G. Barker, J. Lloyd, and R. Reynolds, eds., *Cyrenaica in Antiquity*, Society for Libyan Studies Occasional Paper I: BAR International Series 236 (Oxford 1985) 205–217.
BMCGal	Warwick Wroth, *Catalogue of the Greek Coins of Galatia, Cappadocia, and Syria* [in the British Museum] (London 1899).	DO	Philip Grierson, *Catalogue of the Byzantine Coins in the Dumbarton Oaks Collection and the Whittemore Collection* (Washington, DC 1968).
BMCMoh	Stanley Lane Poole, *Coins of the Mohammedan Dynasties in the British Museum* (London 1876).	Gericke, *Gefässdarstellungen*	H. Gericke, *Gefässdarstellungen auf griechischen Vasen* (Berlin 1970).
BMCPal	George Francis Hill, *Catalogue of the Greek Coins of Palestine* [in the British Museum] (London 1914).	GettyMus Greek Vases	*Greek Vases in the J. Paul Getty Museum* 3 (Malibu 1986).
BMCPtol	Reginald Stuart Poole, *Catalogue of Greek Coins, the Ptolemies, Kings of Egypt* [in the British Museum] (London 1883).	IGCH	Margaret Thompson et al., *An Inventory of Greek Coin Hoards* (New York 1973).
BMCSicily	Reginald Stuart Poole, *A Catalogue of Greek Coins in the British Museum. Sicily* (London 1876).	Langlotz, *GVW*	E. Langlotz, *Griechische Vasen in Würzburg* (Munich 1932).
BMCThes	Percy Gardner, *Catalogue of Greek Coins, Thessaly to Aetolia* [in the British Museum] (London 1883).	Laronde	André Laronde, *Cyréne et la Libye Hellénistique* (Paris 1987).
Bond and Swales	R.C. Bond and J.M. Swales, "Surface Finds of Coins from the City of Euesperides." See above.	Metzger, *Représentations*	H. Metzger, *Les représentations dans la céramique attique du IVe siècle* (Paris 1951).
Bothmer, Amazons	D. von Bothmer, *Amazons in Greek Art* (Oxford 1957).	Milne	J.G. Milne, *Catalogue of Alexandrian Coins* [in the Ashmolean Museum, Oxford] (Oxford 1933, reprinted 1971 with Supplement by Colin M. Kraay).
Burn	L. Burn, *The Meidias Painter* (Oxford 1987).		
Buttrey, "Roman Coinage"	T. V. Buttrey, "Roman Coinage of the Cyrenaica," in *Studies in Honour of Philip Grierson*, C.N.L. Brooke et al. eds. (Cambridge 1983) 23–46.	Moon and Berge, *Midwestern*	W. Moon and L. Berge, *Greek Vasepainting in Midwestern Collections* (Chicago 1979).
Buttrey, "Crete and Cyrenaica"	T. V. Buttrey, "Crete and Cyrenaica," in *The Coinage of the Roman World in the Late Republic*, A.M. Burnett and M.H. Crawford eds. British Archaeological Reports International Series 326 (Oxford 1987).	Moore, *Final Reports III*	M. Moore, *The Extramural Sanctuary of Demeter and Persephone at Cyrene, Libya, Final Reports* III, Part 2: *Attic Black Figure and Black Glazed Pottery* (Philadelphia 1987).
		Mørkholm	Otto Mørkholm, "Cyrene and Ptolemy I," *Chiron* 10 (1980) 145–159.
CB II, III	L. Caskey and J. Beazley, *Attic Vase Painting in the Museum of Fine Arts, Boston* II (Oxford 1954) and III (Oxford 1963).	Naville	Lucien Naville, *Les Monnaies d'or de la Cyrénaïque* (Geneva 1951).
		Newell	Edward T. Newell, *Miscellanea Numismatica: Cyrene to India*. American Numismatic Society, Numismatic Notes and Monographs 82 (New York 1938).
Crawford	Michael H. Crawford, *Roman Republican Coinage* (Cambridge 1974).	Norton	T.V. Buttrey, "The Norton Excavation Coins," in *Apollonia, the Port of Cyrene*. See above.
Cyrenaica in Antiquity	F. Elrashedy, "Attic Imported Pottery in Classical Cyrenaica," in		

Peredolskaya	A. Peredolskaya, *Krasnofigurnye Attischeskie Vazy* (Leningrad 1967).	Smith, *Lewismaler*	H.R.W. Smith, *Der Lewismaler* (Leipzig 1939).
RIC	Harold Mattingly et al., *Roman Imperial Coinage* (London 1926–1994).	*SNG Cop*	*Sylloge Nummorum Graecorum: The Royal Collection of Coins and Medals, Danish National Museum* (Copenhagen 1942–1979).
Robinson, *NC*	E.S.G. Robinson, "Greek Coins Found in the Cyrenaica," *Numismatic Chronicle*[6] 4 (1944) 105–113.	*SNG Milano*	*Sylloge Nummorum Graecorum. Italia: Milano* 13.1 (Egypt), 14 (Cyrenaica) (Milan 1989).
Samuel	Alan E. Samuel, *Ptolemaic Chronology*. Münchener Beiträge zur Papyrusforschung und Antiken Rechtsgeschichte 43 (Munich 1962).	Svoronos	J. Svoronos, Τὰ νομίσματα τοῦ κράτους τῶν Πτολεμαίων (Athens 1904–1908).
		Sydenham	Edward A. Sydenham, *The Coinage of Caesarea in Cappadocia* (London 1933).
Schefold, *UKV*	K. Schefold, *Untersuchungen zu den Kertscher Vasen* (Berlin 1934).	White, *Final Reports I*	D. White, *The Extramural Sanctuary of Demeter and Persephone at Cyrene, Libya, Final Reports* I: *Background and Introduction to the Excavations* (Philadelphia 1984).
Shapiro, *Southern*	H.A. Shapiro, *Art, Myth, and Culture: Greek Vases from Southern Collections* (New Orleans 1981).		
Sidi Khrebish	R. Reece, "Coins," in *Excavations at Sidi Khrebish*. See above.		
Simon and Hirmer	E. Simon, M. and A. Hirmer, *Die griechischen Vasen* (Munich 1976).		

Editor's Preface

Both of the studies presented here were originally intended to be published simultaneously with volume V, which appeared in 1993. Technical problems in producing a text on the coins which presents unusual problems for the printer, together with other circumstances beyond the control of the authors, have regretably led to their delay. I want in particular to thank Ian McPhee for his patience and forbearance and wish to stress that the absence of references to scholarly activity since 1990 is the responsibility of the editor and publishers. At the same time the reader should be aware that many of the acknowledgements included as part of Volume V apply equally here but have not been duplicated in order to avoid unnecessary repetition.[1]

Both authors were able to visit Cyrene in 1978, the project's last season devoted entirely to excavation, and McPhee was able to return for a brief second visit during the 1981 study season, which marks the last time that the Pennsylvania expedition was active at Cyrene before the collapse in relations between Libya and the United States brought about a premature end to the project. At the time the stresses involved in travel in and out of Libya were considerable, and the University of Pennsylvania expedition owes a real debt of gratitude to both of our authors for undertaking their studies under what were less than ideal circumstances.

Coins, for reasons that do not always make sense, are often treated by field excavators as more reliable chronological indexes than other classes of artifacts. This always makes their discovery a welcome event, especially when they are silver or gold which tend to survive in the ground in a more recognizable state than their bronze counterparts. It shall be seen that an unusually large number of local silver issues came to light between 1969 and 1979, with important ramifications for the understanding of regional coin production, particularly before the Hellenistic period, that are discussed in the ensuing text.[2] But the large majority were bronze, which were normally both worn and thoroughly corroded at the time of their recovery as well as heavily stereotypical in appearance, at least in the eye of the non-specialist. This meant that, in addition to requiring considerable pains to conserve,[3] their identification remained often hit or miss until Buttrey was able to undertake his study, the essential elements of which were available in time for inclusion in volume V. As a class of objects the coins have therefore had an important impact on dating the sanctuary's various architectural components,[4] as well as elsewhere on the controversial issue of the site's earthquake destructions.[5]

The Red Figure pottery does not have quite the same chronological relevance as the coins but does on occasion contribute to the dating of archaeological contexts. Its often high quality and interesting variety of shapes has already generated commentary elsewhere in addition to what McPhee offers here.[6] At the same time the reader should be aware that the

---

1 D. White, *University Museum Monograph* 76: *The Extramural Sanctuary of Demeter and Persephone at Cyrene, Libya. Final Reports* III: *The Site's Architecture. Its First Six Hundred Years of Development* (Philadelphia 1993) xxv-xxvi.

2 As well as discussed briefly elsewhere. See T.V. Buttrey, "The Coins and the Cult," *Expedition* 34 (1992) 59-63.

3 See T. Fuller, "Conservation of Objects," *University Museum Monograph* 66: *The Extramural Sanctuary of Demeter and Persephone at Cyrene, Libya. Final Reports* III (Philadelphia 1987) 8-10, pl. 9, A-D.

4 D. White, *University Museum Monograph* 76: *The Extramural Sanctuary of Demeter and Persephone at Cyrene, Libya. Final Reports* V: *The Site's Architecture. Its First Six Hundred Years of Development* (Philadelphia 1993) passim, esp. 187-95

5 D. White "Fresh Reverberations from Cyrene's Later Antique Earthquakes," *Università di Roma* 29: *Studi Miscellanei: Scritti di antichità in onore di Sandro Stucchi* 317-25.

6 G. Schaus, "Pottery from the Sanctuary — A Question of Function," *Expedition* 34 (1992) 32-33.

site's Attic Black Figure has already been the subject of an earlier study.[7]

A final practical note: following initial excavation, the site's 834 coins were catalogued as individual finds. In practical terms this means that a record exists of their three-dimensional location within each separate archaeological context, defined throughout by "area," "trench," and "stratum."[8] Following a different procedure, none of the Attic Red Figure pieces were catalogued individually unless they were either fully intact, inscribed or carried traces of ancient repairs. They are stored instead in numbered wooden boxes organized by area, trench and stratum. The same system has been used for the site's imported Archaic and Hellenistic/Roman fine wares.[9] In an important move to improve the preservation and security of the site's objects Dr. Fadel Ali Mohammed, the Director-General of Antiquities, announced in December of 1996 that he plans to move all the objects, including the boxed pottery whose paper labels have been eaten by vermin to a regretably large extent since 1981, from their present location in the old military garage facility and storage rooms behind the conservation laboratory to safer surroundings in the near future.

All that remains is to express our deep gratitude to Dr. Fadel Ali and his staff for their unassisted efforts to safeguard over the past 16 years not only the objects excavated from the Wadi Bel Gadir sanctuary but also the site itself, a record of dedication to the material remains of the past that can only represent an *auspicium melioris aevi* still to come.

Donald White
1997

---

[7] M. Moore, "Attic Black Figure and Black Glazed Pottery," *University Museum Monograph* 66: *The Extramural Sanctuary of Demeter and Persephone at Cyrene, Libya. Final Reports* III (Philadelphia 1987) i-52.

[8] "Area" refers to location by gridsquare, 'trench" the individual test opening within each gridsquare context, and "stratum" the specific layer or deposit within each trench. See D. White, *University Museum Monograph* 52: *The Extramural Sanctuary of Demeter and Persephone at Cyrene, Libya. Final Reports I: Background and Introduction to the Excavations* (Philadelphia 1984) 1, 56.

[9] *Final Reports* II, xxi and *Final Reports* III, ix.

Preface

A decade has passed since I was first given the opportunity to catalogue and to publish the red-figure pottery unearthed during the excavations in the Sanctuary of Demeter and Persephone at Cyrene. Originally it was intended to combine the red-figure with the black-figure pottery in one volume of the final reports, but it has not been possible to carry out this plan, for the study of the red-figure has taken longer to complete than was expected. For this delay, I alone am responsible, and I apologize.

In order to examine and to record the fragments of red-figure, I made two brief trips to Cyrene (Shahat): the first was in January, 1978, and the second in August, 1981, during the final study-season at the site.

Many people have assisted me during my research both in Cyrene and in Australia. My principal debt is to Donald White: as Director of the excavations, he invited me to undertake this study, and in the years since he has always been ready with advice and encouragement. Without his patient help my work in Libya would have proved impossible. When I visited Cyrene in the winter of 1978, I was alone and could have achieved nothing without the unfaltering cooperation and constant kindness of members of the Libyan Department of Antiquities in Benghazi, Cyrene, and Apollonia. In most cases I never knew their names, but I can at least express my sincere gratitude to Ess. Breyik Attiye, Controller of Antiquities at Cyrene, who facilitated my work in every way.

At various times other people have aided me in one way or another: Miss Rosalind Wood, Dr. Elizabeth Pemberton, Dr. Donna Kurtz, Dr. Adrienne Lezzi-Hafter, Dr. Sally Roberts, Professor Martin Robertson, and Dr. Henry Immerwahr. They all have my deep gratitude. Finally, I would like to record the generous assistance that I received from the Australian Government which financed part of my visit to Cyrene in 1981 through a grant from the Australian Research Grants Scheme.

Since writing the above words, I have been able to carry out some revisions to my original text. I am especially grateful to Dr. Elfriede Knauer and to the late Dr. Kyle M. Phillips, Jr., who read the manuscript and made important suggestions.

Ian McPhee
January, 1989

Note to Preface

This catalogue of the red-figure pottery from the Sanctuary of Demeter and Persephone at Cyrene was completed late in 1986 and revised early in 1989. In the past decade many works have appeared that are relevant to this study, but I have not undertaken any revision of the text, for the alterations would have been extensive and would have delayed the publication even further. I would, however, point out that the work on the Greek pottery from the Sanctuary of Demeter and Kore at Corinth, mentioned in note 22 on p. 78 has appeared: Elizabeth G. Pemberton, *Corinth* XVIII, i, *The Sanctuary of Demeter and Kore, The Greek Pottery* (Princeton 1989).

Ian McPhee
June, 1997

Part I
The Coins from the Sanctuary of Demeter and Persephone

I

Introduction

The interpretation of excavation coins involves several numismatic and archaeological problems simultaneously. First, it has to be assumed, and usually is obvious from the evidence, that the finds are radically skewed toward the smallest and least valuable coins. In the absence of hoards, which might contain anything, the (random) finds will normally include no gold and very little silver, for the obvious reason that people do not lose, or do not allow to remain lost, coins of significant value. We have it on good authority that the frugal housewife who has lost a silver penny lights the lamp, sweeps the floor, and searches zealously until she has found it, whereat she summons the neighbors to rejoice with her.[1] No one in antiquity went about scattering gold or silver coins—or even bronze—carelessly over the ground. The more valuable coins were more earnestly sought if lost, and easier to see; the least valuable were of bronze, which can be difficult to spot against the soil or floors of beaten earth. Even the bronze finds will be skewed, because it is easier to notice the loss of the larger modules, and they are easier to find when sought, so that they were less frequently abandoned. In sum, excavation coins do not provide a representative view of the currency.

Next are two problems that intertwine, the answer to each depending to an extent on the other. On the one hand, a sufficiently large body of excavation coins can be studied as evidence for the history and characteristics of that part of the monetary circulation from which they derive, provided that the nature of the site has not distorted the finds. On the other hand, the numismatic evidence can be of signal importance in the interpretation of the site, provided that the evidence can be independently shown to be characteristic (or not) of the circulation.

In our case, the Demeter Sanctuary attracted for centuries the attendance of the faithful, whose dedications included coined money. The numismatic evidence is virtually continuous from the late sixth century B.C. to the middle of the fourth century A.D., so that we could expect the finds to provide a good survey of the money in use in Cyrene for almost a millennium. At the same time the find coins may reflect intensity of worship rather than of monetary circulation, and the particular denominations present may be of the kind especially appropriate to religious dedication: the prudent worshiper balances expense against benefits anticipated. As will be seen below, we are fortunate to have evidence for the silver of the sixth and fifth centuries B.C., where the relative frequency of drachms and hemidrachms may suggest that they were considered the most appropriate denominations to attract divine favor.

Finally, as archaeological evidence a find coin strictly speaking provides only a *terminus post quem*. Coins are lost sporadically, and individual specimens can survive centuries of use. The recovery of a large number of specimens of a single issue usually indicates that the issue itself was large, but the losses may have occurred over a long period of time and need not reflect intensity of local activity at any one moment of time.

Mindful of these restraints, we can turn to the coins discovered during the excavations of the Demeter Sanctuary at Cyrene between 1969 and 1978. The interpretation of the finds will involve some historical speculations, particularly in Chapter III, on Cyrenaican bronze, and there are historical problems that might have implications for the coinage but that cannot be dissected here. These are thoroughly discussed in Laronde's excellent *Cyrène et la Libye*

The author gratefully acknowledges the assistance of R. A. Hazzard and Catharine C. Lorber, and the support of the Rackham School of Graduate Studies, University of Michigan, through a Faculty Research Grant.

1. *Luke* 15:8–9.

Hellénistique.

The coins found number 834, the largest body of coins from a controlled excavation in Cyrenaica yet to be published. No hoards were identified archaeologically; in fact only two hoards of Greek coins from Cyrenaica have ever been published.[2] All the finds were random in the sense that they occurred in the soil as if they had been casual losses, but it is clear that we have the remains of at least one ancient silver deposit, and it is not impossible that some of the bronze, too, represents deposits that were scattered over time.

The finds are largely archaic, classical, and Ptolemaic coins struck at Cyrene, with a very few from the other Cyrenaican mints. Greek mints abroad, notably the Ptolemaic mint of Alexandria, contribute almost nothing. This is consonant with other Cyrenaican excavations. If the bronze circulation was almost entirely self-contained in Greek times, we might nonetheless assume that silver and gold from foreign mints were in use. In this case we have the evidence of the dozens of pieces of archaic and early classical silver that probably derive from a broken deposit. They include not a single piece struck outside of Cyrenaica, suggesting that at this period the precious metal circulation too was largely self-contained.

Excavation Coins

	Gold	Silver	Bronze
Greek of Cyrenaica			
mint of Cyrene	4	108	613
mint of Barce		2	
mint of Euesperides		1	8
Roman 1st cent. B.C./			
1st cent. A.D. of Cyrenaica			7
Roman 2nd cent. A.D. of Cyrenaica			17
Total coins of Cyrenaica	4	111	645
other Greek mints		1	7
Roman Republican		1	
Roman Imperial		1	26
Roman provincial[3]			6
Byzantine			2
Islamic			1
Modern			3
illegible			26
TOTAL COINS	4	114	716

Greek Coins of Cyrenaica

The broad chronological distribution of the Greek coins of Cyrenaica is as follows:

Greek Coins of Cyrenaica

	Gold	Silver	Bronze
6th–5th cent. B.C.		103	
4th cent. B.C.	4	4	73
3rd/early 1st cent. B.C.		4	548

The most obvious features of the Cyrenaican issues are the large number of bronze coins, relatively low-value pieces of the sort customary in excavations, combined with the unusual and disproportionate amount of early precious metal, quite abnormal for excavations producing no hoards. The silver raises archaeological and monetary questions that are worth considering; the bronze is sufficiently plentiful to permit a separate look at Cyrenaican bronze in general and its historical context, for which see Chapter III, following the Catalogue.

To begin with the silver, any consideration of Cyrenaican coins must be based on the magnificent work by E. S. G. Robinson, *Catalogue of the Greek Coins of Cyrenaica* [in the British Museum] (hereafter *BMC*). It is clear from his survey that the Demeter Sanctuary finds in silver by no means represent a cross-section of Cyrenaican coinage, for they are almost entirely early, are relatively rich in issues not common today, and include some new varieties. It is instructive to compare the material in the *BMC* with the finds. The *BMC* is a deliberate compilation of varieties, but it illustrates the general availability of the issues. The spread of silver denominations in Robinson's first four periods, sixth to mid-third centuries, is as follows (ignoring for the moment the distinction of Attic, Phoenician, and Rhodian standards, and the problem of denomination of a few small pieces):

---

2. *IGCH* 1633, archaic silver; 1686, Hellenistic bronze.

3. That is, coinage of the Imperial period attributed to local mints, conventionally called "Greek Imperial."

Distribution of Silver Denominations in the *BMC*

	Period I	II	III	IV-Civic	Total	%
tetradrachm	31	11	65	3	110	28
didrachm	6	1	18	125	150	38
drachm	28	29	10	1	68	17
hemidrachm	22	9	4	8	43	11
trihemiobol	1	2	6		9	2
obol	4	2	3	7	16	4
hemiobol	1	1			2	1
Total	93	55	106	144	398	
%	23	14	27	36		100

The profiles of the first three periods are similar in that the larger denominations are generally the more frequently cited. Tetradrachms and didrachms account for 52% of the entries. The obvious exceptions are the predominance of drachms in Period II, and the low incidence of didrachms, which were not struck in large quantities in these periods. By contrast, Period IV shows a sharp drop in tetradrachms and drachms, while the dramatic increase in the didrachm causes that denomination to dominate not only Period IV but every denomination in every period.

This is the distribution of the same issues in the Demeter Sanctuary finds:

Distribution of Silver Denominations in the Demeter Sanctuary

	Period I	II	III	IV-Civic	Total	%
tetradrachm	15				15	14
didrachm	2	1			3	3
drachm	29	5	1		35	32
hemidrachm	30	5			35	32
trihemiobol			1		1	1
obol	6	3	4		13	12
hemiobol	3			1	4	4
tetartemorion	2				2	2
Total	87	14	6	1	108	
%	81	13	6	1		100

Chronologically, the emphasis is early; the relatively uncommon archaic and early classical silver of Period I forms the bulk (81%) of our silver finds. There is about the same proportion of finds dated to Period II as in the *BMC*, but the rich issues of civic tetradrachms and didrachms of the later fifth and fourth centuries, Periods III and IV, are completely unpresented.

Period I, 510–475 B.C. (1–87)

The peculiarities of the silver coin finds cannot be explained by casual and random loss, even though the individual pieces were found scattered in the earth. Most of the coins date to Period I; many are of the largest denomination, least agreeably lost (i.e., tetradrachms), whose presence in a hoard would be easily explicable, but not in random debris. Certain varieties are duplicated while others are wanting. The smaller denominations of drachm and hemidrachm appear to be overrepresented. Finally, there are just so many of them. Such large-scale silver losses are never found in excavations.

The explanation must be archaeological, not monetary, namely, that the silver coins of the sixth and the first half of the fifth centuries B.C. derive from an unrecovered deposit (or possibly more than one), broken up owing to earthquake or land-slip. In the archaeological context of a sanctuary one thinks of a votive *stips* rather than a private hoard. Some 31 pieces were concentrated at D12/13, and another 21 at D15/16: these must represent sacred dedications of money. The irregular donations of the faithful would also explain the curious composition of the group, extending as it does over several decades, richest in the middle denominations, yet sporadic in its representation of the large number of issues that must have been struck serially during that period. It is not possible to say with any precision when the *stips* closed, and of course this kind of deposit might well have remained open and been added to from time to time. The distribution of issues suggests that it ran down into Period II, roughly to the middle of the fifth century B.C. Our finds from Periods III and IV are so sparse as to suggest that they actually were random losses.

TETRADRACHMS

In the Catalogue the Period I finds are arranged in four groups, which might represent the order of die development: (1) A] with obverse silphium fruit (not found in the excavations) or plant, and reverse incuse punch; B] as A with fruit, and with the addition of an obverse figuration above; C] as B, but figuration between two fruits; and (2) with reverse type. This is a convenient arrangement, but the evidence is lacking to prove that it is chronologically correct. At the Cyrene mint it is possible that some reverse punches are actually later than some reverse types.[4] Within the groups the order of individual pieces is arbitrary, for there, too, the evidence is still thin. Comparison of the find material, the Asyut hoard, and the museum specimens collected in the *BMC* shows how unsatisfactory our present state of knowledge is. It also shows where the composition of both our finds and the Asyut hoard is skewed.

Period I: Tetradrachms[5]

	BMC	Asyut	Demeter Sanctuary
(1) with reverse incuse			
A. without symbol			
obv. fruit	2		
obv. fruits	1		
obv. leaf	1		
obv. top of plant			2
obv. plant	4	5	5
B. & C. with symbol			
obv. fruit:			
Dolphin			1
Gazelle			3
Lion	1		
obv. plant:			
Bird's head	1		
Gazelle	1		
"Root"[6]	1		
obv. fruits and plant:			
Lion	2		
(2) with reverse type			
Cyrene/Ammon	3		
Ammon		2	
Ammon (Barce?)[7]		8	2
Heracles & nymph	1		
Dolphins	4	6	
Eagle's head	2	5	
Gazelle	3		
Gorgoneion	1	5	2
Lion's head	1		
Pegasus	1		
Barce Bull	2		
Barce Dolphins		11	

The *BMC* listings are a compendium of examples gathered from a number of major collections. Given the scarcity of all early Cyrenaican issues, it is not likely that Robinson's selection was unrepresentative, although he may have forborne to list repetitions of types already known to him. At the least he presented a survey of the varieties as extensive as then possible. The Demeter Sanctuary finds fall more commonly in the first group, less so in the second. The numbers of coins from all three sources that fall into group (1)-A are comparable, though the Cyrene finds contribute two examples of a type unrepresented in either the *BMC* or Asyut. In groups (1)-B & C the *BMC* gives 5 varieties with various obverse symbols; the Demeter Sanctuary finds include none of these, but examples of 2 new obverse symbol issues of comparable shape (**57–60**). Asyut has no coins in these groups at all. In group (2), with reverse types, the representation from both the *BMC* and Asyut is considerably stronger: our finds produced only 4 pieces compared with 18 in the *BMC* and 37 from Asyut; and none of ours derives from the commonest varieties, the issues with 2 dolphins of Cyrene and Barce.

It is clear that the full range of tetradrachm types has yet to be established, and that both the Demeter Sanctuary finds and the Asyut hoard represent only discrete slices from the archaic Cyrenaican coinage. These are not just *disiecta membra*, for the coins form little groups within the type or variety. Two of the tetradrachm find coins in group (1)-A are die-linked (**4, 5**). In the Asyut hoard, 3 tetradrachms without reverse type are from the same pair of dies; the 2 pieces of /Ammon are die-linked; all 8 pieces of /Ammon from Barce (?) are from the same pair of dies; 3 pieces with /dolphins are die-linked, and another 2 are from the same pair of dies; the 11 /dolphins from Barce are die-linked in two groups[8]; of the 5 /eagle pieces, 4 are from the same pair of dies; and the 5 /Gorgoneion coins are all die-linked.

Even the material that is not die-linked is associated. Thus the excavations produced no fewer than three examples of the tetradrachm with gazelle symbol (**57–59**), a variety unknown to the *BMC*; that these are not die-linked suggests an issue of some size. Or again, an /Ammon tetradrachm (**72**) is accompanied in the excavations by a didrachm of identical style (**73**), also hitherto unknown.

The material in the Asyut hoard must have left Cyrenaican circulation in several compact lots at different times; many of the coins show signs of wear, yet had not been dispersed, so that they probably circulated locally rather than in Cyrenaica before hoarding. The distribution of the find material from

---

4. *Asyut* p. 114.

5. *BMC* xviii–xxi, xxii–xxiv, clxvi, 1, 3–5, 91, 123; *Asyut* 818–59; Demeter Sanctuary cat. nos. **1–7, 57–60, 69–72**.

6. *BMC* 2d, more likely a leaping animal.

7. Possible attribution to Barce is suggested in *Asyut* p. 112.

8. The die-link indicated between *Asyut* 848 and 849 is, I believe, incorrect.

the sanctuary *stips* may be a different matter because we have only a selection of indeterminate size. The discovery of more tetradrachms might well provide a wider spread of varieties; but the distribution by period and denomination, as shown in the table above, and the relative scarcity of tetradrachms with reverse types, is not likely to be a distortion. The evidence seems to be that dedications of such value in the sanctuary were sporadic, and that the tetradrachms cannot be taken as a cross-section of the circulation at any particular time.

OTHER DENOMINATIONS

The most obvious peculiarity is the frequency of drachms and hemidrachms. They are relatively common in the collections assembled in the *BMC* and in dealers' sales, but in the context of our finds these two denominations do seem to have been particularly appropriate as offerings. The still smaller denominations are scarcer in the finds, but this may be due to the difficulty of spotting them in the soil during excavation.

Periods II–III, ca. 475–308 B.C. (88–154, 726–732)

There is a rapid falling off of finds, indicating the closing of the *stips,* after which the ordinary circumstances of an excavation apply, namely, little silver coin to be found no matter how plentiful the bronze. The discovery of four gold coins is particularly unusual. They too must have been dedications in the sanctuary, but their relatively late date suggests that they were not associated with the silver treasure.

It is toward the end of Period III that the coinage of bronze begins at the three Cyrenaican mint cities, and only now would we expect to find any coins in a conventional excavation. Almost all the finds from this point on are of bronze. About three-quarters of the known types struck from the late fourth to the early first century B.C. are represented to some extent, though the great bulk of the finds are late.

Period IV to Ptolemy Apion, ca. 308–96 B.C. (155–725, 733–736)

Only four silver coins were found, one an unusual quartering of the didrachm. The bronze provides no real surprises until the reign of Euergetes II, but one curiosity of circulation. By far the largest issues of autonomous bronze ever produced in Cyrenaica, to judge from the *BMC*, were the Apollo/lyre and Ammon/palm tree coinages of ca. 282–261 B.C., of which Robinson listed 25 and 32 examples respectively. The Demeter Sanctuary finds happen to occur issue by issue in roughly comparable quantities to those given in the *BMC*—except in this instance, where the finds include only 5 examples of the Apollo/lyre issue and 3 of Ammon/palm tree. Apollonia produced no example of either.[9] Where are these coins to be found? The answer may be provided by the evidence from Euesperides. Bond and Swales published 90 pieces of autonomous bronzes of Cyrene, covering the whole range of issues; of these, 17 were Apollo/lyre and 8 Ammon/palm tree, together amounting to some 28% of the total. In the Sidi Khrebish (Berenice) finds there were only 8 autonomous bronzes from Cyrene, yet they included 3 Apollo/lyre and 2 Ammon/palm tree. It appears, then, that although the coins were struck at Cyrene (for they bear the city name) their circulation area actually lay to the west.[10]

The archaeological remains of the third and second centuries B.C. from the sanctuary seem to create a conundrum, in that while there was major expansion of the sanctuary there was a falling off of votive items.[11] The expansion had to be financed somehow, and it might be surmised that offerings then more frequently took the form of money. There are, however, virtually no finds of silver or gold coins to document such offerings; and in evaluating the evidence of the bronze we encounter the problems

---

9. Throughout discussion following, references, if not otherwise cited, are to publications in the "Excavations and Finds" bibliography.

10. One piece traveled as far west as could be without falling off the edge of the earth: to the Azores, where it was buried in a hoard ca. 200 B.C. (*IGCH* 2299).

11. Donald White, "Cyrene's Sanctuary of Demeter and Persephone: A Summary of a Decade of Excavation," *AJA* 85 (1981) 25.

described above, namely, that site finds may or may not be reliable indicators of local activity. It is the case that on the attributions suggested in Table I in Chapter III there is a surge of coin production under Ptolemy III Euergetes I, from the middle of the third century; and a much greater one in the last half of the second century under Euergetes II (the latter is certain because some of the coins are signed) and then under Soter II and Apion.

An evaluation of this evidence can only be provisional, given that the comparative material is so slight, for only one other group of excavation coins from Cyrenaica of any size has yet been published, namely the finds from Apollonia. The two excavation groups are different in that the Apollonia coins were excavated from a range of locations all over the city, whereas the Cyrene finds derive from a single institution, the Demeter Sanctuary; yet the finds are reasonably comparable. Both sites produced finds from the whole sweep of Cyrenaican bronze coinage, from the fourth to the first centuries B.C. and on into Roman times. From Apollonia the Greek coins of Cyrene totaled 90 pieces; from the Demeter Sanctuary, 613, a ratio of roughly 1:7. Of these, the Apollonia small /eagle issues of Euergetes II, Soter II, and Apion (I lump them together because they were not well distinguished in the publication) provided 22 pieces; the Demeter Sanctuary, 181, a ratio of roughly 1:8. The /Isiac headdress issue provided 10 and 113 pieces from the two sites, roughly 1:11. Ptolemy Apion's Soter/Libya Group IX-E issue provided 21 and 63 pieces respectively, a ratio of 1:3. On present evidence, then, the finds of these issues from Apollonia and the sanctuary are not wildly divergent, and it seems unlikely that the sanctuary finds are purely dedications rather than just losses. Presumably the sort of commerce in votive offerings known everywhere was conducted on the premises; and as noted above some of the coins might well have been lost long after they were struck. It would be unsafe to draw any conclusions from these finds about unusual monetary activity within the sanctuary during the third and second centuries B.C.

The coins themselves, however, are of importance. About two-thirds of the Demeter Sanctuary bronzes are the small module pieces of the last three Ptolemaic reigns in Cyrenaica, that is, of Euergetes II, Soter II, and Apion. This predominance coincides with the evidence of previous excavation reports and casual Cyrenaican finds. The particular interest lies in enlarging our understanding of late Ptolemaic monetary policy, because the scholarship of this century has attributed few coins of Euergetes to Cyrenaica, and none at all of Soter. For further discussion, see the survey of Cyrenaican bronze coinages in Chapter III, where it is also argued that some large module issues not found in the excavations are to be attributed to Euergetes' Cyrenaican reign. The result of all this is to reveal far more mint activity at Cyrene among the latest Ptolemaic kings of Cyrenaica than would be supposed from the limited attributions of the *BMC*.

Other Greek Mints (760A–773)

Although bronze coins from outside Cyrenaica seem never to have entered in any quantity, the character of the finds suggests that patterns may emerge when more evidence is available. For example, the single piece from Judaea catalogued here (**767**) is matched by another reported from Cyrene by Healy, and a third found at Ptolemais. The Demeter Sanctuary produced one Achaean League hemidrachm (**764**); another was found at Ptolemais, and there is an unpublished hoard of them in the Shahat museum. On the other hand the totals are very small, and what is particularly characteristic of Cyrenaican finds is the virtual absence of Ptolemaic coinage of Egypt until the very latest issues, Cleopatra VII and the subsequent coinage of Augustus. The pattern of the Apollonia finds is similar to ours: only one piece of Ptolemy II, then Cleopatra and Augustus. At Sidi Khrebish, too, bronze coins of Augustus from Egypt were found, but nothing earlier. Although the Asyut hoard, buried in Egypt in the fifth century B.C., included a fair number of Cyrenaican tetradrachms, the difficulties of communication between Cyrenaica and Egypt, whether by land or sea, seem always to have severely restricted the interchange of money.

Coinage from the west was even scarcer. Robinson believed that Carthaginian bronze circulated freely in Cyrenaica.[12] In fact, the huge Carthaginian and Siculo-Punic bronze coinages, which are found all over the western Mediterranean and even in Dalmatia, are virtually unknown. Nothing appeared in the Apollonia or Demeter Sanctuary excavations, nor in Norton's collection. Farther west, some pieces of the first issue of Carthaginian bronze were used as flans at Euesperides,[13] and among the unpublished finds from Euesperides one piece occurs that was not overstruck (**E23**). A second Carthaginian piece was found at Sidi Khrebish, possibly from the same issue, described only as "Obv. female head l., Rev. horse r."

All this confirms the commercial isolation of Cyrenaica from both Egypt and Tripolitania, demonstrated by Fulford.[14]

Roman Coinage of Cyrenaica, 1st Century B.C.–2nd Century A.D. (737–760)

Production of Roman provincial coinage specifically in or for Cyrenaica occurred in two distinct periods. The first began at some undetermined point following the cessation of the Ptolemaic coinage at the death of Apion. The central difficulties of the first period are the lack of any useful information about the officials who signed it, and the consequent problems of relative and absolute chronology. Only the coins of Cleopatra and Antony can be dated with any accuracy before the issues in the name of Augustus and Tiberius.

The provincial coinage is explicable denominationally as keyed to Roman usage, and the halved pieces occasionally found reflect Roman adjustment.[15] But in practice most small change must have continued to be Ptolemaic, now perhaps revalued to accommodate it to the Roman. Evidence of the continuity of use is the scarcity of the provincial coins, which cannot have provided a sufficient monetary stock to substitute for the earlier bronze. The small proportion of provincial coins in the Demeter Sanctuary finds is typical and should not be taken as having any special significance for the activity of the shrine.

There was also one occasion during this period when Republican denarii and quinarii were produced, the first silver struck in Cyrenaica since the middle of the third century. These were the coins produced in 31 B.C. by the general Scarpus, first for Antony and then, after Actium, for Octavian. Scarpus had been stationed in Cyrenaica by Antony, and some of the coins bear the head of Ammon, so that the attribution is secure. Presumably the mint was at Cyrene. The coins are not extraordinarily uncommon, yet as far as I know no find has ever been attested in Cyrenaica. They were obviously a military issue and may well have been shipped out with the troops for whom they were produced as pay.[16]

The other imperial Cyrenaican coinage appeared in the second century A.D., silver and bronze bearing Greek legends and the local type of Ammon. For a long time these issues of Trajan, Hadrian, and Marcus Aurelius were thought to have been struck at Caesarea in Cappadocia, along with similar issues whose types referred to other provinces of the Empire. A closer examination of style, fabric, and circulation patterns now makes it certain that that attribution cannot stand. It is possible that these issues were minted at Cyrene, where striking occurred from dies cut at Rome, but it is perhaps more likely that the coins were produced at Rome itself, for export to Cyrenaica. Current scholarship favors the idea that the conventional distinction between Roman and provincial ("Greek Imperial") coinages may disguise production at Rome of issues intended purely for local use elsewhere.

Roman Empire, 1st–4th Centuries A.D. (776–802)

Finds of imperial coins in the Demeter Sanctuary are not numerous, but they run from Claudius to the middle of the fourth century A.D. Only two post-Augustan non-Cyrenaican provincial pieces were identified (**773**, **760A**). There can be no doubt that Cyrenaica had already entered the Roman monetary

---

12. *BMC* xcvi.

13. *BMC* p. 112, 8–9.

14. Michael Fulford, "To East and West: the Mediterranean Trade of Cyrenaica and Tripolitania in Antiquity," *Libyan Studies* 20 (1989) 169–91.

15. On halving in Cyrenaica, see Buttrey, "Roman Coinage" 30, 36–37.

16. Alföldi's attempt to assign the Roman gold and silver of Cornuficius and Caesarian orichalcum to the mint of Cyrene is, I believe, without merit. See Buttrey, "Roman Coinage" 39, n. 29.

orbit in the first century B.C.

The second-century Cyrenaican pieces were in fact of Roman denomination, silver denarii and quinarii, and bronze of several denominations. There is no knowing their purpose; because the first issue predates the Jewish revolt of A.D. 115, they can have had nothing to do with it or the subsequent Hadrianic rebuilding. One could guess that the relatively large issues of semisses and quadrantes were intended to replace the surviving small-module Ptolemaic bronze, for there is no doubt that Roman coin continued to be pieced out with Ptolemaic, examples of which have been found in the Demeter Sanctuary in contexts as late as the third century A.D. This bears on our awareness of activity in the sanctuary, because the limited number of the imperial coins alone might suggest that worship was less lively than in the Greek past. Note that when the Greek legend coins of second-century A.D. Cyrenaica are added to the Roman the profile of the imperial coinage is greatly altered. For the first century there are only 2 coins, for the second, 25—by far the busiest period until the second and third quarters of the fourth century. Perhaps the coins should be associated with the embellishments provided (e.g., by numerous dedications of statues).[17] In contrast there are no small-module finds at all for about a century between the 170s and 270s A.D. Whatever damage the earthquake of 262 may have done, the coins suggest that the sanctuary had been quiescent for decades.

The small total of imperial coins found might well be owing to their large size: everything up to the 270s A.D. is in bronze, and the usual Roman bronze denominations are much larger in module than the late Hellenistic, hence more difficult to lose. For that reason I would suppose that the coins of largest module, the four third-century sesterces, were likely to have been deposits in the sanctuary rather than losses. By contrast the period from the last years of the third to the middle of the fourth century produced proportionately quite a lot of coins, much smaller in module and easier to lose.

The imperial finds end abruptly with Constantius II and Julian. Something happened to the life of the sanctuary, and the archaeological evidence suggests that it was the earthquake of 365 A.D. In contrast the finds from Apollonia continue not richly but regularly through the next three centuries, coming down to Heraclius and the fall of the city in 642 A.D. The Demeter Sanctuary finds show clearly that worship had ceased there, that even casual visits ceased, for we would expect at least a scattering of odd losses. Instead there is nothing at all until two pieces of Heraclius and, 250 years later, a single Islamic stray.

---

17. Donald White, "Cyrene's Sanctuary of Demeter and Persephone: A Summary of a Decade of Excavation," *AJA* 85 (1981) 21.

II

Catalogue of Coin Finds

Introduction

By far the greatest number of the coins found is of pieces struck at Cyrene. The Catalogue follows the arrangement of the *BMC*, from the late sixth century B.C. to the end of the Ptolemies in Cyrenaica, followed by the few pieces from the mints of Barce and Euesperides, and the coins of Roman Cyrenaica. The non-Cyrenaican material is arranged conventionally: Greek and "Greek Imperial" coins moving clockwise around the Mediterranean; then, chronologically, Roman Republican and Imperial, Byzantine, Islamic, and Modern.

The chronology of the Cyrenaican coins generally follows Robinson's Periods and Groups in the *BMC*, tempered in the early stages by the findings of the Asyut hoard. For the first two centuries of coinage the absolute dates should be used with caution, for there is no independent evidence and other Greek coinages do not offer a sure analogue. Cyrene lagged behind in coinage technology, as is shown by tetradrachm overstrikes with a typeless reverse punch on Athenian coin already bearing two types.[1] The chronology of the late fourth to early first century B.C. is somewhat better. We know more of the attendant history of Cyrene and Cyrenaica, and the coins themselves are more informative, whether in fabric or in type and legend. Still, many problems remain and the chronological attributions suggested here are not certainties. The chronology of the Ptolemies themselves follows Samuel, *Ptolemaic Chronology*.

Excavation coins are normally much more poorly preserved than hoard specimens. For this reason it can be misleading to describe details of the types or the legends of the individual pieces in full when so much is actually missing. The reader should take it as understood that when a reference is cited, the find coin coincides with it as far as it is legible. Legends and monograms as printed do not certify their legibility on the coin.

The present weight of each coin is provided, but little emphasis should be placed on single examples: much of the bronze (e.g., the autonomous Units of the fourth century) suffered severely in circulation; many coins have lost weight (or even gained weight) through the processes of corrosion; some of the silver may have been reduced by vigorous cleaning after discovery. Therefore, a considerable range in weights for a single issue may reflect varying states of preservation rather than inaccuracy at the mint, although there is no doubt that some of the latest Ptolemaic bronze from Cyrenaica was produced very casually.

The die position of each issue is given where the coin bears types on both faces. In a few cases the orientation is not ascertainable, that is, where a symmetrical pattern has no natural orientation or where one face has been obliterated through wear or corrosion.

An asterisk indicates illustration. The plates include all silver and gold coins found, except where poor condition makes illustration impracticable. The minor silver with silphium fruit is usually aligned with the point downward, arbitrarily; at the Cyrene mint itself the orientation was inconsistent.[2] In illustration of the Cyrenaican bronze every type found is represented by at least one example, again insofar as the condition of the coins allows.[3]

---

1. *BMC* 2.
2. Cf. *BMC* pls. 1.4 and 7.
3. The photographs of the coin casts were kindly executed by Fred Anderegg, Kelsey Museum of Archaeology, University of Michigan.

Catalogue

Mint of Cyrene (1–725)

PERIOD I (1–87)[4]

1. CA. 510–490 B.C., WITHOUT REVERSE TYPE (1–68)

A: OBV. SILPHIUM, PLANT OR FRUIT (1–56)

ATTIC TETRADRACHMS (1–7)

Silphium; fruit at l. pointing inward [apparently no fruit at r., but die damaged].
Square incuse.
AR

	weight	diam.	inv. no.
*1	16.84	19/22	77-0782

Silphium crowned by umbel [below which a pair of leaves?] and axillary umbels, below which a pair of very short leaves with 3 leaflets; fruit l. and r. pointing outward.
Deep irregular square incuse.
AR obv. style cf. *Asyut* 836

*2	16.87	20/22	69-0211

Top of silphium; fruit l. and r., pointing outward.
Incuse.
AR obv. cf. *BMC* xxiv, 17c [didrachm]

*3	16.85	21/22	77-0766

Silphium without leaves; fruit l. and r., one outline, pointing downward.
Two-banded lumpy incuse.
AR same rev. punch as **5** below

*4	16.64	22/23	77-0781

Silphium; fruit l. and r., pointing downward.
Two-banded lumpy incuse.
AR same rev. punch as **4** above; obv. cf. *BMC* xx–xxi, 2a–e; p. 1, 2; rev. cf. *BMC* xviii, 1a

*5	16.61	19/23	69-0228

Silphium; in field below, fruit l. and r. pointing inward.
Quadripartite square incuse, lumpy central area with thin crossing lines.
AR *BMC* 2

*6	16.58	20/21	76-1304

Upper part of silphium fruiting; fruit l. and r. with stigma, pointing downward.
Quadripartite square incuse with some diagonal lines.
AR cf. *BMC* xix, 1e

*7	16.76	22/23	77-0686

ATTIC DIDRACHM (8)

1 fruit.
Sexpartite incuse.
AR cf. *BMC* xxi, 5a [drachm]

*8	7.08	15/19	73-1272

ATTIC DRACHMS (9–25)

Silphium.
Shallow incuse square.
AR

*9	3.92	11/14	76-1300

3 fruits pointing inward; central pellet and pellet between each fruit pair.
Lumpy incuse within quartered rectangle.
AR

*10	3.59	11/15	74-0202

1 fruit; above and behind, another fruit (?).
[illegible]
AR cf. *BMC* 7 [hemidrachm] (same obv. die?)

*11[5]	3.42	11/14	69-0368

1 fruit in outline border.
Irregular incuse.
AR

*12	3.87	12	78-0073
*13	3.63	11/12	76-1303

1 large fruit in outline border.
Small square incuse.
AR

*14	4.18	11/14	71-0219

1 large fruit with pedicel.
Large oblong barred incuse in two panels.
AR *BMC* 5; **16** and **17** same dies

*15	4.13	11/13	77-0718
*16	3.46	12	76-1305
*17	3.40	11/13	77-0786
*18	3.39	11/14	77-0688

---

4. The early silver of Cyrene must have been issued in large quantity, as the scarcity of die links suggests. We are far from having a corpus of issues, and it is hopeless to attempt to reconstruct the seriation of what is known through die linkage. The order of issues in the Catalogue generally follows the increasing complexity of types, but within each denomination the arrangement is arbitrary. There has been no attempt to trace die links between the find material and that published elsewhere, but a few are noted that have sprung to the eye in the course of compiling the Catalogue, as an aid to future study.

5. Heavily cleaned.

	*19	3.15	11/14	76-0673

1 small fruit in outline border.
Irregular incuse in two panels.
AR   obv. cf. *BMC* xxi, 5c

	*20	3.99	12	74-0445
	*21[6]	3.39	11/15	74-1028

1 fruit.
Incuse in two panels with crossing bars.
AR

	*22[7]	4.31	10/13	77-0474

1 fruit.
Sexpartite oblong incuse.
AR

	*23	3.12	11/13	74-1090

1 small fruit in outline border.
Incuse with two bars crossing.
AR   cf. *BMC* xxi, 5b

	*24	3.96	12/13	71-0768

1 small fruit in outline border.
Large crossed and messy reverse, not noticeably incuse.
AR   cf. *BMC* 6

	*25[8]	4.30	12/13	74-0616

ATTIC HEMIDRACHMS (26–48)

3 fruits pointing inward, dot in middle.
Squarish incuse, diagonals beginning.
AR   same die pair

	*26	2.17	10/12	77-0993
	*27	2.02	10/11	77-0541

2 fruits.
Irregular incuse in two panels.
AR

	*28	1.89	10	71-0615

1 fruit.
Irregular incuse, two panels with striations.
AR

	*29	1.55	8/10	74-1027

1 fruit with pedicel, 1 outline.
Square incuse, unevenly divided into 4 compartments.
AR

	*30	2.00	10	77-1284

1 fruit with pedicel, 1 outline.
Rhomboid incuse.
AR

	*31	1.92	9/11	77-0785

1 fruit with double outline border and pedicel, and lines outward at either side.
Square four-compartmented incuse.
AR   all same obv. die; same rev. die, **32**, **34**, possibly **33**

	*32	1.97	9/10	71-0614
	*33	1.85	9/10	77-0853
	*34	1.78	9/10	77-0732

1 fruit.
Squarish incuse with lumps.
AR

	*35	1.95	9/10	77-0687
	*36	1.91	10	76-0019

1 fruit with pedicel, irregular outline.
Square, shallow incuse, a few thick diagonals beginning.
AR

	*37	2.00	9/10	77-0784
	*38[9]	1.94	10	71-0215

1 fruit with pedicel, 1 outline.
Shallow rectangular incuse.
AR

	*39	2.00	8/9	78-0422

1 fruit.
Messy incuse.
AR

	*40	1.69	9/10	71-0394

1 fruit with pedicel, 1 outline.
Incuse six-compartmented rectangle with striations.
AR   cf. *BMC* 6 [drachm]; **41** and **43** same rev. die

	*41	1.55	9	71-0282
	*42[10]	1.08	8/9	73-1273
	*43	1.88	9/10	77-0852

1 fruit.
Large crossed and messy reverse, not noticeably incuse.
AR

	*44[11]	1.91	11/13	71-0280

1 fruit.
Incuse seven-compartmented rectangle with diagonal bar.
AR

	*45	1.55	9/10	71-0613

1 fruit.
Square incuse, more neatly five-compartmented.
AR

	*46	2.00	10	74-0771
	*47	1.95	10	71-0281
	*48	1.67	9/10	74-0770

---

6. The low weight is due in part to heavy cleaning.

7. The high weight is due to an unusually thick flan, measuring 6 mm at its maximum.

8. The reverse die is that of **44** below [hemidrachm].

9. The reverse is corroded: possibly type in incuse.

10. Heavily cleaned.

11. The reverse die is that of **25** above [drachm].

ATTIC OBOLS (49–52)

1 fruit with pedicel and stigma.
Quadripartite incuse square.
AR   cf. *BMC* 9 [hemiobol]
    *49   0.87   7   74-0617
    *50   0.77   7   78-0358

1 fruit with pedicel, 1 outline.
Angularly-divided quadripartite incuse.
AR
    *51   0.87   7/8   77-0206

1 fruit.
[illegible]
AR
    *52[12] 0.82   9   73-0419

ATTIC HEMIOBOLS (53 AND 54)

1 fruit with outline.
Irregular incuse.
AR
    *53   0.47   7   74-0398

1 fruit with outline border and pedicel.
Angularly-divided quadripartite incuse with dot in each section.
AR   cf. *BMC* xxii, 8a
    *54   0.46   6   71-0616

ATTIC TETARTEMORIA[13] *(55 AND 56)*

1 fruit.
Irregular incuse.
AR
    *55   0.23   5   74-0400
    *56   0.19   5   74-1091

B: OBV. TYPE ABOVE SILPHIUM FRUIT (57–65)

ATTIC TETRADRACHMS (57–60)

Gazelle kneeling r., above fruit with 1 outline.
Two-banded panels, stippled or partly striated.
AR   cf. *BMC* xix, 1c

    *57   16.39   18/24   77-0765
    *58   15.87   21/22   77-0719
    *59   15.65   19/23   77-0764

Dolphin l., under 2 fruits pointing downward; umbel between, above and below.
Two-banded incuse, partly striated.
AR
    *60   15.83   21/23   77-0735

ATTIC DRACHMS (61–64)

Ram's head r., above 2 fruits with outline pointing downward, pedicel below.
Striated incuse.
AR   cf. *BMC* 4; **62–64** same obv. die; **63** and **64** same rev. die
    *61[14] 4.42   12/15   71-0278
    *62   3.90   11/13   77-0880
    *63   3.76   12/13   77-0783
    *64   3.36   11/14   71-0217

ATTIC HEMIDRACHM (65)

Lion's head l., above 1 fruit pointing downward.
Irregular incuse.
AR   *BMC* 8, same dies
    *65   1.49   9/10   74-0772

C: OBV. TYPE BETWEEN SILPHIUM FRUITS (66–68)

ATTIC DRACHMS (66–68)

Silphium; fruit l. and r. pointing downward.
Deep barrel vault incuse.
AR   rev. cf. *BMC* xxii, 7a–b
    *66[15] 3.96   13/14   71-0393

Two frogs mating, seen from above; fruit l. and r. pointing upward.[16]
Vague, square incuse.
AR   obv. same dies; rev. cf. *BMC* xxi, 5c
    *67   3.78   13/14   69-0229
    *68   3.21   13/14   71-0836

---

12. The relatively broad flan is appropriate to the hemidrachm, but the weight is much too low.

13. The denomination is not otherwise attested for Cyrenaica.

14. The weight is enhanced by adherescent corrosion. Possibly the same obverse die as **62–64**.

15. The obverse type is really quite uncertain.

16. The issue was completely unknown before these excavations, and the type of two frogs, one upon the other, is unexampled anywhere. (The silphium fruit to l. and r. are the sign of Cyrenaican minting, and have nothing to do with the frogs.) Prof. Timothy Halliday of the Open University has kindly examined a photograph. "It seems that they are meant to be in amplexus. However, the limbs of the upper animal (the male?) are splayed out instead of being clasped around the lower animal's neck. Perhaps this was artistic licence or ignorance of what frogs actually do. Frogs have two amplexus positions. The more primitive groups have inguinal amplexus, the male clasping the female around her waist; more advanced frogs have axillary amplexus in which she is clasped under the armpits. The position of these frogs suggests axillary amplexus, consistent with a European *Rana* (frog) or *Bufo* (toad). The overall shape of the animals is consistent with either of these,

PERIOD I

2. CA. 490–475 B.C. WITH REVERSE TYPE (69–87)

ATTIC TETRADRACHMS (69–72)

Silphium, type IB; [ ] l. and r.; fruit below l. and r. pointing outward.
Gorgon facing in dotted border, square incuse.
AR   dies ↖   BMC 10
  *69[17]   17.24   21/22   73-1199

Silphium, type IB; fruit l. and r. pointing inward between two pairs of leaves.
Gorgon facing in dotted border, square incuse.
AR   dies ↘   cf. BMC 10
  *70   15.67   22   76-1302

Silphium, type IB; below l., [ ]; r., fruit pointing to 10:30.
Head of Zeus Ammon r. in square incuse.
AR   dies ↑   BMC xxiii, 12c, same dies
  *71   16.78   20/22   71-0621

Silphium, type IB; fruit below l. and r. pointing upward; in dotted border.
Head of Zeus Ammon l. within light square border, in square incuse.
AR   dies ←   Asyut 837-42, same dies
  *72[18]   16.83   21/22   73-0473

ATTIC DIDRACHM (73)

Silphium, type IB; fruit l. and r. below, with pedicel and stigma, pointing upward and outward.
Head of Zeus Ammon r. in square incuse.
AR   dies →   Overstruck on Corinthian stater, Pegasus l. / Athena head r. in square incuse.
  *73[19]   8.24   18/20   77-0235

ATTIC DRACHMS (74–77)

Head of man-faced bull l.; behind, fruit, pointing outward.
Floral pattern in square incuse.
AR   dies —   BMC 19
  *74   3.18   12   71-0214
  *75   3.18   12/14   73-0766

Dolphin l. under fruit pointing down.
Cock r. in square incuse.
AR   dies ←   BMC xxvi, 21b, same dies; Naville sale 14 (2/VII/1929) 462, same dies
  *76   4.30   12/14   74-1030

Temple façade: 2 Doric columns with capitals supporting lintel and pediment; within, fruit with pedicel, pointing downward.
Palmette, with dot in corners upper l. and r.
AR   dies ↑   rev. cf. BMC 23 [hemidrachm]
  *77[20]   3.36   14   76-1295

ATTIC HEMIDRACHMS (78–83)

1 fruit with stigma.
1 fruit set diagonally.
AR   dies ↗   cf. BMC 22
  *78   2.12   10/11   71-0006

1 fruit with stigma.
1 fruit set diagonally, with pellet in each corner.
AR   dies ↑   cf. BMC 22
  *79   1.35   9/10   74-1098

1 fruit with stigma.
1 fruit with pellet in each corner and pellet for pedicel.
AR   dies ←   BMC xxvi, 22a
  *80   1.46   8/9   71-0619

1 fruit in outline border with stigma.
2 grains in incuse square.
AR   dies —   ANS, Norton 7, same dies

---

though the rather pointed outline of the heads suggests frogs rather than toads." What possible significance the type can have had for Cyrene escapes me, except as it makes part of the zoo created on the coins of Period I. It is probably not useful to recall the village of Batrachos ("Frog") on the coast, east of Derna (Laronde 223).

17. The obverse die is the same as *Asyut* 824, 827; the reverse style is that of *BMC* 17d [didrachm].

18. The variety was unknown before the discovery of this piece and the Asyut hoard, which contained six specimens. All seven coins were struck from the same pair of dies. See also the accompanying didrachm, **73**.

19. The style is exactly that of the tetradrachm, **72**, and like it the didrachm was heretofore unknown. The Corinthian stater on which it is overstruck is probably Ravel Period II Series I or II (ca. 480–470 B.C. on the chronology of *Asyut*) (O. Ravel, *Les "Poulains" de Corinthe* [Basel and London 1936–1948]).

20. Hitherto the earliest numismatic representation of any kind of structure was the fifth-century B.C. fountain house at Himera (Martin Jessop Price and Bluma L. Trell, *Coins and Their Cities: Architecture on the Ancient Coins of Greece, Rome, and Palestine* [London 1977] 53). In the fourth century appear the first roofed buildings, temple-shrines on the coins of Hierapolis-Bambyce and Tarsus. This early fifth-century Cyrenaican drachm, a previously unknown type, is now the earliest architectural representation on Greek coin. (The only other architectural type struck at Cyrene is the well-known late-fourth-century bronze with the Tomb of Battus [**154**]). The temple is simply a distyle façade on a base with pediment. The capitals are obscure but the columns are relatively broad and squat, characteristic of the Doric. Identification of the building can only be conjectural, but one thinks immediately of the archaic temple of Apollo.

Between the columns is the silphium fruit. Although later representations of temple façades, particularly Roman and Roman Provincial, frequently include the sacred image, it would be presumptuous to press such a meaning here. There is no evidence for a cult of the silphium; the fruit here is not shown on a basis or in any way reflecting a physical original; and anyway the fruit appears invariably on the coin in this period as the sign of the Cyrene mint. The engraver simply put it where there was room for it in the design.

*81	1.75	10	71-0392

1 fruit, with two others in profile.
Scorpion in square incuse.
AR dies ↓ *BMC* 41, possibly the same obv. die

*82[21]	0.93	9/10	74-0218

1 fruit.
Head of Zeus Ammon r. in square incuse.
AR dies ↘ *BMC* 26

*83	1.79	10	74-0217

ATTIC OBOLS (84 AND 85)

1 fruit.
Floral pattern in square incuse.
AR dies — *BMC* 33

*84	0.80	7	71-0620
*85	0.50	7/9	69-0209

ATTIC HEMIOBOL (86)

1 fruit with pedicel.
Grain ear in square incuse.
AR dies — cf. *BMC* 32 [obol]

*86[22]	0.50	7	71-0395

ASIATIC DRACHM (87)

2 fruits set base to base, with 4 flanking pellets.
Lion mask facing.
AR dies → *BMC* 38

*87	3.32	11/12	69-0272

PERIOD II (88–99)

CA. 475–435 B.C.

GROUP I

ASIATIC DRACHMS (88 AND 89)

Silphium, type IC.
Head of Zeus Ammon r. in beaded circle, in square incuse.
K   V
V   d
AR dies ↙, ↘ *BMC* 50, same dies as **89**; same obv.
                   die as **88** (later state)

*88	3.27	15	71-0770
*89	3.03	14	74-0773

ASIATIC HEMIDRACHMS (90–93)

Silphium, type IC.
Head of Zeus Ammon r. in dotted circle, in square incuse.
Around,   K   [ ]
           [ ]   [ ].
AR dies ↙, ↘ cf. *BMC* xxxviii, 48c–f [drachm]

*90	1.69	10/11	69-0106
*91	1.44	9/12	71-0313

Silphium, type IC.
Head of Zeus Ammon r. in circular frame. KYPA before head.
AR dies ↓, ↗ cf. *BMC* 58

*92[23]	1.54	11	71-0623
*93	1.52	10	74-1029

ASIATIC OBOLS (94 AND 95)

Silphium, type IB.
Head of Zeus Ammon r. in square incuse.
AR dies ↑

*94[24]	0.30	8/9	76-0327

Silphium, type IB.
Head of Zeus Ammon r. in circle, in square incuse.
Around,
        K   [ ]
        V   [ ].
AR dies ↓ cf. *BMC* 48 [drachm]

*95	0.61	7.5	71-0624

GROUP II

ATTIC DIDRACHM (96)

Silphium, type IC.
Head of Zeus Ammon r. in circular dotted frame, in circular incuse. KYPA before.
AR dies ↑ cf. *BMC* 43 [tetradrachm, same engraver]

*96	8.13	21/22	69-0039

ASIATIC DRACHMS (97 AND 98)

Silphium, type IC.
Head of Zeus Ammon r., in dotted circle in circular incuse. KV.
AR dies ↑, ↘ *BMC* 53

*97	3.17	14	78-0460
*98	2.59	13	74-0216

---

21. The weight is terrible, but the flan and type are appropriate to the hemidrachm. Robinson had originally identified the issue as an Asiatic hemidrachm, but emended it to Attic, *BMC* cclxxv.

22. Denomination is a problem: no. **84** is pretty certainly an obol; no. **85** is light but has a decent obol flan; no. **86** is somewhat heavy for the hemiobol but has a small flan.

23. Apparently no square incuse on reverse, but the piece is badly corroded.

24. The weight is very low for an obol but the flan is appropriate.

ASIATIC OBOL (**99**)

Silphium, type IC.
Head of Zeus Ammon r. in square frame, in circular incuse.
AR   dies ↓   *BMC* 60
   *****99**   0.49   7/8   73-1275

PERIOD III (1) (**100**)

CA. 435–375 B.C. OR LATER

ASIATIC DRACHM (**100**)

Silphium, type IC.
Head of Zeus Ammon r., in beaded circle.
AR   dies ↖   cf. *BMC* lii, 98c (silphium as rev.)
   *****100**   2.53   15   73-0947

PERIOD III (2) (**101–154**)

CA. 375–308 B.C. (**101–108**)

ATTIC GOLD STATER (**101**)

Quadriga r. KYPANAION.
Zeus Ammon standing. ΠΟΛΙΑΝΘΕΥΣ.
AV   dies ↖   Naville 92; *BMC* 117 ff.
   *****101**   8.65   19   73-0089

ATTIC GOLD DRACHMS (**102** AND **103**)

Horseman l.
Silphium. KVPA.
AV   dies ↗   Naville 31; *BMC* 125
   *****102**   4.28   14/15   73-0221

Horseman r. KYPANAION.
Silphium; in field l., jerboa.
AV   dies ↙   Naville 108; *BMC* 124
   *****103**   4.31   14   73-0220

ATTIC GOLD TENTH (**104**)

Head of Zeus Ammon l. ΠΟ.
Head of Libya r.
AV   dies ←   Naville 116; *BMC* 154 ff.
   *****104**   0.86   8   73-0219

ATTIC OBOLS (**105–108**)

Silphium, type IC.
Head of Zeus Ammon r. in circular incuse.
AR   dies ↑   *BMC* lxi, 169a
   *****105**   0.51   10   78-0631

Silphium, type IC.
Head of Zeus Ammon l. in circular incuse.
AR   dies ↓   cf. *BMC* lxi, 169a (silphium as rev.)
   *****106**   0.48   8.5   71-0315

Carneius head facing.
Female head r. (Cyrene?).
AR   dies ↙   rev. cf. e.g. *BMC* 143 [gold]
   *****107**   0.30   7   74-1092

Carneius (?) head facing.
[effaced]
AR
   *****108**   0.47   8   73-1050

CA. 325–313 B.C. (**109–153**)

BRONZE, FIRST SERIES (**109–138**)

BRONZE UNITS (**109–126**)

Head of Zeus Ammon r.
Silphium.   K   Y
             P   A
AE   dies irregular   *BMC* 180-82
   109   14.45   19   69-0271
   110   13.37   20/21   69-0315
   *****111**   10.45   19   71-0029

Head of Apollo r.
Silphium (no legend visible).
AE   dies irregular   *BMC* 183-84
   112[25]   14.79   21/22   69-0325
   *****113**   13.44   20   69-0324
   114   13.03   19/20   73-0549
   *****115**   11.98   20/21   71-0046

[illegible]
Silphium.
AE
   116   16.28   21/22   76-1284a
   117   14.41   21/23   76-1284b
   118   14.17   22   76-1284c
   119   13.20   19/20   73-0645
   120   13.11   18   71-0618
   121   12.77   20   73-0469

Head of Carneius r.
2 silphium plants [prob. with fruit between and above].
AE   dies ↘   BM 1946 12-5-6, 7 = *NC*[6] 4 (1944) p. 108, 80-81
   *****122**[26]   12.79   21   73-0770

Head of Cyrene r. KYPANA.

---

25. The condition of the find specimens makes it difficult to determine in every case whether the head really is Apollo, rather than Carneius or Cyrene.

Triple silphium.
AE　　dies —　　*BMC* 178-79
　　*****123**　　13.40　　　　20　　　　73-0813

[illegible]
[illegible]
AE
　　124　　13.82　　　20/22　　　74-1038
　　125　　13.30　　　21/24　　　69-0327
　　126　　12.75　　　21　　　　74-1033

Bronze Quarter Units (127–138)

Head of Carneius r. (no legend visible).
Silphium.
AE　　dies irregular　　*BMC* 199
　　127　　4.96　　　15　　　　77-1285
　　*****128**　　4.06　　　16　　　　77-0768
　　129　　3.36　　　15　　　　76-1293

Head of Libya r.
Silphium;　　　　　　　[ ]　　Y
　　　　　　　　　　　　[ ]　　[ ].
AE　　dies ↗　　*BMC* lxviii, 201a
　　*****130**　　3.93　　　14　　　　73-0827

Head of Athena r.
Double silphium.
AE　　dies ↑, ↓　　*BMC* 202-203
　　*****131**[27]　　5.02　　　14　　　　77-0771
　　*****132**　　2.63　　　14/15　　　73-0573

Head of Carneius r. (no magistrate's name visible).
Triple silphium.
AE　　dies —　　*BMC* 198
　　*****133**　　4.35　　　15/16　　　78-0315
　　134　　3.86　　　14/15　　　69-0338
　　*****135**　　3.85　　　15　　　　76-1292
　　136　　3.57　　　14　　　　74-0620

Head of Carneius r. (no magistrate's name visible).
Triple silphium.
AE　　dies —　　*BMC* lxviii, 198b
　　*****137**　　4.10　　　14/15　　　77-0682
　　*****138**　　3.86　　　17　　　　76-0680

Second Series (139–153)

Bronze Unit (139)

Head of Zeus Ammon r.
Six-spoked oval wheel.
AE　　dies —　　*BMC* 187
　　*****139**　　13.90　　　23/24　　　73-0120

Bronze Half Units (140–152)

Horse prancing r.; above, star.
Six-spoked oval wheel; ΝΙΚΩΝΟΣ reading upward.
AE　　dies ↙, ↗　　*BMC* 189-93
　　140　　8.60　　　17　　　　73-0640
　　*****141**　　8.16　　　18/19　　　73-0004

Horse prancing r.; above, star.
Six-spoked oval wheel; ΝΙΚΩΝΟΣ reading downward.
AE　　dies ↙　　cf. *BMC* 189-93
　　*****142**　　8.86　　　16/17　　　74-0143

Horse prancing r.; above, star.
Six-spoked oval wheel (no legend visible).
AE　　dies —　　cf. *BMC* 189-93
　　143　　8.81　　　16/17　　　76-1294
　　144　　8.79　　　17/18　　　76-0235
　　*****145**　　8.64　　　17　　　　77-0855
　　146　　8.33　　　17　　　　77-0720
　　147　　7.96　　　19　　　　69-0144
　　148　　7.80　　　18/21　　　74-0144
　　149　　7.53　　　18/19　　　69-0307

Horseman on horse r.
Four-spoked round wheel, silphium between spokes at r.
AE　　dies ↘　　*BMC* 194-96
　　*****150**　　8.06　　　19　　　　73-0637

Horseman on horse r.; below, [ ].
Four-spoked round wheel, silphium between spokes at l.
AE　　dies ↗, ↙　　*BMC* lxvii-lxviii, 194a, 196a
　　*****151**　　8.59　　　18　　　　76-0163
　　*****152**　　7.27　　　18　　　　71-0156

Bronze Quarter Unit (153)

Horse prancing r.
Eight-spoked oval wheel.
AE　　dies —　　*NC*⁵ 4 (1944) p. 108, 83
　　*****153**　　4.39　　　14　　　　71-0218

REVOLT, 313–312 B.C. (154)

Bronze Unit (154)

[Head of Zeus Ammon r.]
Tomb of Battus: column on mound, surmounted by urn (no legend visible).
AE　　dies —　　*BMC* lxvii, 187c-e
　　*****154**　　10.89　　　22/24　　　73-0250

---

26. The identification of Carneius is Robinson's and is followed throughout for convenience. One should note, however, Chamoux' attractive argument that the head represents Hermes Parammon ("Hermès Parammon," in *Études d'archéologie classique* 2 [1959] 31–40).

27. Struck on an unusually thick flan of 4 mm.

PERIOD IV

308–ca. 250 b.c. (155–218)

CIVIC ISSUES, 308–277 B.C. (155)

HEMIOBOL (155)

Stallion r.; above, star.
Lyre.
AR   dies ←   *BMC* 269-72
    ***155**[28]   0.29   8   73-1274

PTOLEMY I SOTER, CA. 308–305 B.C. (156–164)

BRONZE HALF UNIT (156)

Gazelle r. (no symbol or legend visible).
Silphium.
AE   dies ↑   *BMC* 279-85
    156   5.65   18   73-0121

BRONZE QUARTER UNITS (157–164)

Crab; below, EYA
Jerboa r. in circular incuse; above, AYƎ
AE   dies ↓   *BMC* cviii, 285a
    *** 157**[29]   2.54   13/15   71-0119

Jerboa l. (no legend visible).
Crab in circular incuse.
AE   dies irregular   *BMC* cviii, 285c-d
    ***158**   3.96   14   77-0854
    159   3.67   14   73-0348
    160   3.25   13/14   74-0644
    161   3.10   13/14   76-0234
    162   3.02   14   69-0287
    163   2.95   13/14   76-0456
    164   2.41   13/14   77-1288

REVOLT, CA. 305–300 B.C. (165–177)

BRONZE HALF UNITS (165–169)

Head of Libya r.
Gazelle r. KY.
AE   dies ↑, ↗ (2)   *BMC* 287
    165[30]   4.27   15   74-0623
    ***166**   2.86   13   77-0140
    ***167**   2.71   14   77-0770
    168   2.03   14   74-0147

Head of Libya r.
Gazelle r.; above, KY; before, silphium.
AE   dies ↗   cf. *BMC* 287
    ***169**   4.24   15   78-0814

BRONZE EIGHTH UNITS (170–177)

Head of Libya r.
Gazelle r. KVPA.
AE   dies irregular   *BMC* 208-209
    170[31]   1.37   10   74-1050
    ***171**   1.36   11   73-1201
    172   1.17   11/12   73-0092
    173[32]   1.14   11   74-1049
    174   0.86   11   77-0736
    ***175**   0.85   10   77-0769
    176   0.85   10   77-0737
    177   0.56   8/11   74-0626

PTOLEMY I SOTER, CA. 300–282 B.C. (178–185)

BRONZE (178–185)

Head of Apollo r.
Eagle l. on fulmen; before, silphium; at l., ⌾.
ΠΤΟΛΕΜΑΙΟΥ.
AE   dies ↗   cf. *BMC* p. 74, 4; Svoronos 66
    ***178**   3.69   18   76-0677

Head of Apollo l.
Eagle l. on fulmen; before, silphium; at l., Ⓐ.
ΠΤΟΛΕΜΑΙΟΥ.
AE   dies ↑   *BMC* cxli, 5c; Svoronos 65
    ***179**   3.96   17.5   76-0931

Head of Apollo r.
Eagle r. on fulmen; before, silphium (no monograms visible). ΠΤΟΛΕΜΑΙΟΥ.
AE   dies ↑   *BMC* 5; Svoronos 68
    180   3.93   16   69-0244
    181   3.54   16   71-0085
    182   3.47   16/18   69-0339

Head of Ptolemy Soter r.
Eagle r. on fulmen; at r., Ⓐ over ⌾; below, silphium and crab. ΠΤΟΛΕΜΑΙΟΥ.
AE   dies ↑   *BMC* cxli, 5d; Svoronos 70
    183   3.81   16/17   69-0213
    ***184**   3.80   16/17   74-0470

---

28. *BMC*, "Obols (?)." The find piece, and four examples in *BMC*, range from 0.45 to 0.25 grams, averaging 0.36—exactly the weight of the Attic hemiobol.

29. The weight is low but the flan size is sufficient for the Quarter Unit.

30. Thick flan, heavy with corrosion.

31. The type was first catalogued in *BMC* as the Sixteenth Unit of Period III, emended p. cclxxv to Eighth Unit of Period IV. The weight of this piece is enhanced by adherent corrosion.

32. Only on this example can the plow (?) symbol of *BMC* 208 be made out.

Head of Ptolemy Soter r.
Eagle r. on fulmen; below, silphium and crab. ΠΤΟΛΕΜΑΙΟΥ.
AE   dies ↑   *BMC* cxli, 5e; Svoronos 70
  *****185**   3.73   16.5   77-0476

MAGAS IN REVOLT, CA. 282–261 B.C.
(186–196)

BRONZE (186–196)

Head of Apollo r.
Horse prancing r.; above, star; below, crab. KY.
AE   dies ↙   *BMC* 343-46
  *****186**   4.15   14/16   71-0044

Head of Apollo r.
Lyre. [legend and symbol uncertain].
AE   dies ↑   *BMC* 319-25
  *****187**   4.59   15   78-0195
  188   3.95   18   73-0636
  189   3.56   18   73-1049

Head of Apollo r.
Lyre.   K   Y
             crab   A
AE   dies ↑   *BMC* 326-31
  *****190**[33]   5.12   20   74-1185
  191   3.90   17/20   71-0030

Head of Libya r.
Silphium, type IIIA.   K   [ ]
                        P   [ ]
AE   dies ↑   *BMC* 290-91
  *****192**[34]   3.24   19   77-0475

Gazelle r.
Silphium, type IIIA. KVPA.
AE   dies ↑   cf. *BMC* 279 [half unit]
  *****193**   1.89   13/14   73-0621

Head of Zeus Ammon r.
Palm tree; below on r., silphium.   K   Y
                                      P   A
AE   dies ↑   cf. *BMC* 292-96
  *****194**   3.92   17   71-0008

Head of Zeus Ammon r.
Palm tree; below on r., silphium.   [ ]   [ ]
                                      PA   [ ]
AE   dies ↑   *BMC* 308-18
  195   4.90   18/19   69-0157

Head of Zeus Ammon r.
Palm tree; below on r., silphium.   K   Y
                                      PA   Ξ
AE   dies ↗   cf. *BMC* 311-18
  *****196**   6.25   17   71-0026

MAGAS RECONCILED WITH PTOLEMY II PHILADELPHUS, CA. 261–258 B.C. (197–217)

PHOENICIAN DIDRACHMS (197–199)

Head of Ptolemy Soter r.
Eagle standing l. on fulmen; at l., ⚵ ΠΤΟΛΕΜΑΙΟΥ ΒΑΣΙΛΕΩΣ.
AR   dies ↑   *BMC* 7; Svoronos 307
  *****197**   6.76   20   69-0316

Head of Ptolemy Soter r.
Eagle standing l. on fulmen; at l., ᴬ ΠΤΟΛΕΜΑΙΟΥ ΒΑΣΙΛΕΩΣ
AR   dies ↖   cf. *BMC* cxliii, 8b; Svoronos 323a
  *****198**   6.78   19   74-0095

Head of Berenice I r.
Club in wreath. ΒΕΡΕΝΙΚΗΣ ΒΑΣΙΝΣΣΗΣ.
AR, cut quarter   dies ↓   *BMC* 9-13; Svoronos 316–320
  *****199**[35]   1.64   [18]   73-0638

BRONZE (200–217)

Head of Ptolemy Soter r.
Eagle l. on fulmen. ΠΤΟΛΕΜΑΙΟΥ ΒΑΣΙΛΕΩΣ
AE   dies ↑   *BMC* 19-22; Svoronos 327–328
  *****200**   9.57   19/20   74-0632

Head of Ptolemy Soter r.
Eagle l. on fulmen. ΠΤΟΛΕΜΑΙΟΥ ΒΑΣΙΛΕΩΣ
AE   dies ↑   *BMC* 23-24; Svoronos 330
  *****201**   8.18   19   73-0558

Head of Ptolemy Soter r.
Eagle l. on fulmen (no legend visible). ΠΤΟΛΕΜΑΙΟΥ ΒΑΣΙΛΕΩΣ
AE   dies ↑   *BMC* 19-24; Svoronos 327–330
  202[36]   8.55   17/18   74-0643
  203   8.37   18/19   74-1093
  *****204**   7.46   18/19   71-0041
  205   7.43   18   71-0839
  206   6.35   18/21   73-1048

---

33. Wide flan, possibly overstruck.

34. Concave reverse, probably overstruck.

35. The silver and bronze coins with head of Berenice were attributed to Berenice-Euesperides by Poole, *BMCPtol* p. 60, 9–13, a notion entertained uncertainly by Robinson (cliv, clvi), who nonetheless catalogued them under Cyrene. The apple wreath and (Heracles') club of the silver reverse suggest Euesperides, and the bronze would go along on style. I have inconsistently followed *BMC* in placing the one find coin in silver at this point, for convenience, while including the bronze issue, not found in the excavations, with the others of Euesperides on Table III. Certainly it is quite unlike the contemporary bronze of Cyrene.

36. The weight is enhanced by heavy corrosion.

	207[37]	4.96	17/18	73-0767

Head of Ptolemy Soter r.
Fulmen. ΠΤΟΛΕΜΑΙΟΥ ΒΑΣΙΛΕΩΣ

AE	dies —		*BMC* 14-18; Svoronos 324–326	
	208	8.26	20/21	71-0157
	*****209**	7.20	20/21	78-0050

Head of Ptolemy Soter r.
Fulmen. ΠΤΟΛΕΜΑΙΟΥ ΒΑΣΙΛΕΩΣ

AE	dies —		*BMC* cxliv, 18a; Svoronos 326	
	210	4.74	18/19	73-0780

Head of Ptolemy Soter r. [ΠΤΟ ΒΑΣΙΛ].
Protome of winged horse l. (no symbol or legend visible).

AE	dies ↑, ↗ (1)		*BMC* 27; Svoronos 333	
	211	5.49	16/17	71-0327
	212	4.89	16/17	74-0631
	*****213**	4.26	16	76-0230
	214	3.38	16	73-0547
	215	3.28	14/15	69-0280

Head of Ptolemy Soter r.
Horse l. (possibly inscription below).

AE	dies ↑		*BMC* 28; Svoronos 336	
	*****216**	1.79	12	78-0317
	217	1.22	11	77-0799

PTOLEMY II PHILADELPHUS,
CA. 258–250 B.C. (**218**)

Bronze (***218***)

Group I—module B

Head of Ptolemy Soter r.
Head of Libya r.; below chin, double cornucopiae.
ΒΑΣΙΛΕΩΣ ΠΤΟΛΕΜΑΙΟΥ.

AE	dies ↑		*BMC* 30-33; Svoronos 855.	
			Countermark O (?) on obv.	
	*****218**[38]	5.51	17/18	73-0442

KOINON, CA. 250–246 B.C. (**219**)

Bronze (***219***)

Head of Zeus Ammon r.
Silphium. KO
IN
ON.

AE	dies ↗		*BMC* 16-21; Svoronos 862–864	
	*****219**	8.80	20	73-0624

PTOLEMY III EUERGETES, CA. 246–222 B.C.
(**220–234**)

Bronze (***220–234***)

Group II—Module B

Head of Ptolemy Soter r.
Head of Libya r.; below chin, single cornucopiae.
ΒΑΣΙΛΕΩΣ ΠΤΟΛΕΜΑΙΟΥ.

AE	dies ↑		cf. *BMC* cxlv, 33a (double cornucopiae); Svoronos 866	
	*****220**	8.61	22	73-0773
	221	7.95	21/22	73-0550
	222	7.52	23	74-1031

Group II—Module D

Head of Ptolemy Soter r.
Head of Libya r.; below chin, double cornucopiae.
ΒΑΣΙΛΕΩΣ ΠΤΟΛΕΜΑΙΟΥ.

AE	dies ↑		*BMC* 34; Svoronos 867	
	223	2.51	16	73-0247
	*****224**	2.18	15	69-0267
	*****225**	2.14	14/15	76-0221

Group II—Module E

Head of Ptolemy Soter r.
Head of Libya r.; below chin, double cornucopiae.
ΒΑΣΙΛΕΩΣ ΠΤΟΛΕΜΑΙΟΥ.

AE	dies ↑		*BMC* 36; Svoronos 868	
	*****226**	1.66	13	73-0630

Group III—Module B

Head of Ptolemy Soter r.
Head of Libya r.; below chin, single cornucopiae; below neck, silphium-top. ΒΑΣΙΛΕΩΣ ΠΤΟΛΕΜΑΙΟΥ.

AE	dies ↗		*BMC* cxlv, 41a; Svoronos 865	
	*****227**	7.33	21/22	73-1200

Group III—Module D

Head of Ptolemy Soter r.
Head of Libya r.; behind, single cornucopiae. ΒΑΣΙΛΕΩΣ ΠΤΟΛΕΜΑΙΟΥ.

AE	dies ↑ (2), ↖ (4)		*BMC* 42	
	228	2.77	15/16	78-0052
	*****229**	2.66	16	77-0830
	*****230**	2.61	16/17	73-0168
	231	2.55	16	76-0005
	232	2.46	15	73-0805

---

37. The low weight is due to loss through corrosion.

38. The flan has been cut down all around after striking, reducing its weight considerably from the norm of Group I-B, but the style is good and there are no surface holes, so that the attribution to Group I is appropriate.

233	2.21	14	73-0252
234	2.04	broken	78-0477

PTOLEMY IV PHILOPATOR–PTOLEMY VI/VIII, 222–163 B.C. (**235–280**)

Group IV—Module D

Head of Ptolemy Soter r.
Head of Libya r.; below chin, single cornucopiae.
ΒΑΣΙΛΕΩΣ ΠΤΟΛΕΜΑΙΟΥ.

AE dies ↑ (2), ↖ (5)   *BMC* 45; Svoronos 873

235	2.88	15/17	73-0809
236	2.85	15	74-0220
237	2.36	15/16	73-0047
238	2.12	14/16	73-0242
***239**	2.04	14	73-0048
240	2.01	13/14	74-0622
241	1.91	15	74-1046
242	1.83	14	73-0126
***243**	1.80	14	73-0091

Group IV—Module E [i, thin flan]

Head of Ptolemy Soter r.
Head of Libya r.; below chin, single cornucopiae.
ΒΑΣΙΛΕΩΣ ΠΤΟΛΕΜΑΙΟΥ.

AE dies ↑, ↗ (1)   *BMC* 46; Svoronos 869

***244**	1.58	13	69-0284
245	1.40	13.5	73-0003
***246**	1.20	13	73-0122
247	1.14	13	74-1045
***248**	1.04	13/14	73-0212
249	0.97	13	73-0249

Group IV—Module E [ii, thick flan]

Head of Ptolemy Soter r.
Head of Libya r.; below chin, single cornucopiae.
ΒΑΣΙΛΕΩΣ ΠΤΟΛΕΜΑΙΟΥ.

AE dies ↑   *BMC* 46; Svoronos 869

***250**	1.40	13	73-0254
251	1.28	12.5	74-0433
252	1.19	13	73-0808

Group VI—Module B

Head of Ptolemy Soter r.; behind neck, club.
Head of Libya r.; below chin, double cornucopiae.
ΒΑΣΙΛΕΩΣ ΠΤΟΛΕΜΑΙΟΥ.

AE dies ↖   *BMC* 55; Svoronos 1268

***253**	7.70	21/24	73-0564

Group VI—Module C

Head of Ptolemy Soter r.
Head of Libya r.; below chin, double cornucopiae.
ΒΑΣΙΛΕΩΣ ΠΤΟΛΕΜΑΙΟΥ.

AE dies ↑ (2), ↖ (4)   *BMC* 56-59

***254**	4.55	17	74-0469
***255**	3.85	17	69-0093
***256**	3.60	16	77-0358
257	3.53	16/17	76-0681
258	3.45	17	71-0020
259	3.22	16	69-0098

Group VI—Module E [i, thin flan]

Head of Ptolemy Soter r.
Head of Libya r.; below chin, single cornucopiae.
ΒΑΣΙΛΕΩΣ ΠΤΟΛΕΜΑΙΟΥ.

AE dies ↑

***260**[39]	1.38	12.5	71-0043
261	1.31	11.5	73-0167
262	1.08	11	73-0169

Group VI—Module E [ii, thick flan]

Head of Ptolemy Soter r.
Head of Libya r.; below chin, single cornucopiae.
ΒΑΣΙΛΕΩΣ ΠΤΟΛΕΜΑΙΟΥ.

AE dies ↑

***263**	1.40	11/12	73-0420
***264**	1.24	11	73-0037
265	1.18	11	73-0253

Group VII—Module B

Head of Ptolemy Soter r.; behind neck, club.
Head of Libya r.; below chin, single cornucopiae.
ΒΑΣΙΛΕΩΣ ΠΤΟΛΕΜΑΙΟΥ.

AE dies ↑   *BMC* 60

266	5.41	21/22	76-0328
***267**[40]	4.87	20	74-0774

Group VII—Module C

Head of Ptolemy Soter r.
Head of Libya r.; below chin, single cornucopiae.
ΒΑΣΙΛΕΩΣ ΠΤΟΛΕΜΑΙΟΥ.

AE dies ↖   *BMC* 61-65

268	3.56	16	71-0216
269	3.39	16	73-0443
***270**	3.27	16	73-0557
271	3.12	16	73-0804
272	2.93	16	69-0248
273	2.42	15/16	73-0625
274	2.24	15/16	73-0810

---

39. I have attributed to Group VI-E those pieces of the smallest denomination that in *BMC* are categorized as VII-E, on the grounds that their style is too pretty for Group VII. They seem to fall into two issues, the former with thin flans, low relief, fine small lettering, and heads of good style. The dies of the latter are cut with grosser lettering and are struck on thicker flans.

40. The coin is overstruck, the undertype uncertain. *BMC* 60, of the same issue, is described as "doublestruck," but perhaps is overstruck.

Group VII—Module D

Head of Ptolemy Soter r.
Head of Libya r.; below chin, single cornucopiae.
ΒΑΣΙΛΕΩΣ ΠΤΟΛΕΜΑΙΟΥ.
AE dies ↑ (3), ↖ (2)   *BMC* 66-68

*275	2.97	15	78-0318
*276	2.64	15/16	69-0163
277	1.96	14/15	73-0248
*278	1.92	15	78-0053
279	1.80	15	76-0236
280	1.62	13/14	74-1053

PTOLEMY VIII EUERGETES II AS KING IN CYRENAICA, 163–145 B.C. (**281–283**)

Head of Zeus Ammon r.; behind, sceptre.
Eagle on fulmen l. looking r. From lower l., ΕΥΕΡΓΕΤΟΥ ΒΑΣΙΛΕΩΣ ΠΤΟΛΕΜΑΙΟΥ; at l., Φ.
AE dies ↑   *BMCPtol* p. 88, 1; Svoronos 1644

*281	7.31	21	73-0441

Head of Zeus Ammon r.
Eagle on fulmen r. From lower l., ΕΥΕΡΓΕΤΟΥ ΒΑΣΙΛΕΩΣ ΠΤΟΛΕΜΑΙΟΥ.
AE dies ↖   *BMCPtol* p. 95, 88; Svoronos 1653

*282	17.47	32	77-0359

Head of Zeus Ammon r.
Eagle on fulmen l. From lower l., ΒΑΣΙΛΕΩΣ ΠΤΟΛΕΜ[ΑΙΟΥ ΕΥΕΡΓΕΤΟΥ]; at l., M (?).
AE dies ↑   cf. *BMCPtol* p. 95, 86-88; cf. Svoronos 1645

*283[41]	7.30	25	69-0086

PTOLEMY VIII EUERGETES II AS KING IN EGYPT, 145–116 B.C. (**284–358**)

Head of Zeus Ammon r.
Eagle on fulmen l. From lower l., ΕΥΕΡΓΕΤΟΥ ΒΑΣΙΛΕΩΣ ΠΤΟΛΕΜΑΙΟΥ; at l., ΘΕ.
AE dies ↑, ↖ (5), ↗ (1)   *BMCPtol* p. 95, 82-83; Svoronos 1651

*284[42]	6.62	20	73-0643
285	5.66	20	77-0139
286	5.32	20	74-0146
287	5.20	19	73-0838
288	4.94	20	73-0565
*289	4.91	20	74-0145
290	4.89	20	74-0640
291	4.82	19	73-0840
*292	4.59	17	74-0067
293	4.52	20	76-1288
294	4.43	17/18	69-0079
295	4.31	17/20	73-0774
296	4.11	20	73-1280
297	3.91	18	73-0839
298	3.85	19	73-0768
299	3.61	19	71-0042
300	3.55	19	73-0626
301	3.33	20	78-0206
302[43]	3.04	17	73-0642
303[43]	2.95	18	76-0457

Head of Zeus Ammon r.
Eagle on fulmen l. From lower l., ΕΥΕΡΓΕΤΟΥ ΒΑΣΙΛΕΩΣ ΠΤΟΛΕΜΑΙΟΥ; at l., ΘΕ.
AE dies ↑   *BMCPtol* p. 95, 84; Svoronos 1652

*304	3.06	15/16	78-0207
*305	2.76	15	78-0628

Head of Zeus Ammon r.
Eagle on fulmen l. From lower l., ΕΥΕΡΓΕΤΟΥ ΒΑΣΙΛΕΩΣ ΠΤΟΛ (etc.).
AE dies ↑, ↖ (5), ↗ (1)   cf. *BMCPtol* p. 95, 85 [no eponym]; Svoronos 1655

306	3.11	15	74-0454
307	2.92	13	73-0822
308	2.61	13	73-0825
309	2.57	14	73-0641
310	2.57	13	73-0515
311	2.51	13/14	74-0069
312	2.38	12	76-1278
313	2.37	12	73-0817
*314	2.30	12/14	77-0832
315	2.25	14	71-0025
316	2.22	13	73-0570
317	2.21	14	71-0321
*318	2.19	14	76-1290
319	2.17	13	74-0151
320	2.13	12/13	73-0824
321	2.13	12/13	74-0467
322	2.10	12	74-1044
323	2.09	12/13	69-0084
*324	2.08	13/14	77-0990
325	2.07	12/13	77-0733
326	2.07	13	77-0734
327	2.05	12/13	69-0089
328	2.02	13	69-0184
329	2.02	13	69-0245
330	1.97	12	71-0004
331	1.95	11/12	77-0795
332	1.92	12/13	74-1040
333	1.91	14	71-0005
334	1.90	13	73-0562
335	1.87	13/15	73-0559
336	1.81	12/14	73-0046
337	1.80	12	76-0002
338	1.71	11/12	76-1280
339	1.70	12	73-0431

---

41. The style of the eagle is identical with that of the ΘΕ issues below.

42. There may be several subgroups here, since there is variation in flan size matched by variation in die size: **289** at 20 mm has an obverse die of 18 mm; **294** at 17/18 mm, a die of 16 mm; and **292** at 17 mm, a die of 15 mm.

43. Both **302** and **303** are badly worn.

340	1.69	13	73-0627
341	1.61	13	69-0145
342	1.58	12	69-0161
343	1.54	11/13	77-0828
344	1.47	12/13	76-0229
345	1.46	11/13	71-0126
346	1.46	12	77-0991
347	1.46	12/13	73-0826
348	1.43	12	74-0070
349	1.32	11/12	71-0617
350	1.30	12	71-0002

Group VIII—Module B

Head of Ptolemy Soter r.
Head of Libya r.; below chin, single cornucopiae.
ΒΑΣΙΛΕΩΣ ΠΤΟΛΕΜΑΙΟΥ. Below neck, Ἒ.
AE   dies ↑

*351[44]	5.79	21	76-1296
352	5.32	21	76-1274

Group VIII—Module C

Head of Ptolemy Soter r.
Head of Libya r.; below chin, single cornucopiae.
ΒΑΣΙΛΕΩΣ ΠΤΟΛΕΜΑΙΟΥ.
rev. (α): below neck, Ἒ
AE   dies ↑   *BMC* 71-77; Svoronos 1658

*353	4.00	17/18	77-0819
354	3.46	18	71-0625
355	3.36	18	73-0806
356	3.12	15/17	69-0352
357	2.36	18	73-0776
358	2.21	16/17	73-1276

PTOLEMY IX SOTER II, 115–104/1 B.C.
(359–444)

Group VIII—Module C

Head of Ptolemy Soter r.
Head of Libya r.; below chin, single cornucopiae.
ΒΑΣΙΛΕΩΣ ΠΤΟΛΕΜΑΙΟΥ.
rev. (β): below neck, Ĭ (= $\overset{\circ}{\Sigma}$)
AE   dies ↖   *BMC* 78-79; Svoronos 1725

*359[45]	4.22	17	73-0440
*360	3.47	15/17	77-0992

Head of Zeus Ammon r.
Two cornuacopiae; above, stars. ΒΑΣΙΛΕΩΣ ΠΤΟΛΕΜΑΙΟΥ. At sides, Σ Ω / Θ Ε
AE   dies ↑, ↖ (3)   *BMCptol* p. 107, 42-47; Svoronos 1718

*361[46]	6.09	19	73-0244
362	5.88	18	69-0246
363	5.73	19	76-0458
364	5.45	19	73-1279
365	5.37	17	73-0125
366	5.05	19	74-1178
367	4.57	17	69-0343
368	4.37	18	74-0010
369	3.83	17	71-0622
370	3.70	18	69-0297

Head of Zeus Ammon r.
Eagle on fulmen l. From lower l., ΣΩΤΗΡΟΣ ΒΑΣΙΛΕΩΣ ΠΤΟΛ
AE   dies ↑   Svoronos 1717

371[47]	2.57	14/15	74-0150
372	2.35	14/15	74-0225
373	2.29	14/15	73-0575
374	2.29	14	74-0638
375	2.23	14	73-0820
*376	1.87	14	73-0579
*377	1.75	14/15	74-1043

Head of Zeus Ammon r.
Isiac headdress. ΒΑΣΙΛ ΠΤΟΛ. Below, ΣΩ.
AE   dies ↑, ↖ (8), ↗ (1)   Svoronos 1722

378	3.21	16	71-0159
379	3.09	14	77-0966
380	2.94	14/15	73-0423
381	2.92	15	76-1271
382	2.79	14	77-0823
383	2.70	14	69-0091
384	2.68	14	78-0744
385	2.62	13/14.5	77-0861
386	2.52	14	69-0082
*387	2.46	15	77-1286
388	2.42	13/14	76-0003
389	2.40	14/15	77-0356
390	2.40	14	73-0090
391	2.39	13/14	71-0260
392	2.33	14/15	74-0468
*393	2.31	14	71-0007
*394	2.24	14	76-0459
395	2.22	13/14	73-0251
396	2.19	14	74-1182
397	2.19	14	77-0821
398	2.17	15/16	71-0277
399	2.08	14/15	76-0165
400	2.06	14	76-0164

---

44. Not in *BMC*. The hideous style and flat reverse are comparable to Group VIII (cf. *BMC* 74, pl. 32.10), but both weight and diameter are too high for module C. The monogram of **352** is not visible; on **351** enough shows to indicate that the flat top was not capped by a circle (i.e., not Soter's Ĭ) and that the vertical below is off center to the left (i.e., we have here one of the monograms of Euergetes "in various stages of dismemberment" [Robinson, *BMC* 86]). The flans are remarkably beveled.

45. For a clear instance of I for Σ on Soter's coin, see *SNG Cop* Cyprus [*recte* Cyrenaica] 681, reading I Ω / Θ Ε.

46. The variety without ΘΕ, *BMCptol.* 107, 48, Svoronos 1719, appears to be merely the die engraver's aberration.

47. The fabric of the /eagle bronzes of Soter is precisely equivalent to that of Euergetes, but the style and lettering are finer.

CATALOGUE OF COIN FINDS

401	2.04	13/14	77-0862
402	1.58	13	74-0048

Head of Zeus Ammon r.
Isiac headdress. ΒΑΣΙΛ ΠΤΟΛ. [Below, probably ΣΩ].
AE   dies ↑, ↘ (1)   cf. Svoronos 1722

403	2.70	14/15	69-0087
404	2.66	13/14	71-0021
405	2.61	14	73-0777
406	2.37	13/14	73-0566
407	2.31	14	73-0574
408	2.27	13/15	73-0811
409	2.25	14	74-0148
*410[48]	1.92	13	77-0797

Head of Zeus Ammon r.
Eagle on fulmen l. From lower l., ΠΤΟΛΕΜ ΒΑΣΙΛ (etc.).
At l., $\overset{\circ}{\Sigma}$.
AE   dies ↑, ↖ (3), ↗ (1), ↘ (1)

411	2.02	12	71-0317
412	1.92	12	73-0646
413	1.89	13	76-1279
414	1.74	12	78-0745
*415	1.70	12	73-0002
416	1.68	12	69-0148
*417	1.64	11/12	71-0259
418	1.59	11/12	77-0881
419	1.57	11	74-1094
420	1.51	11/12	77-0829
421	1.42	12/13	74-1095
422	1.36	12	71-0837
423	1.35	12	71-0322
424	1.29	11	77-0355
425	1.14	11	73-0823
426	1.14	11	76-1287
427	1.09	10/11	77-0826

Head of Zeus Ammon r.
Eagle on fulmen l. From lower l., ΠΤΟΛΕΜ ΒΑΣΙΛ (etc.).
At l., $\overset{\circ}{I}$.
AE   dies ↖

*428	1.39	12	77-0833

Head of Zeus Ammon r.
Isiac headdress. ΠΤΟΛΕΜΑΙΟΥ ΒΑΣΙΛΕΩΣ. At sides,
  Σ   Ω
  Θ   Ε
AE   dies ↑, ↗ (2)   Svoronos 1720

429	2.07	10/12	69-0367
430	2.04	12/13	74-0452
431	2.00	13	76-0029
432	1.86	13/14	74-0637
*433	1.77	13	74-0635
434	1.74	10/11	77-0888
435	1.67	12	71-0325
*436[49]	1.50	13	74-1177
*437	1.45	12	77-0860
438[50]	1.37	12	77-0824
439	1.35	12	77-0885
440	1.34	11/12	74-0634
441	1.29	13	73-0422

Head of Zeus Ammon r.
Isiac headdress. Below, I (= $\overset{\circ}{I}$ = $\overset{\circ}{\Sigma}$).
AE   dies ↑

*442	1.59	12	71-0154

Head of Tyche r.
Dioscurid caps.
AE   dies ↑, ↖   BM 1946 12-5-15, 16 = NC^6 4 (1944) 109, 49

*443	1.30	10/11	73-0567
*444	1.06	9/10	77-0681

PTOLEMY VIII EUERGETES II OR PTOLEMY IX SOTER II (445–541)

Group VIII—Module C

Head of Ptolemy Soter r.
Head of Libya r.; below chin, single cornucopiae.
  rev. (α) or (β) [monogram uncertain]
AE   dies ↑, ↖ (1)

445	4.31	17/19	73-0934
446	3.53	17	74-0627
447	3.42	17	73-0807
448	3.23	17/18	77-1287
449	3.15	17	73-0554
450	3.07	18	74-0621
451	2.92	17	69-0326
452	2.80	17	74-0149
453	2.64	17	76-0231
454[51]	2.59	15/17	73-0628
455[52]	1.95	17	76-1275

Head of Ptolemy Soter r.
Head of Libya r.; below chin, single cornucopiae.
  rev. (γ): no monogram[53]
AE   dies ↑   BMC 80-83

*456	3.06	16	71-0019
457	2.85	16/17	69-0345

Head of Zeus Ammon r.
Eagle l. on fulmen.
  (uncertain variety)
AE   dies ↑, ↖ (4)

---

48. Overstruck on Ammon/eagle, on which traces of EYEP can be made out.

49. Overstruck by Soter/Libya IX-E of Ptolemy Apion.

50. Overstruck on (or less likely by) Ammon/eagle. The Isiac type is the stronger.

51. Broken.

52. Badly worn.

53. Although this variety bears no monogram, and so might well be ranged with Apion's coinage, I have assigned it to Euergetes or Soter on the grounds that the style and fabric are marginally less terrible than Apion's, as exhibited in his Group IX-E.

458	2.61	13	73-0841
459	2.57	13	71-0086
460	2.56	13/14	78-0105
461	2.47	13/14	77-0722
462	2.42	12/14	77-0863
463	2.42	14	71-0627
464	2.41	13	76-1281
465	2.33	12/13	73-0771
466	2.33	13	73-0560
467	2.32	12/13	69-0153
468	2.25	12	76-1276
469	2.23	13/14	74-1041
470	2.21	13	74-1183
471	2.20	13/14	76-0167
472	2.17	13	73-0568
473	2.07	12/13	73-1271
474	2.05	11/12	71-0040
475	2.02	13	76-1291
476	2.01	12/13	77-0883
477	2.00	12	74-1042
478	1.99	12/14	71-0179
479	1.98	12/13	73-0631
480	1.95	11/12	74-0639
481	1.94	12	76-0004
482	1.94	11/13	69-0090
483	1.93	12	73-1281
484	1.92	11/12	73-0814
485	1.92	12/14	74-0478
486	1.91	11/12	77-0721
487	1.90	13	73-0551
488	1.88	11/12	69-0268
489	1.88	10/11	73-0561
490	1.85	11/12	74-0472
491	1.85	11/13	71-0168
492	1.84	11/12	69-0309
493	1.83	12	71-0840
494	1.81	12/13	73-0576
495	1.78	13	78-0845
496	1.77	12	73-0569
497	1.76	11/12	69-0146
498	1.76	13/14	71-0045
499	1.76	12	71-0158
500	1.72	11/14	73-0578
501	1.72	13	71-0167
502	1.71	10/12	73-0821
503	1.70	12/13	77-0857
504	1.69	11/12	71-0166
505	1.66	9/15	74-1034
506	1.65	11	78-0629
507	1.65	12/13	69-0097
508	1.64	11.5	73-0572
509	1.64	12	73-0639
510	1.63	11	71-0084
511	1.61	12	73-0818
512	1.61	11/13	73-0815
513	1.59	12	71-0118
514	1.57	11/13	71-0320
515	1.57	12/13	77-0189
516	1.53	12/13	69-0216
517	1.52	11	69-0204
518	1.51	12	73-0816
519	1.49	13	74-0049
520	1.49	11/12	76-1277
521	1.47	11/12	77-0831
522	1.45	12	74-0068
523	1.45	10/13	69-0328
524	1.42	11/13	76-0225
525	1.42	11	74-0222
526	1.41	11	71-0120
527	1.40	13	77-0882
528	1.40	10/11	69-0147
529	1.39	11/12	78-0630
530	1.31	11	71-0626
531	1.31	11	74-0465
532	1.29	11/12	69-0176
533	1.28	11	73-0819
534	1.27	12	73-0516
535	1.24	10/11	77-0796
536	1.22	11/12	78-0580
537	1.22	11	73-0563
538	1.18	11	76-0682
539	1.16	11	71-0121
540	1.11	11/12	73-0571
541	1.06	10/11	73-1062

PTOLEMY APION, 104/1–96 B.C. (**542–623**)

Group IX—Module E

Head of Ptolemy Soter r.
Head of Libya r. ΒΑΣΙΛΕΩΣ ΠΤΟΛΕΜΑΙΟΥ.
rev. (α) Neat work
AE dies ↑ *BMC* 84-88

***542**	1.23	11/15	73-0629

Head of Ptolemy Soter r.
Head of Libya r. ΒΑΣΙΛΕΩΣ ΠΤΟΛΕΜΑΙΟΥ.
rev. (β) Crude work, large head
AE dies ↑, ↖ (3) *BMC* 89-94

***543**	1.70	12/14	78-0208
544	1.61	11/13	69-0092
545	1.57	11/12	74-0630
546	1.43	12/14	78-0746
547	1.30	10/11	69-0151
***548**	1.29	11	74-0011
549	1.21	12/15	76-0020
550	1.18	13/14	78-0108
***551**	1.14	12/13	77-0360
552	1.07	10/11	73-0644
553	0.93	10/12	73-0418
554	0.81	11	78-0018

Head of Ptolemy Soter r.
Head of Libya r. ΒΑΣΙΛΕΩΣ ΠΤΟΛΕΜΑΙΟΥ.
rev. (γ) Crude work, small head
AE dies ↑, ↖ (2) *BMC* 95-104

555	2.05	11/13	73-1051
556	1.48	10.5	71-0125
557	1.35	10/12	74-1036
558	1.24	11	76-0094
559	1.21	10/12	76-0678
560	1.20	10/13	77-0030
561	1.20	10/11	77-0884
562	1.16	9.5	78-0104
563	1.15	10/13	74-0629
***564**	1.07	10/12	74-0012

565	1.06	10/11	73-0548
566	1.04	11/12	69-0152
567	1.00	11/12	74-1032
568	0.99	10	74-0453
569	0.95	9/10	71-0324
570	0.95	10/11	76-0237
571	0.86	11	78-0020
572	0.77	10	73-0632

Head of Ptolemy Soter r.
Head of Libya r. ΒΑΣΙΛΕΩΣ ΠΤΟΛΕΜΑΙΟΥ.
rev. (α-γ) [uncertain variety]
AE dies ↑, ↖ (2)

573	1.46	10	69-0154
574	1.41	10/12	76-1298
575	1.40	11/13	73-1268
576	1.40	11/15	76-1297
577	1.39	10/11	73-0124
578	1.35	11	76-0218
579	1.31	10/12	76-0220
580	1.29	10/12	73-0634
581	1.23	11	76-1269
582	1.20	10/12	76-0219
583	1.19	11	69-0288
584	1.18	10/12	73-1270
585	1.17	11/13	76-0021
586	1.15	11/14	73-0123
587	1.15	10/12	73-0622
588	1.14	10	77-0802
589	1.13	10/11	76-0007
590	1.11	9/11	74-0152
591	1.09	11	73-0556
592	1.09	9/13	77-0801
593	1.01	11	73-0772
594	1.01	9/11	76-0095
595	0.97	9.5	77-0680
596	0.95	10/12	78-0314
597	0.94	9/11	73-0421
598	0.82	9/10	77-0234
599	0.78	10/12	76-0674
600	0.78	10	78-0017
601	0.77	10	77-0233
602	0.70	10/11	78-0044
603	0.63	10/12	69-0155

See also **436** and note 49.

Head of Ptolemy Soter r.
[Head of Libya r.]
imitation
AE dies —

*604[54]	0.86	10	77-0835

Head of Zeus Ammon r.
Eagle on fulmen l. From lower l., ΠΤΟΛΕ ΒΑΣΙΛ.
AE dies ↑, ↖ (1)

605	1.93	11/12	71-0323
*606	1.71	12/13	71-0318
607	1.64	11	71-0838

608	1.32	11	77-0858
*609	0.87	10/11	77-0827

Head of Zeus Ammon r.
Isiac headdress, no monograms. ΠΤΟΛΕ ΒΑΣΙΛ (etc.).
AE dies ↑, ↖ (2) Svoronos 1845

*610	2.23	12/13	77-0886
*611	2.13	13/14	77-0798
612	1.98	12/15	78-0316
613	1.95	12	73-0038
614	1.82	11/12	74-0071
*615	1.73	13	69-0298
616	1.71	12	77-0887
*617[55]	1.69	13	78-0051
618	1.69	11/12	76-1289
619	1.65	11/14	69-0346
*620	1.27	13	77-0772
621	1.18	11	76-1272
622	1.08	13	69-0096
623	0.79	11/13	73-0778

PTOLEMY IX SOTER II OR PTOLEMY APION (624–675)

Head of Zeus Ammon r.
Isiac headdress (uncertain variety).
AE dies ↑, ↖ (3)

624	2.79	13/14	78-0045
625	2.67	13	74-1179
626	2.59	14	76-0227
627	2.46	13	77-0889
628	2.31	13/15	73-0503
629	2.13	13	77-0820
630	2.13	13/14	77-0822
631	2.11	13/14	74-0009
632	2.10	11/13	69-0094
633	2.04	11/12	78-0054
634	2.02	12/14	71-0213
635	1.97	12/15	76-1286
636	1.90	14	74-0636
637[56]	1.90	13/14	74-1047
638	1.86	12/14	74-0471
639	1.85	13	74-0641
640	1.84	13	73-0008
641	1.77	13	76-0932
642	1.75	12/14	76-0006
643	1.63	13	69-0206
644	1.62	14	73-0648
645	1.58	11/13	76-1270
646	1.56	12/14	73-0243
647	1.49	12	71-0612
648	1.48	12	71-0568
649	1.46	12	73-0775
650	1.41	12	73-0005
651	1.38	13/14	78-0439
652	1.38	12/13	73-0246

---

54. Ridiculous obverse, the reverse just an indentation where the die missed.

55. Overstruck on Soter/Libya, whose surface holes are still evident.

56. Overstruck on or by Ammon/eagle.

653	1.37	12	73-0647	679	69-0286
654	1.35	11/13	73-0769	680	71-0018
655	1.34	12	76-0092	681	71-0027
656	1.33	12	73-0633	682	71-0028
657	1.31	13	76-0675	683	71-0124
658	1.29	13	74-0642	684	73-0094
659	1.25	10/11	69-0150	685	73-0144
660	1.23	11/12	74-0628	686	73-0211
*661[57]	1.22	11/12	77-0856	687	73-0349
662	0.96	12	76-0226	688	73-0505
663	0.96	10/11	74-1048	689	73-0514
664	0.95	10/12	77-0679	690	73-0517
665	0.93	12	69-0162	691	73-0518
666	0.77	11/12	71-0022	692	73-0519

Head of Zeus Ammon r.
Isiac headdress; dots in lieu of legend.
imitation
AE   dies ↑   Apollonia 51

*667	0.92		10	71-0023	
				693	73-0526
				694	73-0555
				695	73-0577
				696	73-0812
				697	73-1198

Head of Zeus Ammon r.
Isiac headdress; legends garbled.
imitation
AE   dies as shown

*668	↑	2.30	13	77-0859	698	73-1277
669	—	1.54	10/12	78-0579	699	73-1278
*670[58]	↖	1.50	13/14	77-0787	700	73-1282
*671	↗	1.37	10/12	71-0024	701	74-0219
672	↑	1.21	11	77-0825	702	74-0221
					703	74-0223

Head of Zeus Ammon l.
Isiac headdress; legends garbled.
imitation
AE   dies as shown

					704	74-0224
					705	74-0473
*673[59]	↓	2.80	13/14	74-0072	706	74-0474
674[60]	↑	2.29	12/13	74-0050	707	74-0475
675	↑	1.51	11/12	76-0228	708	74-0624
					709	74-0633
					710	74-1035
					711	74-1037
					712	74-1176
					713	76-0001

LATE 2ND–EARLY 1ST CENTURY B.C.
(676–725)

Small Ptolemaic bronzes, type unascertainable: Ptolemy/Libya, Ammon/eagle, or Ammon/Isiac headdress
AE

		714	76-0008
		715	76-0030
		716	76-0031
676	69-0095	717	76-0166
677	69-0195	718	76-0232
678	69-0270	719	76-0679
		720	77-0190
		721	77-0836
		722	77-1289
		723	78-0578
		724	78-0812
		725	78-0043

---

57. Overstruck on or by Ammon/eagle.

58. A fragment of the legend reads ...ИI...

59. Crude Ammon head l., irregularly. The die position is eccentric, the legend garbled: ...ΓΓ ITO...

60. Rev. legend garbled: ...IⱢ OL...

Mint of Barce (726 and 727)

PERIOD II (726)

CA. 475–435 B.C. (726)

ASIATIC HEMIDRACHM (726)

Silphium, type IC; at base l., A; at r., I.
Head of Zeus Ammon r. in circle of dots in round incuse; BA behind head; PKAION before.
AR dies ↗   obv. cf. BMC 8 [tetradrachm]; rev. cf. BMC clxx, 16b [drachm]
    *726   1.70   11/12   77-0767

PERIOD III (727)

CA. 435–308 B.C. (727)

ASIATIC TRIHEMIOBOL (727)

Triple silphium of type IB rising from central pellet.
Head of Carneius l.; under behind, AB, under before, ꟼ.
AR dies —   obv. cf. BMC clxxviii, 46a
    *727   0.84   11   74-0201

Mint of Euesperides (728–736)

PERIOD II (728)

CA. 475–435 B.C. (728)

ASIATIC DRACHM (728)

Silphium, type IC.
Head of Zeus Ammon r. in beaded circle, in square incuse.
  E
  V
AR dies ↙   BMC 4, same dies
    *728   2.75   14/15   76-1301

PERIOD III (729–732)

CA. 325–313 B.C. (729–732)

BRONZE UNITS

Head of Heracles r.
Quiver, club, bow.
AE dies ↑   BMC p. 124, 188 bis ["Cyrene"]
    729   12.36   20/21   69-0158

Head of Heracles r.
Bow, club, quiver.
AE dies ↓   cf. BMC p. 124, 188 bis ["Cyrene"]
    *730   13.76   23/24   69-0344
    731   13.39   21   76-1299
    732[61] 12.01   21/23   71-0319

PTOLEMY I SOTER, CA. 300–282 B.C. (733–736)

BRONZE

[Head of Heracles]
Bow case and club; between, ΒΑΣΙΛΕΩΣ.
AE dies irregular   Bond and Swales 128-35
    733   5.21   17/18   69-0308
    734[62] 3.54   13/14   74-0446
    735[62] 4.14   13/14   76-1268
    *736   3.83   14/16   74-0449

For the 3rd century see also 199 and note 36.

Cyrenaica Under the Romans (737–760)

LATE 1ST CENTURY B.C. (737–741)

L. Lollius
Head of Zeus Ammon r.
Curule chair. ΛΟΛΛΙΟΥ.
AE as, cut quarter   dies ↑   BMC 19-20
    *737[63]   5.45   [34]   77-0834

---

61. Considerably corroded, which accounts for the low weight.

62. Overstruck on uncertain types.

63. For the denominations of the Roman period bronze of Cyrenaica, see Buttrey, "Roman Coinage."

Head of Apollo r., B.
Dromedary r., E.   Λ O Λ
                         Λ   I
                         O   Y
AE semis   dies ↗   *BMC* 22, same dies
  *738   11.81   27   73-0552

  Crassus
Head of Libya r.
Crocodile r. ΚΡΑΣ.
AE as   dies ↗   *BMC* ccvii, 25 bis b
  *739   15.32   28   73-0504

Head of Libya r. Κ Ρ Α.
Silphium,   Κ   Υ
                         Ρ   [ ].
AE quadrans   dies ↑   *BMC* 26
  *740   3.40   16/19   71-0181

  Aulus Pupius Rufus
Ram r. ΠΟΥΠΙΟΣ.
Subsellium. ΡΟΥΦΟΣ ΤΑΜΙΑΣ.
AE semis   dies ↓   *BMC* 33
  *741   4.87   21   73-0623

CLEOPATRA AND ANTONY 31 B.C. (*742*)

ΒΑΣΙΛ / ΘΕΑ / ΝΕ
ΑΝΤΩ / ΥΠΑ / Γ
AE as, cut half   dies ↑   Svoronos 1899
  *742⁶⁴   4.42   25   74-1051

1ST CENTURY A.D.

TIBERIUS, A.D. 14–37
A.D. *19–37* (***743***)

Head of Drusus r. ΔΡΟΥΣΟΣ ΚΑΙΣΑΡ ΑΥΓΟΥΣΤΟΥ
ΥΙΟΣ.
Heads of Tiberius and Germanicus. ΤΙΒ ΓΕΡ ΚΑΙΣΑΡΕΣ.
AE as   dies ↑   *BMC* 51
  *743   6.70   23/24   76-0676

2ND CENTURY A.D.

TRAJAN, A.D. 98–117
A.D. *103–111* (***744–753***)

Bust of Trajan r. ΑΥΤΟΚΡΑ ΚΑΙΣ ΝΕΡ ΤΡΑΙΑΝΟΣ ΣΕΒ
ΓΕΡΜ ΔΑΚ.
Head of Zeus Ammon r. ΔΗΜΑΡΧ ΕΞ ΥΠΑΤ Γ.
AE as   dies ↓, ↙ (2), ← (1)   *BMCGal* p. 59, 116 =
                                        Sydenham 232a
  744⁶⁵   8.44   24   74-0477
  *745   7.98   25   76-1265
  746   7.84   23   69-0149
  747   7.69   24   76-1264
  748   7.53   22/25   78-0209
  749   7.50   21/24   69-0353
  750   7.26   23   78-0846
  751   7.22   23   77-1290
  752   6.57   22   76-1267
  753   6.32   23/24   76-0928

HADRIAN, A.D. 117–138
A.D. *119–138* (***754–756***)

Bust of Hadrian r. HADRIANVS AVGVSTVS.
Head of Zeus Ammon r. COS III.
AE semis   dies ↓   Sydenham 289-289a
  *754   3.42   18   76-1263

Bust of Hadrian r. HADRIANVS AVGVSTVS.
Head of Zeus Ammon r. COS III.
AE quadrans   dies ↓   not in Sydenham
  755   2.69   15/16   78-0581
  *756   2.42   15/16   78-0635

MARCUS AURELIUS, A.D. 161–180 (***757–760***)

Bust of Marcus r. M ANTONINVS AVGVSTVS.
Head of Zeus Ammon r. COS III.
AE semis   dies ↙, ↓   Sydenham 348, 350
  *757   3.43   17   76-0053
  758   2.15   16   71-0083

Bust of Marcus r. M ANTONINVS AVGVSTVS.
Head of Zeus Ammon r. COS III.
AE quadrans   dies ↙   Sydenham 349
  *759   2.95   14   74-0618
  760   2.93   13/14   73-1047

---

64. Not in any *BMC* volume. The find confirms the nineteenth century attribution to Cyrenaica. On the phenomenon of halving in Cyrenaica see Buttrey, "Roman Coinage."

65. **744–760**: The old attribution to Caesarea in Cappadocia is now known to be wrong: the coins must have been struck at Cyrene, or in Rome for Cyrenaica. All examples here are very thoroughly worn and underweight.

Greek Coins Struck Outside Cyrenaica (*760A–774*)

THESSALONICA

MARCUS AURELIUS CAESAR – COMMODUS, A.D. *158–192*

Bust of emperor r. ΑΝΤωΝΙΝΟC ΚΑΙCΑΡ
Nike r. holding palm and wreath ΘΕCCΑΛΟΝΙΚΕωΝ
AE   dies ↖   I. Touratsoglou, *Die Münzstätte von Thessaloniki in der Römischen Kaiserzeit*, Antiken Münzen und Geschnittene Steine 12 (Berlin 1988) p. 191, 16 etc.

  ***760A**   10.13   26/28   76-1261

CORCYRA

CA. *300–229* B.C.

Kantharos. K.
Grapes.
AE   dies irregular   *BMCThes* p. 132, 280
  ***761**[66]   4.03   16   74-1180
  ***762**   3.48   15/17   74-1184
  ***763**[67]   3.92   17   73-0093

ACHAEAN LEAGUE, MINT OF ANTIGONEIA

2ND CENTURY B.C.

Head of Zeus r.
X in wreath; to l. and r., N A; below, Ⓐ
AR hemidrachm   dies ↙   M. Thompson, *The Agrinion Hoard*, Numismatic Notes and Monographs 159 (New York 1968) cf. nos. 354-369
  ***764**[68]   2.00   13/14   76-0929

RHODES

CA. *333–304* B.C.

Head of Rhodos r.
Rose. PO.
AE   dies ↑   *BMCCar* p. 238, 74 etc.

  765   1.82   —   78-0815
  ***766**   1.05   11   74-0448

JUDAEA

A.D. *68/9*

Amphora.
Vine-branch.
AE   dies ↓   *BMCPal* p. 274, 42–54
  ***767**   2.66   16   76-0054

EGYPT

CLEOPATRA VII, 52–30 B.C.

Bust of Cleopatra r.
Eagle l. on fulmen; at l., double cornucopiae; at r., Π. ΚΛΕΟΠΑΤΡΑΣ ΒΑΣΙΛΙΣΣΗΣ.
AE 80 drachms   dies ↑   *BMCPtol* p. 123, 5
  ***768**   19.21   26/27   74-0447

AUGUSTUS, 30 B.C.*–14* A.D.

27–10 B.C.

Altar.
Cornucopia.
AE 20 drachms   dies ↑   Milne 8
  ***769**   3.01   15/16   69-0247

2–1 B.C.

Head of Augustus r.
6 ears of grain, bound.
AE diobol   dies ↑   Milne 12
  ***770**   7.77   24   76-1266

Head of Augustus r.
Cornucopia.
AE obol   dies ↑   Milne 21
  ***771**   5.45   19.5   73-0033

---

66. Overstruck, the undertype uncertain.
67. Overstruck, the undertype uncertain.
68. Another example of Achaean League hemidrachm found at Cyrene was included in Robinson *NC*[6] 4 (1944) no. 6. The Cyrene Museum possesses an unpublished hoard of several hundred pieces.

A.D. 9–10

Head of Augustus r.
LΛΘ in wreath.
AE obol   dies ↑   Milne 24b
  ***772**   5.02   19   73-0032

UNCERTAIN MINT

Head of Athena r.
Figure striding l. (?)
AE   dies ↖   Countermark on obverse, facing
                             head (?) in circular field
  ***773**   4.58   19   73-0034
   774   catalogued as 760A

Roman Republic (775)

P. Clodius
Head of Apollo r.
Diana facing.
  Crawford 494/23
          date   *denomination*   *mint*   *inv. no.*
775   42 B.C.   **AR** denarius   Rome   74-1052
                         (plated)

Roman Empire (776–802)

CLAUDIUS, A.D. 41–54

Hand holding balance.
SC.
  BMCRE 1.190.181
776   42 A.D.   **AE** quadrans   Rome   78-0634

1ST CENTURY A.D.

777   [illegible] **AE** as   —   77-0031

TRAJAN, A.D. 98–117

Bust of Trajan r.
Heracles facing.
  BMCRE 3.225.1058
***778** 98–117 A.D. **AE** quadrans   Rome   69-0104

? HADRIAN, A.D. 117-138

Head of Mars r.
Cuirass.
  RIC 2.218.19 (cf. *BMCRE* 3.534.1856)
***779** ?117–138 A.D. **AE** quadrans   Rome   77-0800

ANTONINUS PIUS, A.D. 138–161

Head of Antoninus Pius r.
Annona r.
  BMCRE 4.217.1356
780   140–143 A.D.   **AE** as   Rome   77-0186

FAUSTINA II, A.D. 147–175

Bust of Faustina r.
Venus l.
  BMCRE 4.377.2170
781   150–152 A.D.   **AE** dupondius Rome   69-0269

MARCUS AURELIUS, A.D. 161-180

Radiate head of Marcus Aurelius r.
Salus l.
  BMCRE 4.606.1
782   168–169 A.D.   **AE** dupondius Rome   71-0760

Radiate head of Marcus Aurelius r.
Aequitas l.
  BMCRE 4.674.1682
783   177–178 A.D.   **AE** dupondius Rome   73-0635

2ND CENTURY A.D.

784	[illegible]	**AE** as	Rome	69-0289

BALBINUS, A.D. 238

Bust of Balbinus r.
Providentia l.
   RIC 4².171.19
*785   238 A.D.   **AE** sestertius   Rome   74-0008

GORDIAN III, A.D. 238–244

Bust of Gordian r.
Apollo standing l.
   RIC 4³.48.301a
786   241–243 A.D.   **AE** sestertius   Rome   76-1262

Bust of Gordian r.
Securitas l.
   RIC 4³.52.335a
787   243–244 A.D.   **AE** sestertius   Rome   74-0560

TREBONIANUS GALLUS, A.D. 251–253

Bust of Trebonianus Gallus r.
Pietas l.
   RIC 4³.172.116a
788   251–253 A.D.   **AE** sestertius   Rome   69-0249

AURELIAN, A.D. 270–275

Radiate bust of Aurelian r.
Sol l. between captives; in exergue, XXIς.
   cf. *RIC* 5¹.272.62 (mintmark of .63)
*789   270–275 A.D.   **AR** antoninianus   Rome   74-0619

DIOCLETIAN, A.D. 284–305

Bust of Diocletian r.
Emperor and Jupiter; officina Γ.
   RIC 6.667.46a
790   296–297 A.D.   **AE** radiate fraction   Alexandria   71-0122

MAXIMIAN, A.D. 286–305

Bust of Maximian r.
Emperor and Jupiter; officina Γ.
   RIC 6.670.59b
791   305–306 A.D.   **AE** radiate fraction   Alexandria   73-1283

CONSTANTINE I, A.D. 306–337

Head of Constantine r.
VOT XX in wreath; officina A.
   RIC 7.446.180
792   321–324 A.D.   **AE** follis   Siscia   74-0399

CONSTANTINE II CAESAR, A.D. 316–337

Bust of Constantine II l.
Camp gate; officina T.
   RIC 7.335.323
793   329–330 A.D.   **AE** follis   Rome   73-0543

VRBS ROMA, A.D. 330–337

Helmeted bust of Roma l.
Wolf and twins.
794   330–337 A.D.   **AE** follis   —   76-1283

CONSTANTIUS II CAESAR, A.D. 324–337

Bust of Constantius II r.
Two soldiers with two standards; officina H.
   RIC 7.693.88
*795   330–335 A.D.   **AE** follis   Antioch   76-0933

CONSTANS CAESAR, A.D. 333–337

Bust of Constans r.
Two soldiers with two standards; officina P.
   RIC 7.339.353
796   333–335 A.D.   **AE** follis   Rome   71-0123

VRBS ROMA, A.D. 336–337

Helmeted bust of Roma l.
Two soldiers with one standard; officina B.
   RIC 7.561.156
797   336–337 A.D.   **AE** follis   Heraclea   73-0544

CONSTANTINE I POSTHUMOUS, A.D. 337–340

Veiled head of Constantine r.
Emperor in quadriga r.; officina S.
   RIC 8.491.19
798   337–340 A.D.   **AE** follis   Cyzicus   78-0016

CONSTANTIUS II, A.D. 337–361

Bust of Constantius r.
Falling horseman 4.
799   351–361 A.D.   **AE** 3   —   76-0930

Bust of Constantius r.
Falling horseman 3.
  RIC 8.545.84
800   355–361 A.D.   **AE** 3   Alexandria   71-0312

CONSTANTIUS II OR JULIAN, A.D. 355–363

Head of Emperor r.
Virtus l.
801   355–363 A.D.   **AE** 4   —   78-0813

JULIAN CAESAR, A.D. 355–361

Head of Julian r.
Virtus l.
802   355–361 A.D.   **AE** 4   —   74-1039

Byzantine Empire (*803* and *804*)

HERACLIUS, A.D. 610–641

Figures of Heraclius and Heraclius Constantine.
M; officina Ɛ.
AE follis   dies ↙   *DO* 2^1·278-286.76e.1   Constantinople
       etc.
*****803**[69]   613–616 A.D.   12.19g   33/34mm   76-1285

Cross on two steps, dot [l.] and r.
S.
AE 6 nummi   dies ↗   *DO* 2^1.341.198.8-9   Alexandria
804   613–618 A.D.   1.86g   15/17mm   78-0632

Islamic (*805*)

AGHLABID
IBRAHIM II, A.D. 874–902/261–289 A.H.

AE   *BMCMoh* 2.63.214   al-Abbasiya
*****805**   874–902 A.D.   0.92g   15mm   74-1181

Kingdom of Italy (*806–808*)

VICTOR EMMANUEL II, 1849–1878

806   1861   **AE** 5 centesimi   Milan   78-0633
807   (1861-1867)   **AE** 5 centesimi   —   71-0001

VICTOR EMMANUEL III, 1900–1946

808   1926   **AE** 5 centesimi   Rome   74-0476

---

69. Overstruck on a follis of Phocas, XX[XX] / CON[ ], DO 2^1.163–165.26a–32b.

Illegible (809–834)

AE			**822**		71-0391
809	Hellenistic	71-0155	**823**		71-0759
810	Hellenistic	71-0276	**824**		71-0835
811	Hellenistic	71-0390	**825**		73-0318
812	Hellenistic	71-0628	**826**		73-0553
813	Hellenistic	74-0625	**827**		73-1061
814	Hellenistic	78-0476	**828**		73-1269
815		69-0175	**829**		74-0466
816		69-0177	**830**		76-0093
817		69-0299	**831**		76-0233
818		71-0279	**832**		76-1273
819		71-0314	**833**		76-1282
820		71-0316	**834**		77-0678
821		71-0326			

III

The Bronze Coinage of Cyrenaica

Introduction

The Demeter Sanctuary excavation has produced a body of material large enough to warrant a survey of the bronze coinage of Greek Cyrenaica. Four tables below present the array of issues from the four mints—Cyrene, Barce, Euesperides, and (possibly) Apollonia—as far as they are currently known, with their suggested chronological and denominational placement. The sequence of the bronze coinage was established in general by Robinson in the *BMC*, although many individual issues are difficult to place and the absolute chronology is very uncertain. In this study I have followed the chronology of the *BMC* except as indicated, understanding that some of its dates are more convenient than persuasive. Issues not known to Robinson have been included in their appropriate setting. What particularly distinguishes the array of coinages here from that of the *BMC* is the inclusion of Ptolemaic issues excluded there: "Several issues attributed to the Cyrenaica by R. S. Poole and by Svoronos have been omitted, because the evidence did not seem sufficient to establish their attribution."[1] Archaeological evidence is now available that demonstrates the validity of some of the earlier attributions and shows how rich the later bronze coinage of Cyrenaica really was.

The Mint of Cyrene

The earliest date of bronze coinage is unknown. Robinson included the first issues in his Period III (2), 375–308 B.C., but concluded from the style of the silphium type and the apparent relation of the horseman type to that of the gold, "that little if any of the bronze is before the time of Alexander, and that the bulk was struck after his death (323)."[2] Consequently he catalogued the bronze under the subheading "Late 4th cent.–308 B.C."[3] It would follow that most of the early autonomous issues were produced only after Ptolemy I gained control of Cyrenaica in 322 through Ophellas' victory over Thibron. From the beginning, then, national Cyrenaican types would have been struck under some form of Ptolemaic authority. This chronology is supported by the common fabric of the earliest bronze from Cyrene, Barce, and Euesperides, and the fact that the Heracles/ obverse of the earliest Euesperides bronze is imitated from tetradrachms of Alexander (see Appendix).

---

1. *BMC* cxxxviii.
2. *BMC* xci.
3. *BMC* 40.

The bronze issues of the Cyrene mint, whether or not represented in the excavation, are laid out in Table I in a proposed sequence and chronology. To begin, Robinson's designation of the "Unit" (the Greek denomination is unknown) and its fractions in the issues to ca. 300 B.C. has been followed here and in the Catalogue. No one can doubt that there was originally a systematic structure, and subsequent issues also appear to fall into groups of related denominations. But it is possible that some issues gathered together here were struck sequentially rather than contemporaneously.

CA. 325–313 B.C.

The theoretical weights appear to have been the 17.2, 8.6, 4.3, and 2.15 grams of the Attic tetradrachm, didrachm, drachm, and hemidrachm. The diameters are characteristically narrower than those of the third century but the flans are thicker. The sequence of /silphium and /wheel types is established by overstrikes (*BMC* 187).

REVOLT, 313–312 B.C.

The unusual reverse type, Tomb of Battus, recalls the foundation of the autonomous city and is appropriate to the revolt of 313–312. Robinson read the signature of Euphris, who also struck gold drachms (*BMC* 170b-d), independently dated by Mørkholm to 314 B.C.[4] Mørkholm associates the Artemis/Nike issue with the revolt;[5] Laronde gives it to the revolt of 305–300,[6] but the fabric is earlier than that on my arrangement.

OPHELLAS' CARTHAGINIAN CAMPAIGN, 309 B.C.

The rare palm tree bronze is probably to be associated with Ophellas' disastrous Carthaginian campaign. It also appears alongside the silphium on silver (*BMC* 173) and gold (Naville 144); and the silver bears the Tanit symbol.[7]

From this point the chronology is particularly difficult to establish. Robinson considers his Period IV, "308–277 B.C.," in great detail,[8] dividing the issues into three stages. In the First Stage of eight types (Table I.16, 25, 26–27, 28, 29, 30, 32, 37) problems arise from the developing fabric of the different issues, and the evidence of overstrikes. No. 16 should be separated out.[9] The gazelle/silphium Halves and the crab/jerboa Quarters must be the next-earliest issues on the basis of fabric: the flans continue dumpy and the reverses incuse, characteristic of the issues of the first series above, but the standard is lighter than that of the first series, perhaps to a drachm weight of ca. 3.20 g. The other issues that Robinson included in his First Stage do not share that fabric to an appreciable degree. Furthermore, one of these, the Ammon/bow case piece (*BMC* 286), is overstruck on an /eagle issue of Ptolemy I. On the basis of fabric no Ptolemy piece can be as early as the two types that open the First Stage. The stage must therefore be divided, and the issues in the name of Ptolemy inserted.

Five issues of Quarters and Eighths remain. Their fabric requires that they be placed after the gazelle/silphium; at the same time they appear to have nothing to do with the issues which certainly follow the Ptolemy types. Therefore they probably precede the Ptolemy /eagle types.

The issues of the other two stages follow. The two types of the Second Stage, Apollo/quiver and Libya/silphium, also occur as overstrikes, some legible examples on Ptolemaic /eagle. The three common issues that constitute the Third Stage—Ammon/palm tree, Apollo/horse, Apollo/lyre—are of relatively broad dies in low relief and so are late in Robinson's Period IV. The large Ammon/palm tree issue is here placed last of all.[10]

This sequence is at variance with the most recent arrangement of the silver issues. Some gazelle/ silphium and jerboa/crab pieces bear the name of Σῶσις, which also occurs with jerboa symbol on a large issue of "Phoenician" didrachms (*BMC* 261–63) dated by Mørkholm to ca. 290–280 B.C.[11] If monograms and symbols that are common to the bronze and silver really do signify simultaneous issue, the bronze or the silver will have to be rearranged.

---

4. Mørkholm 149.

5. Mørkholm 150.

6. Laronde 356–57.

7. Mørkholm 151.

8. *BMC* cxxv–cxxxiii.

9. See Table I.16, note.

10. For the rationale of this arrangement, see discussion below under MAGAS IN REVOLT.

11. Mørkholm 154.

PTOLEMY I, CA. 308–305 B.C.

This date span is suggested with some reservations. The legends on the jerboa/crab excavation coins (**158–164**) cannot be recovered. Robinson read ΣΩΣI on the Berlin piece (*BMC* 285c), surely correctly, though doubted by Newell: the Berlin piece is not from the same obverse die as the piece published by Newell clearly reading ΒΑΣΙΛ.[12] The chronology is very tight; if Mørkholm is correct in dating the next revolt to 305[13] there will have been little time for news of Ptolemy's assumption of the title Βασιλεύς in that year to have been reflected on the local coin.

REVOLT, CA. 305–300 B.C.

The chronology of the revolt follows Mørkholm.[14] The issues included here are relatively uncommon and difficult to date: their failure to refer to Ptolemy I is here taken as indicative. They can hardly be earlier in the relative chronology, given their new, thinner fabric, and little indentation of the reverse, whereas the /eagle and subsequent issues are generally heavier.

PTOLEMY I, CA. 300–282 B.C.

For the opening of this period, I follow Mørkholm's date for the end of the revolt in preference to Naville's date of 304 B.C.[15] The bronze was apparently struck to the "Rhodian" standard with a drachm at ca. 3.90 g; the monogram ⌐ is shared by the Soter/eagle bronze (*BMC* 5a), and "Rhodian" weight didrachms (*BMC* 243–248). There is a chronological problem. None of the /eagle reverses is sufficiently well-preserved to establish the reading ΒΑΣΙΛΕΩΣ, and *BMC* 5d-e appear to omit it. But they are linked by common magistrates, Hippocrates and Clea ..., with gold, which does read ΒΑΣΙΛΕΩΣ, dated by Naville to 304–284,[16] and to silver of the "Rhodian" standard dated by Mørkholm to 300–298.[17]

MAGAS IN REVOLT, CA. 282–261 B.C.

The opening date follows Chamoux, who suggested that Magas' revolt is probably to be dated to the accession of Philadelphus.[18] The date of their reconciliation is quite unknown; Robinson's choice of 261 B.C. is here retained for convenience. As for the coins of this period, Naville argued that the coinage of the revolt of Magas ought not to have borne the portraits of Soter and Berenice (*BMC* Regal 6–29).[19] In his review of Naville, Robinson admitted this argument.[20] The result is to move down in time, to after the reconciliation, the Soter/ issues with Magas' monogram, which Robinson had originally given to the revolt.[21] The issues listed at this point in the Catalogue, mostly given in the *BMC* to 300–277 B.C., take their place as the coins of Magas' independence. This provides a plausible explanation for the overstriking frequently observed in these types: Ammon/bow case, Apollo/lyre, Apollo/quiver, and Libya/silphium are all found overstruck on the regal, that is, they obliterated the earlier Ptolemaic /eagle types. An additional type, Ammon/palm tree, falls later in the period. It seems not to have been used to overstrike earlier issues, and was produced to a somewhat heavier standard similar to that of the restored Ptolemaic bronze following 261 B.C.

It is noteworthy that Magas never struck coin with his own portrait, nor even with his own name—the Soter/Libya pieces reading ΒΑΣΙΛΕΩΣ ΜΑΓΑ (*BMC* Regal 32–33) have been retooled—nor indeed with any sort of regal typology. The types of this period are either traditional Cyrenaican, or general Greek.

MAGAS RECONCILED WITH PTOLEMY II, CA. 261–258 B.C.

All issues bear Magas' monogram. The conventional date of the reconciliation, 261 B.C., seems too late (or Magas' death in 258 too early) to allow for the abundant coinage of this period. There are in any case difficult problems in the chronology of events, both historical and numismatic, from the latter part of Magas' rule to the reign of Ptolemy III Euergetes. The relative chronology of the issues is

---

12. Newell 13–14.
13. Mørkholm 152.
14. Mørkholm 152–54.
15. Naville nos. 241–47.
16. Naville p. 80.
17. Mørkholm 158.

18. F. Chamoux, "Le roi Magas," *Revue Historique* 216 (1956) 18–34.
19. Naville pp. 83–84.
20. E.S.G. Robinson, *NC*[6] 13 (1953) 163.
21. For those coinages, see below under MAGAS RECONCILED.

easy enough:

(1) the various types in silver and bronze bearing the heads of Soter or Berenice I, with Magas' monogram (*BMC* Regal 6–29);

(2) bronze of Soter/Libya, without monogram (*BMC* Regal 30–33, Group I);

(3) bronze of the Koinon with Zeus/silphium, frequently overstruck on the preceding issues of Magas and Soter/Libya (*BMC* Koinon 2–29);

(4) return to Soter/Libya (*BMC* Regal 34–38, Group II).

So Robinson.[22] The sequence is secure: coins of (1) are overstruck on earlier autonomous issues of Cyrene; (2) introduces what became a long-lived sequence of issues of the same type; (3) is overstruck on (1) and (2); and (4) introduces the rest of the Soter/Libya issues, being related to them particularly by the appearance of the surface hole on each face of the coin, which characterizes all of Groups II–IX.

The problem is the absolute chronology, and the relation of the coinages to the fragmentary historical information we possess. Robinson in the *BMC* attributed the issues of (1) above to Magas' revolt and (2) to follow the reconciliation between Magas and Ptolemy II Philadelphus, ca. 261 B.C. Later, however,[23] he accepted that Naville's attribution of non-Ptolemaic type coinage to Magas required moving the issues of (1), with portraits of Soter and Berenice, to after the reconciliation. The reattribution is accepted in this Catalogue. Robinson did not consider the problem of issue (2), but the new chronology of (1) implies that he now would have placed (2) after Magas' death (in 258 B.C., on Robinson's chronology). Indeed there is no better explanation for the disappearance of Magas' monogram from Cyrenaican coin.

Now the two rulers agreed that their children, respectively Berenice and the Ptolemy who became III Euergetes, would marry, and that Cyrenaica would revert to the Egyptian crown after Magas' death. It would seem likely enough that issue (2), whose types unite reference to Cyrenaica and the Egyptian dynasty, was struck in recognition of the return of the province to Ptolemaic control. Subsequently (we know not when) some sort of independence movement seized the area, and Cyrene (or Cyrenaica) called in law-givers from Greece. Robinson not unnaturally associated (3), the Koinon coinage, with that movement, dating it to ca. 250–247 B.C. Finally, Ptolemaic control was reestablished, probably on the succession of Ptolemy III to the throne in 246 B.C., when (4) the Soter/Libya coinage was resumed.

Some scholars have been troubled by the dating of issue (2). At the death of Magas, whenever it was, Berenice and the prince Ptolemy had not yet married. Magas' widow, Apama, herself a Seleucid princess, broke off the Ptolemaic betrothal, preferring for Berenice a Seleucid alliance. She was offered Demetrius ὁ Καλός, who came to Cyrene and took it into his power.[24] But he came to a sudden and embarrassing end, murdered in Apama's chamber in what were said to be tasteless circumstances. We might believe that his intrusion into Cyrenaica was more disturbing than his private habits. In any case, what followed is unknown, but the dynastic difficulties had obvious political implications, and Berenice, who favored the Egyptian liaison, was ultimately driven to reduce the cities that had taken against her (the Koinon?). There is therefore the double problem: where in all this is there political room for a new Ptolemaic coinage in Cyrenaica, issue (2), the Soter/Libya issue, and where chronological room? In Robinson's revised arrangement issue (2) presumably falls somewhere between 258 and 250, whereas the Koinon issue (3) represents the period of Cyrene's autonomy.

Laronde accepts this sequence of issues, but his analysis is different. First, he reminds us of the problem of the foundation of the city Berenice and the abandonment of Euesperides.[25] Solinus relates that Berenice, who was married to Ptolemy III, fortified the city known by her name which lay just to the west of Euesperides: *Berenicem civitatem. . . Hanc Berenice munivit quae Ptolemaeo tertio fuit nupta* (27,54 Mommsen). The new city became the home of the inhabitants of the old. This is usually taken to have occurred after Cyrenaica was reunited to the kingdom of Egypt, that is, no earlier than 246 B.C.

There is numismatic evidence for a relative date, in the surface finds of coins from Euesperides collected and published by Bond and Swales. The coins are a good cross-section of Cyrenaican bronze into the reign of Magas, (1) above, where they stop abruptly. There is nothing later, aside from one Soter/Libya piece (for which see below), and notably nothing of the rather common Koinon issue, (3) above. It would follow that the population of Euesperides moved to the new community that we call Berenice just when the Soter/Libya type was first introduced. This picture of a circulation ending sharply with coins of Magas is confirmed by the unpublished finds from Euesperides (see Appendix).

Bond and Swales suggested that abandonment of Euesperides might have been gradual.[26] Laronde has

---

22. *BMC* cli.

23. See above, n. 20.

24. Eusebius *Chronica* I.237.18ff.

25. Laronde 390–94.

26. Bond and Swales 93.

well replied that the coins in fact indicate the opposite, and that their sharp cessation must mark the move of the entire population to Berenice. Bond and Swales also adverted to Solinus' text, suggesting that if Berenice fortified the new site she must have found there some settlement to fortify, and there is actually no evidence that the new site bore her name at its foundation. That is, the people of Euesperides could have made their move to a new community that only later received both the generosity and the name of Berenice. In response, Laronde provides a serial argument that is perhaps more ingenious than compelling: *munire* is equivalent to the Greek τειχίζειν; Berenice provided the city with walls; normally walls are built before the rest of the city; therefore she must have founded the city that bears her name, and the Euesperides coins are consonant with a foundation dated after reversion of Cyrenaica to Egypt under Ptolemy III.[27]

Second, in Laronde's view, Magas actually died in 250 B.C. It is impossible to disentangle the date of Magas' death, a problem that is still with us after a century and a half of discussion.[28] The evidence is well known, and was reviewed again by Chamoux, who settled for 250 B.C. His argument is essentially this: (1) Negatively, there is no direct evidence for the conventional date of 258 B.C., which is deduced from Eusebius' date for the subsequent death of Demetrius ὁ Καλός in 259/8 B.C. But Eusebius had confused this Demetrius with his nephew Demetrius II, so that this evidence cannot be used. (2) Positively, Athenaeus (12.550b) cites Agatharchides, who says that Magas reigned for 50 years. Chamoux, having argued that Magas first appeared in Cyrenaica in 300 B.C., therefore dates his death to 250. (3) The Açoka inscription appears to mention Magas as known in India in 251 or 248.[29]

To my mind this line of argument is unpersuasive. (1) It is true that the careers of the two Demetrioi are confused in Eusebius, but it does not follow that the details of their careers are wrong. The text says specifically that 259/8 was the year of the death of Demetrius ὁ Καλός, and it is certain that that date has nothing to do with Demetrius II, who died in 230 or 229 B.C. Emendation has been suggested but is superfluous. Since 259/8 cannot refer to Demetrius II, it must be Eusebius' date for the death of ὁ Καλός. (2) The date of Magas' death depends on dating his first arrival in Cyrenaica, which must be separately argued. In any case Agatharchides was commenting on Magas' fatal corpulence, and only remarked in an offhand way that Magas reigned for 50 years. Some may find "50 years" too casual and too round a number to be taken literally. (3) The Açoka inscription was intended to impress Indians, not to provide an exact account of Hellenistic kingship. Whatever Açoka's knowledge of Magas may have been, it is entirely possible, as Chamoux admits, that word of his death had not reached India—hardly surprising.

Acceptance of the 250 B.C. date has been encouraged by the assumption that Berenice would not have remained unmarried for 10 years or more after her father's death. But we know virtually nothing about what went on in Cyrenaica or its ruling family during and after the episode of Demetrius the Fair. On balance I believe that the 250 B.C. date for Magas' death is too fragile to allow as settled, and that Eusebius' date for the death of Demetrius ὁ Καλός, with its implication for the death of Magas, should be maintained until weightier evidence is at hand.

The result of accepting (a) that the Euesperides finds provide a relative date for the transmigration to Berenice, which (b) was founded under Ptolemy III, is to push the post-Magan issues of coin into this Ptolemy's reign. That is Laronde's position: in his view the issues of Magas, including Soter/Libya Group I, run to his death in 250 B.C.[30] No coinage can be attributed to the following four years. The next issue, struck after the accession of Ptolemy III and the reversion of Cyrenaica to Egypt, was the Ammon/silphium bronze with the legend KOINON (evidence, apparently, of regal leniency toward evocation of the old traditions of Cyrenaican independence).[31] The Koinon flans resembled the subsequent Ptolemaic flans in having no surface holes. Finally, at some unknown time, perhaps only with Ptolemy IV, the Soter/Libya type was resumed.[32]

From a numismatic point of view there are serious problems with this reconstruction. First, on a point of fact, Laronde has misunderstood an ambiguous passage in Robinson on the Koinon coins: "E.S.G. Robinson remarque . . . que le point central manque, ce qui apparente ces émissions au bronze ptolémaïque frappé à partir d'Evergète Ier."[33] Robinson wrote, "Details of fabric such as the bevelled edge and the absence of the hole in the flan, characteristic of Ptolemaic bronze issues from

---

27. Laronde 382–83, 393–94.

28. B.G. Niebuhr, *Kleine Schriften* I (Bonn 1828) 233–38; Geyer in *PW* s.v. Magas.

29. Chamoux (n. 18) 30–31.

30. Laronde 392–93. Laronde's dating of the first Soter/Libya issue to the last decade of the 4th century, p. 368, is presumably just an oversight.

31. Laronde 405–406.

32. Laronde 419.

33. Laronde 405.

Euergetes onwards..."[34]—that is, what is characteristic of the subsequent bronze is the hole, not the absence of the hole. Neither Group I nor the Koinon coins have surface holes, while Groups II-IX normally do have them.[35] The Koinon and the subsequent Soter/Libya issues do not manifest the same manufacturing technique—quite the reverse. This point is of significance because the supposed physical similarity of these two types of coin encouraged Laronde to decide that the Koinon issue was struck within the realm of Ptolemaic authority, contrary to Robinson's attribution.

Second, against the Ptolemaic attribution of the Koinon issue is the fact that its Ammon/silphium types recall a type-pairing that had not been seen at Cyrene for perhaps three-quarters of a century, and that was particularly associated with the independent city. It would be very odd indeed if such type-pairing should not simply occur with Ptolemaic acquiesence, but should interrupt the coinage of Ptolemaic types. Worse, examples of the most recent Ptolemaic coinage, the new Soter/Libya issue, were obliterated by being used as flans for Koinon coins.

Perhaps most important, to judge from the non-overstruck Koinon pieces in the *BMC*, the bronze was a one-denomination issue whose weight standard had nothing to do with the Ptolemaic coinages of the preceding 50 years, but replicated the standard of the fourth-century units of independent Cyrene. Twenty pieces in the *BMC* average 11.44 g. An additional eight pieces in the *BMC* are overstruck on Magas and Soter/Libya, issues that never came near to such a standard; these, which admittedly must be somewhat light from earlier circulation, average only 8.13 g. One cannot attribute the phenomenon of overstriking simply to sloppiness at the mint; there has to be some guiding intelligence behind it. Older coins do not leap unbidden upon the die to be re-struck; someone has to make provision for collecting them and conveying them to the mint, and the number of these overstrikes surviving today suggests that this was a considerable operation. It might of course have had a purely fiscal purpose: it costs less to overstrike than to produce new flans, and money was saved additionally by using undersize flans. But the practical effect was to diminish the overtly Ptolemaic coin in circulation while reintroducing a traditional pre-Ptolemaic type and weight standard.

The same difficulty attends the rare Koinon silver. It is much less common than the previous silver issues of Magas—hardly a new imperial coinage. More importantly it "abandons the current Ptolemaic (`Phoenician') standard and reverts to the `Rhodian.'"[36] In type and weight both the silver and the bronze Koinon issues were plainly meant to break with current usage. I see no way to explain them as Ptolemaic, struck in Cyrene under Euergetes. On the contrary, it must be meaningful that the Soter/Libya bronze was subsequently resumed in an Alexandrian technique, and that no silver ever again was struck at the Greek mint of Cyrene.

Robinson must have been correct in understanding the Koinon issues to have been produced during a period when Cyrenaica was not under Ptolemaic control. Obliteration of Ptolemaic coin taken from circulation was a matter of deliberate policy. This accepted, the most economical explanation of the evidence is to assign the issue to the period of autonomy independently attested to in the literature, after Magas' death and before Euergetes' accession. Necessarily, the first Soter/Libya issue precedes the Koinon in the same period.

To return to the finds from Euesperides, they are earlier still. The published attribution of the single Soter/Libya piece (Bond and Swales 136) to Group I is wrong. I have handled it myself, and can certify that the traces of the types are sufficient to show that it is of a later style, and that in any case the flan bears the surface holes unknown to Group I.[37] It is an example of Group IV-B, a later issue of Ptolemy III—that is, it is a stray (as is Bond and Swales 137, dating to the first century B.C.), and does not bear on earlier monetary activity at Euesperides. The surface finds, now confirmed by the unpublished coins from Euesperides (for which, see Appendix), suggest that the move to Berenice occurred before the Soter/Libya issues were begun.

Thus the numismatic evidence for the transmigration is fixed only to the rule of Magas or shortly after his death. Nothing in the coins requires that it fall any later. Bond and Swales wrote of their finds, "This numismatic evidence implies that the transfer to the promontory site had taken place some time before it received the name of Berenice from Euergetes I."[38] I believe that the coins show their case for the pre-Euergetes transfer to be correct. But their assumption about the name of the new site is another matter. Actually Solinus only informs us that Berenice fortified the city, and that she was married to Ptolemy III. He does not connect these two facts, and his identification of her may be intended only to

---

34. *BMC* cxxxvi.

35. See *BMC* clvi–clviii and 80–81, with descriptions at nos. 30 and 34.

36. Robinson, *BMC* cxxxv.

37. The holes are denied by Bond and Swales, on p. 93, but they are there.

38. Bond and Swales 93.

specify her in a world rich in Berenices (*quae* = "the one who"). Even accepting Laronde's argument that "fortified" is equivalent to "founded," nothing requires the conclusion that it was *as Ptolemy's wife* that Berenice (or those who exercised authority in her name) founded the city; on the contrary, had the foundation occurred after 246 B.C. we would expect to be told that it was undertaken on the authority of Euergetes and the city named by him after his wife in analogy to the polinyms Arsinoe and Ptolemais. We might better conclude that the daughter of Magas, who apparently could control military power, was given the credit for the foundation prior to her marriage to Euergetes. This arrangement is in agreement with the sources, the Euesperides finds, and Laronde's interpretation of *munivit*, while avoiding the grave difficulties, numismatic and constitutional, in attributing the Koinon issue to a period of Ptolemaic rule.

PTOLEMY II, CA. 258–250 B.C.

Somewhere in this period the Soter/Libya issues begin. They have been arranged by Robinson in nine Groups (I–IX) of five denominations (A–E), continuing down to the death of Ptolemy Apion. It is convenient to survey them at this point.

SOTER/LIBYA

Robinson distinguished among the issues in part by the symbol of single or double cornucopiae, a distinction that is not consistently observed in the actual coinage. He also separated the issues by fabric, which can be seen to deteriorate as time goes by. The earliest, Group I-B, have no central surface holes on obverse or reverse. The holes were to appear only after the Koinon, and to persist with some exceptions to the end. With Group V/VIII flans begin to be produced open-cast, with a broad flat reverse on which the type and legend are in low relief. The flans of Groups VIII and IX are very carelessly made, the flans irregular and often disfigured by remnants of unclipped scissel.

The denominations fall roughly into the ratio 16–8–4–2–1, although some of the smaller pieces are difficult to place. The structure may be misleading in that it implies an original conception of five modules. Actually, the first and only issue of Group I is in module B, corresponding to the largest bronze then in circulation. There is no indication that any other module was intended until after the interruption by the Koinon coinage when Soter/Libya II-B, D, and E were produced. Module A does not appear until Group III, and perhaps responds deliberately to the Koinon issue in weight and diameter. It is only in Group VI that module C first appears. In short, there seems not to have been a full schedule of modules either in the original conception or in subsequent production.

Denominations A and B seem always to have been relatively scarce, although of course excavation evidence tends to favor the smaller modules. I-B might today be artificially uncommon given that it provided the flans for some of the Koinon coins. But II-B is equally scarce, and indeed it is only in the middle groups that the Soter/Libya type begins to appear in the excavations in any quantity. The finds in the Demeter Sanctuary illustrate the point (the dash indicates that the module is known but is not represented in the excavation):

Module	A	B	C	D	E
Group I		1			
II		3		3	1
III	—	1		7	
IV		—		9	9
V	—				
VI		1	6		6
VII		2	7	6	—
VIII	—	2	21		
IX					62

It is not possible to elicit a specific chronology from the individual issues, or even to be absolutely confident of their sequence. The beginning and end are anchored: as we have seen above, the first Group must precede the issue of the Koinon; part of Group V is signed by Euergetes II; Group VIII is signed by Euergetes II and Soter II; and Group IX can only follow on and must be assigned to Apion. Between the extremes, however, there is real uncertainty as to the chronology, both relative and absolute.

Group I was assigned by Robinson in the *BMC* to the last years of Magas' reign ("ca. 260 B.C."); the attribution is accepted by Laronde but not the date, since he dates Magas' death to 250 B.C. Robinson's later revision of the Magan issues implied that Group I was struck under the authority of Ptolemy II after Magas' death. In my judgment this is inescapable, for if we accept that the agreement between Magas and Philadelphus left Cyrenaica in Magas' hands for his lifetime, it would have been contradictory for him to issue coin that eliminated reference to himself and in its types asserted the close connection between the Egyptian kingship and Cyrenaica. In any case Group I initiates issues without Magas' monogram and is quite different from his in style and fabric (the beveled edge).

Against the attribution to Ptolemy II, it has been maintained that only with the marriage of Berenice and Ptolemy III Euergetes did Cyrenaica revert to

Egyptian control. "It is curious . . . that Euergetes should speak [in the Adoulis inscription] of the Cyrenaica as inherited from his father, for it was in fact through his own marriage to Berenike, the daughter of Philadelphos' half-brother Magas, that the third Ptolemy was able to reunite the Cyrenaica with the Ptolemaic kingdom."[39] But do we really know this to be the case? The agreement between Magas and Ptolemy II included the provisions that the children of the two kings should marry, and that Cyrenaica should revert to the Egyptian crown after Magas' death.[40] We know that the marriage had not taken place by the time of Magas' death. But I believe that we are not told *totidem verbis* that the two conditions were inextricably related, and that Philadelphus' claim would hold *only if and after* the marriage took place. That he delayed asserting his claim after Magas' death until Berenice or her mother should decide whom the girl was to marry is hardly credible, particularly when a Seleucid was being brought in as proposed husband. The period after Magas' death appears to have been tumultuous, and part of the reason for that had to be the assertion of the Egyptian claim. I conclude that in Egyptian eyes Cyrenaica was theirs on Magas' death, that the Soter/Libya type was introduced at some time during this difficult period on the authority of Ptolemy II, and that Euergetes could properly say that he had inherited Cyrenaica from his father.

None of the next Soter/Libya Groups II–IV bears any mark by which they can be assigned to an individual Ptolemy. Presumably they began with Ptolemy III Euergetes after his accession. But Group V, which is distinguished by several monograms, includes a small issue with the legend ΘΕ Ε̇, which can hardly be anything other than the abbreviation of ΘΕΟΣ ΕΥΕΡΓΕΤΗΣ. Robinson took this to be Euergetes II, I believe correctly.[41] But the attribution creates a chronological problem. If we accept Robinson's seriation, at least some of Group V, all of Groups VI–VII, and some of Group VIII were struck under Euergetes II, between 163 and 116 B.C. at the extremes. This leaves only Groups II–IV and some of V to have been struck under Ptolemy III–VIII, between 246 and 163 B.C. It leaves Euergetes signing an issue early on, then not signing, then returning to sign toward the end.

The alternative is to divide Group V so that the larger and heavier modules, V(a), fall in Robinson's order but before the reign of Euergetes, while the somewhat smaller and lighter pieces bearing his monogram fall wholly within his reign. Group V(b) would then provide the A module in the issue in which the B and C modules are represented under Euergetes by Group VIII, all bearing Euergetes' monogram.

The seriation of Groups does not address the difficult question of the mints. For convenience Robinson collected all varieties under Cyrene, but noted two pieces in Group IV bearing monograms of BE or ΠΤ, "which presumably indicate the mints of Berenice and Ptolemais respectively."[42] It may be so, although the monograms of Groups V and VIII plainly indicate either officials or the sovereign. Again, Group III bears the silphium as symbol, which might imply that those *not* so marked were not products of the Cyrene mint; and Group V has the apple-branch elsewhere associated with Euesperides. The symbols aside, Groups VIII and IX characteristically bear surface holes while the apparently contemporary /eagle and /Isiac headdress issues do not. This argues separate minting, and it is my impression that Group IX is more sloppily struck than the other small bronze of Apion. But there are no mintmarks and I see no way of solving this problem.

Group V presents another difficulty in the several magistrates' monograms which it bears. Each is also to be found on proper Ptolemaic /eagle bronze or silver, and Svoronos went so far as to attribute such coinages (and others he considered related) to Cyrenaica because of the connection with Soter/Libya (Svoronos 1140–1151, 1154–1157, 1266). But these /eagle bronzes are attested in Egyptian finds[43] and do not occur in Cyrenaica. Some carry a cornucopiae countermark, while the Soter/Libya with the same monograms never do. An alternative is to suppose that all were struck in Alexandria, the Soter/Libya for shipment to Cyrene. Against this are the practical problems of transportation and communication between Egypt and Cyrene. A third possibility is that the monograms are of mint officials in Alexandria who exercised control over production at a branch mint at Cyrene.

Obviously there was some sort of control, whether or not the dies were signed, for Cyrenaica was, after the Koinon, firmly in Ptolemaic hands. What the coins show is that silver was no longer struck, while the Soter/Libya bronze was revived, now with surface holes. Either this technique was introduced from Alexandria, or the Cyrene mint was closed after 246 B.C.—in reprisal—and the coins were struck at

---

39. R.S. Bagnall, "Archagathos, son of Agathocles, epistates of Libya," *Philologus* 120 (1976) 201.

40. Chamoux (n. 18) 31.

41. *BMC* clix–clx.

42. *BMC* clix.

43. E.g., R.A. Haatvedt et al, *Coins from Karanis* (Ann Arbor, MI 1964): Svoronos 1142 and 5 of Svoronos 1148; unpublished finds from Terenouthis at the University of Michigan: of only 23 identified Ptolemaic bronzes, 2 are Svoronos 1145 and 1149.

Alexandria. In further support of this possibility there is the apparent double flow of coin production later under Euergetes II's Egyptian reign, Soter II, and Apion: each of them has Soter/Libya coins with the holes, other types without.

It is also the case that no Soter/Libya pieces bear the eponym of Euergetes II spelled out, unlike his other Cyrenaican bronze, while those with the name in monogram are so similar in style and fabric to those of Soter II that the one issue must have run on into the other.[44] That is to say, on the arrangement proposed here there is no certain evidence for Soter/Libya production during Euergetes' Cyrenaican reign, only during his subsequent Egyptian reign. If the type was the major small change of Cyrenaica why was it not being struck? The answer may be that up to 163 B.C. it was struck at the Alexandria mint, to which Euergetes in Cyrene did not have easy access subsequently, given his thorny relations with his brother, Philometor. This would also explain Euergetes' introduction of his personal /eagle bronzes, in lieu of the Soter/Libya C and D modules.

KOINON, CA. 250–246 B.C.

I have indicated above that in my judgment Robinson is correct in associating this large issue with a period of city independence that followed (or coincided with) the exercise of the claim of Ptolemy II, and preceded the accession of Ptolemy III Euergetes. We do not know whether the KOINON coins were retired by Ptolemy III or allowed to continue in circulation. Those of good weight served a function which no others did until the introduction of Soter/Libya module A in Group III. I assume that they continued to be used, since neither the III-A nor any other Ptolemaic issue was overstruck on them.[45]

PTOLEMY III–PTOLEMY VI/VIII, 246–163 B.C.

The issues of these years are largely of the repetitive Soter/Libya type. The two issues with the divinities Apollo and Artemis might reflect a regal marriage of brother and sister, Ptolemy VI and Cleopatra II Θεοὶ Φιλομήτορες (Table I. 63–64). The Ammon/two-eagle issue with silphium symbol is appropriate to the joint reign of Ptolemy VI and Ptolemy VIII (Table I.72). No examples were found in the excavation, but Cyrenaican finds are attested.[46] The same type was struck for Euesperides with apple branch symbol (Table III.11).

PTOLEMY VIII EUERGETES II AS KING IN CYRENAICA, 163–145 B.C.

From this point forward the *BMC*'s coverage needs revision and considerable enlargement. The only coinage specifically attributed there to Euergetes II (and without considering which reign) is the Soter/Libya issue with monogram EE; and none at all is given to Soter II. Now, however, several Cyrenaican issues, some large, can be given to each of them. In fact it is at this point that the finds become particularly abundant. The comparative figures are these: from ca. 300 B.C. to the end of the Ptolemies with the death of Apion in 96 B.C. we have a total of 545 bronze coins identifiable to some degree. Of these, 445 (82%) are attributable to the reigns of Euergetes II, Soter II, or Apion. That ratio is the measure of the intensity of local bronze production and circulation in the last two-thirds of the second century B.C. and the first few years of the first century, compared to that of the third century. Further, of the 261 coins of Euergetes and Soter only 26 (10%) are of the Soter/Libya issues; the great majority are of the /eagle, /two cornuacopiae, and /Isiac headdress types not given to Cyrenaica in the *BMC*.

Poole had attributed to Cyrenaica several of Euergetes' bronze issues with /eagle or /two cornuacopiae type, some of large denomination, bearing his eponym and the control letters Φ, ΘΕ, or Κ.[47] These were given to Cyprus by Svoronos[48] and entirely omitted by Robinson. The archaeological evidence confirms Poole's attributions. Some issues are abundantly represented in every excavation; others can be connected with them by style and fabric. The excavations also show that these issues cannot be imports: most are the smallest of small change, and in any case non-

---

44. Compare *BMC* pl. 32.10–11.

45. Robinson claimed such overstrikes in "Quaestiones Cyrenaicae," *NC*⁴ 15 (1915) 289. He had misread the coins, supposing that the overstrikes by, e.g., Soter/fulmen were on KOINON, an interpretation that also required denying that the monogram Ṁ was that of Magas. He acknowledged and corrected his mistake in the *BMC* (cl, n. 2), but the 1915 version was imported into the *CAH* (VII, 713) by Tarn, who speaks of Ptolemaic hostility to the Koinon being demonstrated "by Ptolemaic regal issues being often over-struck upon League coins." In fact the KOINON pieces were often overstruck on the preceding Ptolemaic, but not the other way around (cf.

SNG Milano 13.1, 198 where the description is reversed).

46. One piece was found in an Egyptian hoard along with 104 examples of the same type with cornucopiae symbol, good evidence of their relative distribution (J.G. Milne, "Report on Coins found at Tebtunis, 1900," *JEA* [1935] 211–12).

47. *BMCPtol* lxix–lxx.

48. Svoronos υγ´–υε´; followed in our time by Mørkholm, *SNG Cop* 651–57; divided between Alexandria and Cyprus by Martini, *SNG Milano* 13.1, 377–79, 388–403.

Cyrenaican Ptolemaic bronze coins are otherwise almost never found in Cyrenaica until the issues of the last Cleopatra.

First, the chronology. Poole divided the signed bronze of Euergetes into three classes,[49] but declined to "separate the coins struck after [Euergetes II] Physcon's succession to the whole kingdom B.C. 146 [145] from the earlier currency."[50] Such a separation can be made, however. From 170 B.C. on Euergetes shared the Egyptian throne with his older brother, Ptolemy VI, and briefly ruled alone in 164–163. Ejected in 163 he ruled as king of Cyrenaica until the death of Ptolemy VI in 145, when he again became sole king in Egypt until his own death in 116. It is not possible that coins were struck at Cyrene in his name before 163: he was the junior partner in the kingship; it is not credible that the plentiful /eagle issues bearing his name were struck during the seven months of sole rule in 164–163; and in any case the coinage of a reigning king, unlike the issues which we are about to consider, bore only the undifferentiated title ΠΤΟΛΕΜΑΙΟΥ ΒΑΣΙΛΕΩΣ. Euergetes' issues must fall after 163.

But some must also have fallen before 145. The bronze of Euergetes II for Cyrenaica differs markedly from its predecessors. Contrary to custom he displayed his eponym prominently, usually spelled out—ΕΥΕΡΓΕΤΟΥ ΒΑΣΙΛΕΩΣ ΠΤΟΛΕΜΑΙΟΥ. The eponym of the Ptolemaic kings does not appear on Ptolemaic bronze at Alexandria. Euergetes' name asserted his independent authority and avoided the confusion of the conventional ΠΤΟΛΕΜΑΙΟΥ ΒΑΣΙΛΕΩΣ: that would have been taken to mean the king in Alexandria. It is the peculiarity of the eponym, then, that indicates the Cyrenaican reign, for to introduce it on coin after 145 when he was king in Egypt would have been unparalleled and superfluous.

This interpretation stands against the received view that Ptolemy VIII took his eponym only after the return to Alexandria in 145.[51] That is essentially an argument from silence. The eponym does not occur in the heading of Euergetes' will of 155, in which he blackmailed both his subjects and his brother by leaving his kingdom to the Romans should he die prematurely.[52] Surely (it has been argued) the eponym would have been included in a document of such significance. The earliest preserved use of the name in the papyri or inscriptions is found in Egypt and dated to the late 140s. But it occurs on the Cyrenaican coins, and indeed there are no Cyrenaican coins without the eponym that can be assigned to him. It may have been assumed between 155 and 145 B.C.[53]

In addition to the issues illustrated by the excavations Euergetes produced a range of ostentatious

---

49. *BMCPtol* pp. 88, no. 1; 94–95, nos. 78–84 and 86–88; 98, nos. 132–33.

50. *BMCPtol* lxix–lxx.

51. So Robinson, *BMC* clvii, following Bouché-Leclerq; and generally.

52. *SEG* IX, 7. Cf. H. Belloc: "Always keep ahold of nurse / For fear of finding something worse."

53. For the *epiklesis* Εὐεργέτης as early as 143/2 B.C., see P. dem. Turin 2142 (I owe this reference to the kindness of R. A. Hazzard). That bronzes of Ptolemy VIII as Euergetes were struck in Cyrenaica is certain. Their style and fabric are cruder than anything of the period struck at Alexandria, and the archaeological evidence confirms that these are Cyrenaican issues, not Egyptian. But their chronology is another matter. We have no secure date for Ptolemy's assumption of the title. His Cyrenaican will of 155 does not bear the title; documents dating after his return to Egypt in 145 normally do. The one piece of evidence to suggest that Εὐεργέτης was assumed after his return is P. dem. Cairo 30605, an Egyptian document of the 25th year of "Ptolemy and Cleopatra, children of Ptolemy and Cleopatra the manifest gods [Θεοὶ Ἐπιφανεῖς]".

On the face of it the document could refer to the 25th year of Ptolemy VI and Cleopatra II (156/155 B.C.), or of Ptolemy VIII and Cleopatra II (145/144 B.C.). But Glanville and Skeat have shown that the priesthoods listed are essentially the same as those in another document certainly given to the 36th year (i.e. the last year) of Ptolemy VI (*JEA* 40 [1954] p. 54, 43). There is no real likelihood that the same characters would have resumed their priestly offices in a body after a lapse of eleven years. Rather, since we know that on his return to Egypt in 145 Ptolemy VIII resumed the count of his regnal years from his first accession in 170/169 B.C., so that this was his 25th year, the document must be given to him, his 25th year following immediately upon Ptolemy VI's 36th.

The problem then is that in this document Ptolemy VIII is not given any *epiklesis*, evidence (it is claimed) that he had not yet taken up the title Εὐεργέτης. But he is not given any title at all, although in Egypt he had been Φιλομήτωρ during his sole reign of 164/163 (P.W. Pestman, *Chronologie égyptienne d'après les textes démotiques*, P. Lug. Bat. 15 [1967] 50). And it is interesting that Glanville and Skeat dated P. dem. Cairo 30605 on the internal evidence, not on the heading; the implication is that the absence of eponym was not decisive in distinguishing between Ptolemy VI and Ptolemy VIII. So de Cenival: "Cette expression ['Ptolemy and Cleopatra, children of Ptolemy and Cleopatra Θεοὶ Ἐπιφανεῖς'] peut s'appliquer à Ptolémée VI Philométor comme à Ptolémée VIII Évergète II" (*Revue d'Égyptologie* 17 [1965] 189). The argument from silence is therefore not secure.

As to the coins, if they were attributed to the period of Egyptian kingship post-145, there would be no coinage at all for the twenty years of the Cyrenaican kingship. What then was in use? In the absence of hoards we can say nothing about gold and silver; presumably Egyptian coin was to be had. But as to bronze, which is found in quantity, the archaeological evidence from all Cyrenaican sites is clear: Ptolemaic bronze from Egypt is virtually unknown. Further, a regular output of bronze had been a characteristic of Cyrenaican coinage for a century and more. It is difficult to believe that Ptolemy VIII contributed nothing to the bronze coinage during the two decades of his local reign. On balance, then, I prefer to believe that the *epiklesis* was assumed during his Cyrenaican rule, and to attribute much of his bronze to that period.

bronze denominations. These can now be attributed to Cyrenaica although the largest have not so far surfaced in any reported excavation. This is itself not surprising, because casual coin finds are always weak in the more visible or more valuable denominations. But several important finds of Ammon/eagle in addition to our **281** confirm the attribution.[54] Sidi Khrebish also produced two examples of the K issue (Table I.83), and another was seen at the British Museum in 1980 as from Cyrenaica.[55] The Ammon obverses are appropriate to Cyrenaica, the use of the eponym parallels that on the abundant finds of the smaller /eagle denominations, **284–350**, and of course the coins were found in Cyrenaica. There can be no doubt that they are Cyrenaican in origin. With them must be associated Svoronos 1640-49, large Ammon/eagle types of various modules, some not especially common, connected among themselves by rather rough fabric and style, and by the common occurrence of the Φ or K. All these coins bear the head of Ammon, and, again, the eponym of Euergetes, which is unknown elsewhere in the coinage that can be confidently attributed to him. Their fabric and style also are comparable to the Cyrenaican issues of Euergetes attested to by the excavations; in fact the dies of **282** (without letter) and *BMCPtol* 95, 86 (with K) must be the work of the same engraver. Most of the Φ dies are of equivalent style and must accompany the others.

Finally there are the largest pieces of all, the enormous Ammon/ bronzes with reverse types of /two cornuacopiae, /one cornuacopiae, or /eagle, all measuring 45–46mm and bearing control mark Φ. The /two cornuacopiae type is uncommon in the Ptolemaic coinage, and almost always associated with a feminine obverse; but a notable exception is the only other Ammon/two cornuacopiae issue of the Ptolemies (**361–370**), which was struck in Cyrenaica under Soter and signed with the digram abbreviating Soter's name.[56]

Therefore all of these exceptionally large bronzes, related to one another by style, fabric, and control letter, are to be attributed not to Cyprus but to Cyrenaica. They must fall within the period of Euergetes' sole reign for they are matched by nothing at Alexandria, representing a once-only coinage of high denominations, apparently struck to a weight standard roughly equivalent to 80-40-20-10 grams. They would thus be 5x and 10x multiples of the Cyrenaican denominations already in circulation, which had been produced to a standard of ca. 8–4–2 grams. Were they celebratory pieces, on his taking up the eponym which they bear?[57]

These issues also reintroduced the Ptolemaic /eagle reverse, which had not been struck in Cyrenaica since Magas. I surmise that the traditional Ptolemaic type both legitimized Euergetes' reign and reflected his independence of the administration in Alexandria whose officials had previously been authorizing the Soter/Libya issues for Cyrenaica.

PTOLEMY VIII EUERGETES II AS KING IN EGYPT, 145–116 B.C.

The more usual denominations are assigned in Table I to the Egyptian reign, on the guess that Euergetes' title Θεός, which does not appear on his large denomination bronze, was inappropriate in Cyrenaica and was not taken on until after he had become king in Alexandria. The eponym survived locally on these issues—not elsewhere in the kingdom—and was to be imitated by Soter II in the next reign. Toward the end of the reign the Soter/ Libya coinage was reintroduced: Groups V-A and VIII-B and C with EE monogram, are quite different in style and fabric from Group VII, but VIII-B and C are almost identical with the pieces signed subsequently by Soter II.

The commonest Cyrenaican coins of Euergetes' Egyptian reign are the small change with /eagle reverse type.

AMMON/EAGLE

Small bronzes of this type with Euergetes' name occur extensively in the excavations, and their local origin is no longer in doubt. They were presumably struck over time, for there is a gradual decay in quality of every kind. **289** is struck from large dies of relatively good style on a slightly beveled flan of 2 mm; at the other extreme the dies of **292** are smaller and of poorer style with less careful lettering, struck on a chunky flan (3 mm) with a square projection and a pronounced bevel. Some of the largest pieces have the surface holes; the others of the issue do not.

---

54. Robinson, *NC*[6] 4 (1944) nos. 45–46, five pieces with Φ; and one from Sidi Khrebish.

55. 23.35 g; I owe this helpful information to Andrew Burnett.

56. Poole separated Svoronos 1640 from the other Φ bronze of Euergetes, in part no doubt because it appeared not to have a control mark. The two BM specimens do not show clearly that the reverse bears the letter Φ, but it can be seen in Svoronos' illustration (pl. 56.12). The piece should therefore be associated with the other Φ coins.

57. Poole dated the /two cornuacopiae issue to the Egyptian reign, on the grounds that the reverse type reflected Euergetes' double marriage with his sister and her daughter (*BMCPtol* lxx). But the Φ issues include the equally large /cornuacopiae and /eagle coins, and all must go together, given also their similarity of style and fabric.

The small ΘE issue, which is very much scarcer than the larger, does not seem to be simply a degeneration of it. It never has surface holes, the flans are markedly smaller, and it appears to represent roughly the half denomination of the larger. The /eagle issue here placed third does not bear the ΘE legend, and for that reason might be taken to precede the other two. I place it last because it is so similar to the /eagle issues of Soter that follow. It also is without holes.

The style and fabric of Soter's coins are close to those of Euergetes. The /two cornuacopiae type took the place of Euergetes' larger /eagle, whereas the smaller /eagle continued, signed with Soter's name. Perhaps the point of the new type was to differentiate between two denominations that previously were difficult to distinguish, given their sloppy manufacture. But Soter's /eagle coins, too, appear to fall into two groups by weight and module, perhaps representing the two smallest denominations.

Finally comes a small group of /eagle reverses without signature or monogram. They are here assigned to Apion.

PTOLEMY IX SOTER II, 115–104/1 B.C.

We are told by Justin that Cyrenaica was inherited by the illegitimate Apion from his father, Euergetes II, rather than by the legitimate Soter II, who succeeded to the rule in Egypt (39.5.2). For this reason no modern scholar has followed Poole, who assigned Soter's /two cornuacopiae, and /Isiac headdress types to Cyrenaica.[58] Svoronos gave them to Egypt. In his catalogue he did attribute one Soter issue to Cyrenaica, the Soter/Libya with monogram Ĭ (Svoronos 1725), but apparently thought better of it when he came to write his text, for there the monogram is expanded to ΖΩΙ[ΛΟΣ(?).[59] No Cyrenaican coins at all were assigned to Soter by Robinson in the *BMC*. A decade later a French scholar could write, "[A]ucune monnaie de Cyrénaïque ne peut être rapportée avec quelque certitude à Ptolémée X [i.e., Ptolemy IX Soter II]";[60] and Robinson was still cautious in the face of signed coins of Soter discovered in Cyrenaica.[61] Even today the /eagle, /two cornuacopiae, and /Isiac headdress types are all given to Cyprus in the *SNG Cop* and the British Museum trays.

But Bagnall's study of the Stolos inscriptions showed that in his earlier years as king Soter must have ruled over Cyrenaica;[62] and today his Cyrenaican coins are known in the hundreds. Robinson had actually listed one variety, the Soter/Libya with monograms EE̊ and Ĭ (*BMC Regal* 71–79), attributing the former properly to Euergetes, but saying nothing of the latter; it has to be the monogram of Soter, equivalent to Σ̊.[63]

On Apion's inheritance Justin is probably just wrong; Laronde points to his unreliability in other matters having to do with Cyrenaica.[64] The testamentary division of the kingdom between Euergetes' wife and an illegitimate son who had no claim by virtue of birth or personal power seems unlikely, especially in view of Euergetes' own unhappy experience. Justin might have misunderstood as original a situation which developed out of Soter's struggle with Cleopatra III. The alternative, that Justin was correct and that Apion's inheritance was genuine but was thwarted by Soter for some years, perhaps overrates the possibilities of Soter's own precarious position.

In any case Soter did rule over Cyrenaica for a time, and the coins prove it. The affirmation of his legitimate claim can be seen in the coin types, which are notable in largely following those of his father, and for bearing (as his father's had) either his eponym, an abbreviation of it, or the monogram Σ̊ (or a debased form of it, Ĭ). He also introduced a new /Isiac headdress type, to be struck in large quantities during his and Apion's reigns.

AMMON/ISIAC HEADDRESS

The type occurs under Soter in three varieties, one large and two small, signed in three different ways. Table I reflects the assumption that larger and smaller modules were struck and circulated together, but it is equally possible that they were sequential and that even the small weight of the 14 mm issue fell by almost a third. It is certain that there was a gap of some nature between the larger and the smaller varieties since taken altogether their weights do not compose a Gaussian (standard) distribution.

The reverse legend must have been intended as

---

58. *BMCPtol* 107–108.

59. Svoronos υκδ´–υκε´.

60. P. Roussel, "Ptolémée X Sôter II et Cyrène," *Revue des Études Anciennes* 41 (1939) 9, n. 1.

61. "We must wait for comparative find evidence" (*NC*[6] 4 [1944] 109–110).

62. R.S. Bagnall, "Stolos the Admiral," *Phoenix* 26 (1972) 358–368.

63. See Chapter II, n. 45 to **359**.

64. Laronde 42, 85.

ΠΤΟΛΕΜΑΙΟΥ ΒΑΣΙΛΕΩΣ, but on no example is it complete. Poor condition prevents certain reading in many cases, but where the word endings are visible something is invariably abbreviated. The engraver inserted as much of the legend as he found convenient. On Soter's ΣΩ–ΘΕ issue the legend begins in the reverse exergue with inverted ΠΤ or ΠΤΟ. Under Apion the legend also begins in the exergue, with an upside-down Π as the first letter of ΠΤΟΛ or ΠΤΟΛΕ, presumably in lieu of an eponym signature such as Soter's.

Several /Isiac headdress overstrikes can be recognized in the smaller varieties: e.g., under Soter on Ammon/eagle (**410**), under Apion on Soter/Libya (**617**), under Apion a Soter/Libya on /Isiac headdress (**436**). These are among the very least of Cyrenaican bronze, weighing between 1.92 and 1.50 g. It is difficult to conceive the utility of such an operation.

Imitations are common, although it is not always clear whether the dies of an official piece are just badly cut. Fabric is not a good guide because the official emissions are so irregular. Where the legend is nonsense, or gives way simply to a series of dots, where the style is unendurably crude, or the obverse head faces in the wrong direction, there is little doubt.

Two modules were used for the /eagle issues, and the same two for the /Isiac headdress. Although weights and diameters overlap to a degree because of their rough production, there is no doubt that for each type the two modules are distinct, and they generate different weight distributions. The use and disposition of Soter's eponym, abbreviation, or monogram also shows that they were conceived as distinct. I have arranged the modules in Table I as two simultaneous denominations, but it is possible that they were issued sequentially, and that the smallest pieces are also the latest.

In either case the /eagle and /Isiac headdress types circulated together and must have been issued together. They subsequently appeared together under Apion. They might have been the product of separate mints, but their crude fabric is similar and there is nothing on the coins to indicate differing sources.

Finally, there is the small bronze with the astonishing types of Tyche/Dioscurid caps, so uncharacteristic of the coinage of Cyrenaica. The Tyche of Ptolemais occurs more than half a century later on bronze struck by Crassus at Ptolemais, but nothing on the Hellenistic coin reveals its mint. Although several examples are now known, it has not proved possible to decipher the legend. The flan is the thick, rather ragged product of the end of the Ptolemaic system, but the style is pretty. I have given it arbitrarily to Soter, but it might belong under Apion.

PTOLEMY APION, 104/1–96 B.C.

Soter's unquiet career included the loss of Cyrenaica to Apion at some unknown time. The general period of 104 to 101 B.C. cited here is elicited from Bagnall.[65] Svoronos was doubtful whether any coinage could be attributed to Apion.[66] But there are late issues of Soter/Libya (Group IX), /eagle, and /Isiac headdress that bear no eponym or monogram and are therefore not likely to have been struck under Euergetes or Soter. They also are of the smallest denomination, and wretchedly made, so that they can hardly fall anywhere else.

Apion's coinage is nothing but very small change. The three types carry on from Soter, and like his fall into two groups. All must have been issued in relatively large quantities. Robinson believed that Soter/Libya IX-E was struck in two denominations, D and E, admittedly difficult to distinguish because of the irregularity of their production. But there seems to be no distinction in style or size of types, and a weight table of the *BMC* and Demeter Sanctuary specimens falls into a single Gaussian distribution with a peak of about 1.30 g, so that they must all be module E.

Where a real distinction does occur is in the preparation of Apion's flans. Soter's Soter/Libya coins had the surface holes, whereas his other types did not; about half of Apion's Soter/Libya still have the holes, his other types do not. If two mints were in operation, there is no way of identifying them, and aside from the holes the small, crude flans seem much alike.

AFTER THE DEATH OF APION, 96 B.C.

Scholars seem to agree that Apion's will, leaving his possessions to the Roman people, actually referred to the regal lands and did not involve the cities and their territories. What little we know of the Romans' response for the first 20 years bears this out: apparently they simply collected the royal rents. For a long period there was no Roman coinage for what became the province of Cyrenaica (with Crete), nor any autonomous coinages of the cities. I would now resist the notion that the latest unsigned small

---

65. R.S. Bagnall, *The Administration of the Ptolemaic Possessions outside Egypt*, Columbia Studies in the Classical Tradition 4 (Leiden 1976) 27.

66. Svoronos p. υκε′.

bronzes might be civic strikes, following the death of Apion;[67] for the cities had their own traditions to draw on and there was no need to continue a Ptolemaic typology. But as far as we can see they did not strike, and the Greek coinage of Cyrenaica, of glorious tradition, ended in the lamentable small bronzes of Apion.

Introduction to Tables

The tables survey all the Greek Cyrenaican bronze coinages by type, whether or not examples were recovered in the excavations. Weights and diameters are averages of the *BMC* and our excavation specimens, or of other published or museum pieces as noted. The results are only an approximation, for the body of material is thin at many points, the coins were often struck quite imperfectly, and surviving examples have frequently lost considerable weight through wear or corrosion. The weight standards also varied over time. But it does appear to be the case that throughout the three centuries of bronze coinage many issues were simultaneous and denominationally interrelated.

In the tables double vertical lines separate apparently different standards.

---

67. Buttrey, "Crete and Cyrenaica" 165–66.

TABL...

	ca. 325–313 B.C.	Revolt 313–312 B.C.	Ophellas' Carthaginian campaign, 309 B.C.	Ptolemy I ca. 308–305 B.C.	Revolt ca. 305–300 B.C.	Ptolemy I ca. 300–282 B.C.	Magas in revolt ca. 282–261 B.C.	Magas reconciled with Ptolemy II ca. 261–258 B.C.	Ptolemy II ca. 258–250 B.C.	Koinon ca. 250–246 B.C.	Ptolemy ca. 246–
Unit	Ammon/silphium[1] Apollo/silphium[2] Carneius/silphium[3] Cyrene/silphium[4] Carneius/2 silphium[5] Cyrene/triple silphium[6] 13.53 21.5 mm	Ammon/oval wheel[14] horse's head/oval wheel[15] 12.74 23 mm	Ammon/column[22] 10.86 24 mm Artemis/Nike[23] 15.10 20 mm	Ammon/palm tree[24] 11.87 20 mm					Soter/Libya: I	Ammon/silphium[52] 11.44 23 mm	II
Half		Ammon/oval wheel[16] 8.68 22 mm horse/oval wheel[17] horseman/round wheel[18] horseman/oval wheel[19] 8.02 19 mm		gazelle/silphium[25] 6.13 17 mm			Ammon/bow case[37] 3.10 19 mm	/eagle[44] 7.32 19 mm /fulmen[45] 7.30 21.5 mm	B[51] 7.85 23 mm		B[53] 7.92 22.5
Quarter	Athena/silphium[7] Carneius/silphium[8] Libya/silphium[9] horseman/silphium[10] Athena/double silphium[11] Carneius/triple silphium[12] 4.07 15 mm	horse/oval wheel[20] 4.39 14 mm		crab/jerboa[26] 2.91 15 mm jerboa/crab[27] 3.09 14 mm	Carneius/silphium[28] 2.96 14 mm Libya/gazelle[29] 3.07 14 mm	Apollo/eagle[33] 3.59 17 mm Soter/eagle[34] 3.88 17 mm	Apollo/horse[38] 3.93 16 mm Apollo/lyre[39] 4.22 17 mm	Ammon/palm tree[43] 5.13 18 mm	/fulmen[46] 4.64 19 mm /protome of winged horse[47] 4.31 16 mm		
Eighth		horse/oval wheel[21] 1.98 13 mm			Ammon/Athena[30] 1.24 11 mm Athena/protome of gazelle[31] 1.35 —	Soter/eagle[35] 2.06 13 mm	Apollo/quiver[40] 4.60 17 mm Libya/silphium[41] 3.90 19 mm		/prow[48] 5.09 19 mm /horse[49] 1.66 12 mm		D[54] 1.85 14.5
Sixteenth	Carneius/silphium[13] 0.63 9 mm				Libya/gazelle[32] 1.04 11 mm		gazelle/silphium[42] 1.89 13.5 mm		/prow[50] 2.62 13 mm		E[55] 1.22 13
					Soter/eagle[36] 0.86 12/13.5 mm						

Coinage of Cyrene

	Ptolemy IV/VIII 222–163 B.C.		Ptolemy VI/VIII 170–163 B.C.	Ptolemy VIII Euergetes II as king in Cyrenaica, 163–145 B.C.	Ptolemy VIII Euergetes II as king in Egypt, 145–116 B.C.	Ptolemy IX Soter II 115–104/1 B.C.	Ptolemy Apion 104/1–96 B.C.
IV / V(a)		VI / VII			V(b), VIII	VIII	IX
	A[62] 15.61 27 mm	Apollo & Artemis Soter[63] 16.28 26 mm		Ammon/ 2 cornuacopiae[74] 84.76 Φ / 46 mm			
				Ammon/ cornucopiae[75] 72.68 / Φ 46 mm			
B[59] 7.84 21 mm			B[65] 8.00 23 mm — B[68] 5.79 22 mm	Ammon/two eagles[72] 7.39 21 mm	Ammon/ Eagle[76] 66.57 / Φ 45 mm			
				Ammon/2 cornuacopiae[77] 44.75 Φ / 46 mm			
				Ammon/ eagle[78] 40.91 / Φ 44 mm	Ammon/ eagle[83] 20.82 / K 32 mm — Ammon/ eagle[85] 17.47 32 mm	C[93] 3.90 17 mm — Ammon/2 cornuacopiae[94] 5.00 18 mm	
			C[66] 3.64 17.5 mm — C[69] 3.20 16.5 mm		Ammon/ eagle[86] 10.90 25 mm — A[90] 11.68 25 mm		
				Ammon/ eagle looking back[73] 10.85 Φ / 25 mm — Ammon/ eagle[79] 10.97 Φ / or / Φ 25 mm	Ammon/ eagle[84] 7.30 M / 25 mm		
				Ammon/ eagle[80] 8.20 Φ / 21 mm	Ammon/ eagle[87] 4.43 ΘE 20 mm — B[91] 5.56 21 mm	Ammon/eagle[95] 2.19 14 mm	
D[60] 2.09 14.5 mm		Apollo/Artemis[64] 1.86 14 mm	D[70] 2.13 15 mm		Ammon/ eagle[88] 2.91 ΘE 15 mm — C[92] 3.32 18 mm		
				Ammon/ eagle[81] 2.10 / Φ 15 mm		Ammon/Isiac headdress[96] 2.43 14 mm	
					Ammon/ eagle[89] 2.04 13 mm		
E[61] 1.22 13 mm			E[67] 1.27 11.5 mm — E[71] 0.82 11.5 mm	Ammon/ eagle[82] 1.50 Φ / 10 mm		Ammon/eagle[97,98] 1.52 12 mm	E[102] 1.22 12 mm — Ammon/eagle[103] 1.49 11 mm
						Ammon/Isiac headdress[99,100] 1.65 12 mm	Ammon/Isiac headdress[104] 1.63 12 mm
						Tyche/caps of Dioscuri[101] 1.18 10 mm	

Notes to Table I

CA. 325–313 B.C.

The denominations are as noted by Robinson in the *BMC* (pp. xci-xcii). I have kept for convenience the category of Sixteenth Unit, which he withdrew (p. xci, n. 3). The surviving Units tend to be relatively light, owing to very considerable wear in circulation; even the heaviest, *BMC* 174–75, at 17.83 and 17.39 g, are well worn. The obverse types, and the shape and number of the silphium, vary; it is not practicable to calculate weights by individual type. The other denominations are closer to the standard. Here too the weights of the several earliest issues have been taken together.

1. **109–11**. Ammon head l., *BMC* 181a.
2. **112–15**. Apollo head l., Newell 3.
3. *BMC* 174-77.
4. Robinson, NC^6 4 (1944) no. 78.
5. **122**.
6. **123**.
7. *BMC* 201c.
8. **127–29**.
9. **130**.
10. *BMC* 201b.
11. **131–32**. To judge from the style of the slightly smaller heads, and from the relatively small traces of reverse incuse, this could be a somewhat later issue.
12. **133–38**. To judge from style, and from the relatively small traces of reverse incuse, this too could be a somewhat later issue.
13. The issue is doubtful. It is known only from two examples reported by Bond and Swales as found at Euesperides, nos. 35-36, and firmly assigned by them. Unfortunately neither is illustrated, and the coins cannot now be located. The types are those of Table I.28 below; more importantly, also of Euesperides, Table III.6. But module and weight here are much smaller than either.
14. **139**. Overstrikes of /wheel Units on /silphium establish their sequence, e.g., *BMC* 187.
15. *BMC* 188.
16. *BMC* 277-78. The /wheel type is appropriate to the first series and complements the Ammon/ Unit. Because the obverse style is unusual, while the weight of *BMC* 277 at 9.45 g is apparently too great for the Half, and its flan relatively large and thin, Robinson originally suggested that these were a Three-quarter Unit—a unique denomination—struck in his Period IV, ca. 300 B.C. But two other specimens known to Robinson weigh rather less, 6.88 and 5.85g (*BMC* p. cxxvi and n. 2), and the weights of the BM examples themselves fall within the range of the /wheel Halves of his Period III. It seems best to read the denomination as a Half, as Robinson acknowledges loc. cit., and to include the issue with the rest of the /wheel series.
17. **140–49**.
18. **150–52**.
19. *BMC* 197.
20. **153**. Not in *BMC*. Another example, Robinson, NC^6 4 (1944) no. 83, weighs 3.90 g.
21. *BMC* 204-207.

REVOLT, 313–312 B.C.

22. **154**. The weights are unreliable, as all known examples are both overstruck and badly worn. Ammon/wheel and horse's head/wheel occur as undertypes (*BMC* 187c-e, and Robinson, NC^6 4 [1944] no. 79).
23. *BMC* 188a.

OPHELLAS' CARTHAGINIAN CAMPAIGN, 309 B.C.

24. *BMC* 187b. A second example of the bronze was acquired by Norton (ANS, Norton 22).

PTOLEMY I, CA. 308–305 B.C.

25. **156**. The type is found overstruck on horseman/wheel Halves (*BMC* xciii). Some pieces are linked by a common magistrate EYA to crab/jerboa Quarters.
26. **157**.
27. **158–64**.

REVOLT, CA. 305–300 B.C.

The chronology of the revolt follows Mørkholm. The issues included here are relatively uncommon and difficult to date: their failure to refer to Ptolemy I is here taken as indicative. They can hardly be earlier in the relative chronology, given their new, thinner fabric, and modest indentation of the reverse; while the /eagle and subsequent issues are generally heavier.

28. *BMC* 287a-b, not illustrated, legend illegible. Is it of the Cyrene mint at all? The same types occur, with head l., at Euesperides, *BMC* 10b.
29. **165–69**.
30. *BMC* 288-89.
31. *Atti e Memorie dell'Istituto Italiano di Numismatica* 8 (1934) p. 68, 2 pieces, one of which = *SNG Milano* 31.
32. **170–77**.

PTOLEMY I, CA. 300–282 B.C.

33. **178–82**. The weight of *BMC* 5b, 2.20 g, is apparently erratic and is omitted.
34. **183–85**.
35. BM 1948 6-7-7. Monograms as those of *BMC* 5d, a Soter/eagle Quarter.
36. Svoronos 72. See Appendix, **E13**, below.

MAGAS IN REVOLT, CA. 282–261 B.C.

37 *BMC* 286, overstruck on /eagle.
38 **186**. Poor style, comparable with *BMC* 340 (/lyre) and 346 (/horse).
39 **187–91**. *BMC* 329-31, overstruck on /eagle, and *BMC* 336, on Apollo/quiver.
40 *BMC* 291a, overstruck.
41 **192**. *BMC* 290, overstruck on /eagle.
42 **193**. This rare issue is placed here because of the similarity of reverse style to that of the Libya/silphium issue next above.
43 **194–96**.

From this point on all Cyrene bronze obverses bear the head of Soter unless otherwise indicated.

MAGAS RECONCILED WITH PTOLEMY II, CA. 261–258 B.C.

All issues bear Magas' monogram.
44 **202–207**. *BMC* 19, overstruck on /silphium Half.
45 **208–209**. *BMC* 14, overstruck.
46 **210**.
47 **211–15**.
48 *BMC* 25, overstruck on Ammon/palm tree (not [nymph]/silphium Half of Euesperides, as reported in *BMC*); Svoronos 337.
49 **216–17**.
50 BM 1927 4-12-5.

PTOLEMY II, CA. 258–250 B.C.

Here begin the Soter/Libya issues, displayed according to Robinson's arrangement in nine Groups (I-IX) of five denominations (A-E).
51 **218**. No central surface holes on obverse or reverse. The average of weights does not include *BMC* 32, which has lost weight through tooling, or the excavation piece, whose flan has been cut down.

KOINON, CA. 250–246 B.C.

52 **219**. No holes. Both types and weight are a throwback to the autonomous units of the 4th century. The weight is the average of 20 non-overstruck pieces in the *BMC* and the find piece. Other examples are overstruck on Ptolemaic /fulmen and Group I-B Soter/Libya, issues of lower weight that distort the average.

PTOLEMY III, CA. 246–222 B.C.

53 **220–22**. Holes.
54 **223–25**. Holes.
55 **226**. Holes.
56 *BMC* 39-41; Svoronos 854. Holes. The weight average omits *BMC* 41, 8.54 g, broken.
57 **227**. Holes.
58 **228–34**. Holes.

PTOLEMY IV–PTOLEMY VI/VIII 222–163 B.C.

59 *BMC* 43-44, 47; Svoronos 871. Holes. On the possibility that some of this issue emanated from mints at Berenice and Ptolemais, see *BMC* cxlv, 47a-b; clix.
60 **235–43**. Holes.
61 **244–52**. The issue occurs with and without holes.
62 *BMC* 48–54; Svoronos 1143, 1152, 1266. Robinson's Group V, with module A only, needs to be divided between the earlier pieces bearing various official monograms, entered here, and the later and somewhat smaller ones bearing Euergetes' own monogram. The latter are entered below as the largest denomination of Group VIII (Table I.90).
63 *BMC* 105; BM 1963 11-13-4. Holes. Twelve pieces at Svoronos 1137 average 16.28 g. The type does not occur in published excavations, but it can be attributed to Cyrenaica and placed here by fabric and style: largish flan with a flat reverse, central surface holes characteristic of the Soter/Libya issues, rather heavy lettering as Soter/Libya Group V, and a particular rendition of the portrait of Soter: cf. the reverse of *BMC* pl. 32.18 with the obverse of pl. 31.15 (Soter/Libya)—probably the same engraver.
64 *BMC* 105a; BM 1946 12-5-14 = Robinson, *NC*[6] 4 (1944) no. 48; Svoronos 1138. Holes. Apparently a fraction of the preceding type. The description of types follows Svoronos. The BM specimen is labeled "/Ammon," but the god does not otherwise occur in the Greek Cyrenaican bronze as a reverse type, and the bust does not appear to be bearded.
65 **253**. Holes, much rougher fabric than the preceding issues. On the possibility that some of this issue emanated from a mint at Berenice, see *BMC* clix.
66 **254–59**. Holes.
67 **260–65**. Holes. Not in *BMC*.
68 **266–67**. Holes.
69 **268–74**. No holes on excavation examples, holes on *BMC* pieces.
70 **275–80**. Holes.
71 *BMC* 69-70. Holes.

PTOLEMY VI/VIII, 170–163 B.C.

72 *BMC* 106-108; Svoronos 1158. Holes. Not found in the excavation, but Cyrenaican finds are attested at Apollonia and Sidi Khrebish, and in Robinson, *NC*[6] 4 (1944) no. 44. A piece said to be from Cyrenaica was shown at the British Museum in 1980.

PTOLEMY VIII EUERGETES II AS KING IN CYRENAICA, 163–145 B.C.

73 **281**. Holes. Svoronos 1644. The flan is small and thick. This issue is here placed first among the bronzes with the control letter Φ since it appears to be of marginally better style than the others which follow, and alone bears the eagle with folded wings and head averted. It was taken by Poole *BMCPtol* p. 88, 1 to have been the earliest of Euergetes' Cyrenaican bronzes.
74 *BMCPtol* p. 98, 132–133; Svoronos 1640. Holes. The control letter is not recorded in *BMCPtol* but can be seen on the other specimens. The weight given here is the average of the best specimen each in BM and Svoronos. The average of 13 pieces, often very worn, in BM, Svoronos, *SNG Milano* and the Malter auction (see note 75) is 68.86.
75 The only known example appeared in the Joel L. Malter auction 2 (23–24/II/1978) 240 = Classical Numismatic Group auction 29 (30/III/1994) 395. Holes.

76 Svoronos 1641. Holes. One example in Svoronos weighing high for the group at 68.20 was explained as having been struck on an unusually thick flan. A second such piece, very worn, has now appeared (Joel L. Malter auction 2 [23–24/II/1978] 241), and the weight given here is the average of the two. Plainly intended as the equivalent of the /2 cornuacopiae and /cornucopiae issues. The other examples of Svoronos 1641 are included below under no.78.
77 Svoronos 1640. Holes. It appears that a small issue of the /2 cornuacopiae type was struck at a lower weight. See note 78 below.
78 *BMCPtol* p. 94, 78; Svoronos 1641. Holes. The rest of this group (see note 76) exhibit a large drop in weight without a significant narrowing of the flan, as if the mint were attempting to maintain the earlier value of the coin while contributing less to it. The example in Joel L. Malter auction (23–24 February 1978) lot no.242 is described as having been "found by a British soldier during the battle of El Alamein."
79 Svoronos 1642–43. Holes. The eagle faces either l. or r.
80 Svoronos 1645.
81 Svoronos 1646. Holes.
82 Svoronos 1647.

PTOLEMY VIII EUERGETES II AS KING IN EGYPT, 145–116 B.C.

83 Svoronos 1648–49. Holes.
84 **283**. Holes. Apparently unpublished. The style of eagle is identical with that of the ΘE issues below (Table I.87–88).
85 **282**. Holes. Without control mark, but of identical style to no.82. The dies were probably cut by the same engraver.
86 Svoronos 1654.
87 **284–303**. There may have been several issues of this type. Some examples have holes, others not. Die size varies with the flan, between 15 and 18 mm.
88 **304–305**. No holes. The high weight is the average of only two pieces; five pieces at Svoronos 1652 average 2.64 g. All fall within the limits of **306–50**.
89 **306–50**. No holes.
90 *BMC* cxlv, 54a. Holes. The variety with Euergetes' monogram is somewhat smaller than *BMC* 48–54 (Table I.62): *BMC* 54a and four pieces at Svoronos 1657 average 11.68 g, 25 mm.
91 **351–52**. Group VIII marks a significant change in fabric and style from the earlier Soter/Libya issues. No holes, unusually for the Soter/Libya series. Not in *BMC*.
92 **353–58**. Holes.

PTOLEMY IX SOTER II, 115–104/1 B.C.

93 **359–60**. Holes.
94 **361–70**. No holes. *BMCPtol* 107, 48 with ΣΩ only is presumably an engraver's aberration.
95 **371–77**. No holes.
96 **378–410**. No holes.
97 **411–27**. No holes.
98 **428**. No holes.
99 **429–41**. No holes.
100 **442**. No holes.
101 **443–44**. No holes. First published by Robinson, NC^6 4 (1944) no. 49, six examples, average 1.19 g. The small, thick flan is late, but no eponym or monogram is visible. It is here given arbitrarily to Soter, but might belong under Apion.

PTOLEMY APION, 104/1–96 B.C.

102 **542–603**. Among the find coins about half have the surface holes, half do not. All the examples of Group IX-E in the *BMC*, nos. 84-104, 21 pieces, were presented by the Society of Antiquaries of Scotland. To judge from their state of preservation, and the characteristic scissel which they retain throughout, they probably represent a single hoard.
103 **605–609**. No holes.
104 **610–23**. No holes.

The Mint of Barce

The bronze issues of the city were sporadic, and all are very rare.[68] One example was found in the Apollonia excavations, one appears in the Norton coins, but none in the Demeter Sanctuary.

CA. 325–313 B.C.

The earliest issues are similar in fabric to the earliest Cyrene Units and Quarters, and presumably are contemporary with them. They also share the Ammon/ and, later, the horse/ obverse types.

MAGAS IN REVOLT, CA. 282–261 B.C.

The Apollo/horse type was struck for Barce, Cyrene, and Euesperides with individual mint mark and symbol—BA-cornucopiae, KYP-crab, E-apple branch. Although the weight of *BMC* 48 is rather high, there is no reason to dissociate it from the same type as struck for the other two mints. The dies are of similar style: presumably all three issues were produced simultaneously at the Cyrene mint.

The Ammon/palm tree issue is in the same case, in that the type was issued for both Barce and Cyrene, though not for Euesperides. The quantities of the Cyrenean coins are not matched by the Barcan, however. This piece is the only example reported in the *BMC*; a second is in Copenhagen, *SNG Cop* 1297. The mediocre style of the Barce and Cyrene coins is similar. Presumably both issues were struck at the Cyrene mint; a single moneyer may be represented by the signatures ΔA at Cyrene and ΔAP at Barce (*BMC* 304 and 47b).

PTOLEMY V–PTOLEMY VI/VIII, CA. 200–163 B.C.

Attribution of the Ptolemaic ram/eagle issue to Barce is irresistible, but the chronology is very uncertain. An early *terminus post quem* is provided by the surface holes. Flans so treated first appeared in Cyrenaica ca. 246 B.C., after the Koinon episode. This issue is considerably later, for in module and weight it approximates denomination C in Soter/Libya Groups VI-VII at Cyrene, and shares their relatively neat flan. A date in the first third of the second century B.C. seems appropriate.

No further bronze is given here to Barce, but one additional possibility has been suggested, the small Ammon/eagle with B–A (*BMCPtol* 114, nos. 1–4). "To Ptolemy Apion I have conjecturally assigned the small copper coins apparently of Cyrenaic fabric with the inscription B A for ΒΑΣΙΛΕΩΣ."[69] The types are appropriate, and the thin beveled flans with casting protrusions are similar to those of the late Ptolemaic issues of Cyrenaica. But the inscription is unsatisfactory. BA abbreviating ΒΑΣΙΛΕΩΣ (or ΒΑΣΙΛΕΩΣ ΑΠΙΟΝΟΣ?) is not otherwise found in Ptolemaic Cyrenaica. Considered alternatively as a mintmark, BA alone does not occur at Barce; and the issue is late in the Ptolemaic series, while the city had lost its prominence on the foundation of Ptolemais, probably under Ptolemy III.[70]

Most important, Svoronos attests that both these and a similar issue with KΛ are found in large quantity in Alexandria,[71] where BA perhaps was to be understood as ΒΑΣΙΛΕΩΣ ΑΛΕΞΑΝΔΡΟΥ. In support of that attribution, the Cyrenaican excavations have reported no BA examples—save for Sidi Khrebish. The publication of this last includes a surprisingly large total of 16 BA pieces, but none at all of the really very common small /eagle issues of Euergetes, Soter, and Apion (**306–350, 411–428, 458–541, 605–609**). It is probable that the Sidi Khrebish pieces are actually examples of these regal issues, as their publisher, R. Reece, confirms *per litteras*.

---

68. "Barca subit une éclipse totale à partir du deuxième quart du IV siècle . . . tout se passe comme si la cité avait brusquement disparu, et cette absence . . . se traduit également par l'arrêt total du monnayage" (Laronde 162). Actually at this point the bronze coinage begins, but it is a poor thing after the great days of the silver.

69. Poole, *BMCPtol* lxxx.

70. C.H. Kraeling, 5–6.

71. Svoronos p. υκζ'.

TABLE II: Bronze Coinage of Barce

	ca. 325–313 B.C.		Magas in revolt ca. 282–261 B.C.		Ptolemy V–VI/VIII ca. 200–163 B.C.
Unit	Ammon/ram[1] 13.35 19.5 mm				
Half		horse/ram[3] 6.62 18.5 mm			
Quarter	ram's head/eagle[2] 4.76 14.5 mm	—/ram[4] 2.80 15 mm	Apollo/horse[5] 5.02 18 mm	Ammon/palm tree[6] 3.80 16.5 mm	ram/eagle[7] 4.30 19 mm
Eighth					
Sixteenth					

Notes to Table II

CA. 325–313 B.C.

1   *BMC* 46c, Paris. Two other examples are in Milan, *SNG Milano* "Cyrene" 49 (see *Atti e Memorie dell'Istituto Italiano di Numismatica* 8 [1934] 68), and New York, ANS.
2   BM 1927 4-2-9; two pieces each in Robinson, *NC*⁶ 4 (1944) no. 96 = BM 1946 12-5-10, 11; and Buttrey, *Norton*, no. N77. The good weight and deep circular incuse support attribution to the earliest issue.
3   *BMC* 47, 47a. The type is in a style reminiscent of the Cyrene horse/wheel Half.
4   Bond and Swales 91, the only example noted. The obverse is completely illegible; the ram of the reverse is clear enough, but much of the exergue has broken away. The reverse legend is given as BA in the text of the publication, as AP in the catalogue. I cannot make out anything on the coin itself. The low weight is due to wear and corrosion, but the diameter is appropriate for an early Quarter.

MAGAS IN REVOLT, CA. 282–261 B.C.

5   *BMC* 48.
6   *BMC* clxxxv, 47b, Paris. A second example is in Copenhagen, weight 3.99 g (*SNG Cop* 1297).

PTOLEMY V–VI/VIII, CA. 200–163 B.C.

7   *BMC* 108a. Holes.

The Mint of Euesperides and Berenice

Euesperides

Attribution of most of the issues listed here is secure. Seven bear the mint name, abbreviated as EY or E. Two of these bear the head of Heracles, appropriately, because the adventure of the Apples of the Hesperides was claimed to have occurred here. Aside from a single archaic tetradrachm with the scene of the picking of the fruit (*BMC* 10a), Heracles does not occur on any certain issue of Cyrene. It seems best, therefore, to attribute to Euesperides the two Heracles/ types without mint mark. Two issues (one with mint mark) also bear the apple branch symbol appropriate to the city.[72] However, I have not included the Soter/Libya variety with apple branch (*BMC* Regal 48–54).

CA. 325–313 B.C.

The Unit bears no ethnic. It was attributed by Robinson to Cyrene, although he allowed the possibility of its having been struck at Euesperides.[73] The latter must be the case: the Unit is overstruck by the subsequent Heracles/trident Unit, but not by Cyrenaean Units. The best-preserved example of the unit is the piece found at Euesperides (see Appendix, **E16**). It shows without a doubt that the head of Heracles is imitated from tetradrachms of Alexander. Martin Price has kindly determined that the source will have been a tetradrachm of the Pella mint, dating to ca. 325; not—perhaps surprisingly—the Alexander tetradrachm attributable to Cyrene itself (*BMC* Regal 1–2). Since it appears that the earliest Units of all three Cyrenaican mints are more or less contemporary, a date of ca. 325 B.C. for the beginning of bronze coinage has been adopted in this study for them all.

The Heracles/trident piece makes a set with the Half and Eighth of common reverse type. The style of each is quite unlike anything being produced at this time at Cyrene. Their relative chronology is established by overstrikes, Units in Copenhagen and Athens on the first Euesperides Unit, Heracles/bow[74]; the BM example on Cyrene Ammon/wheel; two Euesperides find coins from Bond and Swales (92–99, seen by me), and two from the unpublished Euesperides finds, on Cyrene horse's head/wheel and ?/wheel (Appendix, **E17**, **E18**). The series must be roughly coeval with the Cyrene /wheel issues; there too the Unit, Half, and Eighth were the major denominations.

---

72.   *BMC* cxv–cxvi.
73.   *BMC* xciv–xcv.
74.   *BMC* cxciii, 5 bis a-b.

PTOLEMY I, CA. 308–305 B.C.

The Half, the only denomination of this issue, appears to parallel the gazelle/silphium Half at Cyrene, and like it is somewhat incuse on the reverse. Three of the four pieces cited by Robinson are overstruck on the Carthaginian Persephone l./free horse r., dated to 370–340 B.C. by Visonà in his study of the Carthaginian bronze.[75] Carthaginian bronze is very rarely found in Cyrenaica: presumably these pieces leaked back to the east with the survivors of Ophellas' expedition.

REVOLT, CA. 305–300 B.C.

The mint mark secures attribution to Euesperides, but the chronology is doubtful. It seems to fit best between the post-Ophellas and the ΒΑΣΙΛΕΩΣ issues. For a possibly related issue see Table I.28.

PTOLEMY I, CA. 300–282 B.C.

The attribution of the Heracles/ issues is good. Table III.7 bears no mint mark, but the reverse is obviously parallel to that of the next variety, which is mint-marked. In addition, several Heracles/ pieces were found at Euesperides by Bond and Swales, included in their nos. 128–33, 135, not all of certain reading; and another appeared among the unpublished pieces from Euesperides (**E19**). On Mørkholm's dating the Revolt of ca. 305 was overcome in 300;[76] only then will coins have been struck with the legend ΒΑΣΙΛΕΩΣ, the title which Ptolemy I assumed in late 305.

Cat. nos. **734–735** are overstruck, apparently on Cyrene Apollo/eagle.

MAGAS IN REVOLT, CA. 282–261 B.C.

The style of the only issue of this period is consistent with that of the same types from Barce and Cyrene—presumably all three varieties were struck at Cyrene.

MAGAS RECONCILED WITH PTOLEMY II, CA. 261–258 B.C.

Poole had attributed this issue to the mint of Euesperides-Berenice,[77] and Robinson acknowledged the possibility while actually listing it under Cyrene.[78] Poole's attribution is accepted here. The point is that stylistically the Cyrenaican silver and bronze portraits of Berenice I go together, and the former is distinguished by an otherwise unique apple-wreath border, appropriate to Euesperides. The style is unlike anything else coming out of Cyrene. The weight of the bronze in Table III is an average of the *BMC* piece and four pieces at Svoronos 321; neither the average nor the range (6.59–5.65 g) is commensurate with that of contemporary Cyrene issues.

Berenice

PTOLEMY VI, 180–163 B.C.

By this time Euesperides had long been abandoned for Berenice. The apple-branch symbol is appropriate to the city, and this attribution was already suggested by Poole. But the /two eagles issue was not catalogued in the *BMC* by Robinson, although he did include the same type with silphium symbol under Cyrene. (The type also occurs at Alexandria with cornucopiae symbol [Svoronos 1412–26, various modules].) Poole gave the apple-branch issue to Soter II,[79] but his other coinage in Cyrenaica is signed, and the /two eagles type is appropriate to the joint rule of Philometor and Euergetes II.

On the possibility that some of Soter/Libya V-A emanated from a mint at Berenice, see *BMC* clix.

---

75. In course of publication.

76. Mørkholm 152–54.

77. *BMCPtol* 60, no. 14.

78. *BMC* cliv, clvi.

79. *BMCPtol* 108, 57–58.

Notes to Table III

Euesperides

CA. 325–313 B.C.

1   **729–32**, anepigraphic. See **E 16**.
2   *BMC* 5 bis, 5 bis a-b, with legend EY. See **E 17–18**.
3   *BMC* 6-7, with legend EY.
4   *BMC* 11, with legend EY.

PTOLEMY I, CA. 308–305 B.C.

5   *BMC* 8-10, 10a, with legend EY. The first two *BMC* pieces were overstruck on Carthaginian Persephone/free horse.

REVOLT, CA. 305–300 B.C.

6   *BMC* 10b, with mint mark EY. The reported weight appears to be at variance with the small diameter. The weight is here disregarded and the issue taken as an Eighth.

PTOLEMY I, CA. 300–282 B.C.

7   **733–36**, no mint mark. See **E 19**.
8   Newell pp. 11-12, no. 3, with mint mark EY.

MAGAS IN REVOLT, CA. 282–261 B.C.

9   *BMC* 12-13, with mint mark E above horse and apple-branch below. See **E 20**.

MAGAS RECONCILED WITH PTOLEMY II, CA. 261-258 B.C.

10   *BMC* Regal 29.

Berenice

PTOLEMY VI/VIII, 170–163 B.C.

11   *BMCPtol* p. 108, 57-58, with apple-branch symbol.

TABLE III: Bronze coinage of Euesperides

	ca. 325–313 B.C.	Ptolemy I ca. 308–305 B.C.	Revolt ca. 305–300 B.C.	Ptolemy I ca. 300–282 B.C.	Magas in revolt ca. 282–261 B.C.	Magas reconciled with Ptolemy II ca. 261–258 B.C.	Bronze coinage of Berenice Ptolemy VI/VIII 170–163 B.C.
Unit	Heracles/bow, club, quiver[1] 14.00 25 mm	Heracles/trident[2] 13.36 24 mm					
Half		Ammon/trident[3] 7.36 21 mm	Nymph/silphium[5] 5.65 18.5 mm			Berenice/sling[10] 6.18 20 mm	Ammon/2 eagles[11] 5.69 19 mm
Quarter					Heracles/bow case and club[7] 4.18 15 mm Heracles/club and bow case[8] 3.09 15 mm	Apollo/horse[9] 4.33 17 mm		
Eighth		dolphin/trident[4] 2.73 13/15 mm		Carneius/silphium[6] 3.40 13 mm			
Sixteenth							

The Mint of Apollonia

No coins are given to Apollonia in the catalogue proper of the *BMC*. However, in the introductory matter Robinson was inclined to accept Müller's attribution to Apollonia of issues with crab, whether as type (crab/jerboa [*BMC* 285a–d]) or symbol (Ammon/palm tree [*BMC* 293–300], Apollo/lyre [*BMC* 326–331], Apollo/horse [*BMC* 343–346]); and certain Regal gold and bronze.[80] This theory can be tested by examining the published finds from Apollonia. Among 95 Cyrenaean bronze coins, covering the entire range from the fourth century /silphium to Ptolemy Apion, there was just one crab/jerboa, one Apollo/horse, and no /palm tree or /lyre coins at all—the two latter issues being otherwise relatively common. The conclusion is inevitable that Apollonia was not their mint, and that the crab symbol does not signify the city. In fact, Apollonia does not appear to have been a city at all until relatively late; it was simply the port of Cyrene, and the name Apollonia, which in our evidence first occurs in Strabo, does not precede the second century B.C.[81]

However, one unusual issue might belong here, struck during a brief period when the port was not under Cyrene's control, during the invasion of Thibron, 323–322 B.C. The discovery of a piece of Thibron among the coins collected by Norton in Cyrenaica enabled Newell to make the first certain identification of his coinage.[82] The dates are secure: Thibron invaded Cyrenaica from Crete in 323, and in the following year (or early 321, according to Laronde)[83] after a series of brutal encounters was defeated, captured, and killed. His mint city is not certain: Thibron was not successful in his siege of Cyrene, so he did not strike there. He gained control of Barce, Euesperides, and Apollonia, but attribution to either Barce or Euesperides would move the coins from his primary area of operation. (Newell was disinclined to see in the Heracles/ type a reference to Euesperides, for Thibron had been a lieutenant of Harpalos, Alexander's treasurer, and the Heracles types are reminiscent of Alexander's bronze.) Apollonia was Thibron's base for the siege of Cyrene. Sixty talents were extorted from the Cyrenaeans while he was there, and the property of the merchants in the port was plundered.[84] Here might be the source of funds for his coinage. The Athena/ type too may be significant; it is rare in Cyrenaica, otherwise appearing only at Cyrene, including early bronze which is more or less contemporary with Thibron. For these reasons I hesitatingly assign the two Thibron pieces to Apollonia.

On present evidence there appears to be no other coinage of the city.

---

80. *BMC* cxcviii–cc.

81. Laronde 457.

82. Newell 3–11.

83. Laronde 46.

84. Diodorus 18.19–20.

Table IV: Bronze coinage of Apollonia

	Thibron 323–322 B.C.
Unit	
Half	Heracles/spearhead and club[1] 8.51 19 mm Athena/spearhead and club[2] 4.70 19 mm
Quarter	
Eighth	
Sixteenth	

Notes to Table IV

THIBRON, 323–322 B.C.

1 New York, ANS. Newell 3–11, no. 2.
2 Paris. L. Robert, "La Monnaie de Thibron," *Hellenica* 10 (1955) 167–71. The coin is of the same diameter and struck from the same reverse die as the piece above. Its low weight is due to its unusually thin flan.

APPENDIX

Unpublished Finds from Euesperides

Introduction

Excavations at Euesperides in 1954, conducted by C.N. Johns and Basil Wilson, and supported by the Ashmolean Museum, Oxford University, produced a small number of coins. They are today deposited in the Ashmolean's Heberden Coin Room, whose Keeper, Dr. D.M. Metcalf, has kindly made them available for study.

These coins confirm the picture independently drawn by Bond and Swales. Like their surface finds, the unpublished coins run from the late fourth century to the time of Magas, then abruptly stop at the point when Euesperides was abandoned for the new city of Berenice, save for one fragmentary stray from the Roman coinage of the first century B.C.

Several of the coins are individually of importance, most obviously the one example of the earliest bronze issue of the city, the Heracles/bow, club, and quiver Unit (**E16**). Aside from being beautifully produced it is the best-preserved specimen known, and shows that the head of Heracles is imitated from tetradrachms of Alexander, specifically a tetradrachm of the Pella mint, dating to ca. 325 B.C.

This group also includes a tiny Soter/eagle coin, of a module rarely found (**E13**). There is an additional example of the small Heracles/club and quiver piece with legend ΒΑΣΙΛΕΩΣ (**E19**), several of which had already been found by Bond and Swales, reaffirming Newell's attribution of the issue to the mint of Euesperides.[1] The one silver coin is an apparently unpublished variety of the fifth-century B.C. tetradrachm of Barce (**E15**).

From beyond the borders of Cyrenaica comes a Carthaginian bronze, very rarely found so far to the east (**E23**).

Catalogue

Mint of Cyrene

CA. 325–313 B.C.

BRONZE, FIRST SERIES

BRONZE UNITS

Head of Cyrene r.

Triple silphium.
AE   dies —   *BMC* 178

	weight	diam.
E1[2]	8.06	20/21

Head of Cyrene r.
[illegible]
AE   dies —   cf. *BMC* 178

---

1. Newell 11–12.

2. The unusually low weight is due to severe corrosion.

E2	11.39	24

BRONZE QUARTER UNIT

Head of Carneius r. (no magistrate's name visible).
Triple silphium.
AE   dies —   *BMC* 198b
   E3   2.33   16

SECOND SERIES

BRONZE HALF UNITS

Ammon head r.
Oval wheel.
AE   dies ↑ or ↓   *BMC* 277-278
   E4³   5.81   19/20

Horseman on horse r.; below [ ].
Four-spoked round wheel, silphium between spokes at r.
AE   dies ↘   cf. *BMC* 194
   E5   5.63   19

Horseman on horse r.; below, ΘA.
Four-spoked round wheel, silphium between spokes at l.
AE   dies ↙   *BMC* 194 obv., 195 rev.
   ***E6**   5.59   20

PTOLEMY I SOTER, CA. 300–282 B.C.

Head of Apollo r.
Eagle l. on fulmen.
AE   dies ↑   *BMC* Regal 4
   E7   3.15   17/19

Head of Apollo l.
Eagle r. on fulmen; before, ꟼ and silphium visible.
AE   dies ↘   cf. *BMC* Regal 5c
   E8   2.19   16
      (broken)

MAGAS IN REVOLT, CA. 282–261 B.C.

Head of Apollo r.
Lyre.
AE   dies ↖   *BMC* 319-25, 332 etc.
   ***E9**⁴   3.28   17/19

MAGAS RECONCILED WITH PTOLEMY II PHILADELPHUS, CA. 261–258 B.C.

Head of Ptolemy Soter r.
Eagle l. on fulmen.
AE   dies ↑   *BMC* 20-23
   E10   6.17   18/20
   E11   7.03   19/20
   E12   6.06   18

Head of Ptolemy Soter r.
Eagle l. on fulmen.
AE   dies ↑
   ***E13**⁵   0.86   12/14

Head of Ptolemy Soter r.
Protome of winged horse r.
AE   dies ↑   *BMC* 26
   E14   2.78   15

Mint of Barce

PERIOD II

CA. 475–435 B.C.

ATTIC TETRADRACHM

Silphium, type IC; at base l., [ ]; at r., A.
Head of Zeus Ammon r. in circle of dots; BAP before.
AR   dies ↓   cf. *BMC* 5-7
   ***E15**   13.43   26

---

3. The flan resembles that of BMC 278 with its projections. Both may have been struck from spheres of metal.

4. The piece is overstruck, but the undertype is not recoverable.

5. The module is not reported elsewhere.

Mint of Euesperides

CA. 325–313 B.C.

BRONZE UNITS

Head of Heracles r.
Bow, club, quiver.
AE   dies ↓   cf. *BMC* 188 bis
    *E16[6]   Pl. 12   11.52   23/26

Head of Heracles r.
Trident; dolphin to l. and r. of haft.
AE   dies ↗, ↙   cf. BMC 5 bis
    *E17[7]   12.23   23
    *E18[8]   12.10   24

PTOLEMY I SOTER, CA. 300–282 B.C.

Head of Heracles.
Bow case and club; between, ΒΑΣΙΛΕΩΣ.
AE   dies ↙   Bond and Swales 128-35
    *E19[9]   4.33   15

MAGAS IN REVOLT, CA. 282–261 B.C.

Head of Apollo r.
Horse prancing r.; above, E and star; below, crab.
AE   dies ↙   BMC 12
    E20   1.81   17

Cyrenaica Under the Romans

LATE 1ST CENTURY B.C.

L. Lollius
Club.
Wreath.
AE   quadrans   dies ←   *BMC* 16 bis etc.
   E21   (fragment)

Greek Coins Struck Outside Cyrenaica

MACEDON ?

CA. 336–323 B.C.

Head of Heracles.
Bow, quiver, and club; between, ΑΛ[Ε]ΞΑΝ.
AE   dies ↗
    *E22[10]   8.55   16/20 x 5/6

CARTHAGE

CA. 370–340 B.C.

Head of Persephone l.
Horse running r.
AE   dies ↗   *BMCSicily* p. 255, 1-5
    *E23[11]   3.50   15/16

---

6. This is the finest example of the issue yet to be published, the dies beautifully designed and cut (compare *BMC* 188 bis) and the coin carefully struck. Although the obverse type is obviously taken from the Alexander tetradrachms, the style is not that of the tetradrachms struck at Cyrene (*BMC* 72, 1-2), but as Martin Price kindly informs me is a direct imitation of the tetradrachms of the main Macedonian mint, Pella, from ca. 325 B.C. The narrow reverse die was probably designed to obliterate an original type in overstriking. The deep incuse of the reverse makes it appear that the piece is indeed overstruck, but the undertype is not visible. In the Catalogue the indicated die position assumes the reverse club to be upright on its handle.

7. The strike is weak, but enough is visible to show that the type is a variety not noted in *BMC*: the trident is accompanied by a dolphin downward on either side of the haft. Overstruck on Cyrene ?/wheel. The reverse types of Bond and Swales 92 and 97 are also described as including a dolphin at r.

8. Overstruck on Cyrene horse's head/wheel.

9. The issue is the same as that found in several examples by Bond and Swales at Euesperides.

10. The type is a regular Alexander bronze, whose symbol (if there was one) cannot be read. The flan is very dumpy and un

Uncertain Mint

Head r.
Prow r.; above ΑΛΕ...
AE   dies →
   *E24   2.71   13

even—20 x 16 x 5-6 mm— and the striking poor. The reverse legend abbreviates the name, ΑΛΕΞΑΝ, unusually; the letters are unevenly horizontal, and the second Α is only the height of the top two lines of the Ξ. The striking is careless. It is altogether a poor production. At 8.55 g the piece is considerably heavier than any of its type in *SNG Cop*, Macedonia 1034-1061, and the reverse, somewhat incuse, gives the impression of an overstrike although no undertype can be seen. The weight is exactly within the range of the Half Unit /wheel issues of Cyrene. I assign the piece to Macedon in order not to disturb the display of known issues of Cyrenaica, but I wonder whether it was not actually produced at Euesperides and overstruck on Cyrene.

11. The date follows Paolo Visonà's unpublished study of the Carthaginian bronze. Robinson identified this issue, the earliest in bronze, as the undertype for *BMC* Euesperides 8-9, nymph/silphium. Carthaginian coins are otherwise virtually unknown in Cyrenaica. The Apollonia and Demeter Sanctuary excavations, together with Norton's campaign, produced over 1600 coins, of which not one was Carthaginian. This piece is the first evidence for circulation of the issue un-restruck in western Cyrenaica, although another may have surfaced in the same area, at Sidi Khrebish, where the one Carthaginian coin found in the excavations is described as "Obv. female head l., Rev. horse r." (p. 229).

Concordance of Inventory and Catalog Numbers

69-0039	**96**	69-0195	**677**	69-0328	**523**	71-0084	**510**
69-0079	**294**	69-0204	**517**	69-0338	**134**	71-0085	**181**
69-0082	**386**	69-0206	**643**	69-0339	**182**	71-0086	**459**
69-0084	**323**	69-0209	**85**	69-0343	**367**	71-0118	**513**
69-0086	**283**	69-0211	**2**	69-0344	**730**	71-0119	**157**
69-0087	**403**	69-0213	**183**	69-0345	**457**	71-0120	**526**
69-0089	**327**	69-0216	**516**	69-0346	**619**	71-0121	**539**
69-0090	**482**	69-0228	**5**	69-0352	**356**	71-0122	**790**
69-0091	**383**	69-0229	**67**	69-0353	**749**	71-0123	**796**
69-0092	**544**	69-0244	**180**	69-0367	**429**	71-0124	**683**
69-0093	**255**	69-0245	**329**	69-0368	**11**	71-0125	**556**
69-0094	**632**	69-0246	**362**	71-0001	**807**	71-0126	**345**
69-0095	**676**	69-0247	**769**	71-0002	**350**	71-0154	**442**
69-0096	**622**	69-0248	**272**	71-0004	**330**	71-0155	**809**
69-0097	**507**	69-0249	**788**	71-0005	**333**	71-0156	**152**
69-0098	**259**	69-0267	**224**	71-0006	**78**	71-0157	**208**
69-0104	**778**	69-0268	**488**	71-0007	**393**	71-0158	**499**
69-0106	**90**	69-0269	**781**	71-0008	**194**	71-0159	**378**
69-0144	**147**	69-0270	**678**	71-0018	**680**	71-0166	**504**
69-0145	**341**	69-0271	**109**	71-0019	**456**	71-0167	**501**
69-0146	**497**	69-0272	**87**	71-0020	**258**	71-0168	**491**
69-0147	**528**	69-0280	**215**	71-0021	**404**	71-0179	**478**
69-0148	**416**	69-0284	**244**	71-0022	**666**	71-0181	**740**
69-0149	**746**	69-0286	**679**	71-0023	**667**	71-0213	**634**
69-0150	**659**	69-0287	**162**	71-0024	**671**	71-0214	**74**
69-0151	**547**	69-0288	**583**	71-0025	**315**	71-0215	**38**
69-0152	**566**	69-0289	**784**	71-0026	**196**	71-0216	**268**
69-0153	**467**	69-0297	**370**	71-0027	**681**	71-0217	**64**
69-0154	**573**	69-0298	**615**	71-0028	**682**	71-0218	**153**
69-0155	**603**	69-0299	**817**	71-0029	**111**	71-0219	**14**
69-0157	**195**	69-0307	**149**	71-0030	**191**	71-0259	**417**
69-0158	**729**	69-0308	**733**	71-0040	**474**	71-0260	**391**
69-0161	**342**	69-0309	**492**	71-0041	**204**	71-0276	**810**
69-0162	**665**	69-0315	**110**	71-0042	**299**	71-0277	**398**
69-0163	**276**	69-0316	**197**	71-0043	**260**	71-0278	**61**
69-0175	**815**	69-0324	**113**	71-0044	**186**	71-0279	**818**
69-0176	**532**	69-0325	**112**	71-0045	**498**	71-0280	**44**
69-0177	**816**	69-0326	**451**	71-0046	**115**	71-0281	**47**
69-0184	**328**	69-0327	**125**	71-0083	**758**	71-0282	**41**

71-0312	**800**	73-0034	**773**	73-0504	**739**	73-0634	**580**
71-0313	**91**	73-0037	**264**	73-0505	**688**	73-0635	**783**
71-0314	**819**	73-0038	**613**	73-0514	**689**	73-0636	**188**
71-0315	**106**	73-0046	**336**	73-0515	**310**	73-0637	**150**
71-0316	**820**	73-0047	**237**	73-0516	**534**	73-0638	**199**
71-0317	**411**	73-0048	**239**	73-0517	**690**	73-0639	**509**
71-0318	**606**	73-0089	**101**	73-0518	**691**	73-0640	**140**
71-0319	**732**	73-0090	**390**	73-0519	**692**	73-0641	**309**
71-0320	**514**	73-0091	**243**	73-0526	**693**	73-0642	**302**
71-0321	**317**	73-0092	**172**	73-0543	**793**	73-0643	**284**
71-0322	**423**	73-0093	**763**	73-0544	**797**	73-0644	**552**
71-0323	**605**	73-0094	**684**	73-0547	**214**	73-0645	**119**
71-0324	**569**	73-0120	**139**	73-0548	**565**	73-0646	**412**
71-0325	**435**	73-0121	**156**	73-0549	**114**	73-0647	**653**
71-0326	**821**	73-0122	**246**	73-0550	**221**	73-0648	**644**
71-0327	**211**	73-0123	**586**	73-0551	**487**	73-0766	**75**
71-0390	**811**	73-0124	**577**	73-0552	**738**	73-0767	**207**
71-0391	**822**	73-0125	**365**	73-0553	**826**	73-0768	**298**
71-0392	**81**	73-0126	**242**	73-0554	**449**	73-0769	**654**
71-0393	**66**	73-0144	**685**	73-0555	**694**	73-0770	**122**
71-0394	**40**	73-0167	**261**	73-0556	**591**	73-0771	**465**
71-0395	**86**	73-0168	**230**	73-0557	**270**	73-0772	**593**
71-0568	**648**	73-0169	**262**	73-0558	**201**	73-0773	**220**
71-0612	**647**	73-0211	**686**	73-0559	**335**	73-0774	**295**
71-0613	**45**	73-0212	**248**	73-0560	**466**	73-0775	**649**
71-0614	**32**	73-0219	**104**	73-0561	**489**	73-0776	**357**
71-0615	**28**	73-0220	**103**	73-0562	**334**	73-0777	**405**
71-0616	**54**	73-0221	**102**	73-0563	**537**	73-0778	**623**
71-0617	**349**	73-0242	**238**	73-0564	**253**	73-0780	**210**
71-0618	**120**	73-0243	**646**	73-0565	**288**	73-0804	**271**
71-0619	**80**	73-0244	**361**	73-0566	**406**	73-0805	**232**
71-0620	**84**	73-0246	**652**	73-0567	**443**	73-0806	**355**
71-0621	**71**	73-0247	**223**	73-0568	**472**	73-0807	**447**
71-0622	**369**	73-0248	**277**	73-0569	**496**	73-0808	**252**
71-0623	**92**	73-0249	**249**	73-0570	**316**	73-0809	**235**
71-0624	**95**	73-0250	**154**	73-0571	**540**	73-0810	**274**
71-0625	**354**	73-0251	**395**	73-0572	**508**	73-0811	**408**
71-0626	**530**	73-0252	**233**	73-0573	**132**	73-0812	**696**
71-0627	**463**	73-0253	**265**	73-0574	**407**	73-0813	**123**
71-0628	**812**	73-0254	**250**	73-0575	**373**	73-0814	**484**
71-0759	**823**	73-0318	**825**	73-0576	**494**	73-0815	**512**
71-0760	**782**	73-0348	**159**	73-0577	**695**	73-0816	**518**
71-0768	**24**	73-0349	**687**	73-0578	**500**	73-0817	**313**
71-0770	**88**	73-0418	**553**	73-0579	**376**	73-0818	**511**
71-0835	**824**	73-0419	**52**	73-0621	**193**	73-0819	**533**
71-0836	**68**	73-0420	**263**	73-0622	**587**	73-0820	**375**
71-0837	**422**	73-0421	**597**	73-0623	**741**	73-0821	**502**
71-0838	**607**	73-0422	**441**	73-0624	**219**	73-0822	**307**
71-0839	**205**	73-0423	**380**	73-0625	**273**	73-0823	**425**
71-0840	**493**	73-0431	**339**	73-0626	**300**	73-0824	**320**
73-0002	**415**	73-0440	**359**	73-0627	**340**	73-0825	**308**
73-0003	**245**	73-0441	**281**	73-0628	**454**	73-0826	**347**
73-0004	**141**	73-0442	**218**	73-0629	**542**	73-0827	**130**
73-0005	**650**	73-0443	**269**	73-0630	**226**	73-0838	**287**
73-0008	**640**	73-0469	**121**	73-0631	**479**	73-0839	**297**
73-0032	**772**	73-0473	**72**	73-0632	**572**	73-0840	**291**
73-0033	**771**	73-0503	**628**	73-0633	**656**	73-0841	**458**

73-0947	**100**	74-0218	**82**	74-0638	**374**	76-0002	**337**
73-1047	**760**	74-0219	**701**	74-0639	**480**	76-0003	**388**
73-1048	**206**	74-0220	**236**	74-0640	**290**	76-0004	**481**
73-1049	**189**	74-0221	**702**	74-0641	**639**	76-0005	**231**
73-1050	**108**	74-0222	**525**	74-0642	**658**	76-0006	**642**
73-1051	**555**	74-0223	**703**	74-0643	**202**	76-0007	**589**
73-1061	**827**	74-0224	**704**	74-0644	**160**	76-0008	**714**
73-1062	**541**	74-0225	**372**	74-0770	**48**	76-0019	**36**
73-1198	**697**	74-0398	**53**	74-0771	**46**	76-0020	**549**
73-1199	**69**	74-0399	**792**	74-0772	**65**	76-0021	**585**
73-1200	**227**	74-0400	**55**	74-0773	**89**	76-0029	**431**
73-1201	**171**	74-0433	**251**	74-0774	**267**	76-0030	**715**
73-1268	**575**	74-0445	**20**	74-1027	**29**	76-0031	**716**
73-1269	**828**	74-0446	**734**	74-1028	**21**	76-0053	**757**
73-1270	**584**	74-0447	**768**	74-1029	**93**	76-0054	**767**
73-1271	**473**	74-0448	**766**	74-1030	**76**	76-0092	**655**
73-1272	**8**	74-0449	**736**	74-1031	**222**	76-0093	**830**
73-1273	**42**	74-0452	**430**	74-1032	**567**	76-0094	**558**
73-1274	**155**	74-0453	**568**	74-1033	**126**	76-0095	**594**
73-1275	**99**	74-0454	**306**	74-1034	**505**	76-0163	**151**
73-1276	**358**	74-0465	**531**	74-1035	**710**	76-0164	**400**
73-1277	**698**	74-0466	**829**	74-1036	**557**	76-0165	**399**
73-1278	**699**	74-0467	**321**	74-1037	**711**	76-0166	**717**
73-1279	**364**	74-0468	**392**	74-1038	**124**	76-0167	**471**
73-1280	**296**	74-0469	**254**	74-1039	**802**	76-0218	**578**
73-1281	**483**	74-0470	**184**	74-1040	**332**	76-0219	**582**
73-1282	**700**	74-0471	**638**	74-1041	**469**	76-0220	**579**
73-1283	**791**	74-0472	**490**	74-1042	**477**	76-0221	**225**
74-0008	**785**	74-0473	**705**	74-1043	**377**	76-0225	**524**
74-0009	**631**	74-0474	**706**	74-1044	**322**	76-0226	**662**
74-0010	**368**	74-0475	**707**	74-1045	**247**	76-0227	**626**
74-0011	**548**	74-0476	**808**	74-1046	**241**	76-0228	**675**
74-0012	**564**	74-0477	**744**	74-1047	**637**	76-0229	**344**
74-0048	**402**	74-0478	**485**	74-1048	**663**	76-0230	**213**
74-0049	**519**	74-0560	**787**	74-1049	**173**	76-0231	**453**
74-0050	**674**	74-0616	**25**	74-1050	**170**	76-0232	**718**
74-0067	**292**	74-0617	**49**	74-1051	**742**	76-0233	**831**
74-0068	**522**	74-0618	**759**	74-1052	**775**	76-0234	**161**
74-0069	**311**	74-0619	**789**	74-1053	**280**	76-0235	**144**
74-0070	**348**	74-0620	**136**	74-1090	**23**	76-0236	**279**
74-0071	**614**	74-0621	**450**	74-1091	**56**	76-0237	**570**
74-0072	**673**	74-0622	**240**	74-1092	**107**	76-0327	**94**
74-0095	**198**	74-0623	**165**	74-1093	**203**	76-0328	**266**
74-0143	**142**	74-0624	**708**	74-1094	**419**	76-0456	**163**
74-0144	**148**	74-0625	**813**	74-1095	**421**	76-0457	**303**
74-0145	**289**	74-0626	**177**	74-1098	**79**	76-0458	**363**
74-0146	**286**	74-0627	**446**	74-1176	**712**	76-0459	**394**
74-0147	**168**	74-0628	**660**	74-1177	**436**	76-0673	**19**
74-0148	**409**	74-0629	**563**	74-1178	**366**	76-0674	**599**
74-0149	**452**	74-0630	**545**	74-1179	**625**	76-0675	**657**
74-0150	**371**	74-0631	**212**	74-1180	**761**	76-0676	**743**
74-0151	**319**	74-0632	**200**	74-1181	**805**	76-0677	**178**
74-0152	**590**	74-0633	**709**	74-1182	**396**	76-0678	**559**
74-0201	**727**	74-0634	**440**	74-1183	**470**	76-0679	**719**
74-0202	**10**	74-0635	**433**	74-1184	**762**	76-0680	**138**
74-0216	**98**	74-0636	**636**	74-1185	**190**	76-0681	**257**
74-0217	**83**	74-0637	**432**	76-0001	**713**	76-0682	**538**

76-0928	753	77-0140	166	77-0799	217	78-0016	798
76-0929	764	77-0186	780	77-0800	779	78-0017	600
76-0930	799	77-0189	515	77-0801	592	78-0018	554
76-0931	179	77-0190	720	77-0802	588	78-0020	571
76-0932	641	77-0206	51	77-0819	353	78-0043	725
76-0933	795	77-0233	601	77-0820	629	78-0044	602
76-1261	760A	77-0234	598	77-0821	397	78-0045	624
76-1262	786	77-0235	73	77-0822	630	78-0050	209
76-1263	754	77-0355	424	77-0823	382	78-0051	617
76-1264	747	77-0356	389	77-0824	438	78-0052	228
76-1265	745	77-0358	256	77-0825	672	78-0053	278
76-1266	770	77-0359	282	77-0826	427	78-0054	633
76-1267	752	77-0360	551	77-0827	609	78-0073	12
76-1268	735	77-0474	22	77-0828	343	78-0104	562
76-1269	581	77-0475	192	77-0829	420	78-0105	460
76-1270	645	77-0476	185	77-0830	229	78-0108	550
76-1271	381	77-0541	27	77-0831	521	78-0195	187
76-1272	621	77-0678	834	77-0832	314	78-0206	301
76-1273	832	77-0679	664	77-0833	428	78-0207	304
76-1274	352	77-0680	595	77-0834	737	78-0208	543
76-1275	455	77-0681	444	77-0835	604	78-0209	748
76-1276	468	77-0682	137	77-0836	721	78-0219	104
76-1277	520	77-0686	7	77-0852	43	78-0314	596
76-1278	312	77-0687	35	77-0853	33	78-0315	133
76-1279	413	77-0688	18	77-0854	158	78-0316	612
76-1280	338	77-0718	15	77-0855	145	78-0317	216
76-1281	464	77-0719	58	77-0856	661	78-0318	275
76-1282	833	77-0720	146	77-0857	503	78-0358	50
76-1283	794	77-0721	486	77-0858	608	78-0422	39
76-1284a	116	77-0722	461	77-0859	668	78-0439	651
76-1284b	117	77-0732	34	77-0860	437	78-0460	97
76-1284c	118	77-0733	325	77-0861	385	78-0476	814
76-1285	803	77-0734	326	77-0862	401	78-0477	234
76-1286	635	77-0735	60	77-0863	462	78-0578	723
76-1287	426	77-0736	174	77-0880	62	78-0579	669
76-1288	293	77-0737	176	77-0881	418	78-0580	536
76-1289	618	77-0764	59	77-0882	527	78-0581	755
76-1290	318	77-0765	57	77-0883	476	78-0628	305
76-1291	475	77-0766	3	77-0884	561	78-0629	506
76-1292	135	77-0767	726	77-0885	439	78-0630	529
76-1293	129	77-0768	128	77-0886	610	78-0631	105
76-1294	143	77-0769	175	77-0887	616	78-0632	804
76-1295	77	77-0770	167	77-0888	434	78-0633	806
76-1296	351	77-0771	131	77-0889	627	78-0634	776
76-1297	576	77-0772	620	77-0966	379	78-0635	756
76-1298	574	77-0781	4	77-0990	324	78-0744	384
76-1299	731	77-0782	1	77-0991	346	78-0745	414
76-1300	9	77-0783	63	77-0992	360	78-0746	546
76-1301	728	77-0784	37	77-0993	26	78-0812	724
76-1302	70	77-0785	31	77-1284	30	78-0813	801
76-1303	13	77-0786	17	77-1285	127	78-0814	169
76-1304	6	77-0787	670	77-1286	387	78-0815	765
76-1305	16	77-0795	331	77-1287	448	78-0845	495
77-0030	560	77-0796	535	77-1288	164	78-0846	750
77-0031	777	77-0797	410	77-1289	722		
77-0139	285	77-0798	611	77-1290	751		

Part II
Attic Pottery from the Sanctuary of Demeter and Persephone

I

Introduction

The American excavations in the extramural Sanctuary of Demeter and Persephone at Cyrene have brought to light a considerable quantity of broken pottery, including many fragments of red-figured vases imported from Athens. These red-figured sherds are the principal subject of the present study. It must be emphasized that the catalogue below incorporates not a mere selection from a larger quantity of red-figure but almost all the fragments known to me from the site; I have omitted only a few scraps of which so little remains that neither the date nor the shape can be determined with any precision. It is important, however, to remember that, although the fill in the sanctuary has not been completely cleared and no doubt contains more red-figure, the excavation has been extensive and the fragments presented below probably provide a reasonably representative sample of the total amount of red-figure pottery to be found at the site.[1]

All the items in the catalogue are fragments: there are no complete vases such as one might expect from a cemetery. Moreover, the fragments are often lamentably small and were found widely scattered, a situation brought about by continuous use of the temenos and by widespread destruction wrought by severe earthquakes. As an example I may cite the fine, large skyphos, no. **87**, of ca. 410 B.C., attributable to the Meidias Painter, which is preserved in at least twenty sherds that have been unearthed "over a large part of the eastern half of the Middle Sanctuary."[2] Yet, despite the existence of these twenty sherds, it is still not possible to reconstruct the two pictures on this important vase. Given such circumstances, I have been especially careful about assigning sherds from different findspots to a single vase. Unless I have been reasonably certain that two non-joining sherds belong together, I have catalogued them separately, but have noted any possible connection.[3]

The catalogue lists 138 items, all of which seem to be Attic with the possible exception of **138**, a bell-krater which may be Elean. **1** to **129**, and **138**, belong to red-figured vases; **130–132** are epinetra, either bilingual or black-figure; **133** is a white-ground alabastron; **134–136** are fragments of head vases; and **137** comes from a vase with relief figures. The fragments of Attic red-figure (**1–129**) are organized by shape following, in the main, the order adopted by J.D. Beazley in ARV^2.[4] I have, however, placed at the end of the red-figure a group of sherds (**113–129**) which clearly belong to vases of "closed shape" but which I have usually not been able to categorize more accurately. Fragments of each specific shape are arranged so far as possible chronologically. The exact findspot of each sherd is given in terms of Area, Trench, and Stratum.[5] In a few instances this findspot is preceded by an inventory number, but this is unusual, for relatively little of the pottery could be inventoried by the excavators. Where a single vase is represented by more than one sherd, I have designated these fragments with letters of the alphabet and have not employed "storage box" numbers.[6] As a rule I have refrained from describing the fabric of each piece unless it seems unusual for Attic red-figure. I have illustrated as many fragments as possible; unfortunately, a few (**1, 40, 41, 43, 59, 60, 76, 104, 136**) were never photographed.

---

1. See White in *Final Reports* 1, ix–x.

2. White, *Final Reports* 1, 62 and n. 12.

3. This follows the practice adopted by Mary Moore in her publication of the black-figure pottery from the site: see Moore, *Final Reports* 3, 1.

4. ARV^2 xlix–li.

5. A plan of the site with the trenches indicated is given in Fig. 1. See also White, *Final Reports* 1, 54–116.

6. In this I differ from Mary Moore in her publication of the black-figure: see *Final Reports* 3, 1.

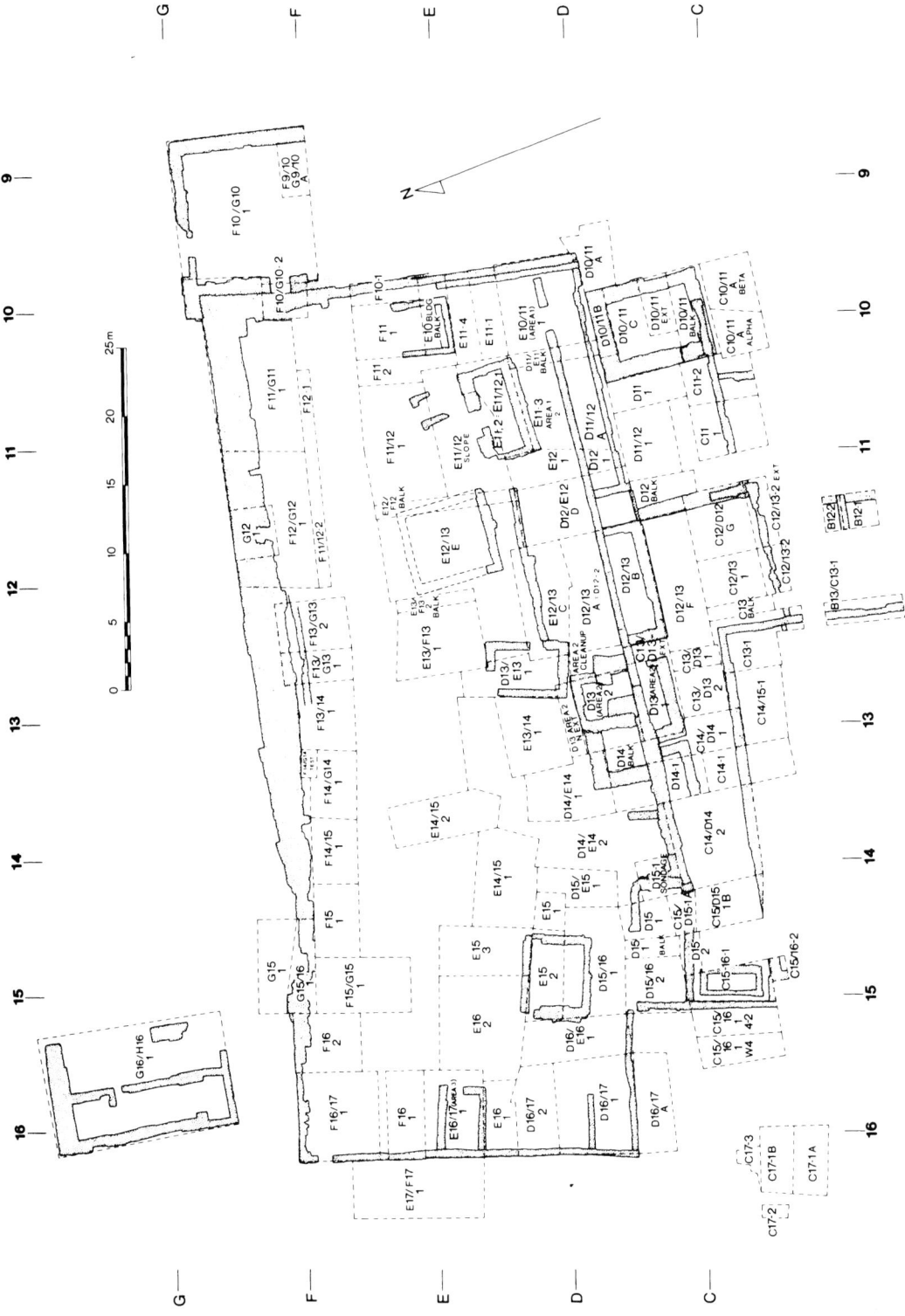

Figure 1. *Trench Plan of the Site (by Carl Beetz).*

Attic Red-figure

Chronology

The fragments from the Wadi Bel Gadir sanctuary span almost the entire chronological range of Attic red-figure, from the last quarter of the sixth century to the third quarter of the fourth. No sherds in the collection date to the earliest phase of red-figure; the first fragments may be dated ca. 520–500. The neck of an amphora of type A (**1**) and part of a pelike (**5**) seem to be products of the Pioneer Group, but most of the fragments of this period belong, as one would expect, to vases of small size—cups (**92–95**), plates (**110–112**), and mugs (**78–80**)—and were decorated by painters who specialized in these shapes. A number of cups (**96–98**, and **109**) may be either late sixth or early fifth century. Moreover, the bilingual epinetron **130** must be placed about 500 or a little later (together with the other epinetra fragments **131–132**).

Some fifteen fragments may be assigned to the first two decades of the fifth century (Late Archaic Period): **3**, an amphora perhaps of Panathenaic shape; **6**, a pelike; **18–23**, column-kraters or stamnoi; perhaps **31** and **32**, column-kraters; **61**, probably a hydria; **99–101**, cups; and the perhaps the fragment **114**.

More numerous are the red-figure fragments of the Early Classical Period (ca. 480–450). In this phase we may place the amphora **2**, the pelikai **7**, **8**, and perhaps **9**, the lebes gamikos **15**, the fragments of column-kraters or stamnoi **24–29**, the column-kraters **33–36**, the bell-kraters **42–43**, the volute-krater(?) **53** and the bell- or column-krater **54**, the hydriai **62–64**, the skyphos **83**, the cups **103** and **105**, the closed shapes **115–121**, and perhaps **124** and **125**. The calyx-krater **37**, the cups **102**, **104**, and **106**, and the closed shapes **113** and **122** probably belong to the first half of the fifth century, but their date cannot be fixed more definitely. A similar problem occurs with the column-krater or stamnos **30**, the bell-krater **44**, the bell-krater or calyx-krater **55**, the lid **82**, the skyphoi **84–86**, the stemless(?) cups **107–108**, and the closed shapes **123–127**—all are dated to the second or third quarter of the fifth century, though most are perhaps earlier than, or close to, 450. Even if some of these pieces do date after 450, a drop in the number of fragments is noticeable in the third quarter of the century: only the neck-amphora **4**, the bell-krater **45**, the krater **56**, the hydria **65**, the pyxis-lid **81**, and the oinochoe or hydria **129** can be attributed with any degree of assurance to the High Classical phase of red-figure.

In the last quarter of the fifth century may be dated the bell-kraters **47–48**, and perhaps **46**, the hydriai **66–72**, and the skyphoi **87–91**, in all some fifteen fragments which may, however, come from only four to six vases. The bell-krater **49** and the krater **57** are perhaps early fourth century rather than late fifth. Attic red-figure of the fourth century is also represented by the pelikai **10–14**, the lebetes gamikoi **16–17**, the calyx-kraters **38–41**, the bell-kraters **50–52**, the bell- or calyx-kraters **58–60**, and the hydriai **73–77**. Most of these fragments fall in the first half of the fourth century, but **41**, **52**, and perhaps **75–77** may belong to the third quarter.

Shape

The range of shape exhibited by these red-figured fragments from Cyrene is considerable. Vases of large size and of thick wall predominate. Most common is the bowl (krater or stamnos, **18–60**), in particular the column-krater (**18–36**—some may be stamnoi) and the bell-krater (**42–52**). Hydriai (**61–77**) and pelikai (**5–14**) are well represented, but there are few amphorai (**1–4**). Doubtless most of the fragments of closed shape (**113–129**) come from vases of large size, whether hydriai, pelikai or amphorai of various types. Among vessels of smaller size, cups or stemless cups (**92–109**) and skyphoi (**83–91**) are most numerous, but some examples of mugs (**78–80**) and plates (**110–112**) are also present. Clearly, wine-mixing bowls and drinking vessels form the bulk of the red-figured fragments of the sanctuary. While banqueting may well have constituted a part of the ritual, it is not possible to be sure whether these vases were employed for cult-purposes or dedicated as votive-offerings.[7] On the other hand, the lebetes

---

7. On this question, see White in *Final Reports* 3, xi. There was certainly ritual dining in the Demeter Sanctuary at Corinth.

gamikoi **15–17**, the pyxis of which the lid **81** formed the cover, the epinetra **130–132** were perhaps dedications considered suitable to female divinities.

Let us now examine the shapes in more detail. Only four fragments of amphorai (**1–4**) have been identified, though others may be concealed among the sherds of closed shapes **113–129**. There are two one-piece amphorai (**1, 2**), both of type A: **1** was made in the last twenty years of the sixth century, but **2** is later, dating perhaps to the second quarter of the fifth century. Two other varieties of amphora are probably represented at Cyrene: the amphora of Panathenaic shape in the sherd (**3**) of the first quarter of the fifth century; and the neck-amphora in a fragment (**4**) from the Polygnotan workshop, of ca. 440–420. More common than the true amphora is the pelike (**5–14**): **5** is a very early red-figured pelike decorated by one of the Pioneers about 520–510; **6** is Late Archaic; **7–9**, which may be from a single vase, are Early Classical. There is then a hiatus until the fourth century: **10–14** may be dated between 390 and 350.[8]

Of the lebetes gamikoi (**15–17**), **15** is a fairly early red-figured example of the shape, but **16** and **17** belong to the first half of the fourth century when the shape enjoyed a certain vogue.

I have not been able to identify definitely any stamnoi, but **18–30** must come from stamnoi or column-kraters: **18–23** belong to the first two decades of the fifth century; **24–28**, and perhaps **29** to the second quarter; **30** is perhaps closer to the second quarter than the third. Of the column-kraters, **31** and **32** are probably to be dated in the first quarter of the fifth century, **33** to **36** in the second quarter. It will be observed that, with the possible exception of **30**, none of the Cyrene stamnoi or column-kraters is later than 450, though the stamnos does not cease to be decorated in red-figure until the last quarter of the fifth century, and the column-krater disappears from the repertoire only in the first quarter of the fourth.[9] As elsewhere, for example at Corinth,[10] in the last thirty or so years of the fifth century and during the fourth century the bell-krater and the calyx-krater took the place of the column-krater and stamnos.

The earliest calyx-krater seems to be **37**, a small lip-fragment, of the late sixth or first half of the fifth century. With this exception, the calyx-kraters all belong to the fourth century: **38–40**, to the first half; **41**, perhaps to the third quarter.

More frequent than the calyx-krater is the bell-krater. **42–44** are relatively early, from the second quarter and middle of the fifth century; **45** may be dated to the third quarter, **46–48** probably to the last quarter; **50–52** and perhaps **49** are fourth-century examples of the shape.

A few fragments, **54–60**, may be either bell-kraters or calyx-kraters. Of these, **54** and **55** may be assigned to the second quarter or middle of the fifth century, **56** to the third quarter; the remainder (**57–60**) are probably all fourth century.

The fourth type of krater, the volute-krater, may be represented by **53**, to be dated ca. 460–440.

The earliest hydria is **61**, of ca. 490–480. **62–64** belong to the second quarter of the fifth century; **65** probably to the third quarter; **66–72** to the last quarter. **73–77** are fourth century in date. Again, one should probably add some of the closed vases **113–129**, most of which are probably Early Classical.

81 is the lid of a pyxis, no doubt of type A, a cosmetic (or trinket) box, a typical work of ca. 450–440. **82** is also a fragment of a lid, of a pyxis or lekanis, and was made about 460–440.

78–80, though classed as oinochoai, shape 8A, are really small, one-handled mugs, for drinking, ladling or measuring, and all were produced in one workshop in the years 510–490. There are no true oinochoai except for **123**, of ca. 460–440, which may be an example of shape 5B, and for **129**, of ca. 430, which may be an oinochoe of shape 4.

There are nine fragments (**83–91**) of skyphoi, though **87–91** may all come from a single, imposing vase decorated by the Meidias Painter about 410. However, the earliest example is **83**, of ca. 460 B.C., and **84–86** must also be placed in the second or third quarter of the fifth century. Somewhat surprisingly, there are no skyphoi of the fourth century.[11]

The commonest drinking vessel is the cup (**92–106**). Most (**92–101**) seem to find a place in the last twenty years of the sixth century or in the first twenty years of the fifth. **103** may be dated ca. 480–470, and **104** perhaps goes with it; **105** is probably second quarter of the fifth century; **102** and **106** cannot be placed more closely than late sixth or first half of the fifth century. Unfortunately, not enough is preserved of any piece to allow an attribution to a known potter. **95** may come from a cup of type B; **98**, from one of Bloesch's type C; **107** (together with **108**) is perhaps a stemless cup rather than a cup of type C—the date is about 450. **109**, of the late sixth century, could be a cup or stemless cup. There are no cups or stemless cups from the sanctuary after the

---

8. There may also be pelikai among the fragments of closed shapes (**113–129**).

9. On the latest column-kraters, see *Hesperia* 45 (1976) 381, n. 3.

10. See *Hesperia* 56 (1987) 276.

11. One might say the same of the oinochoe of type 2. Oinochoai and skyphoi of the F.B. Group have been found in North Africa: Sèvres 7090.2, ARV^2 1484, 17; Madrid 11506, ARV^2 1486, 85; Carthage, ARV^2 1487, 99; Louvre MN758, ARV^2 1489, 153; Carthage, skyphos, *AntAfr* 15 (1980) 66, fig. 53.

middle of the fifth century.

The three plates, **110–112**, are all early; **110** must be one of the earliest red-figured vases from the excavation, ca. 520–500, and **111** and **112** are only slightly later, ca. 500.

The epinetra **130–132** are examples of a special and uncommon shape. They probably all derive from a single workshop active around 500 and normally working in black-figure.

Style

The Wadi Bel Gadir sanctuary has not produced any vases by the first practitioners of the new red-figure technique, such as the Andokides Painter and Psiax, but the work of the Pioneer Group who were active in the last twenty years of the sixth century may be seen on the pelike-fragment **5**, and probably on **1**, the neck of a type A amphora. However, this formative phase of Attic red-figure, the last quarter of the sixth century, is mainly represented by the products of artists who specialized in decorating small vases, especially cups, plates, and mugs. The plate **110** shows a symposiast, and the drawing recalls the work of Epiktetos. **111** and **112**, which are also fragments of plates, may be attributed to the Heraion Painter, a minor decorator of cups and plates in the years around 500. The cup **96** was also painted by one of the less significant artists of this time, perhaps the Pithos painter. We may add, as well, the fragments of mugs **78–80**, all with male figures and all closely related in style to similar mugs by the Painter of Berlin 2268. The bilingual epinetron **130** (cf. also **131**), which may be dated ca. 500, must come from a workshop producing both black-figure and, at least on occasion, red-figure vases, and the connections, though tenuous, are with the Sappho Painter.

Though red-figure of the Late Archaic and Early Classical Periods is reasonably plentiful in the sanctuary, little has yet been attributed. **20**, which preserves the heads of Dionysos and Ariadne (or a maenad) is close to Myson; and **36** is probably by an Early Mannerist. **33** (together with **34**), a column-krater with part of a symposion, may be compared with vases by the Harrow Painter and the Flying-Angel Painter. The skyphos **83**, showing a portion of a woman, was decorated by the Lewis Painter about 460. **81**, the lid of a pyxis, has ornamental zones that allow it to be placed within the Penthesilea Workshop. And the fragments of a stemless cup, **107**, have horsemen rendered in the manner of the Sotades Painter (cf. Hippacontist Painter).

One of the principal pictorial traditions during the second half of the fifth century is that which begins with the Altamura and the Niobid Painters, and continues first in the Group of Polygnotos and then in the Kleophon and Dinos Painters. The palmette-floral on **4**, a neck-amphora of ca. 440–420, may be assigned to a painter of the Polygnotan Group or to the Keophon Painter. The hydria **65** is also comparable with work of this Group. The *gynaikeion* scene on the hydria **66** (to which **67** and **68** may belong) is certainly in the manner of the Dinos Painter, and not far from the Chrysis Painter. A contemporary of the Dinos Painter during the turbulent years of the Peloponnesian War was the Kadmos Painter. The fragments catalogued under **47** and **48**, which come from one or two bell-kraters, are certainly in the manner of the Kadmos Painter, and probably by the Kekrops Painter. The hydria **69** (cf. **70**, **71**) must also be a work of a pupil of the Kadmos Painter. The most tantalizing red-figured vase from Cyrene, and one which well illustrates even in fragments the florid, elaborate drawing of the late fifth century, is the large skyphos **87** (cf. also **88–91**) which may be attributed to the Meidias Painter.

For the most part the red-figured pottery of the fourth century is so poorly preserved that few stylistic connections can be made. There seems to be very little from the first decade or two, certainly nothing attributable to the Meleager or Erbach Painters or to the Jena Workshop, though **58** (and perhaps **59**, **60**), from a bell-krater or calyx-krater, comes from the Plainer Group of painters active at this time and is stylistically akin in particular to the Nostell and Dublin Painters. The bell-krater fragment **50** is also connected with the Plainer Group. The draped youth on the pelike **10** is by the same hand as the youths on the reverse of London, B.M. E 429 and perhaps also Geneva 4793, and close to the draped figures on pelikai by the Pasithea Painter. Though no certain example has come to light of the mature "Kerch" style from the third quarter of the fourth century, the excavations have produced two fine representatives of the early phase of this style in the years 380–350, namely the lebes gamikos **16**, which preserves the heads of a man and a woman flanked by Erotes, and the hydria **73** with the delicately drawn head and body of a female figure (queen or goddess).

Iconography

The red-figured pottery from the Cyrene excavations cannot be said to provide a rich source of mythological representations. Only one story can be recognized with any confidence. On the calyx-krater **38**, which may be dated ca. 380–360, a male, probably Herakles, leans against a tree-trunk, asleep; his club is purloined; two satyrs are involved, and one already holds what ought to be the quiver and bow of the hero. This is the latest appearance in Attic red-figure of a scene—the robbery of Herakles—that first enters the vase-painter's repertoire about 500 B.C. A fragment of a column-krater or stamnos of ca. 500–490 (**18**), also shows Herakles, but on this occasion participating in a fight, and his missing opponents may have been Amazons. The quadriga that is partly preserved on the bell-krater fragment **51**, from the first half of the fourth century, brings to mind the apotheosis of Herakles, a popular theme at that time, but Herakles is not preserved, and there are other possible interpretations. Among individual deities Eros makes an appearance on **16**, **47**, **74**, and perhaps **48**; Nike (or at least a winged female) on **15** and **120**; Nike or Eros on **14**. The helmeted figure on **127** may be Athena but could be a hero or mortal warrior. There are rather more Dionysiac scenes among the fragments: Dionysos himself appears on **20**, **23**, and probably **19** (unless the figure is an Anacreontic komast), which are column-kraters or stamnoi of ca. 490–480; and what remains of the pictures on **42**, **49**, **50**, and **75** certainly suggests the world of Dionysos. The creature on the lid **82** looks like a Siren. The female figure on **73** must be a queen or goddess. The head with Oriental cap on **5** may belong to an Amazon rather than a Trojan or Scythian archer.

If we turn to scenes of everyday life, we meet banqueters on **21**, **33**, **95**, **106**, and **110**; revellers perhaps on **24**, **36**, **58** (or Dionysos?), and **114**; komasts or athletes perhaps on **79**, **80**, and **92** (cf. also **19**); and female flute-players probably on **7** and **26**. The arm grasping a javelin on **122** may have belonged to an athlete about to throw. One sherd (**107**), probably from a stemless cup, was decorated with young men on horseback, perhaps hunters, each wearing a chlamys and carrying spears. The picture on **118** may have shown the departure or return of a warrior. The scene on the hydria **66** is set in the women's quarters, and included a woman dressing. Finally, the epinetron **130** was decorated, at least on one side, with a black-figure picture that included a fountain-house.

In a few instances the iconography deserves special consideration. Two fragments of an amphora perhaps of Panathenaic shape (**3**) appear to preserve a cock upon a column beside an altar, and it may not be too fanciful to imagine that the original scene was like that found on amphorai of Panathenaic shape decorated by the Nikoxenos Painter.[12] On **113**, fragments of a closed shape (amphora or pelike?, ca. 500–450), an owl seems to be perched amid olive-sprays. One may well ask who is the seated youth represented on the bell-krater **47** (ca. 420–400) and whether **48** (perhaps the reverse of **47**) once showed Dionysos reclining on an animal-skin surrounded by satyrs, maenads, and Erotes. The hydria **69**, which may also be dated in the last quarter of the fifth century, was decorated with female figures—one holding a *trigonon*—at an altar: are they to be interpreted as Muses, perhaps with Apollo (contest with Marsyas?) or some famous singer such as Thamyras or Musaios?

It is particularly unfortunate that we are unable to identify the scenes on the Meidian skyphos **87**. The remaining figures, which may come from one or both sides of the vase, seem mainly female, and one woman holds a tortoise-shell lyre; part of a thyrsos is also preserved. A thyrsos suggests that some of the female figures may be maenads, and a lyre is also occasionally carried by a maenad (but also by Muses). Another skyphos-sherd, **88**, may belong to the same vase: here the remaining female, who is identified by an inscription, was probably called Kymodoke, the name of a Nereid in Hesiod and on at least two other red-figured vases.

Attic White-ground

Only one Attic white-ground vase is included in this publication,[13] an alabastron (**133**), preserved in two non-joining fragments, one of which shows the head and shoulders of an Amazon, the other, part of a draped youth seen from behind. The vase belongs to the small series of alabastra painted in outline

---

12. See *ARV*^{2}, 220–221, 5–8bis.

13. I omit **132**, an epinetron fragment, on which white slip is employed for a zone next to the outer edge of the vase.

technique against a white slip with an Amazon,[14] who is normally dressed in a black vest or, later, cuirass over the sleeved and trousered garment typical of the Scythian archer, and who may be armed with bow and/or battle-axe. To balance the Amazon, other elements are normally added: a draped youth as on the Cyrene vase, a negro, heron, palm-tree, helmet upon a stool.

These Amazon alabastra, and the closely related group of the Negro alabastra, first came into vogue at the very end of the sixth century apparently in the workshop of the potters Pasiades and Paidikos (a single individual perhaps, as Beazley suggests in ARV^2 102) and continued to be produced until about the middle of the fifth century in the workshop of the potter Syriskos. The Cyrene fragments are clearly early in the series and are related stylistically both to the Group of the Paidikos Alabastra and the Painter of New York 21.131.

Only a few of the Amazon alabastra have a known provenience, but it is interesting that two examples (ARV^2 269, 4 and 5) have been found at Selinus and Locri in Magna Graecia, and now this one (**133**) from Cyrene in Libya,[15] in view of the tradition, preserved by Diodorus Siculus (3.52.1-3.55.11), that "Libya" had once been inhabited by Amazons.

Attic Plastic Vases

Fragments of two or three Attic head-vases (**134–136**) have been discovered in the Wadi Bel Gadir sanctuary. **134** is part of a negro-head vase. The exact shape is not certain but a mug or kantharos seems most probable, perhaps with two janiform heads. The date is perhaps late sixth or first quarter of the fifth century. Plastic vases in the form of negro-heads might be thought an obvious item to export to the Greek settlements in North Africa, but **134** is the only Attic example that I can find with such a provenience.

The other two fragments (**135–136**) formed part of one, or perhaps two, vases having the form of a woman's head. Enough remains of **135** to suggest that it is perhaps another example of Class N, the Cook Class, the most common series of such head-vases made in Athens, a series which begins in the late Archaic Period and continues well into Early Classical. The vase is normally an oinochoe of shape 1, and **135** was probably of this form. The Cook Class was exported to Italy, Sicily, and Spain, but **135** seems to be the first found in North Africa.

Relief Ware

Among the fragments from Cyrene is one (**137**) that was adorned with figures in relief. Only one figure remains, a woman, who wears a heavy himation over a chiton. She is shown in frontal view, and her head was probably turned to the left (her right). Traces are still preserved of white slip and gilding on the himation. The date must be somewhere in the second half of the fourth century, possibly in the third quarter. The Cyrene fragment may come from a hydria rather than the more common squat-lekythos. It seems to be only the third relief-vase from Cyrenaica; the other two are a chous, today in Paris, Louvre N 2881, of the late fourth century, and perhaps a neck-amphora in the Bibliothèque Nationale.[16]

---

14. On these Amazon alabastra, see in particular J. Neils, "The Group of the Negro Alabastra: A Study in Motif Transferal," *AntK* 23 (1980) 13–23, and Bothmer, *Amazons* 152, 157–159.

15. See also *Final Reports* 3, 28, no. 148, and what is said about this fragment in catalogue entry for **133**.

16. E. Zervoudaki, *AM* 83 (1968) 35, no. 72 and pp. 61–62; T. Dohrn, "Schwarzgefirnisste Plakettenvasen," *RM* 92 (1985) 101.

Uncertain Fabric

With one possible exception all the red-figured fragments from Cyrene are Attic. Only **138**, a small piece of a bell-krater, may have been made outside Athens. Very little of the decoration is preserved, just the foreleg of a feline above a zone of arcs, and I could not be sure whether the fabric was Attic or perhaps Elean.[17] It is, however, true that the distinctive band of arcs is much more frequent on the local red-figured kraters found in Olympia and at ancient Elis than on Attic vases made in the fourth century, and this may suggest an Elean origin for **138**. The date is likely to fall somewhere in the first half of the fourth century.

Conclusion

The Attic red-figured pottery from the Sanctuary of Demeter and Persephone at Cyrene is less abundant than the Attic black-figure from the site. This may not be, however, a phenomenon of this particular sanctuary, for the same general pattern is reported by Luciana Pandolfi in her summary account of the Greek pottery discovered in the Agora at Cyrene.[18] Moreover, at Tocra the British excavations yielded very few red-figured sherds in comparison with the mass of black-figured fragments.[19] In the latter instance, however, we should be wary of reading too much into the apparently dramatic decrease in imports, for the pottery came from votive deposits associated with a sanctuary of Demeter, and the principal deposits of the Classical Period may still be unexcavated.

Though the Attic red-figure from the Wadi Bel Gadir Sanctuary ranges over about two hundred years, from ca. 520 to ca. 330, the greatest number of fragments, as Chart 1 shows, belongs to the first half of the fifth century, a minimum of 47 (columns 3 and 4), a maximum of 71 (columns 2 to 5). There seems to have been a decline in imports during the second half of the fifth century, but the number of fragments increases again after 400 B.C. This pattern may be compared with that revealed in Chart 2 which tabulates by shape and date the red-figure from Cyrenaica attributed by Beazley (ARV^2 and *Paralipomena*), supplemented by the unattributed vases published in the British and French *Corpora Vasorum Antiquorum*. Here the picture is somewhat different. There is no sixth century red-figure, and only two examples of the Late Archaic phase. The second and third quarters of the fifth century are represented by six and eight vases respectively. The number more than doubles in the last quarter of the fifth century, and increases dramatically in the fourth.[20] The vases listed in Chart 2 must come mainly from tombs, not from settlement or sanctuary. The absence, or at least infrequency, of red-figure during the later sixth and first half of the fifth centuries is probably explained by a preference for the cheaper, mass-produced black-figure pottery. On the other hand, we might well expect the occasional dedication of a more expensive and unusual red-figure vase in a sanctuary.

Cyrenaica obviously provided an important market for Attic red-figure in the fourth century, especially in the second and third quarters, with pelikai and hydriai of Group G, and the occasional oinochoe of the F.B. Group.[21] One shape, the squat-lekythos, decorated usually with a single figure or a palmette, seems to have been appropriate as a funerary offering in tombs of the late fifth and first half of the fourth centuries, but does not appear among the red-figure pottery from the Sanctuary of Demeter at Cyrene.

---

17. To the references for Elean red-figure given in the catalogue under **138**, add now Ian McPhee and A.D. Trendall," The Painter of Louvre M85," *NumAntCl* 15 (1986) 155–167; and Ian McPhee, "The Painter of the Large Egg-Patterns: An Elean Red-Figure Vase Painter," *NumAntCl* 15 (1986) 169–177.

18. L. Pandolfi, "La Ceramica" in S. Stucchi (ed.), *Cirene 1957–1966. Un decennio di attività della missione archeologica italiana a Cirene* (Tripoli 1964) 149–163.

19. J. Boardman and J. Hayes, *Excavations at Tocra 1963–1965* II (Oxford 1973) 91.

20. The red-figure pottery from a tomb at Cyrene published by Luigi Beschi in *ASAtene* n.s. 31–32, 1969–70 (1972) 156–160 belongs to the end of the fifth century or early years of the fourth, and includes at least five oinochoai, a hydria, a stemless cup, and a lekanis. The illustrated red-figure from the Manchester excavations at Cyrene, again from the cemetery, belongs to the last quarter of the fifth century, and to the first half of the fourth: A. Rowe, *Cyrenaican Expeditions of the University of Manchester 1955, 1956, 1957* (Manchester 1959) frontispiece and p. 26, pls. 1c, 12c, 13b, 32b, 36d, 37a-e.

21. See ARV^2 1462, 6, 7; 1464, 39; 1465, 74, 75; 1466, 88, 91, 100–103; 1467, 109, 110, 116, 121, 123; 1468, 124, 126, 129–131, 133, 134, 136; 1471, 5; 1471, 2, 3; 1484, 17; 1486, 85; 1489, 153, 156.

Chart 1. Attic Red-figure from the Sanctuary of Demeter and Kore at Cyrene

	520–500	c. 500	500–480	480–450	480–425	450–425	425–400	400–320
Plates	1	2						
Cups, st. cups	5	3	3	3	2			
Mugs		3						
Amphorai	1		1	1		1		
Pelikai	1		1	2	1			5
Column-Kraters or Stamnoi			6	5	2			
Column-Kraters			2	4				
"Closed" Vases			2	7	5	2		
Hydriai			1	3		1	7	5
Skyphoi				1	3		5	
Lids					1	1		
Bell-Kraters				2	1	1	3	4
Kraters				2	1	1		4
Lebetes Gamikoi					1			2
Calyx-Kraters								4
	8	8	16	30	17	7	15	24

This chart omits nos. 37, 102, 106, 122, 130–138

Chart 2. Attic Red-Figure from Cyrenaica

	530–500	500–480	480–450	450–425	425–400	400–320
Cups		2				1
Pelikai			2	1	1	32
Column-Kraters			1			
Hydriai			2	2	8	22
Skyphoi				1		
Lekanides						1
Pyxides				1		
Bell-kraters			1	2	1	2
Kraters				1		
Oinochoai					2	5
Squat-Lekythoi					6	3
Loutrophoroi					1	
Askoi						1
	0	2	6	8	19	67

Finally, one would like to know how comparable the red-figure from the Wadi Bel Gadir Sanctuary is to that from other sanctuaries of Demeter and Kore in the Greek world. Unfortunately, there is very little published evidence. However, the Sanctuary of Demeter and Kore on the lower slopes of Acrocorinth has been extensively excavated,[22] and the red-figure, though less common than the Corinthian and Attic black-figure, shows a similar range of shapes to the red-figure pottery from Cyrene. At the latter site we have noted that wine-mixing bowls and drinking vessels predominate; at Acrocorinth the picture is not dissimilar: the most common shapes are kraters, skyphoi, and cups.

---

22. For preliminary reports, see *Hesperia* 34 (1965) 1–24; 37 (1968) 299–330; 38 (1969) 297–310; 41 (1972) 283–331; 43 (1974) 267–307. The volume of the final publication that deals with the Greek pottery is in press. I am most grateful to Dr. Elizabeth G. Pemberton for allowing me to comment upon this material ahead of publication. N. Bookidis and R. Stroud, *American Excavations in Old Corinth. Corinth Notes No. 2: Demeter and Persephone in Ancient Corinth* (Princeton 1987) opp. p. 3.

II

Catalogue

Attic Red-figure

Amphorai

1   Amphora (Type A)   E12/13   E   2
Not illustrated
H. 0.041; W. 0.038; Th. 0.006–0.008

Single fragment from the bottom of the neck. Reserved inside except at the lower break.

At the upper break, the lefthand end of a band of pattern across the neck: parts of two circumscribed palmettes set horizontally to left are preserved, with buds in the spandrels.

The palmette-band was similar to that below the main scene on Euphronios' volute-krater Arezzo 1465, *ARV* ^{2} 15, 6, Arias, Hirmer, Shefton, pl. 113. The Cyrene fragment probably came from an amphora of Type A; the picture on the body was almost certainly framed.

About 510 B.C.

2   Amphora (Type A)   E12   1   1
Pl. 13
H. 0.095; W. 0.075

Single fragment of the handle and the adjacent neck; the sherd has broken off above at the junction with the lip. Black glaze on the inside of the neck, thinning out below.

The side of the handle is decorated with a pattern of black ivy (wavy stem). On the neck, one end of a horizontal floral-band: part of a circumscribed palmette, and, to left, a spiral tendril.

It is unclear whether the pattern on the neck consisted of circumscribed palmettes alone or of such palmettes alternating with lotus: the latter is more likely. The picture on the body of the amphora was not framed. The great period of the amphora of type A in red-figure is the last thirty years of the 6th century. At this time the pictures are always framed. Unframed scenes on type A amphorae begin about 500 B.C., for example Berlin 2160, *ARV* ^{2} 196, 1, Berlin Painter, Simon and Hirmer, pls. 136–137, but a red-figure palmette-band is not found on the neck, I think, until the beginning of the Early Classical Period, e.g. Los Angeles 50.8.21, *ARV* ^{2} 500, 28, Deepden Painter, *CVA* 1 [18], pl. 23 [863].

Second quarter of the 5th century B.C.

3   Amphora (Panathenaic Shape?)   F12/G12   1   2
Pl. 13
A: Max. dim. 0.062; Th. 0.004–0.006
B: Max. dim. 0.075

Two fragments (**B** mended from two sherds) of the body of an amphora, probably of Panathenaic shape. Reserved on the inside. The glaze on the outside is a lustrous brownish-black.

Fragment **A** gives the top of the vertical band of net-pattern forming the lefthand frame of the picture; to right, the tail of a cock in profile to right. Fragment **B** gives the bottom of the vertical band of net-pattern and, to the right, the left side of an altar (rather than a stele). Below, two horizontal lines in added red.

Fragment **A** should be positioned further above **B** than in the photograph. Given the thinness of the wall and the curve of **A**, the fragments probably came from an amphora of Panathenaic shape. The cock presumably stood upon a column, the bottom of which was hidden by the altar. Red-figure amphorae of Panathenaic shape showing cocks are not common: see the examples decorated by the Nikoxenos Painter, *ARV* ^{2} 220–221, 5-8bis; see also the remarks of K. Schauenburg, JdI 94 (1979) 69 and n. 93.

About 500–480 B.C.

4   Neck-amphora   D16/17   2   3
Pl. 13
H. 0.034; W. 0.055; Th. 0.008

Single fragment from the lower neck. The upper half of the neck inside is glazed black, the lower covered with a wash of glaze, fired red.

What remains are the tips of four leaves from the righthand side of a palmette (perhaps the lower of two), and part of the spiralling tendril at one side.

The floral is just like that which appears on the necks of neck-amphorae belonging to the Polygnotan Group, e.g. Oxford (Miss.), University of Mississippi 1977.3.97, *ARV* ^{2} 1058, 116, Shapiro, *Southern* 83; or Ferrara T. 422, *ARV* ^{2} 1039, 11, *AntK* 23 (1980) pl. 27, 1, Peleus Painter. The same type is also found on neck-amphorae by the Kleophon Painter, who continues the style of the Polygnotans: see Syracuse 47834, *ARV* ^{2} 1146, 45, *CVA* 1 [17], pl. 9 [823], 1.

About 440–420 B.C.

Pelikai

5   Pelike   C15/16   1   4
Pl. 14
H. 0.056; W. 0.053; Th. 0.006 (bottom)–0.009 (top)

Single fragment from the shoulder and lower neck. The fired clay is fine but quite soft, and paler than is usual for Attic: Munsell 7.5YR 7/4-6. Where the glaze has flaked on the outside, the surface shows a pale red miltos. The inside is reserved.

Head, in profile to left, of a figure wearing a tall Scythian cap. The picture was framed: above, key meander running to right; at the right only a tiny bit of the vertical frame (uncertain pattern—net?) is preserved. Relief contour for the cap.

Pioneer Group. The vertical frame may have consisted of net-pattern or of key meander. The horizontal band of key meander finds a parallel on the Boston pelike of the Pioneer Group published by M. Robertson, *Burlington Magazine* 119 (1977) 78–86, though there the key runs in the opposite direction. The Cyrene pelike might have had a palmette tendril on the neck like the Boston vase. The head with cap is that of the righthand figure in the picture, an Amazon perhaps or an archer in Scythian costume. The form of the cap recalls that worn by the Amazon Toxis on Arezzo 1465, Arias, Hirmer, Shefton, pl. 114, *ARV* ^{2} 15, 6, Euphronios. For the cap, see M.F. Vos, *Scythian Archers in Archaic Vase-painting* (Groningen 1963) 40–48. On early red-figured pelikai, see D. von Bothmer, *JHS* 71 (1951) 40–47; Becker, 1–4; and Robertson, op. cit. 81–82.

About 520–510 B.C.

6   Pelike   E11/12   Balk   2/3
Pl. 14
Max. dim. 0.045; Th. 0.003 (bottom)–0.007 (top)

Single fragment from the junction of shoulder and neck, thickening towards the upper break. Reserved on the inside.

Along the upper break, a band of pattern: a tendril of black palmettes, rightwards, with small black buds in the spandrels. Below, a reserved area with undulating contour and "hatching"—perhaps the back of an animal (boar?—the short strokes along the contour would represent the bristles along the animal's back).

The use of a black palmette tendril on the necks of pelikai continues into the Early Classical period. It is a favorite motif of the Syleus Painter, e.g. Louvre G228, *CVA* 6 [9], pl. 45 [424], 2–3, *ARV* ^{2} 250, 14; compare also a pelike by the Argos Painter, Leningrad 614, Peredolskaya, pl. 41, *ARV* ^{2} 288, 11. These two vases (Becker, 50, no. 142 and 58, no. 167) belong to what Becker terms the "Workshop of the Syleus Potter," on which see also M. Robertson, *Greek Vases in the J. Paul Getty Museum* 3 (Malibu 1986) 76–78. But the drawing of the palmettes on the Cyrene fragment seems closer, if anything, to that of the black floral on the Berlin Painter's early pelikai in Vienna and Florence, *ARV* ^{2} 204, 109–110, Becker, 304, nos. 9–10.

First quarter of the 5th century B.C.

7   Pelike   F11   1   3
Pl. 14
Max. dim. 0.060; Th. 0.006

Single fragment from the junction of shoulder and neck. The inside is reserved.

Head, to right, of a female figure, her hair covered by a sakkos. She was no doubt standing, and probably playing the flute, for a little of what appears to be the mouthpiece is preserved. The woman was the lefthand figure in the picture which was framed: the top lefthand corner of the frame remains, including part of the net-pattern (two knots) that was used for the vertical element. Near the righthand break is the tip of a stick(?): if so, the picture will have shown a komos with fluteplayer. Diluted glaze for the hair of the woman.

About 480–460 B.C.

8   Pelike   F13/G13   1   2
Pl. 14
Max. dim. 0.082; Th. 0.005–0.006

Two joining(?) fragments from the wall of a pelike. The inside is reserved.

The fragment preserves the upper body of a male figure draped in a himation, and, at the right, a section of net-pattern which forms the vertical frame of the picture. These fragments and the handle **9** may belong to the same vase. See also **117**.

About 480–460 B.C.

9   Handle (of a pelike?)   F13/G13   1   2
Pl. 14
H. 0.065; W. 0.023; Th. 0.010

Single fragment of a handle, segmental in section, perhaps from a pelike.

The handle is completely glazed except for a palmette at the base. Possibly there were originally two palmettes, addorsed. Relief contour for the leaves. I do not know whether this may come from the same vase as **8**.

Second or third quarter of the 5th century B.C.

10   Pelike   E11   3   3
Pl. 15
H. 0.060; W. 0.052; Th. 0.005–0.006

Single fragment from the junction of the shoulder and neck. The upper half of the inside is glazed, the lower reserved.

The fragment preserves the head and shoulders of a youth who stands in profile to right. He wears a himation.

Above, a part of a horizontal band of egg-pattern.

The Cyrene fragment is by the same hand as a pelike in the British Museum, E 429, which has Dionysos riding a leopard in the presence of a maenad on the main side, and two draped youths on the other. Compare also an unattributed pelike in Geneva, 4793, *CVA* 1 [1], pl. 20 [20], 5–6. All these are close to the reverses of pelikai by the Pasithea Painter, for example Louvre MN 734, *CVA* 8 [12], pl. 48 [528], 3–5, *ARV* ^{2} 1472, 2. Perhaps from the same vase as the next (**11**).

About 390–370 B.C.

11   Pelike   E11   3   3
Pl. 15
Max. dim. 0.047; Th. 0.003–0.004

Single fragment of the lower wall. Reserved on the inside.

The fragment preserves a section of the horizontal band of egg-pattern below the picture.

Perhaps from the same vase as the preceding (**10**).

First half of the 4th century B.C.

12   Pelike   E11   3   3
Pl. 15
Max. dim. 0.072; Th. 0.005–0.009

Single fragment from the junction of shoulder and neck. On the inside the upper half is glazed, the lower, reserved. The surface is incrusted.

What remains is the head, in profile to left, of a woman, the first figure on the right of the picture. Traces of added white for her flesh. Above, the righthand end of a horizontal band of egg-pattern.

First half of the 4th century B.C., probably second quarter.

13   Pelike   F12 — 2
Pl. 15
H. 0.070; W. 0.075; Th. 0.006 (top)

Single fragment, mended from two, of the shoulder and neck. The neck is glazed on the inside, the shoulder is reserved.

Head, in profile to left, of a standing(?) youth probably wearing a himation. A white dot appears behind the head. Above, the left half of a horizontal band of egg-pattern.

The youth may have been one (the middle?) of the draped youths on a reverse. The Cyrene fragment comes from a pelike contemporary with those decorated by the Herakles Painter and the Pasithea Painter, *ARV* ^{2} 1472.

About 390–360 B.C.

14   Pelike?   E11   3   3
Pl. 15
Max. dim. 0.050; Th. 0.004–0.007

Single fragment from the shoulder of a closed vase, probably a pelike. Ridged on the inside and glazed.

The sherd preserves one wing, outspread, of Eros or Nike and, to the right, the top of a head. The wing was originally gilded or painted in added color. Diluted glaze for the hair of the head.

Perhaps from a Dionysiac scene like that on the pelike Leningrad B 2232, Schefold, *UKV* pl. 8, right.

About 370–340 B.C.

Lebetes Gamikoi

15   Lebes gamikos   E11   1   2
Pl. 16
Max. dim. 0.090; Th. (handle) 0.008

Single fragment preserving part of the bowl and one handle. Reserved on the inside.

Below the handle, the head, and part of the wings, of a Nike, no doubt flying to left. White for the cord binding her hair.

The lebes gamikos is not decorated by red-figure artists until the Early Classical period. Among the early examples in red-figure are those by the Mykonos Painter, *ARV* ^{2} 514, 1–2 and 516, middle; and those by the Sabouroff Painter, *ARV*^{2} 841, 70–72. The Cyrene fragment is also quite early. The Nike seems to have been flying with wings behind her, not running with a wing on either side as on Geneva H 239, *CVA* 1 [1], pl. 17 [17], 6, *ARV* ^{2} 548, 44, Painter of London E 489.

About 450 B.C.

16   Lebes gamikos   D13 (Area 2) — 1-2
Pl. 16
Max. dim. 0.080; Th. 0.004

Single fragment of the bowl. Reserved on the inside.

The fragment preserves parts of four figures from the center of the picture: the head, in profile to right, of a woman; the head, in three-quarter view to left, of a male, his hair adorned with ivy-leaves; parts of two Erotes, wings outspread, as flankers: the righthand Eros was probably seated to right, looking back. At the upper break is a section of the horizontal band of egg-pattern on the shoulder of the vase. White for the flesh of the Erotes and that of the woman. Added clay, probably gilded originally, for the preserved wings of the Erotes. Diluted glaze for the hair of all figures.

The male figure wearing an ivy-wreath may be Dionysos. On lebetes gamikoi of the 4th century the bride is usually flanked by Erotes. Good examples are provided by the vases of the Painter of Athens 1370, *ARV* ^{2} 1506, 1–6. The Cyrene fragment is finer than these and the Erotes flank two figures, female and male, perhaps in this instance Ariadne and Dionysos, rather than mortal bride and groom.

About 380–350 B.C.

17   Lebes gamikos   F14/G14   1   2
Pl. 16
Max. dim. 0.065; Th. 0.003

Single fragment of wall, slightly convex. Reserved on the inside.

Parts of the lower wing (above) and the flowing garment (below) of a Nike flying to left. Some preliminary sketch.

Compare the Nike flying to left on Toronto 916.3.11 (R 432), D.M. Robinson, C.G. Harcum, J.H. Iliffe, *A Catalogue of the Greek Vases in the Royal Ontario Museum of Archaeology* (Toronto 1930) pl. 81, or the similar figures on Agora P 28056, *Hesperia* 43 (1974) pl. 35, 24 and a lebes in the Kerameikos, *AM* 81 (1966) pl. 50.

First half of the 4th century B.C.

Column-kraters or Stamnoi

18   Column-krater or stamnos   C14 1 3
Pl. 17
H. 0.086; W. 0.085; Th. 0.006

Single fragment, mended from two sherds, from the shoulder and upper body. Streaks of glaze on the inside.

Head and upper body of Herakles. The hero strides to the right, his left arm originally thrust forward, his right drawn back and bent upwards. He wears a sleeveless chiton, and a lion-skin knotted on his chest. A baldric passes over his right shoulder. Relief contour throughout. White for the teeth of the lion.

Herakles is no doubt shown in battle, a popular subject in the later 6th century and the beginning of the 5th. If his opponents were Amazons, the scene might have been like that on Rome, Conservatori 185, a column-krater by the Harrow Painter, *CVA* Musei Capitolini 2 [39], pl. 18 [1750], *ARV*^{2} 274, 41. The object in front of Herakles' face may be the point of a spear, despite the angle (the spike of an axe or the end of a long helmet-crest seem less likely). For the subject of Herakles and Amazons in early red-figure, see Bothmer, *Amazons*, 131–143.

About 500–490 B.C.

19   Column-krater or stamnos   F11 2 1-2
Pl. 17
H. 0.045; W. 0.073; Th. 0.006

Single fragment from the upper wall and shoulder. Dull black glaze on the inside.

The fragment preserves the head, in profile to right, the torso, in three-quarter view, the left shoulder, and the right arm of a bearded male. He carries a black kantharos in his right hand. Part of the horizontal stem and one leaf of a grape-vine are visible in the background to left of the figure's head. The man's hair seems to have been bound up with a headcloth. He wears a short-sleeved chiton. Relief contour throughout. White for the single grape-leaf. Traces of preliminary sketch.

Illustrated in *Cyrenaica in Antiquity* 210, fig. 2. A bearded man wearing some form of head-covering might be an Anacreontic komast. Such figures have been discussed most recently by J. Boardman, *Greek Vases in the J. Paul Getty Museum* 3 (Malibu 1986) 47–70. I do not, however, know of any instance in which such a komast holds a kantharos, which is the drinking vessel *par excellence* of Dionysos; nor do I know of an Anacreontic scene in which a grape-vine appears, unless it be the reverse of Florence 3987, *CVA* 2 [13], pl. 33 [617], 2, where the figure may in any case be Dionysos (see Boardman, op. cit. 48). Grape-vine (which the figure may be holding) and kantharos suggest Dionysos. It may be objected that the figure is wearing some form of headcloth: it is true that this is rare for Dionysos, but see the Nikosthenes Painter's kantharos in Boston, *CB* III, pl. 68, *ARV*^{2} 126, 27, and Boardman's comment, op. cit. 53. For Dionysos holding vine-branch and kantharos, see among many examples Leningrad B 3199, Peredolskaya, pl. 38, 1, *ARV*^{2} 290, 8; for the kantharos, Gericke, *Gefässdarstellungen* 22. Elrashedy (*Cyrenaica in Antiquity* 211) claims that the Cyrene fragment is "by the hand of one of the mannerists and he is likely to be the Pan Painter." I am not persuaded by this.

About 490–480 B.C.

20   Column-krater or stamnos   F11 2 3
Pl. 17
Max. dim. 0.10; Th. 0.007 (lower break)

Single fragment of the shoulder, broken above at the junction with the neck of the vase. Dull black glaze on the inside.

At the right, the head, to left, of Dionysos. The god was bearded and probably held a grape-vine, part of which, with reserved stem and white leaves, may be seen in the background. Facing the god was a female figure—a maenad or Ariadne—who is completely lost except for part of the kerchief around her hair, and some loose locks (lampadion style: cf. R. Higgins, *Tanagra and the Figurines* [London 1986] 123). She was looking down. Behind the head of Dionysos, close to the break, are three fingers of a third figure. White for the leaves of the vine (including the leaf behind the maenad's head), and for the wreaths worn by both figures. Relief contour for the brow-nose line of the god and for the stem of the vine. The kerchief is ornamented with small crosses in diluted glaze.

Illustrated in *AJA* 80 (1976) 170 and pl. 25, fig. 13, and in *Cyrenaica in Antiquity* 207, fig. 3. For the subject, one may perhaps compare the obverse of the pointed amphora by the Kleophrades Painter in Munich, *ARV*^{2} 182, 6, *CVA* 4 [12], pl. 201 [579]. Elrashedy (*Cyrenaica in Antiquity* 207–208) remarks that the Cyrene fragment is "very close to the style of Myson," comparing the forms of the eye and ear and the wavy contour of the hair. The style is related, it seems to me, both to Myson and the early work of the Pan Painter. For Myson, compare the head of Dionysos on New York 07.286.73, G.M.A. Richter and L.F. Hall, *Red-figured Athenian Vases in the Metropolitan Museum of Art* (New Haven 1936) pl. 23, 20, *ARV*^{2} 240, 45, or that of Apollo on Florence 3982, A.-B. Follmann, *Der Pan-Maler* (Bonn 1968) pl. 15, 4, *ARV*^{2} 238, 2; compare also Ariadne and Dionysos on Naples 2410, L. Stella, *Mitologia Greca* (Turin 1956) 377, *ARV*^{2} 239, 18. For the Pan Painter, compare the head of Poseidon on Bari 4402, Follman, op. cit. pl. 12, 1, *ARV*^{2} 550, 4, or that of Dionysos on Boston 95.58, J.D. Beazley, *Der Pan-Maler* (Berlin 1931) pl. 13, 3, *ARV*^{2} 552, 21. On the whole, the fragment does seem closest to Myson.

About 490–480 B.C.

21 Column-krater or stamnos E10 bldg. Balk 3 (**A**)
F11 1 1 (**B**)
Pl. 18
A: Max. dim. 0.086; Th. 0.007–0.008
B: Max. dim. 0.078

Two non-joining fragments: **A** comes from the upper wall; **B** is from the upper wall and shoulder. **A** is glazed on the inside, **B** is reserved.

Fragment **A** gives the face, in profile to right, the left shoulder and arm of a bearded man who reclines against a striped cushion. He wears a himation. Just to the right of the man's nose, at the break, is a horizontal relief-line which may form part of the contour of whatever (cup?) the man was holding in his upraised left hand. Fragment **B** preserves the head, to right, of a youth. Above, a section of the tongue-pattern on the shoulder. Relief contour for the face, shoulder and arm of the man. Diluted glaze for the hair-fringe of each figure as well as the iris and pupil of the eyes.

Fragment **A** must come from the obverse of the vase which showed a symposion. **B** might come from the same side, but might just as well be from the reverse of the vase. The style recalls the Eucharides Painter (*ARV*^{2} 226–232): compare the head on **B** with the head of the youth on the Bastis oinochoe, *Antiquities from the Collection of Christos G. Bastis* (New York 1987) 283. See also 22.

About 490–480 B.C.

22 Column-krater or stamnos F11 1 2
Pl. 18
Max. dim. 0.050; Th. 0.005–0.006

Single fragment from the upper wall curving over into the shoulder. Reserved on the inside. The glaze on the outside has fired a dull grayish-black.

Head, in profile to left, and right shoulder of a bearded man. Three relief-lines across the shoulder of the man suggest a garment. Some preliminary sketch. Relief contour for the man's nose. Diluted glaze for the fringe of his hair, for his moustache and beard. The man seems to have worn a wreath in added red. His eye was of the Archaic frontal type.

This may come from the same vase as the preceding fragments (**21**); the treatment of the hair and of the ear is very similar.

About 500–480 B.C.

23 Column-krater or stamnos E10 bldg. Balk 2-3 (**A**)
E10 bldg. 1 2 (**B**)
Pl. 18
Max. dim. 0.105; Th. 0.004–0.005

Two joining fragments from the upper wall and shoulder. Streaky glaze on the lower half of the inside. On the outside the glaze has fired red in places.

The lower part of the face (bearded), the throat, right arm (except the hand) and right side of Dionysos. The god looks to the left but may have been moving to the right. He wears a long-sleeved chiton, and he originally held the vine which is visible in the field. Relief contour for the lips, right shoulder and arm of Dionysos. Diluted glaze for the wing of his nose.

The fragment is illustrated in *Cyrenaica in Antiquity* 210, fig. 3: Elrashedy compares the composition on the obverse of the Palermo bell-krater by the Pan Painter, *ARV*^{2} 550, 2, Arias, Hirmer, Shefton, pl. 163, and the style is not far removed either.

About 480 B.C.

24 Column-krater or stamnos E11 1 2
Pl. 19
Max. dim. 0.046; Th. 0.005

Single fragment of the upper wall and shoulder. Reserved on the inside.

Head and left shoulder of a figure standing to left. The person seems to wear a chiton (the two parallel relief-lines which intersect the line of the throat should represent its upper border), as well as a himation which covers the left shoulder. The figure's hair was bound up at the back (*krobylos*). To the right is the right hand of a second figure grasping a stick. Relief contour for the throat of the first figure and for the wrist of the second.

About 480–470 B.C.

25 Column-krater or stamnos F11 2 3B
Pl. 19
Max. dim. 0.050; Th. 0.004

Single fragment of the wall. Dull black glaze on the inside.

Torso and left arm of a male figure standing in three-quarter view to the left, a himation over his left shoulder and arm, leaving his torso bare.

For the arrangement of the himation over the left arm, compare the man on the reverse of a pelike in Oxford, 282, *CVA* 1 [3], pl. 19 [111], 4, *ARV*^{2} 555, 87, Pan Painter.

About 480–470 B.C.

26 Column-krater or stamnos F11 1 3
Pl. 19
H. 0.074; W. 0.068; Th. 0.005

Single fragment of the wall curving in at the top. The upper half of the inside is reserved, the lower half has a wash of black glaze.

What remains is the body, from neck to waist, of a woman standing in profile to the right. She is dressed in a chiton and himation, and plays a flute (a bit of the flute remains near the upper righthand break). Considerable preliminary sketch. Diluted glaze for the three beads of her necklace.

About 480–460 B.C.

27 Column-krater or stamnos C10/11 A, Sect. B 7
Pl. 19
H. 0.085; W. 0.064; Th. 0.006

Two joining fragments of the wall. Black glaze on the inside.

The fragment preserves part of a standing figure draped in a himation—perhaps one of the draped figures from a reverse. Three fragments of a column-krater from the same deposit may belong to this vase: the first two fragments come from the rim and are black on top, with dot-ivy on the outer edge; the third fragment comes from the neck and is decorated with linked buds.

About 480–460 B.C.

28 Column-krater or stamnos E10/11 (Area 1) 1 3
Pl. 19
Max. dim. 0.070; Th. 0.005–0.006

Single fragment from the junction of the body and shoulder. The lower half of the inside is glazed, but thinly.

The fragment preserves the left shoulder and arm of a male figure with body in frontal or three-quarter view. He is draped in a himation, and holds a stick in his left hand and a black phiale in his right.

For the subject, see the komast (who holds a black skyphos) on the reverse of Adlophseck 74, *CVA* 1 [11], pl. 44 [522], 6, *ARV*² 564, 16, Pig Painter. Phialai on vases are considered by Gericke, *Gefässdarstellungen* 27–31.

Second quarter of the 5th century B.C.

29   Column-krater or stamnos   F14/G14   1   1
Pl. 20
Max. dim. 0.045; Th. 0.005–0.006

Single fragment of the wall. Dull black glaze on the inside.

The fragment preserves part of the body of a female figure who wears a peplos, girt at the waist and open down the side, with a black border. At the right and overlapping the woman is the back-rest of a chair(?). Relief contour for the peplos.

About 460–440 B.C.

30   Column-krater or stamnos
                                      E10/11 (Area 1)   1   3
Pl. 20
Max. dim. 0.058; Th. 0.008–0.009

Wall fragment. Dull black glaze on the inside. Much of the glaze on the outside has worn off.

Upper half of the leg of a table(?). Doubtful if this fragment could come from the same vase as **21**.

Second or third quarter of the 5th century B.C.

Column-kraters

31   Column-krater   E10/11 (Area 1)   1   3
Pl. 20
Max. dim. 0.094; Th. 0.005–0.006

Single fragment of wall. Dull black glaze on the inside. On the outside the glaze has fired reddish-brown, and the surface has been rubbed away in places.

The fragment preserves a left hand holding a kantharos. Relief contour for the hand and the vase. The picture was not framed, and the figure was the first on the right.

First half of the 5th century B.C., probably first quarter.

32   Column-krater   E10 bldg.   Balk   1-2
Pl. 20
Max. dim. 0.078

Single fragment from the shoulder, broken at the junction with the neck: at the lefthand break there is the beginning of a handle. The underside is reserved except at the base of the neck and at the lower break which are glazed.

The fragment preserves part of the head, in profile to left, of a male figure. He wears a wreath in added red. At the left, a vine(?) with leaves in red. On the shoulder, a band of tongue-pattern.

About 490–470 B.C.

33   Column-krater   E10/11 (Area 1)   1   3
Pl. 20
Max. dim. 0.098; Th. 0.006–0.009

Single fragment, mended from three, of the wall. Dull black glaze on the inside.

The picture on the vase was framed: at the left, a section of the vertical frame of ivy-pattern. To the right, the legs, covered by a himation, of a symposiast, and, below, part of the mattress covering the couch.

What remains is close in style to symposia-scenes by the Flying-Angel Painter (*ARV*² 279–282): compare, for example, the obverse of Chiusi 1849, *CVA* 2 [60], pl. 2 [2644], *ARV*² 281, 33. It has, however, been pointed out to me that the ivy-frame on **33** is drawn with more care than is usual for the Flying-Angel Painter and that the fragment is perhaps rather by the Harrow Painter (*ARV*² 272–277): compare the symposion on Florence 3999, *CVA* 2 [13], pl. 42 [626], 3, *ARV*² 275, 47.

About 480–470 B.C.

34   Column-krater?   E10/11 (Area 1)   1   3
Pl. 21
Max. dim. 0.11; Th. 0.008–0.011

Single fragment, mended from two, of the wall of a column-krater(?). Streaky black glaze on the inside.

What remains is the foot of one figure, and the feet and hem of the himation of a second figure. Both figures were standing in profile to right, and the righthand figure was no doubt male.

This fragment may come from the same vase as the preceding (**33**), but from the reverse: compare the reverse of Florence 3999, *CVA* 2 [13],
pl. 42 [626], 2, *ARV*² 275, 47.

About 480–470 B.C.

35   Column-krater   E10/11 (Area 1)   1   3
Pl. 21
Max. dim. 0.097; Th. 0.008

Single fragment of the wall. Dull black glaze on the inside.

At the lefthand break is a section of the leg of a table; then, the leg of a couch; at the right, a part of the vertical frame of ivy-pattern. Relief contour for the table- and couch-legs. The picture must have represented a symposion: this fragment may come from the same vase as **33** above.

About 480–450 B.C.

36   Column-krater   D10/11   C   6
Pl. 21
Max. dim. 0.054; Th. 0.005

Single fragment of the wall. Wash of dull black glaze on the inside; outside, the surface has been burnt a grayish black, and the reserved area is discolored.

The fragment preserves the left side, and the left arm as far as the wrist, of a naked male figure—a komast perhaps or an athlete. His torso was shown in three-quarter view to the left; his left arm is bent down. At the right, part of the vertical frame of ivy that bordered the picture.

Early Mannerist. Compare the righthand komast on the reverse of a column-krater by the Leningrad Painter in Detroit, Moon and Berge, *Midwestern* 168, no. 96, *ARV*² 569, 43.

About 480–460 B.C.

Calyx-kraters

37   Calyx-krater   C13/D13 — 2
Pl. 22
Max. dim. 0.038; Th. 0.010

Single fragment, broken on all sides, of the lip. Black glaze on the inside.

On the lip, part of a palmette tendril. Relief contour throughout. Below, the reserved offset between the lip and the body of the vase.

Late 6th or first half of the 5th century B.C.

38   Calyx-krater   E12/13 E 2 (**A**)
                       E11 1 2 (**B**)
Pl. 22
A: H. 0.074; W. 0.052; Th. 0.006
B: H. 0.070; W. 0.036

Two non-joining fragments of the wall. Dull black glaze on the inside. On the outside the glaze has misfired a brownish-black.

Fragment **A** gives part of the chest, stomach, and left arm holding bow and quiver, of a male figure standing or moving in profile to right; in front of this figure, the torso (in three-quarter view), the right thigh and calf (in profile), part of the left thigh (seen frontally), and the tail of a satyr who moves to right. Fragment **B** preserves the bearded head, wreathed and in three-quarter view, the left side, and the left arm of Herakles, who seems to be shown asleep, to judge especially from his eye. He cradles his club in his left arm, is seated upon a garment, and leans against some object (tree?—a small portion remains above the hero's left shoulder). A second figure, of whom the hands alone are preserved, purloins Herakles' club. Relief contour generally. Some preliminary sketch.

Published in *AJA* 80 (1976) pl. 27, fig. 26 (the findspot given on p. 173 for **A** is incorrect); in *AntK* 22 (1979) pl. 15, figs. 4, 5; and in *Expedition* 34 (1992) 33, fig. 15. The scene can only be the robbery of Herakles: one satyr removes his club, a second has his bow and quiver, a third capers gleefully. See most recently *AntK* 22 (1979) 33–42. The theme begins at the end of the 6th century in Athenian art; the Cyrene fragments represent the last example of the subject in Attic red-figure.

About 380–360 B.C.

39   Calyx-krater   E12/13 E 2
Pl. 22
H. 0.043; W. 0.048; Th. 0.005 (top)

Single fragment from the junction of the wall and the cul below. Dull black glaze on the inside.

Left foot, in frontal view, and part of the garment of a female figure moving to the left. I cannot identify what little remains of the pattern on the cul. See the next, **40**.

First half of the 4th century B.C.

40   Calyx-krater   E12/13 E 2
Not illustrated
H. 0.028; W. 0.046

Single fragment of the cul. Dull black glaze on the inside.

A section of the pattern-band remains: laurel or myrtle, to right, with berries. This might belong to the same vase as **39**.

First half of the 4th century B.C.

41   Calyx-krater
             C17 2 2 (cubic meter test, Terrace 5)
Fig. 2
Max. dim. 0.055

Single fragment of the lip. Black glaze on the inside and the outside.

On the upper edge of the lip, an egg-pattern (solid black heart, relief-line for the outer contour). The lip was of the type that occurs on calyx-kraters by the Painter of the London Griffin-calyx, for example Paris, Petit Palais 328, *ARV* ^{2} 1455, 4, *CVA* 1 [15], pl. 24 [664], 5, 7–9.

About 350–320 B.C.

Bell-kraters

42   Bell-krater   F12 — 2
Pl. 23
Max. dim. 0.087; Th. 0.005

Single fragment, mended from two, of the wall. Brownish-black glaze on the inside; the glaze on the outside has fired a reddish-black.

The fragment preserves the head of a thyrsos and, to the left and right, sections of drapery.

For the type of thyrsos-head, which is not uncommon in red-figure of the Early Classical Period, see Louvre G188, *CVA* 2 [2], pl. 21 [91], 3–4, *ARV* ^{2} 508, 1.

Second quarter of the 5th century B.C.

43   Bell-krater   C13 1 4A
Not illustrated
H. of lip 0.035; W. 0.12; Th. of rim 0.030; Diam. est. of rim 0.30–0.32

Single fragment of the lip, with the beginning of the wall.

Dull black glaze on the inside and the outside of the lip. On top of the lip, a laurel wreath, to right, the leaves contoured in relief. Below the lip, a reserved groove; then, part of an egg(?)-pattern.

Second quarter of the 5th century B.C.

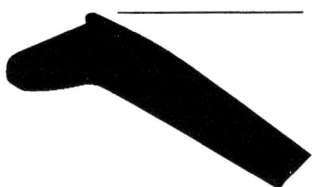

Figure 2. Profile of **41**.

44   Bell-krater (small)   E10 bldg.   Balk   3
Pl. 23
W. 0.052; Th. at rim 0.012

Single fragment of the lip and upper wall. Black glaze on the inside except for reserved bands at the top and bottom of the lip.

On the outside of the lip, a laurel wreath, to left, bordered above and below by a reserved band; at the top of the wall, a zone of vertical strokes with dots below. For the shape of the lip and the zone of strokes, compare the bell-krater, Ferrara 20299, Alfieri, *Spina* 45, fig. 100.

About 460–440 B.C.

45   Bell-krater or stamnos   E11   1   2
Pl. 23
H. 0.052; W. 0.056; Th. 0.008

Single fragment of the lower wall. Black glaze on the inside.

Handle-floral: the left side of a circumscribed palmette with spiral tendril on the left; below, a section of the pattern-band: stopped meanders running to left.

Polygnotan Group? For the lyroid palmette, see B. Philippaki, *The Attic Stamnos* (Oxford 1967) pl. 57, 1–2 and the remarks on p. 124. When I looked at this fragment in Cyrene, I thought that it came from a bell-krater, but perhaps the shape was really a stamnos.

Third quarter of the 5th century B.C.

46   Bell-krater   E11   1   2
Pl. 23
H. 0.029; W. 0.040; Th. at lower break 0.005

Single fragment of the lip and the upper wall; reserved groove at base of lip. The inside is glazed.

The lip was decorated on the outside with an egg-pattern. All that remains of the picture below is the head, to left, of a youth.

Last quarter of the 5th century B.C.?

47   Bell-krater   D12/E12   D   2 (**A**)
                        E12   1   5 (**B–E**)
Pl. 24
A: Max. dim. 0.067; Th. 0.006–0.007
B: Max. dim. 0.057; Th. 0.007–0.008
C: Max. dim. 0.056
D: Max. dim. 0.037
E: Max. dim. 0.065

Five fragments from the body of a bell-krater. The glaze on the inside of all the fragments has fired red.

A: a youth (chin to thighs, left hand) is seated in three-quarter view to the left. He seems to have been looking up slightly and his right arm was raised. He wears a sleeveless, decorated chiton; a himation passes over his upper left arm and hangs down his left side; his hair was bound with a broad fillet one end of which is preserved. Relief contour along the right side of the youth.

B: the legs of a female(?) figure seated to left and wearing a garment with decorated hem.

C: one leg (left?) of a standing female(?) figure wearing a garment with ornamented border (including a band of horse-heads as on the tunic of the seated youth on fragment **A**). Relief contour along the outer edge of the leg.

D: part of the torso and the upper left arm of a female(?) figure wearing a garment which was girdled at the waist and had a decorated yoke.

E: a small Eros (lower half of the head, torso, arms, thighs) stands or hovers to left, his arms outstretched. Relief contour generally.

Kekrops Painter. The patterns used here on the garments will also be found on vases close to the Kadmos Painter and especially by his pupils such as the Suessula Painter and the Kekrops Painter: see J.D. Beazley, *JHS* 59 (1939) 19, no. 51. Compare a pelike in San Francisco, Palace of the Legion of Honor 1811, *ARV*² 1187, 1, *CVA* San Francisco Collections 1 [10], pls. 21–22 [480–481], Manner of the Kadmos Painter. Compare also the fragmentary pelike(?) in Heidelberg, 221, W. Kraiker, *Die rotfigurigen attischen Vasen* (Berlin 1931) pl. 45; and the hydria fragments in Athens, Agora Museum, Pnyx 45, L. Talcott and B. Philippaki, *Hesperia*, Supplement X (1956) pl. 9, 118. The style, especially the drawing of the horse-heads, the hand of the youth and the peculiar double fold-lines on the garment of the seated figure, indicates that the Cyrene fragments are by the Kekrops Painter: cf. Adolphseck 78, *CVA Schlosss Fasanerie* 1 [11], pls. 49–50 [527–528], *ARV*² 1346, 2. See the next entry (**48**).

About 420–400 B.C.

48   Bell-krater   D11/12   1   2
Pl. 25
Diam. est. of rim 0.40
A: Max. dim. 0.066
B: Max. dim. 0.068
C: H. 0.13; W. 0.11; Th. 0.007
D: Max. dim. 0.045
E: Max. dim. 0.051
F: Max. dim. 0.055
G: H. 0.095; W. 0.085

Seven fragments of a bell-krater. **A**, **B**: two rim fragments; **C**: single fragment, mended from seven, of the wall with the base of a handle; **D-F**: single fragments of the wall; **G**: single fragment, mended from four, of the lower wall. Reddish black glaze on the inside.

A, **B**: sections of the laurel and berry, to left, on the lip.

C: lower body and legs of a woman standing to left, in a peplos with belted overfall which has an embattled border. The woman was the righthand figure in the picture. It might seem at first sight that there was something beneath the woman but compare the treatment of this area of the maenad on Adolphseck 78, *CVA Schloss Fasanerie* 1 [11], pl. 52 [530], 1. Around the base of the handle, a pattern of egg-and-dot. Traces of preliminary sketch.

D: feet of an Eros(?) flying to right; below and to the right, the knees, covered by a garment, of a female(?) figure. Relief contour for the top of the feet and for the knees.

E: the right leg and a bit of the left knee of a male figure (satyr?) creeping to right. Then, the decorated hem of a woman's chiton or peplos. Below, the horizontal reserved line above the normal band of pattern (not preserved). Relief contour along the legs.

F: the lower legs, in frontal view, of an Eros(?). To the right, the stem of a plant. Relief contour generally.

G: a section of the pattern band: at least three stopped meanders to left, and a checker-square. What remains of the picture above the pattern-band is difficult to interpret but the dotted object ought to be the tail of a feline—perhaps a panther skin upon which someone (Dionysos?) is reclining, with maenads, satyrs, and Erotes.

Manner of the Kadmos Painter. It is possible that these fragments come from the same vase as those in **47**: the style is very similar and so is the glaze on the inside. The reverse of Adolphseck 78, *CVA* Schloss Fasanerie 1 [11] pl. 52 [530], 1, *ARV*² 1346, 2 may be compared: the Cyrene fragments would have come from a similar Dionysiac scene, with the god himself perhaps, one or more satyrs and maenads, and Erotes.

About 420–400 B.C.

49   Bell-krater   F11   1   2
Pl. 26
Max. dim. 0.055; Th. 0.004–0.005

Single fragment of the upper wall, with the beginning of the lip at the top and the beginning of a handle at the right. The inside is glazed except for a horizontal reserved band at the upper break.

Head of a thyrsos.

Probably last quarter of the 5th or first quarter of the 4th century B.C.

50   Bell-krater   C15/16   1   2
Pl. 26
H. 0.050; W. 0.054; Th. 0.008

Single fragment of the upper wall with the beginning of the lip. The inside is glazed except for a reserved band above the lower break.

At the left, the hair of a female figure (maenad?); then, the head and one side-shoot of a thyrsos; above, the reserved groove marking off the lip, and a bit of a laurel-leaf. Added white for the berries in the head of the thyrsos. Relief contour for the thyrsos.

Plainer Group (*ARV*² 1418–1424). The thyrsos-head is characteristic: cf. London, B.M. F1, *ARV*² 1421, 1. As on the Cyrene fragment, there is usually a side-shoot below the head of the thyrsos, to which one or two bunches of grapes may be attached.

First quarter of the 4th century B.C.

51   Bell-krater   E10/11 (Area 1)   1   3
Pl. 26
Max. dim. 0.059; Th. 0.006

Single fragment of the wall of a bell-krater. Black glaze on the inside much abraded.

Chariot moving to left. The surface is partly abraded and the remains are not easy to interpret in detail: the off-wheel, part of the axle and cab of a chariot, and the hindlegs of the near trace-horse painted in white.

For the general scheme, see, for example, Ruvo, Jatta 422, *ARV*² 1420, 4, H. Sichtermann, *Griechische Vasen in Unteritalien* (1966) pl. 37.

4th century B.C., probably first half.

52   Bell-krater   D10   A   3
Pl. 26
H. 0.070; W. 0.090; Th. 0.005–0.007

Single fragment of the wall. Brownish black glaze on the inside.

What remains is the lower righthand side of the floral below a handle and, below, a bit of the horizontal band of pattern (eggs?).

For this type of floral below the handle of a bell-krater, see *Celti ed Etruschi nell'Italia centro-settentrionale dal V sec. a.C. alla Romanizzazione* (Imola 1987) 195, fig. 5, a bell krater which may be attributed to the Filottrano Painter, *ARV*² 1453–1455.

Middle or third quarter of the 4th century B.C.

Kraters of Uncertain Shape

53   Krater   E10/11 (Area 1)   1   3
Pl. 27
H. 0.045; W. 0.110; Th. 0.007–0.009

Single fragment of the wall of a large open shape, perhaps a volute-krater. Dull black glaze on the inside.

The fragment preserves the lower legs of a female figure standing to right. She wears a chiton and a himation (the lower border indicated by a line in diluted glaze). The vertical object near the righthand break is perhaps the end of a thyrsos or scepter rather than the leg of a stool (diphros) or table. Below, a section of the horizontal pattern-band: meanders (to right?).

For the general scheme, compare the lower part of the woman on the reverse of Oxford 522, *CVA* 1 [3], pl. 29 [121], 4, *ARV*² 1028, 3, Polygnotos. The hem of the himation ends in an S-like squiggle, which is common in the Polygnotan Group: see also London B.M. E 280, *CVA* 3 [4], pl. 16 [181], 1c, *ARV*² 1030, 35.

About 460–440 B.C.

54   Krater   F11   1   2
Pl. 27
Max. dim. 0.050; Th. 0.005–0.006

Single fragment from the wall of an open shape, probably a bell- or column-krater. Glazed on the inside.

The remains are not easy to interpret: the vertical lines appear to be the folds of a garment; over this we have the paws of an animal-skin used as a cloak; the object which crosses the vertical fold-lines seems to be a bent arm encased in a long sleeve with wrist and part of the hand protruding, however unconvincing the arm may appear.

Second quarter of the 5th century B.C.?

55   Krater   D15/16   1   1
Pl. 27
H. 0.052; W. 0.070

Fragment from the lip of a bell-krater or calyx-krater. Reddish black glaze on the inside (no reserved bands).

On the lip, a laurel wreath, to left, the leaves and stem contoured with relief-line.

For the form and decoration of the lip, cf. Ferrara T. 44C, Alfieri, *Spina* 46, fig. 101.

About 460–440 B.C.

56   Krater   C17   1B   3
Pl. 27
Max. dim. 0.052; Th. 0.006

Single fragment of the wall of a bell-krater or calyx-krater. Dull black glaze on the inside.

The fragment preserves parts of the heads and necks of horses pulling a quadriga to the right: the neck and top of the horse; the mane of the near trace-horse.

Third quarter of the 5th century B.C.

57 Krater   E12/F12 Balk 3
Pl. 27
W. 0.068

Single fragment from the lip of a bell-krater or calyx-krater. The inside is glazed except for a reserved band near the top.

On the lip, a wreath of laurel and berry, to left.

Last quarter of the 5th or first quarter of the 4th century B.C.

58 Krater   E12/13 E 2
Pl. 27
H. 0.020; W. 0.050; Th. 0.006

Single fragment of the upper wall of a bell- or calyx-krater. The glaze on the inside has fired reddish; on the outside, a dull black.

The fragment preserves the head, in profile to the left, of a youthful male figure, his hair bound with a broad fillet. At the right, the hand, outstretched to left, of a second figure. Relief contour for the hand.

The head might be that of a mortal komast or symposiast, or perhaps that of Dionysos (cf. London, B.M. 1917.7-21.1, Metzger, *Représentations* pl. 35). The style, so far as one can tell, recalls the Plainer Group of painters working in the early 4th century, in particular the Nostell Painter and the Dublin Painter: *ARV* ^{2} 1422. See, for example, the fragment Oxford G 731, *CVA* 2 [9], pl. 67 [431], 7, *ARV* ^{2} 1422, 3, Dublin Painter. See also **59** and **60**.

First quarter of the 4th century B.C.

59 Krater   E12/13 E 2
Not illustrated
A: H. 0.031; W. 0.033; Th. 0.005
B: H. 0.023; W. 0.028

Two non-joining fragments from the lower wall of a bell- or calyx-krater. Black glaze on the inside.

Fragment **A** gives part of the pattern-band: a checker-square and a meander; fragment **B** preserves a meander with dot center. The fabric suggests that these pieces might belong to the same vase as **58**.

First half of the 4th century B.C.

60 Krater   E12/13 E 2
Not illustrated
A: Max. dim. 0.080; Th. 0.007
B: Max. dim. 0.070

Two non-joining fragments from the lip and upper wall of a bell- or calyx-krater. Dull black glaze on the inside.

A: on the lip, laurel running to left; below, the top of the head (tip of one ear, two leaves of an ivy wreath) of a satyr. Relief contour for the ivy leaves. **B**: part of the laurel wreath on the lip. This may also come from the same vase as **58** and **59**.

First half of the 4th century B.C.

Hydriai

61 Hydria(?) F13/G13 2 2 (upper sherd)
                   D14/E14 2 2 (lower sherd)
Pl. 28
H. 0.095; W. 0.110; Th. 0.005–0.006

Two joining fragments from the wall of a closed shape, probably a hydria. The inside is unglazed.

Right(?) foot, and pleated chiton, of a female figure moving to the left. Below, a reserved ground-line. Some preliminary sketch.

Illustrated in *Cyrenaica in Antiquity* 210, fig. 1: Elrashedy sees the drawing of the himation as "reminiscent of the Pan Painter." I am unable to attribute the fragment, and do not see any connection with the Pan Painter: compare, however, Kansas City 30.13, Moon and Berge, *Midwestern* 156, *ARV* ^{2} 249, 1, Syleus Painter.

About 490–480 B.C.

62 Hydria   F14/G14 1 2
Pl. 28
Max. dim. 0.078; Th. 0.004

Single fragment (mended from two) of the body of a hydria. Reserved on the inside.

Part (waist to knee) of a female(?) figure is preserved. She wears a decorated garment with a kolpos, and seems to be moving to right. Diluted glaze for the pleats of the garment and for the decorative elements.

The type of decorated garment worn by the woman on the Cyrene fragment is not uncommon on vases of the second quarter and middle of the 5th century. Two examples: Houston, Museum of Fine Arts 80.95, hydria, Shapiro, *Southern*, 132–133; Ferrara T. 577, Alfieri, *Spina* 27, fig. 65, *ARV* ^{2} 541, 3, Florence Painter.

About 470–450 B.C.

63 Hydria   E10 bldg. N. of N. wall
Pl. 29
A: H. 0.042; W. 0.057; Th. 0.006–0.007
B: H. 0.032; W. 0.046

Two non-joining fragments of the wall. **A** is reserved and slightly ridged on the inside; **B** is abraded on the inside.

Fragment **A** preserves part of a klismos (back-leg, horizontal bar), a cushion on the chair, and to the right, on the near side of the chair, a section of the chiton and himation of a woman who seems to have been standing to the left. Fragment **B** gives a part of a himation, perhaps from the woman on **A**; at the right, unintelligible reserved area. Relief contour throughout. Diluted glaze for the decoration on the cushion, and for the cords of the chair-seat. See the next, **64**.

For the drawing of the border of the himation, compare the lefthand woman on the obverse of Munich 2324, *CVA* 5 [20], pl. 215 [930], *ARV* ^{2} 604, 55, Niobid Painter.

About 460–450 B.C.

64   Hydria(?)   E11   1   2
Pl. 29
Max. dim. 0.050; Th. 0.005–0.006
   Single fragment from the wall of a closed vase, probably a hydria. Reserved on the inside.
   In the center, the curved back and a bit of the back-rest of a klismos. A small section of the decorated cushion placed on the seat remains at the lower break. To the right, one end of a himation(?) with black stripe at the hem. Two reserved verticals at the lefthand break. This may come from the same vase as the last, **63**.
   About 460–450 B.C.

65   Hydria   D16/17   1   3
Pl. 29
A: H. 0.072; W. 0.046; Th. 0.007–0.009
B: H. 0.067; W. 0.054
   Two non-joining fragments from the neck of a hydria. Dull black glaze on the inside.
   Fragment **A** gives the lefthand end of a horizontal pattern-band: part of a circumscribed palmette. Fragment **B** comes from the righthand end of the same band: an open lotus and, to the left, a bit of a circumscribed palmette. The two sherds should be positioned further apart than in the photograph.
   Polygnotan Group? For the general form of the floral pattern, compare the hydria London, B.M. E 170, *CVA* 5 [7], pl. 75 [325], 2, *ARV* ^{2} 1042, 2, Coghill Painter; or Leiden 1956/6, 7, *CVA* 3 [5], pl. 143 [237], Group of Polygnotos.
   Third quarter of the 5th century B.C.

66   Hydria   E13/14   1   2, around statue (**A**)
                        D14/E14   2   stratum beneath statues (**B**)
Pl. 30
A: Max. dim. 0.090; Th. 0.004–0.005
B: Max. dim. 0.064
   Two fragments (**A** mended from two) of a hydria: **A** comes from the shoulder, with the upturn to the neck and the downturn to the body; **B** comes from the shoulder, with the upturn to the neck. Both fragments are reserved on the inside.
   A: torso, in three-quarter view to left, and head, in profile to right, of a standing woman who is dressed in a peplos and who holds a plemochoe in her left hand; at the right is the shoulder and right breast of a second woman who wears a short-sleeved garment decorated with a pair of black stripes. Relief contour for the face of the first woman. Diluted glaze for the necklace of the same woman.
   B: head and upper body of a woman standing to right. She is in the process of dressing, gripping the end of the overfall of her garment with her teeth. She wears a headband and earring. Relief contour for her face and neck. Traces of preliminary sketch. Diluted glaze for her necklace.
   Gynaikeion scene. The woman on **B** was tying or untying her girdle. The picture ran over from the body onto the shoulder of the vase. In style the drawing is in the manner of the Dinos Painter, not far indeed from the work of the Chrysis Painter, *ARV* ^{2} 1158–1159, especially *CVA* Castle Ashby [15], pl. 45 [700], 4–5. For the figure of a woman holding a plemochoe, see Munich 6452, *CVA* 5 [20], pl. 231 [946], 9–10, *ARV* ^{2} 1147, 62, and Gericke, *Gefässdarstellungen*, 82–85. The motif on **B** is an old one: compare for example a pelike in Münster, K. Stähler, *Eine unbekannte Pelike des Eucharidesmaler* (Köln 1967) pl. 2; and E. Buschor, *ÖJh* 39 (1952) 12–17. See the next, **67**, and **68**.
   About 430–410 B.C.

67   Hydria   E13/14   1   S. balk
Pl. 30
Max. dim. 0.060
   Single fragment, mended from two, of the neck of a hydria. Glazed on the inside except towards the lower break.
   The fragment preserves a section of the horizontal pattern-band on the neck of the vase: tendril with addorsed palmettes set obliquely. Relief contour for the leaves of the palmettes and the stem of the tendril. This fragment may well come from the same vase as **66**.
   About 430–410 B.C.

68   Hydria   C17   1B   3
Pl. 30
Max. dim. 0.072; Th. 0.004
   Single fragment from the junction of the body and the shoulder of a hydria. Reserved on the inside.
   Lower legs, crossed, of a woman seated to left but probably looking back to right, for she was the first figure on the left side of the scene. She wears a chiton. Relief contour for the feet except the toes of the left foot. This fragment may also come from the same vase as **66**.
   About 430–410 B.C.

69   Hydria   E12   1   3
Pl. 31
A: Max. dim. 0.056; Th. 0.004
B: Max. dim. 0.035
C: Max. dim. 0.056
D: Max. dim. 0.056
   Four fragments from the body of a hydria. Reserved on the inside except for **A** which has a wash of thin glaze.
   A: part of the torso, and the upper right arm, of a female figure, in profile to right, probably seated. She wears a chiton and holds a harp (trigonon), the strings of which have been rendered with incised lines below the glaze. Relief contour for the outer edge of the trigonon.
   B: part of a garment with decorated border—foreparts of horses (chariot?) below two zones of wave-pattern.
   C: part of an altar on a two-step base and, below, a bit of the horizontal band of egg-pattern. Relief-lines to define the heart and outer arc of each egg.
   D: two leaves and the lefthand spiral from the upper palmette of a two-tier palmette floral, and, at the left, the stem and spiral of a side-tendril.   Female figures, a harp, an altar—all these suggest a picture of the Muses, perhaps with Thamyras or some other notable singer such as Musaios or even Apollo. The style is not Meidian; the connections are rather with such followers of the Kadmos Painter as the Kiev Painter: for the pattern-border on fragment **B**, compare the himation of Herakles on Leningrad 43 f, *ARV* ^{2} 1346, 1, Schefold, *UKV* fig. 71. On harps, see R. Herbig, *AM* 54 (1929) 164–193. See **70** and **71**.
   About 420–400 B.C.

70   Hydria   D11/12   1   2
Pl. 31
A: Max. dim. 0.052; Th. 0.004
B: Max. dim. 0.041
   Two non-joining fragments from the body of a hydria. Reserved on the inside.
   Two sections of the floral below the vertical handle: **A**, a

lotus-bud; **B**, a spiral-tendril. Perhaps from the same vase as **69**.

Last quarter of the 5th century B.C.?

71   Hydria(?)   C15/16   1   4
Pl. 31

Max. dim. 0.030; Th. 0.004

Single fragment of wall, slightly convex. Wash of brown glaze on the inside.

Part of the head, the neck and the left shoulder of a female figure. She seems to lean forward to the left, her head in profile. She was dressed in a peplos, her hair was bound up with a sphendone decorated with black palmettes, her jewelry consisted of an earring and a necklace of white beads. Diluted glaze for the fringe of hair along the forehead. Possibly from the same vase as **69**.

Compare the head of the woman standing to left of Phaon on the Palermo calyx-krater, *ARV* ² 1321, 9. For a spendone decorated with palmettes, see that worn by Arniope on London B.M. E 224, Burn, pl. 8a, *ARV* ² 1313, 5.

About 420–400 B.C.

72   Hydria   F11   1   2
Pl. 31

Max. dim. 0.060; Th. 0.003 (bottom)–0.005 (top)

Single fragment of the shoulder; at the lefthand break, the beginning of a handle. Reserved on the inside.

A woman (neck to knee) leans forward to right, her right arm akimbo; she is dressed in a girdled peplos.

The woman bears some resemblance in style to the figures that appear on the hydriai belonging to the Class of Brussels A 3099, *ARV* ² 1340–1341, 1, and 2. Another hydria formerly in the Zurich Market (1980), Galerie Nefer (seated woman with swan, seated woman, and two standing women), belongs to the same Class, and the floral design at the back is by the same hand as those on the Brussels and Harvard hydriai.

About 420–400 B.C.

73   Hydria   D11/E11   Balk   2
Pl. 31

Max. dim. 0.060; Th. 0.005

Single fragment from the shoulder of a hydria. Reserved on the inside.

Head, to right, and upper body, in three-quarter view to left, of a female figure, a queen no doubt or a goddess, for she holds a scepter in her right hand. Difficult to be sure whether she was seated or standing, though her pose suggests the former. She wears a peplos over an ornamented chiton, and a wrap passes over her right arm and behind her back. Traces of preliminary sketch. Relief contour generally except for her hair and the wrap. Added clay, gilded, for the earring, the necklace of beads, the double bracelet, the buttons along the sleeve of the chiton, the bands on the scepter, and the uncertain object (spear-point?) below the woman's right forearm. Her hair is rendered in diluted glaze.

A beautiful fragment with delicate drawing, but I cannot make a definite attribution: one might compare, however, Istanbul 2576, Schefold, *UKV* pl. 1, 2 and figs. 26, 34, and Leningrad St. 1924, Schefold, *UKV* fig. 22, both of which Schefold atributes to his Helen Painter.

About 370–350 B.C.

74   Hydria   E11   3   2
Pl. 32

Max. dim. 0.14; Th. 0.006 (neck)

Single fragment (mended from two) of the shoulder and neck. The neck is glazed on the inside, the shoulder reserved.

The horizontal pattern on the neck consists of a narrow band of egg-and-dot above a broad band of egg-and-dart. Below, a small Eros (head, to right, outspread wings, left shoulder, and right arm outstretched) is in attendance upon a female figure of whom there remains only the top of the head. This figure must have been the first on the right of the picture because part of a circumscribed palmette from the handle-floral is preserved behind the woman. To the left of the Eros a fillet hangs in the field. Just to the right of the fillet at the lower break is a bit of the head of a third figure. Below Eros' right wing is the tip of a thyrsos-head. Relief contour for the brow-nose line of Eros, his chin, the nape of his neck, his wings except the tips of the quills, and the brow-nose line of the woman. Diluted glaze for the hair of both figures, and the coverts of Eros' wings.

Illustrated in *LibAnt* 9–10 (1972–1973) pl. 89b. For the pattern on the neck, compare the hydria in Leningrad illustrated by Schefold, *UKV* pl. 13, 1–2.

About 370–350 B.C.

75   Hydria   D12/13   F   2b
Pl. 32

Max. dim. 0.062; Th. 0.005

Single fragment from the body of a hydria. Reserved on the inside.

In the foreground, the leg of a male figure who seems to have been seated to left; below his thigh are the bunched folds of a garment upon which he was seated; below the garment is a reserved area which was painted white—an altar or offering-table? At the left are the feet, in white, and the hem of the dress of a female figure (the dress has an interrupted black border). The woman's right foot is seen in profile to the left, her left foot in frontal or three-quarter view but largely hidden by the leg of the male. Some traces of preliminary sketch. It is possible that the male is Dionysos, the female Adriadne or a maenad, as often on vases of this period.

Second or third quarter of the 4th century B.C.

76   Hydria   D12/E12   D   2, balk
Not illustrated

Max. dim. 0.074; Diam. est. of lip 0.19

Single fragment from the lip of a hydria.

The top of the lip and the inside of the neck are reserved. The ridge between the top and the side of the lip is glazed. The side is decorated with an egg-and-dart pattern (a dot between each egg and dart).

4th century B.C., probably second or third quarter.

77   Hydria   D16/17   2   3
Pl. 32

Max. dim. 0.085; Diam. est. at outer edge 0.14

Single fragment from the lip of a hydria.

The upper surface is reserved; the edge is grooved: the upper element is glazed, the lower has an egg-pattern; the underside is glazed.

4th century B.C., perhaps second or third quarter.

Oinochoai

78   Oinochoe (Shape 8A, mug)   C15/16   1   4
Pl. 33
W. 0.052; Th. 0.005; Diam. est. of mouth 0.10–0.11

Single fragment of the lip and wall, with the beginning of the handle at the lower righthand break. Dull, black to brownish-black glaze on the inside.

The fragment gives the back of the head, the right side of the back, and the right arm of a male figure leaning forward to left and seen from behind. Relief contour along the right side of the male.

With regard to the shape, J.D. Beazley, *Greek Vases in Poland* (Oxford 1928) 60 remarks: "I have called this kind of vase an oinochoe, but evidently it might serve more than one purpose—as a dipper, a measure, a taster, or a portable drinking-cup." See also B. Sparkes and L. Talcott, *The Athenian Agora* Vol. XII: *Black and Plain Pottery* (Princeton 1970) 70–71; and J. R. Green, *BICS* 19 (1972) 8. What remains of the figure recalls figures by the Painter of Berlin 2268, for example, the warriors on Warsaw 142349, ARV^2 156, 62, *CVA* Goluchow 1 [1], pl. 23 [23], 2. Our figure, however, was not a warrior but perhaps a youth leaning upon a staff, his right hand akimbo: a trainer or a komast. For a new mug by the Painter of Berlin 2268, see Sotheby, *Sale Cat.* 5 July 1982, no. 316. There are useful remarks on the painter by B. Cohen in Moon and Berge, *Midwestern* 154, no. 89. See now for the shape K. Schauenburg in W. Moon (ed.), *Ancient Art and Iconography* (Madison 1983) 259 and idem, *Boreas* 6 (1983) 95–97; and for a mug by the same painter, *CVA* Basel 3 [7], pl. 45 [357], 4–7 and p. 70.

About 510–490 B.C.

79   Oinochoe (Shape 8A, mug)   E10/11 (Area 1)   1   3
Pl. 33
A: Max. dim. 0.058
B: Max. dim. 0.040; Th. 0.005

Two non-joining fragments (**A** mended from two sherds) of the lower wall. The glaze both on the inside and the outside has fired a reddish-brown.

Komasts or athletes. **A** gives the legs and part of the abdomen of a naked male moving to right. The long, tapering object that passes behind the right ankle of this figure is hard to identify: is it the foot of a second male? **B** preserves the legs of a naked male who seems to be kneeling to left. Relief contour throughout for the male on **A** and at least for the thigh of the figure on **B**.

Though little remains, the style suggests the Painter of Berlin 2268: compare New York 06.1021.172, ARV^2 156, 64, G.M.A. Richter and M. Milne, *Shapes and Names of Athenian Vases* (New York 1935) fig. 186; Riehen, Kuhn, ARV^2 156, 68: *Vente publique* X (Basel 1951) pl. 20, no. 414; London Market, Sotheby, *Sale Cat.* 5 July 1982, no. 316.

About 510–490 B.C.

80   Oinochoe (Shape 8A, mug)   F13/G13   2   2
Pl. 33
A: W.(chord) 0.095; Th. 0.005 (upper break)
B: W. 0.048

Two non-joining fragments (**A** mended from two sherds) of the wall. Dull reddish-black glaze on the inside.

Fragment **A** preserves the lower body and legs of a male figure who runs to the right; below, a reserved ground-line. **B** gives the back leg of a second male who runs to left; behind this figure is part of a chlamys with one end hanging down; below, the reserved ground-line. Traces of preliminary sketch.

Painter of Berlin 2268, ARV^2 153–158. The subject was probably a komos rather than an athletic scene, but for a picture of two jumpers with a chlamys in the field, see Berlin F 2319, *CVA* 3 [22], pl. 144 [1073], 1–3, ARV^2 157, 78.

About 510–490 B.C.

Lids

81   Lid of a pyxis (Type A)
E10/11 (Area 1)   1   3 (lefthand sherd)
E11   1   2 (righthand sherd)
Pl. 34
Diam. est. 0.13; Max. dim. 0.12

Single fragment (two joining) of the lid of a pyxis (type A): about half the lid remains, with the stump of the knob. The underside and the edge are glazed. On the upper surface, near the edge, is a reserved groove.

The lid has three zones of decoration: groups of stopped meanders (five or more) to left interspersed with checker-squares; circumscribed palmettes with buds in the spandrels; short black strokes with dots along the outer border. The side of the knob is glazed so far as preserved.

The combination of decorative elements occurs on pyxis-lids from the Penthesilean Group: this is confirmed by Dr. S. Roberts who compares for the general scheme Berlin F 2261, *CVA* 3 [22], pl. 136 [1065], 2, ARV^2 906, 116, Veii Painter, and regards the Cyrene lid as "late rather than early within the workshop."

About 450–440 B.C.

82   Lid   F12 — 2
Pl. 34
Max. dim. 0.051; Th. 0.005–0.006

Single fragment of a lid, thickening at the upper break. On the underside there was a black center, with a reserved zone around it.

The fragment preserves the head, upper body, and the arms of a Siren shown in profile to right, playing the flute. Above, a band of egg-pattern which originally encircled the knob-handle. Relief contour for the face and neck of the Siren, and the flute. Dilute glaze for markings on the wings, and for feathers over the chest of the Siren.

The best work on Sirens remains E. Buschor, *Die Musen*

des Jenseits (Munich 1944), but some remarks on musical Sirens will be found in K. Schauenburg, *Praestant interna. Festschrift für Ulrich Hausmann* (1982) 233, and in W. Hornbostel, *Aus Gräbern und Heiligtümern* (Mainz 1980) 107–108, no. 64. Another instance of Sirens employed on a lid will be found on the early 4th century pyxis from Elteghen now in Leningrad: Buschor, op. cit. 55, fig. 42. Professor A.D. Trendall reminds me of the Campanian lekanis in Sorrento, which at least comes from Sirenland: A.D. Trendall, *The Red-figured Vases of Lucania, Campania and Sicily* (Oxford 1967) 242, no. 124. One should not forget N. Douglas, *Siren Land* (1911) chap. 1.

About 460–440 B.C.

Skyphoi

83   Skyphos (probably Type A)   D16/17   1   3
Pl. 35
H. 0.042; W. 0.057; Th. 0.004

Single fragment of the rim and the wall. Dull black glaze on the inside.

The fragment preserves the back of the head, and the shoulders, of the lefthand figure in the picture, a woman, probably standing, in profile to right, wearing sakkos, earring, chiton, and himation off her left shoulder. To judge from the line of the shoulder, her right arm was extended forward. Relief contour for the nape of the woman's neck, and her himation.

Lewis Painter. Compare the lefthand woman on the obverse of Vienna 1773, *ARV*² 972, 2, Smith, *Lewismaler* pl. 2b; or the similar female figure on the reverse of Rome, Villa Giulia 9205, *ARV*² 973, 4, Smith, *Lewismaler* pl. 4b.

About 460 B.C.

84   Skyphos   E11/12   Balk   2/3
Pl. 35
H. 0.070; W. 0.072; Th. 0.005; Diam. est. of rim 0.26–0.28

Single fragment of the rim. Black glaze on the inside.

Circumscribed palmette from the side-tendril of the floral design below a handle. For the type of floral, compare the skyphos in the Vatican, by the Lewis Painter, *ARV*² 974, 28, Smith, *Lewismaler* pl. 33e-f.

About 460–440 B.C.

85   Skyphos   E10/11 (Area 1)   1   3
Pl. 35
H. 0.032; W. 0.045; Th. 0.005; Diam. est. of rim 0.15

Single fragment from the rim of a skyphos. Brownish-black glaze on the inside.

Below the lip, three reserved ivy-leaves joined by a white (faded) tendril; below, the top of a drinking-horn(?).

For ivy below the lip of a skyphos, see Boston M.F.A. 01.8032, *CB* II, pl. 52, *ARV*² 588, 103, Penthesilea Painter.

Second or third quarter of the 5th century B.C.

86   Skyphos   C15/16   1   4 tank
Pl. 35
Max. dim. 0.045; Th. 0.004

Single fragment of the wall. Dull, brownish-black glaze on the inside.

Part of a vertical olive-spray.

No doubt from an owl-skyphos, on which see F.P. Johnson, *AJA* 59 (1955) 119–124, and *ARV*² 982–984. For another, complete glaux from Cyrenaica (Benghazi), see Sèvres 4166, 20, *CVA* 1 [13], pl. 21 [550], 12.

5th century B.C., probably second or third quarter.

87   Skyphos   D11/12   1   2
                        D12/13   A   2 E [**N**, righthand sherd]
                        D12/E12   D   2A
                        D12/E12   D   5
                        E11   2   2
                        E11   3   3 (**A, G, I, L**)
                        E11/12   Balk   2
                        E12   1   3 (**K, S**)
                        E12/13   E   2
                        E14/15   1   1-2 (**T**)
                        F12   —   2 (**D**)
                        F13/G13   1   2
Pls. 36–37
Diam. est. of rim 0.27–0.29; Th. 0.005–0.010
A: H. 0.105; W. 0.095
B: H. 0.077; W. 0.098
C: H. 0.050; W. 0.038
D: Max. dim. 0.072
E: Max. dim. 0.090
F: Max. dim. 0.078
G: Max. dim. 0.037
H: Max. dim. 0.035
I: Max. dim. 0.053
J: Max. dim. 0.043
K: Max. dim. 0.052
L: Max. dim. 0.035
M: Max. dim. 0.048
N: Max. dim. 0.077
O: Max. dim. 0.075
P: Max. dim. 0.065
Q: Max. dim. 0.053
R: Max. dim. 0.042
S: H. 0.045; W. 0.042
T: Max. dim. 0.055

Twenty non-joining fragments from the rim and body of a large skyphos. Lustrous black glaze on the inside. **A-C**: rim fragments (**A** mended from five sherds; **B** mended from three sherds). **D–T**: body fragments (**D** mended from two sherds; **E** mended from two sherds; **N** mended from two sherds; **O** mended from two sherds).

A: on the lip, myrtle-wreath running to left; below, the head, slightly inclined to left, the torso, in three-quarter view, the right arm, and the left hand of a young woman who is shown in the process of binding her hair with a narrow fillet. She wears a finely-pleated chiton which is held by a black girdle and by shoulder-straps. **B**: this must come from the center of one side, for the floral on the lip shows the ends of the myrtle-wreath meeting; below, the head of a thyrsos, with a side-shoot and a bit of the stem; at the lower, lefthand break, a trace of drapery. **C**: on the lip, myrtle running to right; below, the hands of a figure holding up a laurel(?)-wreath. **D**: part of the back, a bit of one leg, and the left arm of a female figure seated to left on rocky ground. She wears a finely pleated chiton and a himation, and holds a tortoise-shell lyre; above the lyre, a laurel(?)-shoot. **E**: shoulder to ankle of a woman bending forward to left with one leg propped up (no doubt on a rock); she wears a peplos with girdled overfall; two unintelligible reserved areas at the righthand break above and below. **F**: legs of a female figure dressed in a peplos(?) over a chiton; to left, a vertical sprig of laurel. **G**: torso and upper left arm of a woman, in three-quarter view to left, dressed in a girdled chiton. **H**: at the lefthand break, the upper arm of a woman dressed in a chiton; sprig of laurel (perhaps held by somebody—cf. Burn, pl. 20d). **I**: at the left, a section of drapery; then, the thighs of a female figure dressed in a chiton. **J**: at the left, a section of chiton; then, the toes of a right foot. **K**: knees and lower legs of a figure seated to right, dressed in a decorated garment (dotted circles, palmettes at the hem); to right, a wreath (ivy?). **L**: at the right, a section of a garment; to left, a lotus-flower from the floral under one handle. **M**: bit of a garment (peplos?), and a lotus-flower from a handle-floral. **N**, **O**, **P**, **Q**, and **R**: sections of the floral designs below one or both handles. **S**: akanthos-base for the floral below one handle; horizontal band of stopped meanders to left broken by a checker-square. **T**: two stopped meanders from the horizontal pattern-band. Relief contour generally except for drapery, the thyrsos on **B**, and the wreath on **K**. Some preliminary sketch. Diluted glaze in places for shading in the folds of garments, for the hair of the woman on A and for the akanthos on **S**. Ground-lines and plants(?) on **D**, **J**, and **K** are lightly incised.

Fragments **A** and **B** are illustrated in *LibAnt* 9–10 (1972–1973) pl. 89d and c; **A** also in *Cyrenaica in Antiquity* 213, fig. 2; and in *Expedition* 34 (1992) 32, fig. 14; see also White, *Final Reports* 1, 62 and n. 12. Fragment **H** may join at the right side of **G**, completing the woman's arm, but the edges of the two sherds are worn, and the join is not certain. One of the anonymous readers of the manuscript has suggested that fragment **K** may not belong, on the grounds that the form of the wreath is unusual (but compare the shoots at the top of the Hesperides' tree on London, B.M. E 224, Burn, pl. 2b); also because the dot-and-circle pattern on the drapery is more frequent in the work of Aison. I did not notice any difference in the clay or glaze of the sherd, however, and though crosses or asterisks are more usual as dress ornaments in the Meidias Painter, the dot-and-circle motif does occur: cf. Leto on Florence 81947, Burn, pl. 27b, or Mousaios on New York 37.11.23, Burn, pl. 37a.

The shape, as fragments **A–C** reveal, was a skyphos of large size, probably of Beazley's type A. The diameter at the rim seems to have been about 27–29 cm. It has been noted (*CB* II, 61) that in skyphoi the rim diameter is not uncommonly in the ratio of 1.236 to the height of the vase. If this ratio held true for the Cyrene skyphos, its height must have been about 21.5 to 23.5 cm. Our skyphos is to be dated about 410 B.C. Earlier by a decade or two is the large skyphos recently acquired by Toledo, 1982.88, and attributed by D. von Bothmer to the Kleophon Painter: *CVA* Toledo 2 [20], pls. 84–87 [967–970]. Until now only one large skyphos was known from the Circle of the Meidias Painter, a very fragmentary example in the Cahn Collection in Basel, published by E. Simon, "Kratos und Bia," *WürzJbb* n.s. 1 (1975) 177–186, figs. 1–5; see also K. Schefold, *Die Göttersage in der klassischen und hellenistischen Kunst* (Munich 1981) 155, fig. 206. The Cahn skyphos was of colossal size, if the figure of 42.5 cm. for the diameter is correct. The Cyrene skyphos was decorated with a wreath of myrtle at the lip on one or both sides: as the Cahn skyphos shows, the design might vary slightly between the two sides of the vase. The Cahn skyphos had elaborate florals below the handles, and this was also the case with the Cyrene vase. It has not been easy to recompose the exact form of the handle florals, and there is no certainty that the two were precisely the same. Plate 37 gives the floral as I have recomposed it; fragment **R** belongs to the same floral as **N**. The core of the floral consisted of an akanthos base surmounted by a three-tiered lotus flower topped by a palmette with sprung leaves. For the form compare the reconstruction of the floral of the Brauron acorn-lekythos in A. Lezzi-Hafter, *Der Schuwalow-Maler* (Mainz 1976) pl. 58: the author provides important comments on the akanthos-lotus type on pp. 47–49. The type is most common on squat-lekythoi or acorn-lekythoi, but Louvre CA 1588, by the Shuvalov Painter and dated 420–410 by Lezzi-Hafter, op. cit. 109 with pl. 58, shows its early use on a skyphos (Corinthian shape). For the akanthos base and the sprung palmette, compare the squat-lekythos by the Xenophantos Painter in Leningrad, *ARV*[2] 1407, P. Jacobsthal, *Ornamente griechischer Vasen* (Berlin 1927) pl. 110a. The Cyrene vase is so fragmentary that it is, unfortunately, not possible to identify the pictures on the two sides. The only certain figures are female; the lefthand figure on **I** may have been male, but this is unclear. That the picture or pictures should have been largely made up of women is hardly surprising, given that our skyphos is Meidian. On **B** there is a thyrsos, which suggests a Dionysiac scene, perhaps with maenads. The seated woman on **D** holds a tortoise-shell lyre and may be a maenad or a Muse. See also the fragment in the next entry (**88**). With regard to style, the most useful fragment of the Cyrene skyphos is **A**, for that preserves not only drapery but also the head of a female figure. The drawing of the florid drapery, of the profile of the face (with short mouth-line, delicate lips and chin), of the distinctive eye, hands and hair shows that this skyphos is a work by the Meidias Painter in his mature phase. Compare, for example, the figures on Florence 81947, Simon and Hirmer, pls. 217–218 and L. For recent discussion of the Meidias Painter and his Circle, see D. Cramers and E. Simon, "Ein neues Werk des Meidias-Malers," *AA* 93 (1978) 67–73; J. Neils, "A Greek Nativity by the Meidias Painter," *Bulletin of the Cleveland Museum of Art* 70 (1983) 274–289; M. True, "A New Meidian Kylix," *Greek Vases in the J. Paul Getty Museum* 2 (Malibu 1985) 79–88; Burn, passim. Our skyphos is not the only vase from the Circle of the Meidias Painter to have come from Cyrenaica: apart from the hydria London B.M. E 226, *ARV*[2] 1318, 3, and the loutrophoros Louvre MN 558, *ARV*[2] 1320, 3, listed by Beazley, there is also a fragment of a hydria which was excavated by the Italians at Cyrene, S. Stucchi et al., *Cirene 1957-1966. Un decennio di attività della missione archeologica italiana a Cirene* (Tripoli 1967) 159, fig. 174. L. Pandolfi, in publishing the pottery from the Italian dig, connects the hydria with the Meidias Painter and Aristophanes. The drawing is certainly in the manner of the Meidias Painter and perhaps by his own hand. The standing woman seems to be an Oriental—perhaps Medea? For the woman tying her hair on the Cyrene skyphos, compare a figure on the Washing Painter's pyxis in Wurzburg, L 541,

ARV ² 1133, 196, *LIMC* II, pl. 126, 1251. See also **88–91**.
About 410 B.C.

88 Skyphos (Inv. no. 74-908)   C10/11 A, Sect. B 5
Pl. 38
H. 0.055; W. 0.042; Th. 0.008

Single fragment from the rim and wall of a skyphos. The glaze on the inside has fired reddish; the glaze outside has flaked in places.

Head, in profile to left, and right shoulder of a female figure who was dressed in a peplos. Her body was seen in frontal view or three-quarter view to left. She may have held some object in her lowered right arm. It is not clear whether she was seated or standing. An inscription, in white, runs from left to right at the level of the woman's forehead: ΜΟΔΟΚΗ, incomplete at left, letters unevenly spaced. Above, band of egg-and-dot pattern (a white stroke at the center of each egg). Relief contour for the woman's face.

Inv. no. 74-908 may come from the reverse of the Meidian skyphos (see the previous entry, **87**), as the technique and the date are very similar, but, if so, the pattern on the lip was different on each side of the vase, and the glaze on the inside fired differently. The name was perhaps ΚΥΜΟΔΟΚΗ, which is the name of a Nereid in Homer, *Iliad* 18.39, and in Hesiod, *Theogony*, 252. On red-figure vases a Nereid with this name appears in a scene of wedding-preparations on London, B.M. E 774, a pyxis by the Eretria Painter, *ARV* ² 1250, 32, S. Roberts, *The Attic Pyxis* (1978) pl. 79; and amid other Nereids on a pyxis, by the Painter of London D 14, in New York, 40.11.2, *AJA* 44 (1940) 428–430, *ARV* ² 1213, 1. The name has also been tentatively restored, as Henry Immerwahr points out to me, on New York, 31.11.13, *ARV* ² 1248, 9, G. Richter and L. Hall, *Red-figured Athenian Vases in the Metropolitan Museum of Art* (New Haven 1936) 175, n. 139; see also Bothmer, *Amazons* 162, no. 15, and R. Lullies, *Eine Sammlung griechischer Kleinkunst* (Munich 1955) 29, no. 64. The style of the Cyrene fragment, insofar as it is possible to tell from the little that remains, seems to be Meidian.

About 420–400 B.C.

89 Skyphos(?)   F12 — 2
Pl. 38
Max. dim. 0.039; Th. 0.006

Single fragment from the wall of a large skyphos or possibly a bell-krater. Lustrous black glaze on the inside.

The fragment preserves the border of a garment (himation?) decorated with black palmettes.

It is possible but not certain that this fragment belongs to the Meidian skyphos **87**. It was found in the same deposit as fragment **D**, the glaze on the inside is not unlike that of the Meidian skyphos, and the black palmettes have a parallel on the garment of the seated figure on **87**, fragment **K**.

About 420–400 B.C.

90 Skyphos   F11/G11 wall cleaning 2
Pl. 38
Max. dim. 0.076; Th. 0.005–0.006

Single fragment from the wall of a skyphos. The inside is slightly ridged and covered with a reddish-brown glaze applied somewhat thinly.

A female figure (waist to ankle preserved) stands in three-quarter view to right, dressed in a peplos with overfall. Two parallel black lines run down the garment along the figure's right leg. At the upper lefthand break are the tips of three leaves (relief contour). Incised ground line and plant between the figure and the left break.

The fragment may come from the Meidian skyphos **87**, but the surface and the glaze on the inside are somewhat different; it is closer, at least in the glaze, to Inv. no. 74-908, **88**. The drawing shows that the fragment must be placed in the manner of the Meidias Painter. Compare the figure of Leto on Florence 81947, Simon and Hirmer, pl. 217; the figure of Chrysothemis on London, B.M. E 224, Arias, Hirmer, Shefton, pl. 214; or Hera on the Karlsruhe hydria, FR 1, pl. 30, *ARV* ² 1315, 1.

About 420–400 B.C.

91 Skyphos   E15 3 3
Pl. 38
Max. dim. 0.045; Th. 0.006

Single fragment from the wall of a skyphos. Black glaze on the inside. Surface slightly abraded.

The remains are difficult to interpret: they appear to represent an animal with furry mane; there seems to be a cord around its neck. Incised ground-lines in the glaze between the animal and the righthand break. I do not know whether this fragment could come from the Meidian skyphos **87**.

About 420–400 B.C.

Cups

92 Cup   F12 — 2
Pl. 39
A: Max. dim. 0.095; Th. 0.004–0.005
B: Max. dim. 0.070
C: Max. dim. 0.030

Three non-joining fragments (**A** mended from three sherds) of the bowl; B preserves the beginning of one handle at the upper break. Black glaze on the inside of all three fragments.

Fragment **A** gives the left leg, with foot raised off the ground, the upper part of the right leg (bent), and the genitals of a naked male figure moving to right. The reserved area at the upper break may be part of an object held by this figure. Below the right knee of this male is a foot and ankle of a second male figure who was also moving to the right. Fragment **B** preserves the back foot, with heel off the ground, and the lower leg of a male figure moving to right. The object with vertical side at the righthand break might be a block-seat or a stele. Fragment **C** (not illustrated) gives the calf of one leg and the shin of a second, overlapping leg. Below the picture on **A** and B is a reserved ground-line. Relief contour generally except for the right knee of the male on **A**.

There is no evidence that the figures are satyrs. They

must be athletes or komasts—athletes, rather, if the object on **B** is a stele. For the feet, compare Louvre Cp 11219 and 11220, *ARV*² 62, 78 and 79, Oltos, *CVA* 19 [28], pl. 39 [1244], 1; or Florence 81601, *CVA* 3 [30], pl. 74 [1338], 1, *ARV*² 64, 96, Oltos.

About 520–500 B.C.

93   Cup   D12/13   B   4 W.
Pl. 39
Max. dim. 0.090; Th. 0.005–0.006

Two joining fragments of the bowl. Black glaze on the outside.

The tondo is bordered by a reserved band. The head, in profile to right, of a youth is preserved from the picture. Relief contour for the youth's face. Red wreath about his head.

Illustrated in *LibAnt* 9–10 (1972–1973) pl. 88b. For the head, compare Louvre F 129, *BSA* 46 (1951) pl. 16b, *ARV*² 84, 20, Skythes.

About 510 B.C.

94   Cup (Type C)   F14/G14   1   2/3
Pl. 39
Diam. of foot 0.075; Pres. H. of cup 0.039

Single fragment preserving the foot, the stem, and part of the bowl. The hollow of the stem is reserved; the underside of the foot is glazed; the resting surface and the side of the foot are reserved; the upper surface of the foot is glazed; the stem is glazed except for a tooled groove on either side of the fillet that separates the stem from the foot; the bowl is glazed on the underside.

Tondo: right arm (as far as the wrist), right side, and right thigh of a naked female figure, seated or kneeling to left, body in three-quarter view. Some traces of preliminary sketch. Relief contour generally. Diluted glaze for the line of the left hip.

For the position, especially of the right arm, torso, and right leg, compare Leningrad B 9104, Peredolskaya, pl. 158, 5, *Paralipomena* 510.

About 510–500 B.C.

95   Cup   C10/11   A, Sect. B   4
Pl. 40
Max. dim. 0.085; Th. 0.003–0.005

Single fragment of the bowl. Lustrous black glaze on the outside.

The tondo is defined by a reserved band. What remains of the picture is the right end of the horizontal beam of a couch; a striped cushion above; and the back, seen in three-quarter view, of a symposiast, with a himation wrapped around his waist. Relief contour for the upper and lower edges of the beam, the cushion, and the back of the symposiast.

Two fragments of the foot of a type B cup (Diam. of foot 0.080) and two fragments of handles, from the same deposit, might well come from this vase. For the pattern on the cushion, see what is said by Beazley in *CVA* Oxford 2 [9], p. 110 on pl. 57 [421], 3.

About 520–500 B.C.

96   Cup   C17   2   2
Pl. 40
Max. dim. 0.043; Th. 0.006–0.007

Single fragment of the bowl. Black glaze on the underside. Red miltos preserved on the reserved areas.

The remains of the picture in the tondo are unclear. Some preliminary sketch.

The style is akin to the coarse work of the Pithos Painter (*ARV*² 139–141): see J.D. Beazley, *JHS* 59 (1939) 2–3. If this connection is valid, the scene might have shown a banqueter wearing a kidaris, and the cup would almost certainly have been of type C.

About 510–490 B.C.

97   Cup   1978, surface of dump
Pl. 40
Max. dim. 0.068; Th. 0.005

Single fragment of the bowl. The clay has been burnt a grayish-yellow through secondary firing. The outside is covered with black glaze.

The tondo is bordered by a narrow, reserved band. All that remains of the picture is the hem of a chiton with stacked folds forming a zigzag edge. Relief contour along the hem.

About 510–490 B.C.

98   Cup   D10/11   C   5
Pl. 40
Max. dim. 0.042

Single fragment of the bowl, with the beginning of the stem: the hollow of the stem was glazed; at the junction of stem and foot-plate there was a fillet. What remains of the underside is glazed.

Tondo: below, a section of the exergue; overlapping this, the foot and part of the garment of a draped figure. At the hem of the garment is an object in added red. At the left above the exergue is the curving end of an unidentified object. Relief contour throughout.

The object in red might, I suppose, be a vine-leaf hanging on a stem from a table, as on Makron's cup in Boston, 01.8022, *ARV*² 469, 149, *CB* III, pl. 78, 141. The stem is characteristic of a cup of Bloesch's Type C: cf. H. Bloesch, *Formen attischer Schalen* (Bern 1940) pls. 33–34.

About 520–480 B.C., earlier rather than later.

99   Cup   C12/13   2, Ext.   2
Pl. 40
H. 0.023; W. 0.034; Th. 0.003

Single fragment of the lip. Grayish-black glaze on the inside except for a reserved band at the rim; the glaze on the outside has burnt a grayish-brown through secondary firing.

The fragment preserves, from the outside of the cup, the head, to left and bent forward, the chest, in three-quarter view, and the upper left arm of a naked youth, an athlete perhaps. Diluted glaze for the fringe of the youth's hair. Though this is not very visible in the photograph, the contour of the hair over the crown is indented.

About 500–490 B.C.

100   Cup   C14/D14   2   2
Pl. 40
H. 0.025; W. 0.023; Th. 0.002–0.003

Single fragment of the lip of a cup rather than a stemless cup. Reserved band on the inside and the outside at the rim; otherwise, the inside is glazed.

Head, to right, and shoulders of a youth. Relief contour for neck, chin, and brow. Wreath in added red (faded) around the youth's head.

About 490 B.C.

101 Cup F15 1 1
Pl. 40
Max. dim. 0.037; Th. 0.004

Single fragment of the bowl of a cup rather than a stemless cup. The inside is covered with black glaze except for a bit of the narrow reserved band defining the tondo.

On the outside, the right shin and foot, in three-quarter view, of a male figure who was moving to the right. The reserved area with undulating contour, in front of the foot, must represent uneven ground. The picture was bordered below by a reserved band. Relief contour for the foot, the leg, and the ground.

About 500–480 B.C.

102 Cup D10/11 C 5
Pl. 40
Max. dim. 0.031; Th. 0.005

Single fragment of the bowl. The outside is glazed.

Tondo: what remains is a horizontal object which is joined by two narrow objects set obliquely, but I cannot interpret the remains. Relief contour throughout.

Late 6th century or first half of the 5th century B.C.

103 Cup E11 3 2
Pl. 40
Max. dim. 0.037; Th. 0.003–0.004

Single fragment of the bowl. Dull black glaze on the outside.

The tondo is bordered by stopped meanders running to left. There is no exergue. What remains of the picture is the slippered feet of a figure seated or standing to right, and a small part of a person's garment. The figure could be female, but an old man would also be possible.

Dr. E. Knauer suggests to me that this fragment is close to the Briseis Painter (*ARV* ^{2} 406–410) and to the Stieglitz Painter (*ARV* ^{2} 827–830).

About 480–470 B.C.

104 Cup E11 3 2
Not illustrated
Max. dim. 0.050; Th. 0.005–0.007

Single fragment of the bowl. The outside is glazed.

Of the scene in the tondo only the top of a lyre (tips of the arms, cross-bar, strings) remains. The seven strings are incised. Relief contour for the lyre. This fragment might come from the same cup as the last (**103**).

5th century B.C., probably first half.

105 Cup E11 1 2
Pl. 41
Max. dim. 0.061; Th. 0.004

Single fragment of the bowl. Black glaze on the outside, rubbed away in places.

The tondo is bordered by stopped meanders running to left. Below, the top of a head (to right?) bound with a broad fillet. My notes do not record whether the contour-stripe was bordered with relief-lines, though that is the impression given by the photograph.

Second quarter of the 5th century B.C.

106 Cup E10/11 (Area 1) 1 3
Pl. 41
Max. dim. 0.050; Th. 0.004–0.007

Two joining fragments of the bowl; underneath, the beginning of the stem.

Tondo: symposiast on a couch—parts of the horizontal frame and one leg of the couch remain, as well as folds of a himation over the thighs(?) of a banqueter. Below, a bit of the border of the tondo. Relief contour for the couch.

First half of the 5th century B.C.

Stemless Cup

107 Stemless cup (Inv. no. 76-50)
E10 1 1-2 (left half of **A**)
E11/12 1 2 (right half of **A**)
C10/11 A, "beta" stray (**B** and **C**)
Pl. 41
Diam. est. of lip 0.24
A: W. 0.090; Th. (lower break) 0.004
B: W. 0.045
C: W. 0.052

Three non-joining fragments (**A** mended from two sherds) of the lip and bowl of a stemless cup rather than a cup with offset lip. A reserved line emphasized the junction of lip and bowl on the outside. The inside is glazed. The glaze on the outside has fired red in places.

Fragment **A**: youth on horseback riding to right. He wears a chlamys off his right shoulder, and holds a levelled spear. Fragment **B**: head, to right, of one horse and, at the righthand break, the tip of the tail of a second horse. Fragment **C**: spiralling tendril from the floral below one handle. Relief contour generally except for the tails of the horses and the tendril.

Fragment **B** does not join at the left of **A**; it must come from the other side of the cup; and the pictures on the two sides will have been similar, with perhaps two riders on each side. The fragments are illustrated in D. White, "Excavations in the Sanctuary of Demeter and Persephone at Cyrene, Fifth Preliminary Report," *LibAnt* 13–14 (1976–1977) 289–330 and A is illustrated in *AJA* 80 (1976) pl. 26, fig. 14, with p. 170; see also White, *Final Reports* 1, 80. In point of style the fragments seem to be in the manner of the Sotades Painter. For the type of stemless cup and the handle-floral, compare Florence 3928, *ARV* ^{2} 770, 4, related to the Sotades Painter, *CVA* 4 [38], pl. 144 [1716]. The stemless cups of the Hippacontist Painter, *ARV* ^{2} 769–770, have a somewhat similar scene on the outside. See also the next (**108**).

About 460–440 B.C.

Cups or Stemless Cups

108 Stemless cup or cup of type C   E14/15   1   1-2
Pl. 42
Max. dim. 0.055; Th. at lip 0.008

Single fragment of the wall with a section of the offset lip on the inside, and the stump of a handle. The inside is glazed.

The outside is glazed except for part of a spiralling tendril which belonged to the floral below a handle. Perhaps from the same vase as the hippacontist fragments (**107**).

5th century B.C., probably second or third quarter.

109 Cup or stemless cup   D12/13   F   2b
Pl. 42
Max. dim. 0.035; Th. 0.004

Single fragment of the bowl. The inside is glazed.

The fragment preserves, from the outside of the cup, a hand with fingers outstretched, and the wrist of a male(?) figure. Relief contour throughout.

Late 6th century B.C.

Plates

110 Plate   E10/11 (Area 1)   1   3 (**A**)
                  D11/E11   Balk   2 (**B**)
Pl. 42
A: Max. dim. 0.072
B: Max. dim. 0.075; Th. 0.008; Diam. est. of foot 0.12

Two non-joining fragments preserving parts of the tondo and the ring-foot. The foot is reserved on the inner side but glazed on the outer side; the area within the ring-foot is reserved so far as preserved.

A reserved band defines the tondo. Fragment **A** gives the back of the head of a symposiast, in profile to right, and most of the striped cushion against which he was reclining. Fragment **B** preserves the legs (covered by a himation) of the symposiast, and the lower half of a leather flute-case which hangs in the field, with, to left, a corner of the box for the mouthpieces; at the upper break is a narrow reserved area crossed by a relief-line. Relief contour generally except for the symposiast's head. Diluted glaze for lines between the stripes on the cushion, and for short strokes (fur) over the surface of the flute-case.

The reserved area at the upper break on **B** is not, I think, part of an object in the field but a section of the forearms, bent upwards, of the symposiast who was probably playing the flute. The style suggests Epiktetos. Compare the symposiast on the interior of Epiktetos' cup London B.M. E 37, *ARV* ^{2} 72, 17, E. Pfuhl, *Malerei und Zeichnung der Griechen* (Munich 1923) fig. 324; or Oberlin 67.61, Moon and Berge, *Midwestern* 132–133, *Paralipomena* 329, 14bis. Notice in particular the group of three fold-lines at the ankle.

About 520–500 B.C.

111 Plate   F13/G13   1   2
Pl. 42
Max. dim. 0.078; Th. 0.005–0.006
Ring-foot: H. 0.002; W. 0.006

Single fragment (mended from two), preserving a section of the low ring-foot; the fragment turns up slightly at the top. The resting-surface of the ring-foot is glazed. Outside the foot, the underside is reserved; inside the foot, there is a band of glaze (W. 0.010), then a reserved area (Diam. 0.055).

The tondo was probably framed by two reserved bands, but the glaze has worn off. Within the tondo are preserved the head, upper body, arms, and left thigh of a youth who kneels to right, leaning forward. He holds, in his left hand, a stick, I think, rather than a flute-case, and he wears a cloak. Thick relief contour throughout except for the hair and parts of the garment.

Heraion Painter. See *ARV* ^{2} 142–144. The Cyrene fragment must have come from a plate of the same shape as the painter's namepiece, Delos 658, *ARV* ^{2} 143, 19, C. Dugas, *Délos X, Les Vases de L'Heraion* (Paris 1928) pl. 54, 658, which has a diameter of 0.168. The attitude of the youth on our fragment must have been like that of the youth on Würzburg 478, *ARV* ^{2} 143, 1, Langlotz, *GVW* pl. 217. The coarse style is also similar.

About 500 B.C.

112 Plate   F13/G13   1/2   2
Pl. 42
Max. dim. 0.045; Th. 0.004–0.006
Ring-foot: H. 0.002; W. 0.007

Single fragment, preserving a section of the ring-foot. The resting-surface of the low ring-foot is lightly grooved and reserved. Outside the foot, the underside is glazed; inside the foot, there is a band of glaze (W. 0.012), then a reserved area with cord marks.

The tondo was framed by at least one reserved band. What remains within the tondo is part of the right side and the right arm of a male figure who leans forward to right. He wears a cloak.

Heraion Painter. See the previous entry (**111**).

About 500 B.C.

"Closed" Shapes

113 Closed shape   E16/17 (Area 3) 1 2a (**A**)
                        F11 2 1-2 (**B** and **C**)
                        E11 4 2 (**D**)
Pl. 43; fragment **C** not illustrated
A: Max. dim. 0.054
B: Max. dim. 0.060; Th. 0.005–0.006
C: Max. dim. 0.042
D: Max. dim. 0.045

Four non-joining fragments from the convex wall of a closed vase, perhaps an amphora or pelike. The inside is reserved.

Fragment **A** preserves a section of a curving olive-branch and, at the right, the furled wings and tail of a bird. Fragment **B** gives a section of olive-branch with parts of seven leaves. **C** and **D** also preserve sections of olive-branch, with five and six leaves respectively. Relief contour for the stem and the leaves, as well as for the bird. The leaves of the olive-spray are joined to the stem by incised stalks.

Fragment **A** is illustrated in R. Goodchild, *Kyrene und Apollonia* (Zurich 1971) fig. 119. I do not know whether the bird is an owl, though that is likely enough, surrounded by and perched upon sprigs of olive as, later, on the necks of oinochoai of Shape 7: for example, Mannheim 61, *ARV* ^{2} 1066, 9, *CVA* 1 [13], pl. 24 [610], 3. For an amphora decorated with an owl, see the vase now in the Hashimoto Collection in Kyoto, *CVA* Japan 1 [1], pl. 1 [1], with Beazley's delightful comment in *AJA* 31 (1927) 348.

First half of the 5th century B.C.

114 Closed shape   F11 2 1-2
Pl. 43
Max. dim. 0.064; Th. 0.003–0.004

Single fragment from the convex wall of a closed shape. The inside is reserved.

What remains is one end of a cloak and, at the right, part of a male figure: komast with wrap? Some preliminary sketch. Relief contour along the body of the male. Diluted glaze for the weighted end of the cloak.

About 490–470 B.C.

115 Closed shape   F11/G11 wall cleaning 2
Pl. 43
H. 0.056; W. 0.063; Th. 0.005–0.006

Wall fragment of a closed shape, perhaps a pelike. The inside is largely abraded but seems to have been reserved.

What remains is the foot, and the lower part of the himation, of a figure standing in profile to left; to the right, the back foot and ankle of a male(?) figure who walks to right; below, the top of the horizontal pattern-band of key-meander running to right.

Perhaps from a pelike with komos like Braunschweig 269, *CVA* 1 [4], pl. 21 [167], 3, *ARV* ^{2} 569, 53, Leningrad Painter; or Munich 2346, *CVA* 2 [6], pl. 70 [266], 1, *ARV* ^{2} 565, 32bis, Pig Painter. See also 116.

About 480–460 B.C.

116 Closed shape   F11/G11 wall cleaning 2
Pl. 43
Max. dim. 0.080; Th. 0.005 (top)–0.007 (bottom)

Wall fragment of a closed shape, perhaps a pelike. The inside is abraded but seems to have been reserved.

Figure (thigh to shin) standing to left, draped in a himation. I do not know whether this is from the same vase as **115**.

About 480–460 B.C.

117 Closed shape   F13/G13 1 2
Pl. 44
H. 0.065; W. 0.050; Th. 0.005

Single fragment from the wall of a closed vase. Reserved on the inside.

Part of the slippered foot, to right, the pleated chiton, and the himation of a female figure. It is just possible, I suppose, that this fragment might belong with **8**.

About 480–460 B.C.

118 Closed shape   E10/11 (Area 1) 1 3
Pl. 44
A: Max. dim. 0.046; Th. 0.006
B: Max. dim. 0.087

Two non-joining fragments of the wall of a closed shape. Reserved on the inside.

Fragment **A** preserves the foot of a warrior standing to the left, and two diamond-shaped ends of the apron that hung down from his shield; the narrow reserved area at the right may be the toes of a second foot; below, a section of the horizontal pattern-band consisting of two meanders to right separated by a dotted saltire-square. Fragment **B** comes from the right side of the picture: below, two stopped meanders to right—the end of the pattern-band; above, perhaps the toes of a foot, to right.

The picture may have represented the departure of a warrior. For the shield-apron, see P.E. Corbett, *BMQ* 24, 97–98, with ns. 4 and 5 on p. 99, and Oxford 1917.60, *CVA* 1 [3], pl. 23 [115], 4, *ARV* ^{2} 649, 47.

Second quarter of the 5th century B.C.

119 Closed shape   C15/16 1 4
Pl. 44
H. 0.052; W. 0.058; Th. 0.005–0.006

Single fragment of the wall of a closed shape, perhaps a pelike. Reserved on the inside.

Legs, and lower part of the himation, of a male figure who stands in profile to right. Below and to the left, a short section of the horizontal reserved band forming the groundline, and the base of the vertical frame for the picture on the left.

About 470–450 B.C.

120 Closed shape   E11 3 2
Pl. 44
Max. dim. 0.080; Th. 0.005 (top)

Single fragment (mended from three) of the shoulder of a closed vase, with the curve up into the neck, perhaps a pelike. Reserved on the inside except at the upper break. On the outside the surface has been abraded in places.

Head, to left, and upper body of Nike, and parts of her outspread wings. She wears chiton and himation, and her hair is bound up with a fillet. Her right arm was outstretched.

For the band of dots on each wing, compare Louvre G 137, *CVA* 6 [9], pl. 34 [413], 1, *ARV* ^{2} 307, 6, Dutuit Painter, or Florence 4017, *CVA* 2 [13], pl. 29 [613], 1, Dresden Painter.

About 470–450 B.C.

121 Closed shape
          E10 bldg.   Balk between E. wall and terrace E. wall
Pl. 44
Max. dim. 0.052; Th. 0.005

Single fragment of the convex wall of a closed shape. The inside is reserved. The surface is much abraded.

Body and arms of a female(?) figure bending forward to the right. The figure seems to wear a himation over a short-sleeved chiton.

Second quarter of the 5th century B.C.

122 Closed shape (hydria?)   E10/11 (Area 1)   1   3
Pl. 45
Max. dim. 0.107; Th. 0.005

Two joining fragments of the wall and shoulder of a closed shape, perhaps a hydria. Reserved on the inside.

Athlete about to throw a javelin. What remains is most of the javelin, as well as the right hand and wrist of the athlete.

For the attitude of the akontist, compare Brussels A721, *CVA* 2 [2], pl. 14 [67], *ARV* ^{2} 226, 5, or Florence 3981, *CVA* 2 [13], pl. 40 [624], 4, *ARV* ^{2} 240, 41.

First half of the 5th century B.C.

123 Closed shape (oinochoe, shape 5B?)
          F13/G13   1   2
Pl. 45
A: Max. dim. 0.088; Th. (lower break) 0.005
B: Max. dim. 0.055

Two non-joining fragments from the upper wall (convex) and shoulder (concave) of a closed vase (oinochoe, shape 5B?). **A** preserves the upper wall and the shoulder; **B**, part of the upper wall. Streaks of glaze on the wall inside; the shoulder is reserved on the inside.

Fragment **A** preserves asection of the horizontal band of floral at the top of the wall: circumscribed palmettes alternating with open lotus-blossoms; above, on the shoulder of the vase, are the feet, to right, and a bit of the chiton of a female figure and, at the right, the legs and tail of a bird. Fragment **B** gives a part of the floral-band. Relief contour for most of the floral. Diluted glaze for the feathers of the bird.

Hard to see what the shape can be except an oinochoe, shape 5B: compare Munich 2445, *CVA* 2 [6], pl. 85 [281], 4–6, *ARV* ^{2} 307, 12, Dutuit Painter; also J.R. Green, *BICS* 19 (1972) 7. For the standing woman and bird, compare the picture on Vienna 383, *ARV* ^{2} 669, 50, Painter of London E 342.

About 460–440 B.C.

124 Closed shape   E10/11 (Area 1)   1   3
Pl. 45
H. 0.040; W. 0.050; Th. 0.007–0.008

Single fragment from the wall of a closed shape. The inside is reserved and ridged.

The fragment preserves a foot, in profile to right, and the butt of a stick(?). Below, a section of the horizontal pattern-band: stopped meanders to right and a dotted saltire-square attached to the lower bounding-line. Relief contour for the foot. For the pattern-band, compare that used on the neck-amphora Wurzburg 503, *ARV* ^{2} 611, 32, Langlotz, *GVW* pl. 170.

5th century B.C., second or third quarter.

125 Closed shape   C14/D14   2   2
Pl. 46
Max. dim. 0.056; Th. 0.005 (bottom)–0.008 (top)

Single fragment from the shoulder and lower neck of a closed shape, perhaps a one-piece amphora. The upper part of the inside is glazed, the lower reserved.

The fragment preserves part of the head, bent forward to right, of a male. Above, two narrow, horizontal bands. Along the lower, righthand break and above the chip, unintelligible reserved areas. Relief contour for the brow-nose line of the male.

Second or third quarter of the 5th century B.C.

126 Closed shape
          E10   Balk   1-2, along S.E. edge of bldg.
Pl. 46
Max. dim. 0.040; Th. 0.004

Single fragment of the convex wall of a closed vase; the inside is reserved and slightly ridged.

The fragment preserves part of the left hand of a figure holding three sprigs of ivy. The stalk of each leaf is painted red.

Second or third quarter of the 5th century B.C.

127 Closed shape   D14/E14   2   1
Pl. 46
Max. dim. 0.047; Th. 0.005

Single fragment of the wall of a closed shape, perhaps a pelike. Slight wash of glaze on the inside. Red miltos on the reserved areas.

The fragment preserves the back of the helmet (neck-guard, bit of the bowl, crest-holder, and crest), and the right forearm, raised, of a warrior or Athena, advancing to left. The figure probably grasped a spear in the raised hand. Just below the forearm at the break is a tiny piece of the garment which was draped over the figure's upper arm. Relief contour for the neck-guard, outer edge of the crest, and the arm.

5th century B.C., probably second or third quarter.

128 Closed shape (hydria?)   E10/11 (Area 1)   1   3
Pl. 46
H. 0.045; W. 0.055; Th. 0.005

Single fragment of the wall of a closed shape, probably a hydria. The inside is reserved. The surface on the outside has been partly abraded.

Woman seated to right in a chair (klismos). Her lower legs are preserved, and one leg of the chair. She wears a chiton and a himation. Below, the top of the horizontal pattern-band: a bit of a meander. The pleats of the chiton were drawn with diluted glaze.

For the drawing of the seated figure, compare Munich 6452, *CVA* 5 [20], pl. 231 [946], 2, *ARV* ^{2} 1147, 62, Kleophon Painter.

Third quarter of the 5th century B.C.

129 Closed shape   E12   1   3
Pl. 46
A: Max. dim. 0.065; Th. 0.003
B: Max. dim. 0.053
C: Max. dim. 0.064

Three fragments from an oinochoe (type 4) or a small hydria: **A** comes from the junction of the body and shoulder; **B**, from the junction of shoulder and neck; **C**, from the lower body. Fragments **A** and **C** are reserved on the inside,

B is glazed inside on the neck.

Fragment **A** preserves part (shoulders to knees) of a female figure who stands in frontal or three-quarter view to left, dressed in chiton and himation, her right arm outstretched. **B** gives a section of the egg-and-dot pattern at the base of the neck. **C** preserves part of the similar pattern below the picture on the body of the vase.

The woman on the Cyrene vase was no doubt the right-hand figure in the picture, her head turned to the left. For a woman in similar attitude and dress, see Naples RC 117, A. Lezzi-Hafter, *Der Schuwalow-Maler* (Mainz 1976) pl. 92 b. When I examined the fragments in Cyrene, I thought that they came from an oinochoe of type 4, but Adrienne Lezzi-Hafter points out to me that they may also belong to a small hydria.

About 430 B.C.

Attic Bilingual and Black-figure Epinetra

130 Epinetron D12/E12 D 1-2, N. of Polygonal Wall
Pl. 47
H. 0.050; W. 0.057; Th. 0.005–0.006

Single fragment from an epinetron, preserving parts of one side and the rounded end.

At the top, a section of incised scales with dot-centers—part of the roughened topside of the vase; below, a strip of checkerboard marking off the top from the side of the vase (not, I think, part of the architecture below): the central row of black checkers was overpainted in white. Below this strip, part of a fountainhouse rendered in black-figure: entablature with frieze of triglyphs and metopes, pilaster- or column-capital to left, panther-head water-spout, wall (the central section in added white) at the right. The rounded end of the epinetron is decorated with a scene drawn in red-figure: waves, with the tail of a dolphin at the left. Also illustrated in *Expedition* 34 (1992) 29, fig. 10b.

On epinetra, see *ABL* 104–106, D.M. Robinson, *AJA* 49 (1945) 480–490, G. Bakalakis, *ÖJh* 45 (1960) cols. 199–207; I have not seen P. Benbow, *Epinetra* (Ph.D. diss., Harvard Univ. 1975). The form of the scale-pattern (imbrication) suggests that our fragment comes from the same vase as another sherd from Cyrene published by M. Moore (Moore, *Final Reports* 3, no. 253, pl. 41). If so, the open end of our epinetron was decorated with a broad band of lotus buds and a narrower band of ribbon pattern. The picture along one side of the Cyrene vase ended, at the right, with a fountain-house: the only other epinetron known to me that shows a fountain-house is Athens, Akropolis coll. 2599, B. Graef and E. Langlotz, *Die antiken Vasen von der Akropolis zu Athen* I (Berlin 1925) pl. 111, *ABV* 481,d. The Akropolis fragment has women at the fountain, and that may have been the scene on the Cyrene vase. It is possible that we have one of the figures: Moore, *Final Reports* 3, no. 251, pl. 41, shows a woman with hands raised—perhaps she had a hydria on her head. In contrast to the side panels, the picture on the rounded end of the Cyrene vase was painted in red-figure, so that the epinetron was bilingual, the only example of which I am aware. A dolphin gambols amid the waves. It is likely that this picture encircled a molded female head which may be preserved among the terracottas from the site. As so little of our vase remains, it is not possible to make a firm attribution. In the years around 500 B.C. epinetra were painted by both the Sappho and Diosphos Painters. Both artists employed checkerboard on their lekythoi. Panther-head spouts appear on the Sappho Painter's lekythos in Athens, 552, *ABL* pl. 35, 3, though the resemblance is not particularly close. But if the fragment published in Moore, *Final Reports* 3, no. 251 belongs to the same epinetron, the black-figure panels were painted by the Sappho Painter. And given that the Sappho Painter was clearly prepared to experiment in technique (see D. Kurtz, *Athenian White Lekythoi* [Oxford 1975] 119), an occasional bilingual vase would not be surprising.

About 500 B.C.

131 Epinetron E10/11 (Area 1) 1 3
Pl. 47
A: Max. dim. 0.098; Th. 0.007–0.008
B: Max. dim. 0.041

Two fragments of an epinetron, **A** from the topside, **B** from the rounded end. Reserved on the inside.

The topside was decorated with a pattern of incised scales. The top was marked off from the side of the vase by a black band bordered by black lines; the band is ornamented with a wavy line in white. Fragment **B** preserves a section of incised arcs with white dots on a black ground, and unintelligible decoration apparently in red-figure.

Fragment **A** is illustrated in *LibAnt* 9–10 (1972–1973) pl. 90e, and in Elrashedy, *Cyrenaica in Antiquity* 213, fig. 3. This fragment clearly belongs to the same epinetron as a sherd published by M. Moore, *Final Reports* 3, no. 254, pl. 41. If fragment **B** also belongs, as I think, the scene on the closed end of the vase was apparently in red-figure. See also **132**.

Early 5th century B.C.

132 Epinetron F13/G13 1 2
Pl. 47
Diam. est. of rim ca. 0.16
A: H. 0.042; W. 0.047; Th. 0.003 (inner edge)–0.007 (outer edge)
B: H. 0.030; W. 0.043

Two fragments (**A** mended from two sherds) from the lip of an epinetron. Reserved on the inside. Moulding at rim glazed black.

A zone about 0.023 wide is covered with a creamy-white slip on which is painted a wreath of ivy leaves alternating with berries, bordered above and below by black lines. On **A** at the lower break are incised scales from the roughened topside of the vase.

These fragments may come from the same vase as **131**. For ivy-berry tendrils, see D. Kurtz, *Athenian White Lekythoi* (Oxford 1975) 154, and n. 9.

Early 5th century B.C.

Attic White-ground Alabastron

133 White-ground alabastron   F13/G13 1 2 (**A**)
                                   F13/G13 2 2 (**B**)
Pl. 48
A: Max. dim. 0.040
B: H. 0.057; W. 0.044; Th. 0.004

Two non-joining fragments from the wall of an alabastron. The inside is reserved. The slip on the outside has fired a creamy-white color.

Fragment **A** preserves the head, inclined to left, and the shoulders, in three-quarter view, of an Amazon who wears an Oriental cap and at least two garments. Above and partly overlapped by the cap is a horizontal band of continuous meanders to right. Fragment **B** gives part (chin, back, buttocks, left arm as far as the wrist) of a youth, leaning forward to left, seen in three-quarter view from behind. The line below the left forearm of the youth, which runs obliquely to the lines of the himation, perhaps represents the upper contour of a walking-stick. The youth wears a himation off his left shoulder. A blob of glaze has disfigured the surface.

These two fragments must come from an "Amazon alabastron" like New York M.M.A. 21.131 ARV^2 269, 1, $AntK$ 23 [1980] pl. 6, 8–9) and Basel Kä 403 (ARV^2 269, 2, $AntK$ 23 [1980] pl. 6, 10–11, CVA 3 [7] 82–83, pl. 55 [367]), both of which have an Amazon archer on one side, a youth leaning against a stick on the other. For such alabastra, see most recently J. Thimme, "Griechische Salbgefässe mit libyschen Motiven," *Jahrbuch der Staatlichen Kunstsammlungen in Baden-Württemberg* 7 (1970) 7–30; and J. Neils, "The Group of the Negro Alabastra: A Study in Motif Transferal," *AntK* 23 (1980) 13–23. The Amazon on fragment **A** will have been moving to the right but looking back, as on the New York and Basel vases. She wears an undergarment (perhaps a short chiton) and an overgarment, probably a black vest like that of the Amazon on the Basel alabastron, though a black, sleeved garment might be possible, similar to that worn by the Amazon on Berlin 3382 (ARV^2 269, bottom, *AntK* 23 [1980] pl. 3, 1), who also sports a comparable cap.

It is possible that a fragment from the bottom of an alabastron, illustrated in Moore, *Final Reports* 3, no. 148, pl. 28 and in Elrashedy, *Cyrenaica in Antiquity* 207, fig. 5, left, may come from the same vase; it is attributed by both Moore and Elrashedy to the Group of the Negro Alabastra.

The New York and Basel vases are works of the Painter of New York 21.131, and the Cyrene fragments are at least very close in style to this painter, as Martin Robertson and Donna Kurtz have also seen. They also point out the resemblance to the Atitas alabastron in Athens, Kerameikos Mus. 2713, *AM* 779 (1964) pl. 59, *Paralipomena* 331. See also the important remarks by M. Ohly in *MuJb* 26 (1975) 211–212.

For more general discussion of white-ground alabastra, see J.R. Mertens, *Attic White-Ground: Its Development on Shapes Other than Lekythoi* (New York 1977) 128–136; and I. Wehgartner, *Attisch weissgrundige Keramik* (Mainz 1983) 112–134. See also Bothmer, *Amazons*, especially 152, 157–158.

About 510–500 B.C.

Attic Plastic Vases

134 Plastic vase in the form of a Negro head (Inv. no. 71-808)   E11 4 2
Pl. 48
H. 0.062; W. 0.078

Single fragment preserving the upper left side of the mold-made head, and the base of the wheel-made mouth of the vase. At the righthand break above the negro's ear there is some evidence to suggest the attachment of a handle.

Most of the left eye of the negro is preserved together with the forehead above, the upper half of the proper left ear, and the hair both over the forehead and at the side in front of, and behind, the ear. The hair consists of pellets of clay covered with a wash of dilute glaze. Red was used for the eyebrows, white for the eyeball.

The fragment does not appear to have come from an oinochoe or aryballos but rather a mug or kantharos. As the hair is not continuous above the preserved ear, I wonder whether the vase may not have been janiform. For negro-head vases, see J.D. Beazley, *JHS* 49 (1929) 38–78, with a list of such vases on pp. 77–78; ARV^2 1529–1539, 1697; *Paralipomena* 501–505; and F. Croissant, *BCH* 97 (1973) 205–223, W.R. Biers in *Ancient Greek Art and Iconography* (Madison 1983) 119–126.

Late 6th century or first quarter of the 5th century B.C.

135 Plastic vase (oinochoe) in the form of a woman's head   D11/12 1 2
Pl. 48
Max. dim. 0.070

Two joining fragments from a plastic vase (oinochoe, no doubt with mouth of shape 1) in the form of a woman's head. The inside is reserved.

Part of the forehead remains and much of the hair over the crown of the head. The hair, apart from the fringe, is glazed and decorated with an ivy-wreath in added white. The fringe is composed of four rows of clay pellets.

Cook Class. See J.D. Beazley, *JHS* 49 (1929) 61–65 and 78; ARV^2 1539–1544, 1698, and 1704; *Paralipomena* 503–504; W. Hornbostel et al., *Aus Gräbern und Heiligtümern* (Mainz 1980) 122–123. The Cyrene vase must have been like Berlin F 2192, *JHS* 49 (1929) 64, fig. 15. See also the next (**136**).

About 490–460 B.C.

136 Plastic vase in the form of a woman's head
                                    F13/G13 1 1
Not illustrated
H. 0.049; Diam. of base 0.045–0.050

Fragment of the base, the nape of the neck, and the back of the head. Black band (W. 0.008) around the base of the neck.

A section of the hair from the proper right side remains, glazed black. The fragment certainly comes from a vase in the form of a woman's head but not enough is preserved to assign it to any class. Possible that it belongs to the same vase as the preceding fragment (**135**).

First half of the 5th century B.C.

Relief-vase

137 Relief-vase (hydria?) (Inv. no. 78-842)
                                    F11/G11 wall surface 2
Pl. 48
H. 0.078; W. 0.078; Th. 0.005 (sherd)
H. 0.071; W. 0.048; Th. 0.010 (figure)

Single fragment from the wall of a hydria(?), with relief figure; a slight thickening at the righthand break may indicate the beginning of a handle. The fragment is reserved on the inside; the black glaze on the outside is much abraded.

Relief figure: the body, from neck to knees, of a woman seen in frontal view, and dressed in chiton and himation (off the left shoulder). Remains of white slip on the himation. Traces of gilding in the folds of the himation below the figure's left arm.

The female figure may have been the first on the right of the picture, in which case her head was probably turned to the left. Her right arm, like her left, seems to have been bent forward. The clay of the vase appears to be Attic. For Attic relief-ware, see E.A. Zervoudaki, "Attische polychrome Relief-keramik des späten 5. und des 4. Jahrhunderts v. Chr.," *AM* 83 (1968) 1–88. Interestingly, there are very few relief-vases with a Cyrenaican provenience: see *AM* 83 (1968) 35, no. 72 and pp. 61–62; and T. Dohrn, *RM* 92 (1985) 101. I have not found a close parallel on relief-vases to the figure on the Cyrene fragment, but, in large-scale sculpture, the drapery of our figure may be compared with that seen on the so-called Artemisia from the Mausoleum, and related female figures of the middle and second half of the 4th century: see G.B. Waywell, *The Free-Standing Sculptures of the Mausoleum* (London 1978) 103–105, no. 27, and pl. 13; also R. Kabus-Jahn, *Studien zu Frauenfiguren des vierten Jahrhunderts vor Christus* (Darmstadt 1963) 23ff.

Second half of the 4th century B.C.

Uncertain Fabric

138 Bell-krater   C12/13 2, Ext. 3
Pl. 48
H. 0.037; W. 0.048; Th. 0.005

Single fragment from the lower wall of a bell-krater. Dull reddish-black glaze on the inside. Red miltos over reserved areas.

The fragment preserves the foreleg of a feline(?), to right, and, below, a section of a horizontal band of arcs.

This fragment may be Attic, for the fired clay and the glaze recall Attic vases of poorer quality produced during the 4th century, but a reasonably hard fabric, orange to light brown in color, and a dull glaze are characteristic of the local red-figure found at Olympia and Ancient Elis. The pattern of arcs is also not infrequent on Elean kraters but would be unusual on an Attic bell-krater. For Elean red-figure, see W. Schiering in *OlForsch* V, *Die Werkstatt des Pheidias in Olympia* (Berlin 1964) 248–266; A.D. Trendall and Ian McPhee, "An Elean Red-figured Pelike in Liverpool," *Aparchai* (Pisa 1982) 471–472; illustrations of isolated pieces in *ArchDelt* 18 (1964) Chronika, pl. 144b, *ArchDelt* 19 (1965) Chronika, pl. 175c, *ArchDelt* 24 (1969) Chronika pl. 160a, *AR* 1963–1964, 12, *Ergon* 1970, 135, *BCH* 95 (1971) 908, fig. 236, *ÖJhBeibl* 49, 113, fig. 16. Note that some red-figured fragments from the British excavations at Tocra may likewise be non-Attic: see J. Boardman and J. Hayes, *Excavations at Tocra 1963–1965: The Archaic Deposits II and Later Deposits* (Oxford 1973) 93, nos. 2354 and 2355, with pl. 41 (no. 2355 must be South Italian, and 2354 does not seem Attic from the photograph). A small squat-lekythos found in the Manchester excavations at Cyrene, A. Rowe, *Cyrenaican Expeditions of the University of Manchester 1955, 1956, 1957* (Manchester 1959) pl. 37d-e, is certainly South Italian. A pelike in Leiden, KvB 56, *CVA* 3 [5], pl. 138 [232], 3–4, said to be from Cyrenaica, has recently been published as Attic, but must be Corinthian.

First half of the 4th century B.C.

Findspot Index

Area	Trench	Stratum	Cat. No.	Approx. Date	Remarks
C10/11	A, Sect. B	4	95	Ca. 520–500	
C10/11	A, Sect. B	5	88	Ca. 420–400	
C10/11	A, Sect. B	7	27	Ca. 480–460	
C10/11	A, "beta"	stray	107B-C	Ca. 460–440	Same vase as **107**A left: E10 1 1/2; **107A** right: E11/12 1 2
C12/13	2, Ext.	2	99	Ca. 500–490	
C12/13	2, Ext.	3	138	1st half 4th	
C13	1	4A	43	2nd quarter 5th	
C13/D13		2	37	late 6th/1st half 5th	
C14	1	3	18	Ca. 500–490	
C14/D14	2	2	100	Ca. 490	
			125	2nd–3rd quarter 5th	
C15/16	1	2	50	1st quarter 4th	
C15/16	1	4	5	Ca. 520–510	
			71	Ca. 420–400	
			78	Ca. 510–490	
			86	5th (2nd–3rd quarters?)	
			119	Ca. 470–450	
C17	1B	3	56	3rd quarter 5th	
			68	Ca. 430–410	
C17	2	2	41	Ca. 350–320	
			96	Ca. 510–490	
D10	A	3	52	Middle–3rd quarter 4th	
D10/11	C	6	36	Ca. 480–460	
			98	Ca. 520–480	
			102	late 6th/first half 5th	
D11/E11	balk	2	73	Ca. 370–350	
			110B	Ca. 520–500	Same vase as **110**A: E10/11 (Area 1) 1 3
D11/12	1	2	48	Ca. 420–400	
			70	Last quarter 5th?	
			87	Ca. 410	Same vase as **87**: D12/13 A 2; D12/E12 D 2A; D12/E12 D 3; E11 2 2; E11 3 3; E11/12 Balk 2; E12 1 3; E12/13 E 2; E14/15 1 1-2; F12 - 2; F13/G13 1 2

Area	Trench	Stratum	Cat. No.	Approx. Date	Remarks
D11/12	1	2	**135**	Ca. 490–460	
D12/E12	D	1-2	**130**	Ca. 500	Same vase as Moore, *Final Reports* 3 No. 253: F11 1 2
D12/E12	D	2	**47**A	Ca. 420–400	Same vase as **47**B-E: E12 1 3
D12/E12	D	2, balk	**76**	4th (2nd or 3rd quarter?)	
D12/E12	D	2A	**87**	Ca. 410	Same vase as **87**: D11/12 1 2; D12/13 A 2; D12/E12 D 3; E11 2 2; E11 3 3; E11/12 Balk 2; E12 1 3; E12/13 E 2; E14/15 1 1-2; F12 - 2; F13/G13 1 2
D12/E12	D	5	**87**	Ca. 410	Same vase as **87**: D11/12 1 2; D12/13 A 2; D12/E12 D 2A; E11 2 2; E11 3 3; E11/12 Balk 2; E12 1 3; E12/13 E 2; E14/15 1 1-2; F12 - 2; F13/G13 1 2
D12/13	A	2	**87**	Ca. 410	Same vase as **87**: D11/12 1 2; D12/E12 D 2A; D12/E12 D 3; E11 2 2; E11 3 3; E11/12 Balk 2; E12 1 3; E12/13 E 2; E14/15 1 1-2; F12 - 2; F13/G13 1 2
D12/13	B	4	**93**	Ca. 510	
D12/13	F	2b	**75**	2nd–3rd quarter 4th	
			109	Late 6th	
D13 (Area 2)		1-2	**16**	Ca. 380–350	
D14/E14	2	1	**127**	5th (2nd–3rd quarters?)	
D14/E14	2	2	**61** lower	Ca. 490–480	Same vase as **61** upper: F13/G13 2 2
D14/E14	2	stratum beneath statues	**66**B	Ca. 430–410	Same vase as **66**A: E13/14 1 2
D15/16	1	1	**55**	Ca. 460–440	
D16/17	1	3	**65**	3rd quarter 5th	
			83	Ca. 460	
D16/17	2	3	**4**	Ca. 440–420	
			77	4th (2nd–3rd quarters?)	
E10 Building, N of N wall			**63**	Ca. 460–450	
E10	1	1-2	**107**A left	Ca. 460–440	Same vase as **107**A right: E11/12 1 2; 107B-C: C10/11 A, "beta" stray
E10	1	2	**23**B	Ca. 480	Same vase a 23A: E10 Balk 2-3
E10	Balk	1-2	**32**	Ca. 490–470	
			126	2nd–3rd quarters 5th	
E10	Balk	2-3	**23**A	Ca. 480	Same vase as **23**B: E10 1 2

Area	Trench	Stratum	Cat. No.	Approx. Date	Remarks
E10	Balk	3	23A	Ca. 490–480	Same vase as 21B: F11 1 1
			44	Ca. 460–440	
E10 Balk, between E Wall and Terrace E Wall			121	2nd quarter 5th	
E10/11 (Area 1) 1		3	28	2nd quarter 5th	
			30	2nd–3rd quarter 5th	
			31	1st half 5th (1st quarter?)	
			33	Ca. 480–470	
			34	Ca. 480–470	
			35	Ca. 480–450	
			51	4th (1st half?)	
			53	Ca. 460–440	
			79	Ca. 510–490	
			81 left	Ca. 450–440	Same vase as 81 right: E11 1 2
			85	2nd–3rd quarter 5th	
			106	1st half 5th	
			110A	Ca. 520–500	Same vase as 110B: D11/E11 Balk 2
			118	2nd quarter 5th	
			128	3rd quarter 5th	
			122	1st half 5th	
			124	5th (2nd–3rd quarters?)	
			131	Early 5th	Same vase as Moore, *Final Reports* 3 No. 254: E11 4 2
E11	1	2	15	Ca. 450	
			24	Ca. 480–470	
			38B	Ca. 380–360	Same vase as 38A: E12/13 E 2
			45	3rd quarter 5th	
			46	Last quarter 5th?	
			64	Ca. 460–450	
			81 right	Ca. 450–440	Same vase as 81 left: E10/11 (Area 1) 1 3
			105	2nd quarter 5th	
E11	2	2	87	Ca. 410	Same vase as 87: D11/12 1 2; D12/13 A 2; D12/E12 D 2A; D12/E12 D 3; E11 3 3; E11/12 Balk 2; E12 1 3; E12/13 E 2; E14/15 1 1-2; F12 - 2; F13/G13 1 2
E11	3	2	74	Ca. 370–350	
			103	Ca. 480–470	
			104	5th (1st half?)	
			120	Ca. 470–450	
E11	3	3	10	Ca. 390–370	
			11	1st half 4th	
			12	1st half 4th (2md quarter?)	
			14	Ca. 370–340	
			87	Ca. 410	Same vase as 87: D11/12 1 2; D12/13 A 2; D12/E12 D 2A; D12/E12 D 3;E11 2 2; E11/12 Balk 2;

Area	Trench	Stratum	Cat. No.	Approx. Date	Remarks
E11	3	3	**87**	Ca. 410	E12/13 E 2; E 14/15 1 1-2; F12 - 2; F13/G13 1 2; E12 1 3
E11	4	2	**113**D	Late 6th–1st quarter 5th	Same vase as **113**A: E16/17 (Area 3) 1 2a; **113**B-C: F11 2 1-2
			134	Late 6th–1st quarter 5th	
E11/12	1	2	**107**A right	Ca. 460–440	Same vase as **107**Aleft: E10 1 1-2; **107**B-C: C10/11 A, "beta" stray
E11/12	Balk	2	**87**	Ca. 410	Same vase as **87**: D11/12 1 2; D12/13 A 2; D12/E12 D 2A; D12/E12 D 3; E11 2 2; E11 3 3; E12/13 E 2; E14/15 1 1-2; F12 - 2; F13/G13 1 2; E12 1 3
E11/12	Balk	2/3	**6**	1st quarter 5th	
			84	Ca. 460–440	
E12	1	1	**2**	2nd quarter 5th	
E12	1	5	**47**B-E	Ca. 420–400	Same vase as **47**A: D12/E12 D 2
			69	Ca. 420–400	
			87	Ca. 410	Same vase as **87**: D11/12 1 2; D12/13 A 2; D12/E12 D 2A; D12/E12 D 3; E11 2 2; E11 3 3; E11/12 Balk 2; E12/13 E 2; E14/15 1 1-2; F12 - 2; F13/G13 1 2
			129	Ca. 430	
E12/13	E	2	**1**	Ca. 510	
			38A	Ca. 380–360	Same vase as **38**B: E11 1 2
			39	1st half 4th	
			40	1st half 4th	
			58	1st quarter 4th	
			59	1st half 4th	
			60	1st half 4th	
			87	Ca. 410	Same vase as **87**: D11/12 1 2; D12/13 A 2; D12/E12 D 2A; D12/E12 D 3; E11 2 2; E11 3 3; E11/12 Balk 2; E12 1 3; E14/15 1 1-2; F12 - 2; F13/G13 1 2
E12/F12	Balk	3	**57**	Last quarter 5th/1st quarter 4th	
E13/14	1	2	**66**A	Ca. 430–410	Same vase as **66**B: D14/E14 2 stratum beneath statues
E13/14	1	S Balk	**67**	Ca. 430–410	
E14/15	1	1-2	**87**	Ca. 410	Same vase as **87**: D11/12 1 2; D12/13 A 2; D12/E12 D 2A; D12/E12 D 3; E11 2 2;

FINDSPOT INDEX

Area	Trench	Stratum	Cat. No.	Approx. Date	Remarks
E14/15	1	1-2	**87**	Ca. 410	E11 3 3; E11/12 Balk 2; E12 1 3; E12/13 E 2; F11 - 2; F13/G13 1 2
E14/15	1	1-2	**108**	5th (2nd–3rd quarters?)	
E15	3	3	**91**	Ca. 420–400	
E16/17	1	2a	**113A**	1st half 5th	Same vase as **113**B-C: F11 2 1-2; **113**D: E11 4 2
F11	1	1	**21B**	Ca. 490–480	Same vase as **21**A: E10 Balk 3
F11	1	2	**22**	Ca. 500–480	
			49	Last quarter 5th/1st quarter 4th	
			54	2nd quarter 5th?	
			72	Ca. 420–400	
F11	1	3	**7**	Ca. 480–460	
			26	Ca. 480–460	
F11	2	1-2	**19**	Ca. 490–480	
			113B-C	1st half 5th	Same vase as **113**A: E16/17 (Area 3) 1 2a; **113**D: E11 4 2
			114	Ca. 490–470	
F11	2	3	**20**	Ca. 490–480	
F11	2	3B	**25**	Ca. 480–470	
F11/G11	Wall cleaning	2	**90**	Ca. 420–400	
			115	Ca. 480–460	
			116	Ca. 480–460	
F11/G11	Wall surface	2	**137**	2nd half 4th	
F12		2	**13**	Ca. 390–360	
			42	2nd quarter 5th	
			82	Ca. 460–440	
			87	Ca. 410	Same vase as **87**: D11/12 1 2; D12/13 A 2; D12/E12 D 3; E11 3 3; E11/12 Balk 2; E12 1 3; E12/13 E 2; E14/15 1 1-2; E11 2 2; F13/G13 1 2; D12/E12 D 2A
			89	Ca. 420–400	
			92	Ca. 520–500	
F12/G13	1	2	**3**	Ca. 500–480	
F12/G13	1	1	**136**	1st half 5th	
F13/G13	1	2	**8**	Ca. 480–460	
			9	2nd–3rd quarter 5th	
			87	Ca. 410	Same vase as **87**: D11/12 1 2; D12/13 A 2; D12/E12 D 2A; D12/E12 D 3; E11 2 2; E11 3 3; E11/12 Balk 2; E12 1 3; E12/13 E 2; E14/15 1 1-2; F12 - 2
			111	Ca. 500	
			117	Ca. 480–460	
			123	Ca. 460–440	
			132	Early 5th	

Area	Trench	Stratum	Cat. No.	Approx. Date	Remarks
F13/G13	1	2	**133A**	Ca. 510–500	Same vase as **133B**: F13/G13 2 2
F13/G13	1/2	2	**112**	Ca. 500	
F13/G13	2	2	**61** upper	Ca. 490–480	Same vase as **61** lower: D14/E14 2 2
F13/G13	2	2	**80**	Ca. 510–490	
			133B	Ca. 510–500	Same vase as **133A**: F13/G13 1 2
F14/G14	1	1	**29**	Ca. 460–440	
F14/G14	1	2	**17**	1st half 4th	
			62	Ca. 470–450	
F14/G14	1	2/3	**94**	Ca. 510–500	
F15	1	1	**101**	Ca. 500–480	
1978, surface of dump			**97**	Ca. 510–490	

Arabic Summary
Parts I and II

هوامش

1- L. Pandolfi, "La Ceramic" in S. Stucchi (ed.), *Cirene 1957 - 1966. Un decennio di attivita della missione archeologica a Cirene (Tripoli 1964) 149 - 163*.

2- J. Boardman and J. Hayes, *Excavations at Tocra 1963 - 1965 II (Oxford 1973) 9*.

3- See *ARV2, 220 - 221, 5-8 bis*.

الديونيزية هي الأكثر شيوعا . وقصة واحدة فقط هي سرقة هيراقليس المصورة على كايليكس كريتر (٣٨) تؤرخ بحوالي ٣٨٠ - ٣٦٠ ، يمكن التعرف عليها بقدر كبير من الثقة . وإناء آخر لون عليه شكل أدمي يعتمر خوذة والذي يعتقد أنها أثينا (١٢٧) . وتتركز مشاهد من الحياة اليومية في معظمها على المآدب / العربدة ، الرياضيين والمحاربين . وجرة واحدة فقط (٦٦) صور عليها حجرات النساء وتضمنت مشهدا لإمرأة تلبس ملابسها .

وتستحق عملية التصوير إعتبارا خاصا من خلال عدد محدود من الأمثلة . وتظهر كسرتان من جرة ربما من الشكل البانأثيني (٣) أنهما حفظتا صورة ديك أعلى عمود بجانب مذبح ، ولعله ليس غريبا أن نتخيل أن المشهد الأصلي كان مثل ذلك الذي وجد على امفورا من الشكل البانأثيني والتي رسمها نيقوكسينوس ٣٠ وعلى شكل ١٣٣ يبدو أن كسرا من إناء مغلق (حوالي ٥٠٠ - ٤٥٠) ، صور طائر البومة يحط بين أغصان الزيتون .

وفي الختام يحب المرء أن يعرف كيف يقارن الفخار الأحمر من حرم وادي الغدير المقدس مع الحرم المقدسة الأخرى لديميتر وكوري في العالم الإغريقي . ولسوء الحظ فقد نشر القليل من الأدلة بهذا الخصوص . وعلى أي حال ، فإن حرم ديمتير وكوري المقدس على منحدرات اكروكورنث المنخفضة قد جرى التنقيب فيه بشكل مكثف ، ويبين طراز الفخار الأحمر ، مع أنه أقل شيوعا من الفخار الكورينثي وطراز الفخار الأسود الأتيكي ، يبين عددا من الأشكال تشابه طراز الفخار الأحمر في قوريني . ولاحظنا في الموقع الأخير أن دوارق خلط النبيذ وأواني الشرب هي السائدة ، وفي اكروكورنث فإن الصورة ليست غير متشابهة ، وأكثر شيوعا هي الدوارق ، سكيفوي والكؤوس .

٤

فقط ، ويمثل الربعين الثاني والثالث من القرن الخامس ستة وثمانية أواني على التوالي . ويرتفع العدد إلى أكثر من الضعف في الربع الأخير من القرن الخامس ، ويزداد بصورة مذهلة في القرن الرابع . ولابد أن الأواني الفخارية المسجلة في شكل ٢ قد أتت من مقابر بصورة أساسية ، وليس من مستوطنة أو حرم مقدس . وغياب ، أو عدم شيوع على الأقل ، طراز الفخار الأحمر في أواخر القرن السادس والنصف الأول من الخامس ربما يفسر على أنه تفضيل الفخار الأسود الأرخص والذي ينتج بكميات كبيرة . ومن جهة أخرى لعلنا نتوقع تقدمات نذرية عرضية لأواني أغلى ثمنا وأقل شيوعا من الفخار الأحمر في الحرم المقدس .

لم ينتج الحرم المقدس أي أواني فخارية من عمل الجيل الأول من الملوينين لطراز الفخار الأحمر مثل أندوكيديس وبسياس ، ولكن ظهرت أعمال مجموعة بيونير التي كانت نشطة في العشرين سنة الأخيرة من القرن السادس (٥ و ١) . ومهما يكن ، فإن هذه المرحلة المشكلة لطراز الفخار الأحمر الأتيكي يمثلها بصورة أساسية إنتاج الفنانين الذين تخصصوا في تلوين الأواني صغيرة الحجم خاصة الكؤوس والأطباق والفناجين .

بالرغم من أن فخار الطراز الأحمر من العصر القديم المتأخر والمراحل الأولى من العصر الكلاسيكي يوجد بوفرة في الحرم المقدس ، فإن القليل منه جرى نسبته إلى فنانين معينين . مع أن معظم الفخار الأحمر من القرن الرابع بقي في حالة رديئة بحيث أمكن عمل عدد قليل من روابط مبنية على الطراز ، إلا أنه تم نسبه كرتير واحد (٥٨ وربما ٥٩ ، ٦٠) إلى مجموعة بلينر من الملوينين وكذلك كسرة من كريتر جرس (٥٠) .

ولا تزودنا هذه المجموعة بمصدر غني من الرسومات الأسطورية . والمشاهد

كؤوس (٩٢ - ٩٥) ، أطباق (١١٠ - ١٢٠) ، وفناجين (٧٨ - ٨٠) وزخرفها ملونون تخصصوا في هذه الأشكال . وهناك عدد من الكؤوس ربما تعود إلى أواخر القرن السادس أو أوائل القرن الخامس . ولابد أن ثنائي إبينيترون (١٣٠) يؤرخ حوالي ٥٠٠ أو بعد ذلك بقليل . ويمكن تأريخ خمس عشرة جرة إلى العقدين الأولين من القرن الخامس (العصر القديم المتأخر) وأما الكسر الفخارية من الطراز الأحمر من العصر الكلاسيكي المبكر حوالي (٤٨٠ - ٤٥٠) فهي كثيرة جدا . وتتضمن أمثلة من القرن الرابع وعلى دوارق على شكل جرس (٤٧- ٤٩) ، جرار ماء (٦٦ - ٧٢) وسكيفوي (٨٧ - ٩١) ، وكذلك بيليكاني (١٠ - ١٤) ، ليبيتيس جاميكوي (١٦ - ١٧) ، دوارق من نوع كايلكس (٣٨ - ٤١) ، دوارق على شكل جرس (٥٠ - ٥٢) ، دوارق على شكل جرس أو كاليكس (٥٨ - ٦٠) ، وجرار ماء (٧٣ - ٧٧) . ويمكن تأريخ معظم هذه الأشكال إلى النصف الأول من القرن الرابع ، ولكن ٤١ ، ٥٢ ربما ٧٥ - ٧٧ تعود إلى الربع الثالث .

يرجع أكبر عدد من الكسر الفخارية إلى النصف الأول من القرن الخامس (أنظر شكل أ) أقل عدد هو ٤٧ وأقصى عدد هو ٧١ . ويبدو أنه كان هناك إنخفاض في عدد الأواني المستوردة خلال النصف الثاني من القرن الخامس ، ولكن يزداد عدد الكسر الفخارية مرة ثانية بعد عام ٤٠٠ ق.م. ويمكن مقارنة هذه الظاهرة مع تلك التي كشفها شكل ٢ والتي تجدول بالشكل والتاريخ الفخار الأحمر من منطقة برقة حسب تصنيف بيزلي (ARV2 and Paralipomena) ، مضافا إليها الأواني الفخارية غير المنسوبة التي نشرها البريطانيون والفرنسيون في Corpora Vasorum Antiquorum . وتختلف الصورة هنا تقريبا . ولا يوجد فخار أحمر من القرن السادس سوى مثالين من أواخر العصر القديم

خلاصة ٢

كشفت حفريات البعثة الأمريكية في حرم ديميتير وابنتها بيرسيفوني الواقع خارج أسوار قوريني عن كمية كبيرة من الفخار المهشم ومن ضمنها كسر من أواني الطراز الأحمر المستورد ومن أثينا. وحيث أنه لا توجد أواني كاملة فإن هذا المجلد يقدم جميع الكسر الفخارية التي يعرفها الباحث من هذا الموقع. وكانت هذه القطع، في الغالب جميعها صغيرة جدا، وقد إنتشرت بصورة كبيرة عبر الموقع بسبب الإستخدام المتواصل للحرم المقدس والزلازل البركانية الشديدة.

ولم يتم بعد تنظيف الرديم بالكامل في الحرم المقدس، وبما أن الحفريات كانت مكثفة، فإن هذه الكسر الفخارية تزودنا بنموذج ممثل بصورة معقولة لفخار الطراز الأحمر الذي يمكن وجوده في الموقع. وعموما فإن الفخار الإتيكي من الطراز الأحمر من حرم ديمتير وبيرسيفوني المقدس في قوريني أقل وفرة من طراز الفخار الأسود الأتيكي: ونفس النمط العام قد ثبت وجوده في السوق العام (الأجورا) في قوريني ١ والحفريات البريطانية في توكرة ٢.

وتمتد الكسر الفخارية تقريبا طوال العمر الزمني لطراز الفخار الأحمر الأتيكي من حوالي ٥٢٠ إلى حوالي ٣٣٠ ق.م. ولا توجد كسر فخارية في المجموعة تؤرخ في أقدم فترات الطراز الأحمر، ويمكن تأريخ أقدم الكسر الفخارية إلى حوالي ٥٢٠ - ٥٠٠. ويبدو أن رقبة جرة (أمفورا) من طراز أ(١) وجزء من بيليكي (٥) هما من إنتاج مجموعة بيونير، ولكن معظم الكسر الفخارية من هذه المرحلة تعود إلى أواني صغيرة الحجم مثل

١

الإمبراطورية الرومانية القرن الأول حتى القرن الرابع الميلادي (٧٧٦ – ٨٠٤)

إن العملات الإمبراطورية التي عثر عليها في حرم ديمتير المقدس ليست كثيرة ، وجرى التعرف على قطعتي عملة يعود تاريخهما إلى ما بعد عصر أغسطس وهما قطعتان ليستا من ولاية برقة (٧٧٣ ، ٧٦٠ أ). وليس هناك أدنى شك أن برقة قد دخلت في فلك النظام المالي الروماني في القرن الأول ق.م. وفي الواقع كانت عملات برقة في القرن الثاني الميلادي تتكون من فئات رومانية مثل الدينار الفضي وفئات عديدة أخرى من البرونز.

ولعل العدد الإجمالي الصغير للعملات الإمبراطورية الذي عثر عليه يعود إلى حجمها الكبير : وكل قطعة عملة حتى عام ٢٧٠ ميلادية هي من البرونز ، وأن فئات العملة الرومانية البرونزية المعروفة هي أكبر حجما من عملات العصر الهلينستي المتأخرة ، ولذا فمن الصعب ضياعها . وبالمقارنة فإن الفترة الواقعة في السنوات الأخيرة من القرن الثالث وحتى منتصف القرن الرابع قد أنتجت عددا كبيرا من العملات ، وأصغر حجما ومن السهل ضياعها .

تنتهي العملات الإمبراطورية فجأة مع قدوم قسطنطين الثاني وجوليان . شيء ما حدث للحياة في الحرم المقدس ، ويدل الدليل الأثري أن ذلك كان بفعل زلزال عام ٣٦٥ ميلادي .

وتبين عملات حرم ديمتير المقدس بوضوح أن العبادة قد توقفت هناك وحتى الزيارات العرضية ، ولهذا فإننا نتوقع على الأقل العثور على بعض المفقودات الغريبة المتبعثرة وبدلا من ذلك لا يوجد شيء على الإطلاق سوى قطعتي عملة من عهد هرقل وأخرى قطعة عملة واحدة إسلامية طائشة بعد ٢٥٠ عام .

التأكد من تأريخها الزمني . وبإستطاعتنا تأريخ عملات كليوباترة وأنطونيوس بشيء من الدقة فقط وذلك قبل العملات التي صدرت بإسم كل من أغسطس وتيبيريوس .

ولا بد أن معظم فئات العملات الصغيرة التي إستمرت كانت تلك العملات البطلمية ، ولكن ربما جددت قيمتها من جديد كي تتناسب مع النظام الروماني . والدليل على إستمراية إستخدامها هو ندرة عملات الولايات الرومانية والتي لم تستطع أن تزود الدعم المالي الكافي كي تكون البديل للبرونز الأقدم . وأن نسبة عملات الولايات الصغيرة بين عملات حرم ديمتير المقدس شيء مألوف ويجب أن لا ينظر إليه بأهمية خاصة بالنسبة للنشاطات في الحرم المقدس .

والمرحلة الثانية التي ظهرت فيها العملات الإمبراطورية في منطقة برقة كانت في القرن الثاني الميلادي ، ومنها العملات الفضية والبرونزية تحمل على وجهيها أساطير إغريقية وأنماط محلية للألـه آمون . ولفترة طويلة كانت عملات تراجان وهادريان وماركوس اوريليوس يعتقد أنها سكت في قيسارية في كبادوشيا ، وذلك إلى جانب عملات شبيهة كانت أنماطها ترجع إلى ولايات أخرى في الإمبراطورية .

وأما الآن وبعد الفحص الدقيق للطراز والمادة وأنماط الإنتشار يجعل من المؤكد أن نسبتها إلى تلك الأقاليم فرضية لا يمكنها الثبات . ومن الممكن أن هذه العملات كانت قد سكت في قوريني ، حيث جرى سكها على قوالب قطعت في روما ، ولكن ربما أن الإحتمال الأقوى أن هذه العملات سكت كي تصدر إلى منطقة برقة . وتنبذ الدراسات الحديثة الرأي القائل بأن التقسيم التقليدي بين العملات الرومانية وعملات الولايات الرومانية ("اليوناني الإمبراطوري") ربما تخفي سك روما لعملات كان الغرض منها في الأساس الإستخدام في مواطن أخرى .

٥

الغالب . وعلى أية حال لا توجد عملات فضية أو ذهبية على الإطلاق كي تثبت مثل تلك التقدمات .

مسكوكات إغريقية أخرى (٧٦٠أ – ٧٧٣)

. مع أن العملات البرونزية من خارج منطقة برقة تبدو كأنها لم تدخلها بأية كمية فإن خصائص العملات تبين أن الأنماط ربما تظهر عندما يتوفر المزيد من الأدلة . توجد قطعة عملة من يهودا (٧٦٧) ، وأخرى نصف دراخمة من العصبة الأخية (٧٦٤) . ومن الخصائص المميزة لعملات منطقة برقة هو الغياب الكامل لعملات مصر البطلمية حتى السكات المتأخرة جدا أي عهد كليوباترة السابعة والإمبراطور أغسطس . ويبدو أن صعوبة الإتصال بين منطقة برقة ومصر ، سواء كان بالبر أو بالبحر ، كان قد حد بشدة من عملية تبادل العملات .

وكانت العملات القادمة من الغرب أقل ندرة . وفي الواقع أن العملات العديدة من قرطاجة وصقلية البونيقية ، التي توجد في جميع أرجاء غرب البحر المتوسط وحتى في دالماشيا ، فهي غير معروفة بالكامل . ويدل هذا على العزلة التجارية لمنطقة برقة عن كل من مصر ومنطقة المدن الثلاث (طرابلس) التي أشار اليها فولفورد ١٤ .

عملات برقة الرومانية ، القرن الأول ق.م إلى

القرن الثاني الميلادي (٧٣٧ – ٧٦٠)

ظهر إصدار العملات الرومانية للولايات بصورة خاصة في قوريني أو لأجل منطقة برقة على مرحلتين . بدأت المرحلة الأولى في وقت غير محدد بعد توقف إصدار العملات البطلمية . وبسبب نقص معلوماتنا عن الحكام الذين وقعوا على عملات هذه فلا نستطيع

٤

الفترتان الثانية والثالثة حوالي ٤٧٥- ٣٠٨ ق.م
(٨٨-١٥٤ ، ٧٢٦-٧٣٢)

يوجد تضاؤل سريع للعملات مما يشير إلى إنتهاء التقدمات المالية ، وبعدها عثر على القليل من العملات الفضية مهما كانت وفرة البرونز . وإن إكتشاف أربع قطع عملة ذهبية شيء غير مألوف بصورة خاصة . وأن تاريخها المتأخر يدل على أنه ليست لها علاقة بكنز العملات الفضية .

ومع نهاية الفترة الثالثة تبدأ العملات البرونزية في مدن برقة الثلاثة ، وجميع العملات منذ هذا التاريخ من البرونز تقريبا . وحوالي ثلاثة أرباع الأنماط المعروفة سكت مع نهاية القرن الرابع وحتى بداية القرن الأول ق.م ممثلة إلى درجة ما ، مع أن الغالبية العظمى من العملات متأخرة .

الفترة الرابع بطليموس آبيون : حوالي ٣٠٨ – ٩٦ ق.م
(١٥٥ – ٧٢٥ ، ٧٣٣ – ٧٣٦)

أكتشفت أربعة عملات فضية فقط ، واحدة غير مألوفة قسمت فيها قطعة من فئة الدراخمتين إلى أربع أرباع . وحوالي ثلاثة أرباع العملات البرونزية من حرم ديمتير المقدس هي وحدات صغيرة تعود إلى عصر الملوك الثلاثة المتأخرين الذين حكموا في منطقة برقة وهم يوايرجيتيس الثاني ، سوتير الثاني ، وآبيون .

وتشير البقايا الأثرية من القرنين الثالث والثاني ق.م إلى أنه بينما كان هناك توسع كبير في الحرم المقدس كانت التقدمات النذرية أقل !! وكان لا بد من تمويل عملية التوسع بشكل ما ، وربما يمكننا التخمين أن التقدمات عندها قد أخذت شكل الدعم المالي في

٣

عثرنا عليها . وتؤرخ نفس النسبة تقريبا من العملات في الفترة الثانية . وعملاتنا من الفترتين الثالثة والرابعة قليلة جدا مما يجعلنا نعتقد أنها مفقودات عشوائية .

المرحلة الأولى : ٥١٠ - ٤٧٥ ق.م (١ - ٨٧)

تعود معظم عملات المجلد إلى الفترة الأولى ، والعديد منها من فئة الثلاث دراخمات وبعض الفئات الصغيرة الكثيرة الأخرى . وجاءت عملات القرن السادس والنصف الأول من القرن الخامس من موقع أو أكثر غير مكتشف . وتفسر التقدمات غير المنتظمة للمؤمنين بالأهلة تركيب المجموعة اللافت للنظر ، والتي تمتد طوال عشرات السنين ، وهي الأغنى من الفئات المتوسطة ، ولكنها متفرقة في تمثيلها للعدد الكبير للفئات التي لا بد أنها كانت سكت بصورة متسلسلة خلال تلك الفترة . وليس بالإمكان أن يحدد بدقة متى توقف سك هذه التقدمات المالية . ويدل توزيع العملات أنها إستمرت حتى الفترة الثانية أي منتصف القرن الخامس ق.م.

رتبت عملات الفترة الأولى في أربع مجموعات والتي ربما تمثل نظام تطور سكها :
١ -أ) على وجه العملة ثمرة نبات سلفيوم (لم يعثر عليه في الحفريات) أو نبات ، وعلى ظهر العملة ضربه سندان ، ب) كما هو الحال في أ مع إضافة شكل في أعلى وجه العملة ج) و كما هو الحال في ب لكن الشكل بين حبتي فاكهة،و٢) له نمط الوجه الخلفي للعملة

وأن الدراخمة ونصف الدراخمة شائعة نسبيا في المجموعات المرتبة في كتالوج المتحف البريطاني الذي وضعه روبنسون ولكن ليس من حرم ديمتير المقدس . وما زالت فئات العملة الأصغر أكثر ندرة من بين العملات وربما يعزى ذلك إلى صعوبة ملاحظتها في التربة أثناء عملية الحفر .

خلاصة ١

منذ أواخر القرن السادس ق.م وحتى منتصف القرن الرابع الميلادي كان حرم ديميتر المقدس يجذب المؤمنين بعبادتها والذين تضمنت تقدماتهم عملات . وكشفت أعمال التنقيب في حرم ديمتير المقدس في قوريني بين عام ١٩٦٩ و ١٩٧٨ عن ٨٣٤ قطعة عملة . وكانت جميع العملات في حالة إنتشار عشوائية وكأنها حالات ضياع عادية ، ولكن من الواضح أنه يوجد لدينا على الأقل بقايا لعملات فضية مجتمعة ، وأنه ليس من المستحيل أن بعض العملات البرونزية أيضا تمثل تلك العملات المجتمعة في مكان واحد .

ترجع معظم العملات إلى العصر القديم الكلاسيكي والبطلمي فقد سكت في قوريني . ومثل الحفريات الأخرى في منطقة برقة فإن القليل جدا من عملاتها أتى من أماكن سك أخرى في منطقة برقة أو بلاد اليونان ، وبصورة ملحوظة سكة البطالة في الإسكندرية . وحتى عشرات القطع الفضية من العصر القديم وأوائل العصر الكلاسيكي لا تتضمن قطعة عملة واحدة سكت خارج قوريني مما يشير إلى أنه في هذه الحقبة الزمنية كان المعدن الثمين مثل البرونز واسع الإنتشار ويوجد محليا بصورة كبيرة .

عملات يونانية من برقة

أكثر ظاهرة واضحة من مسكوكات منطقة برقة هي العدد الكبير للعملات البرونزية - من القطع قليلة القيمة نسبيا والتي يقترن وجودها بكمية غير عادية وغير متناسبة من المعدن الثمين المبكر . وتشكل العملات الفضية من العصرين القديم والكلاسيكي المبكر من الفترة الأولى الغير مألوفة نسبيا ٨١,٥٪ من العملات الفضية التي

١

Plates

MINT OF CYRENE (1–25)　　　　　　　　　　　　　　　　　　　　　　　PLATE 1

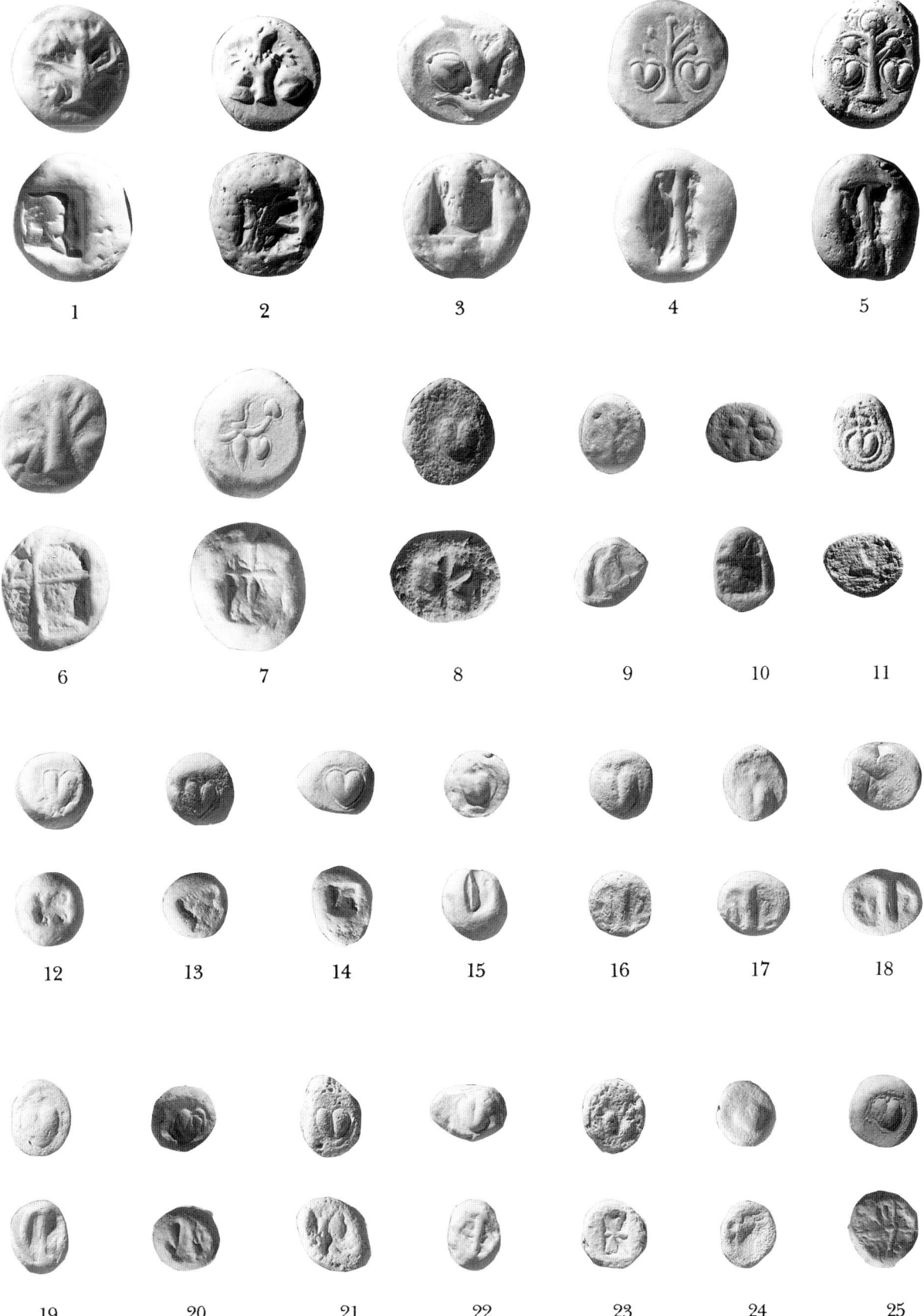

PLATE 2 — MINT OF CYRENE (26–56)

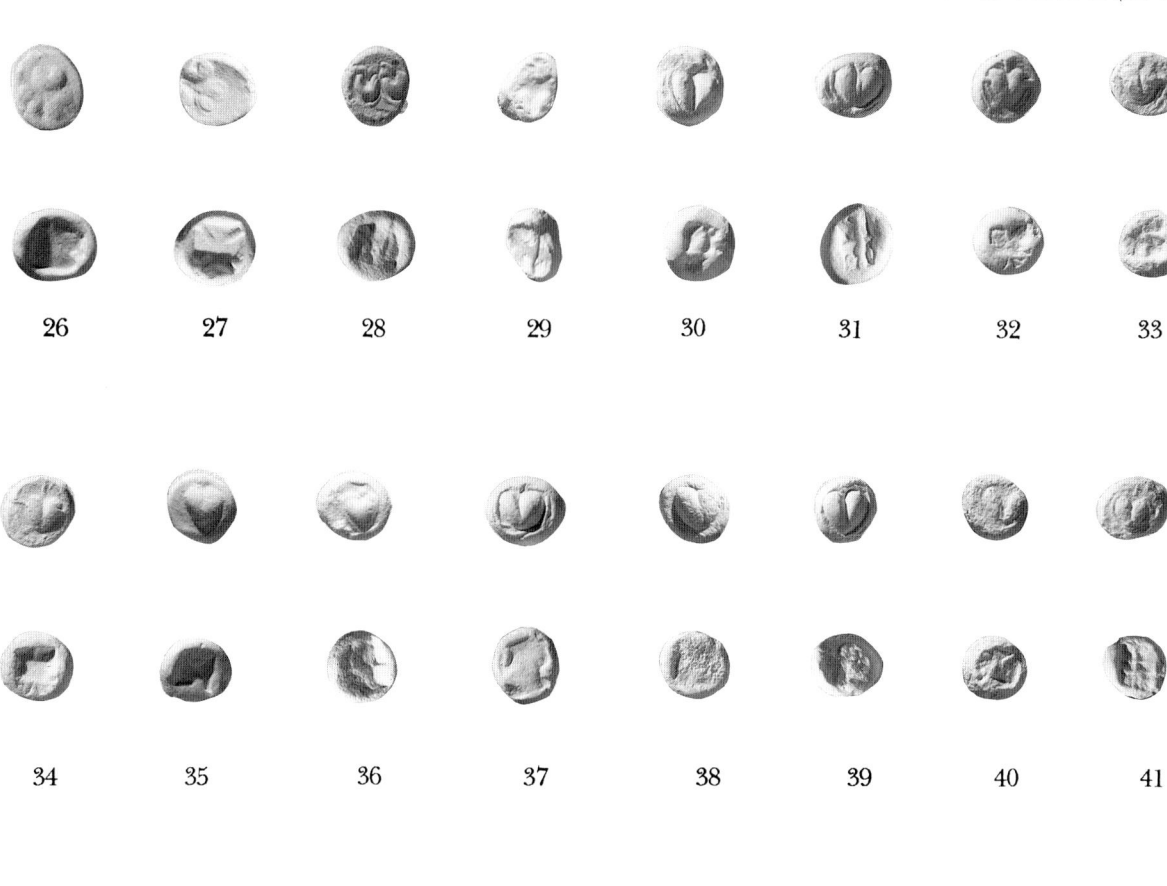

26   27   28   29   30   31   32   33

34   35   36   37   38   39   40   41

42   43   44   45   46   47   48

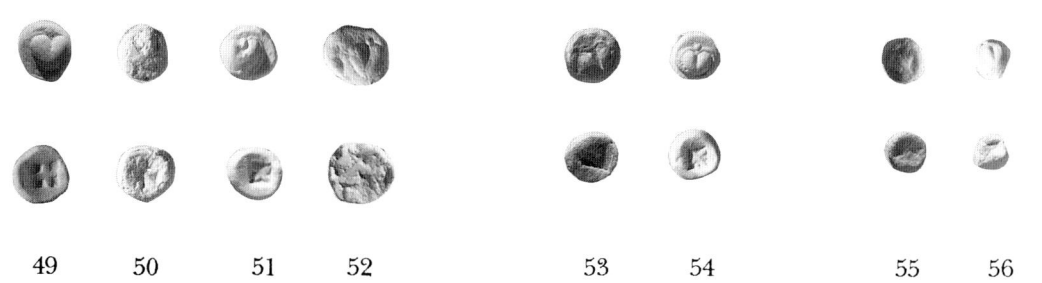

49   50   51   52   53   54   55   56

MINT OF CYRENE (57–80) PLATE 3

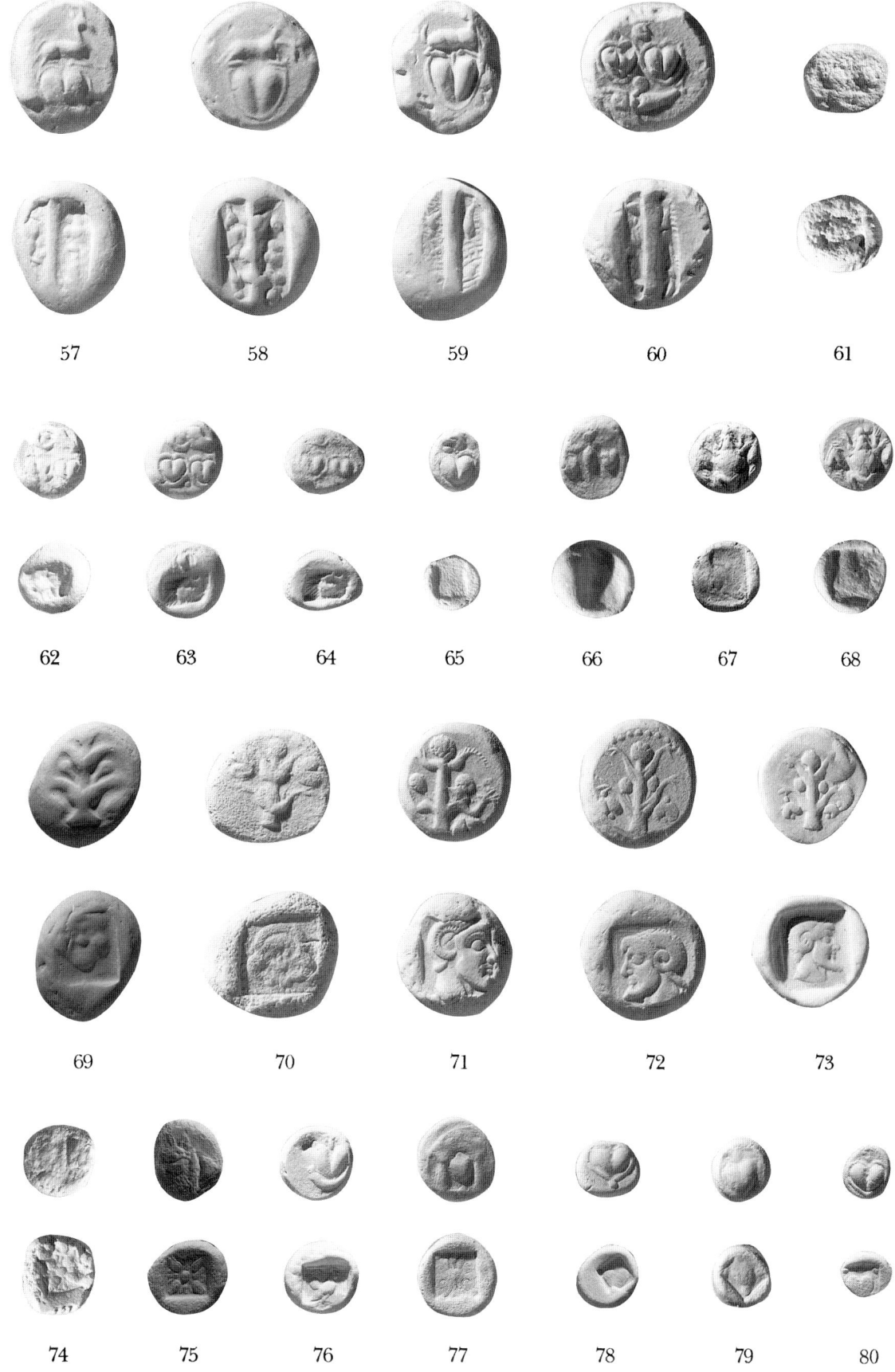

PLATE 4 MINT OF CYRENE (*81–108*)

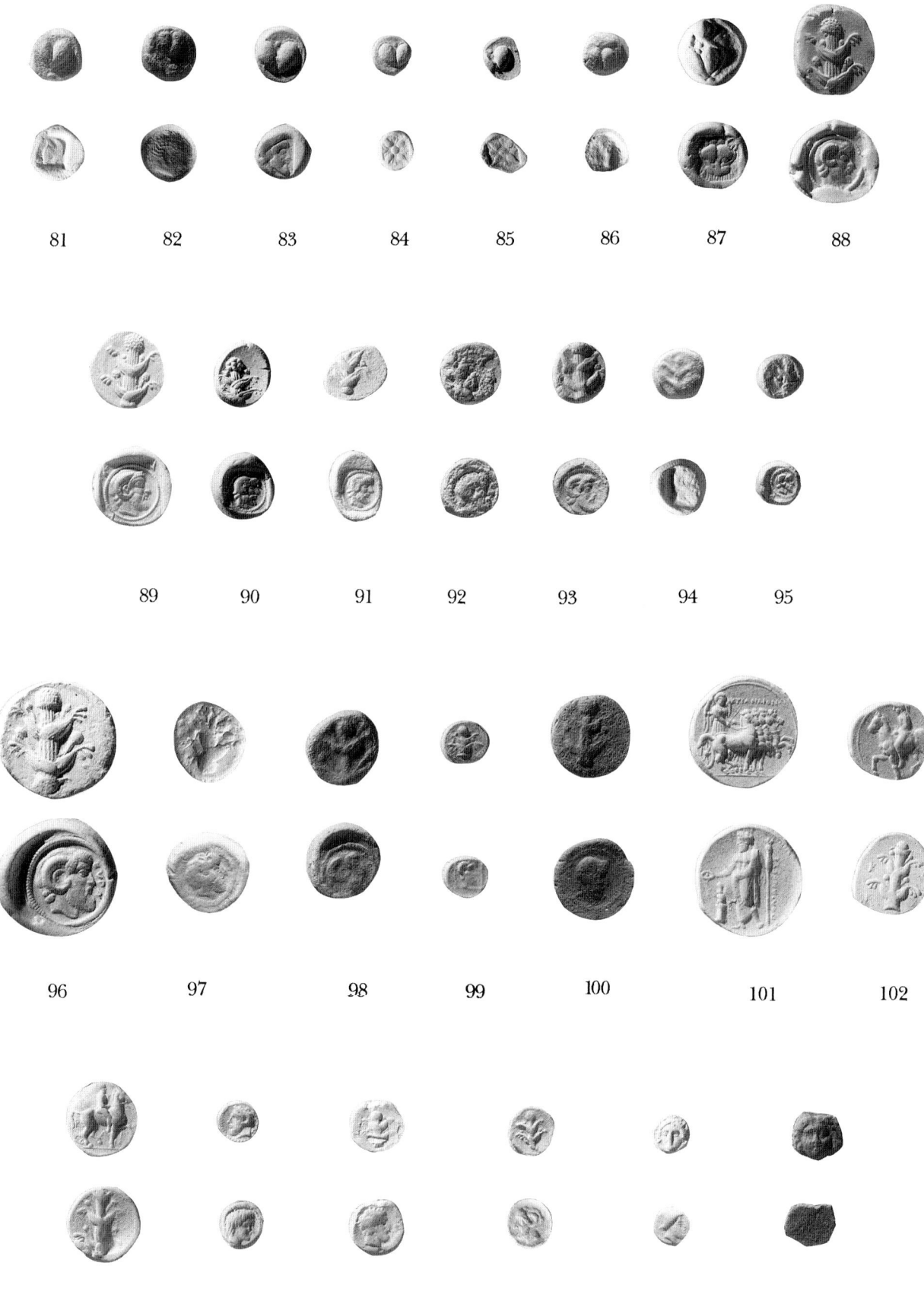

MINT OF CYRENE (111–158) PLATE 5

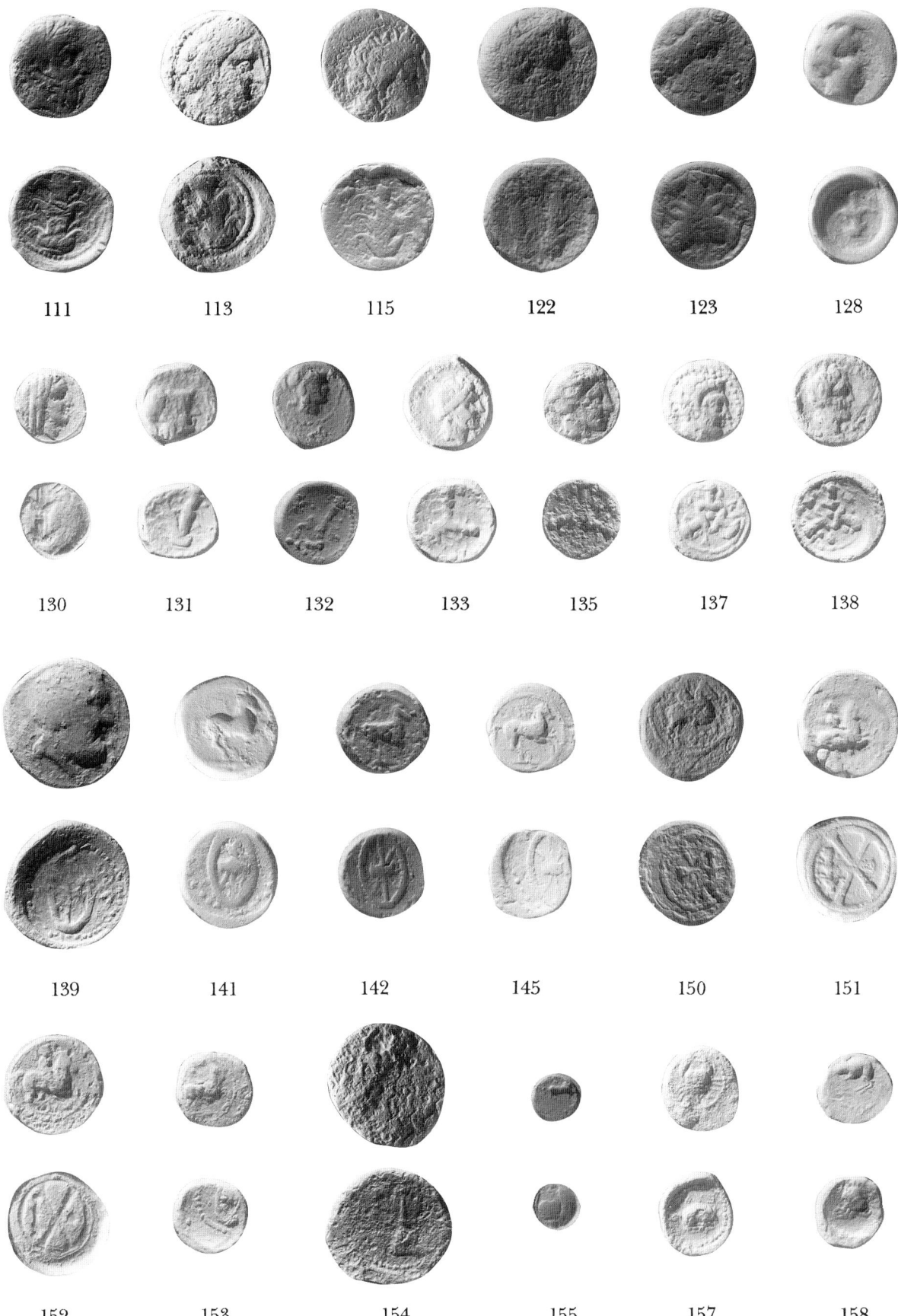

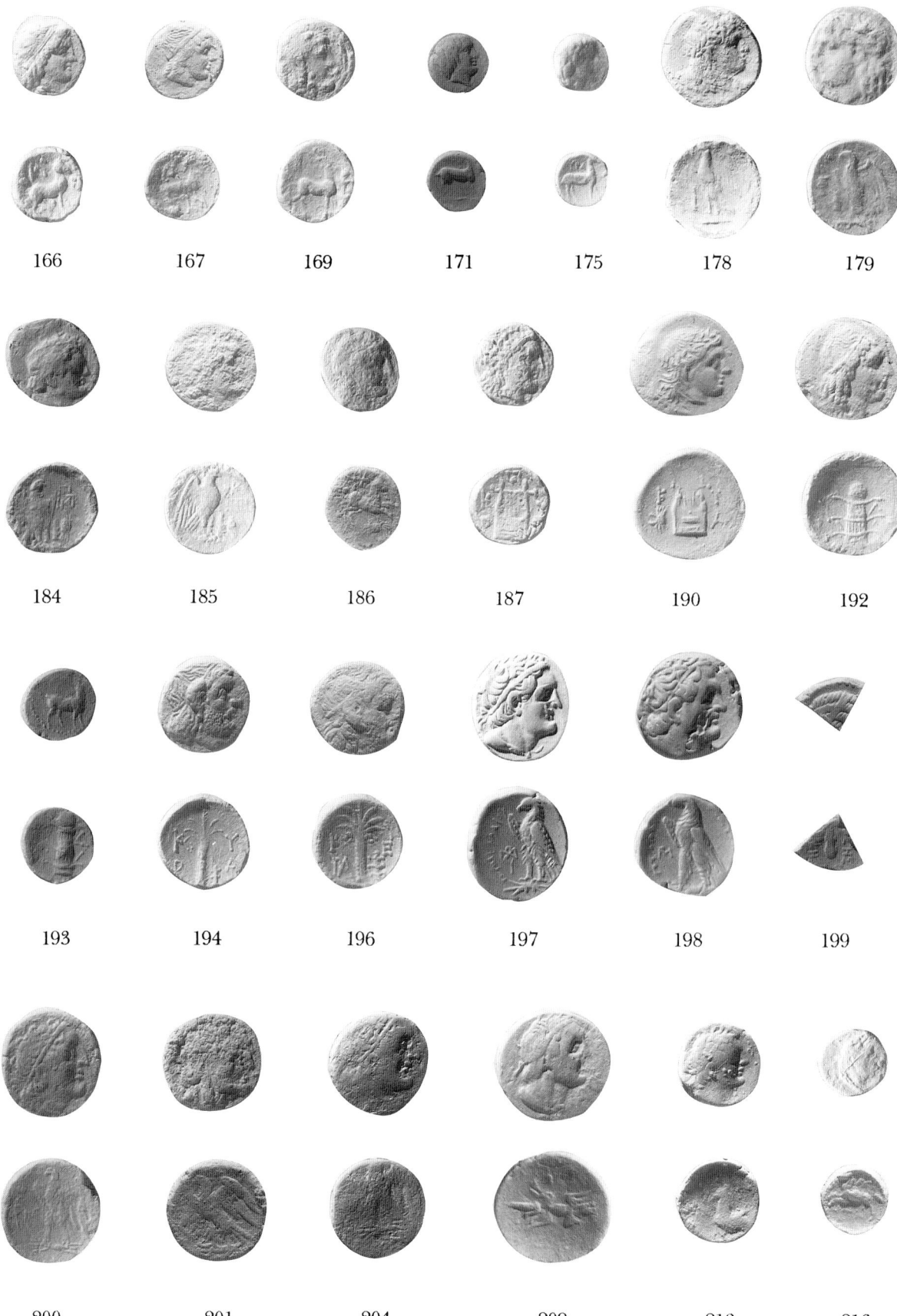

MINT OF CYRENE (*218–278*) PLATE 7

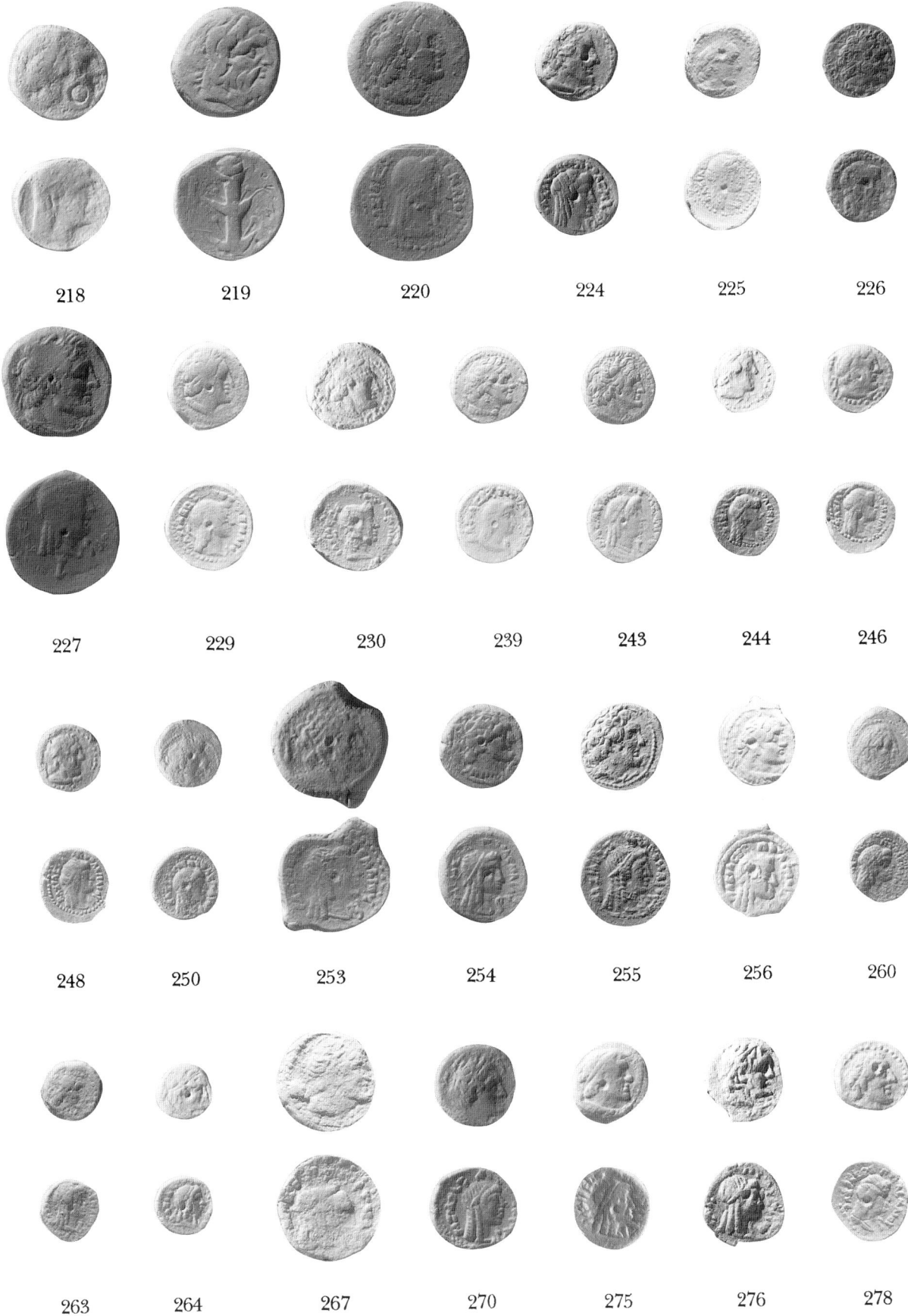

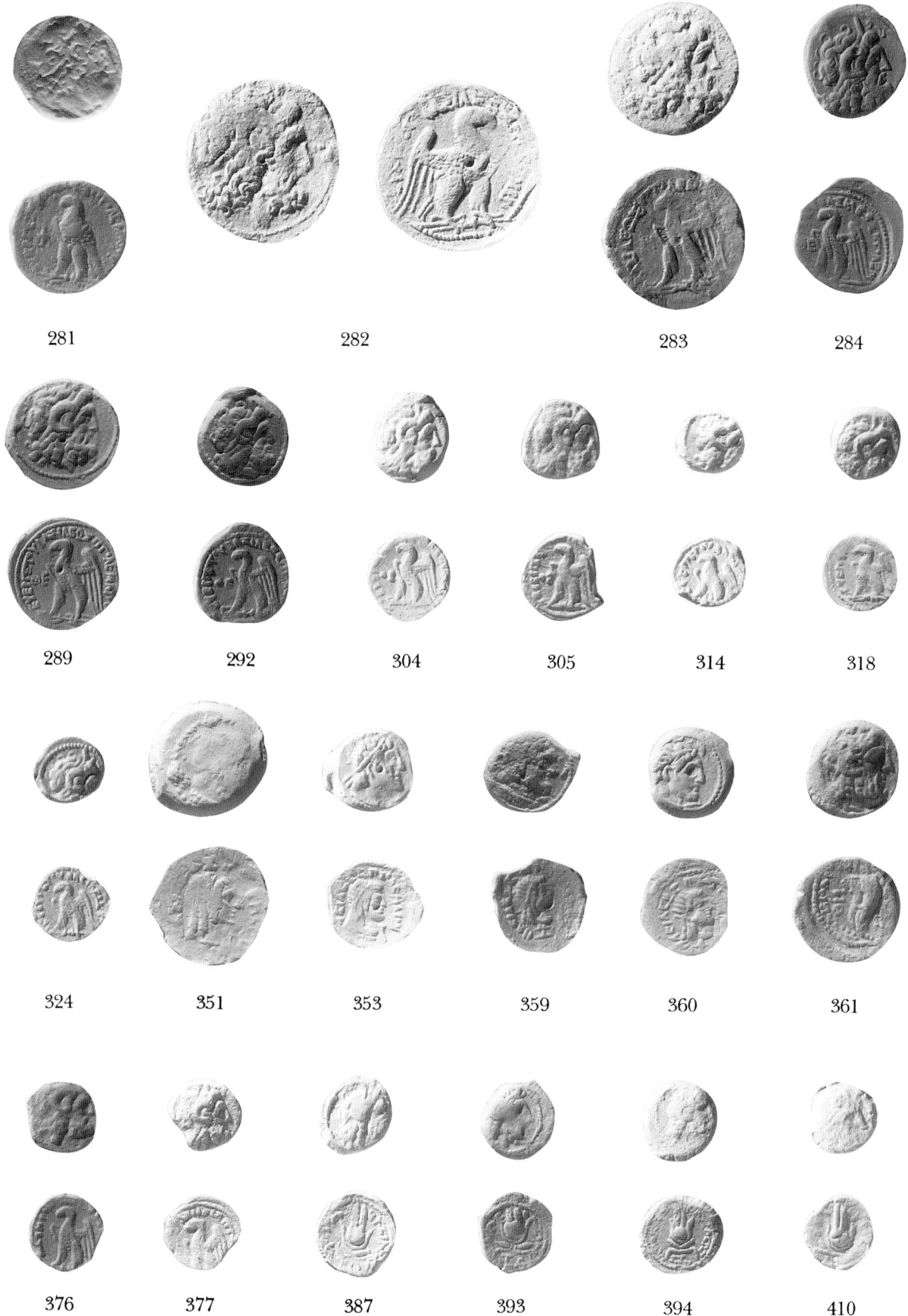

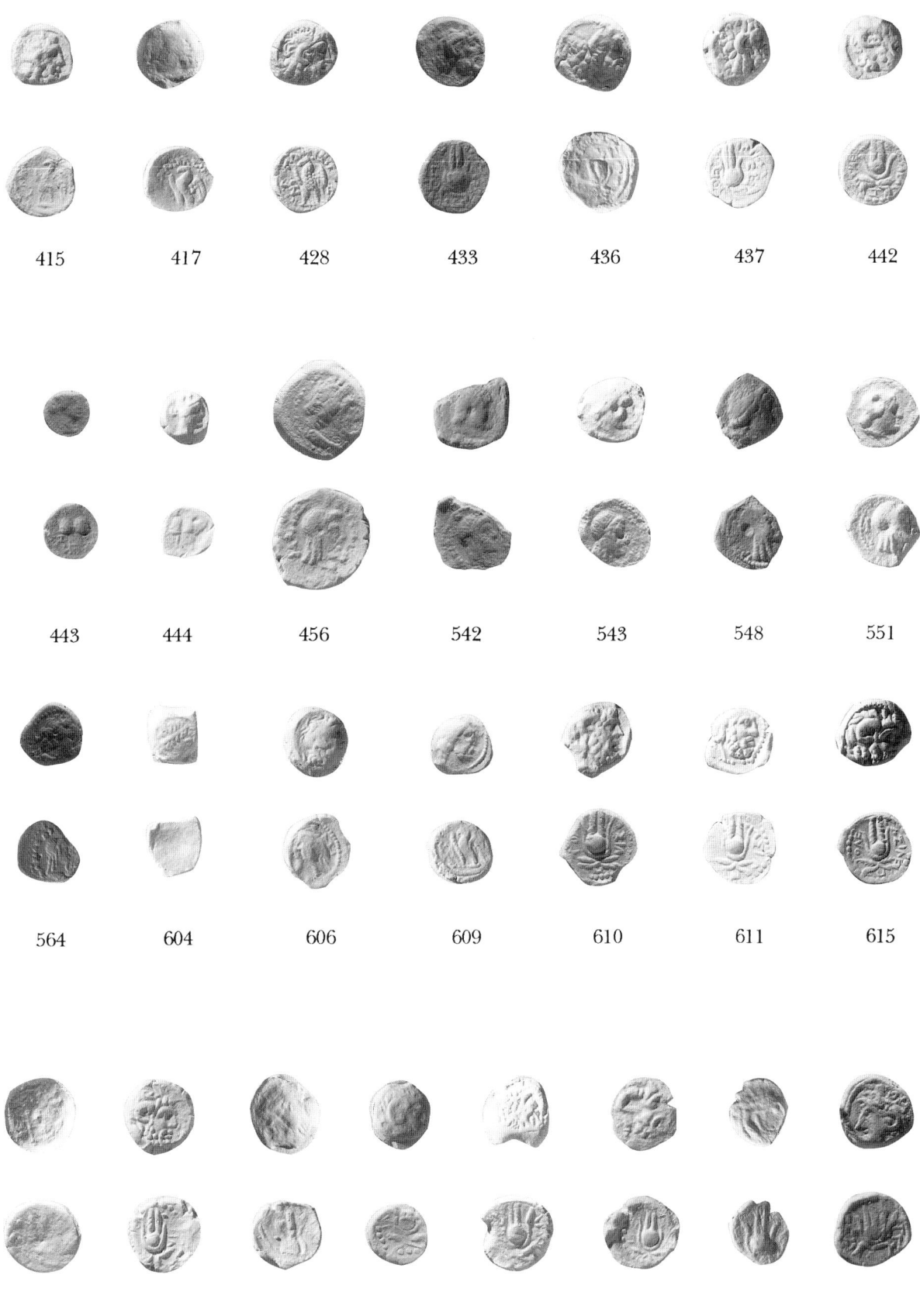

PLATE 10   MINT OF BARCE (*726, 727*), EUESPERIDES (*728–736*), ROMAN CYRENAICA (*737–759*)

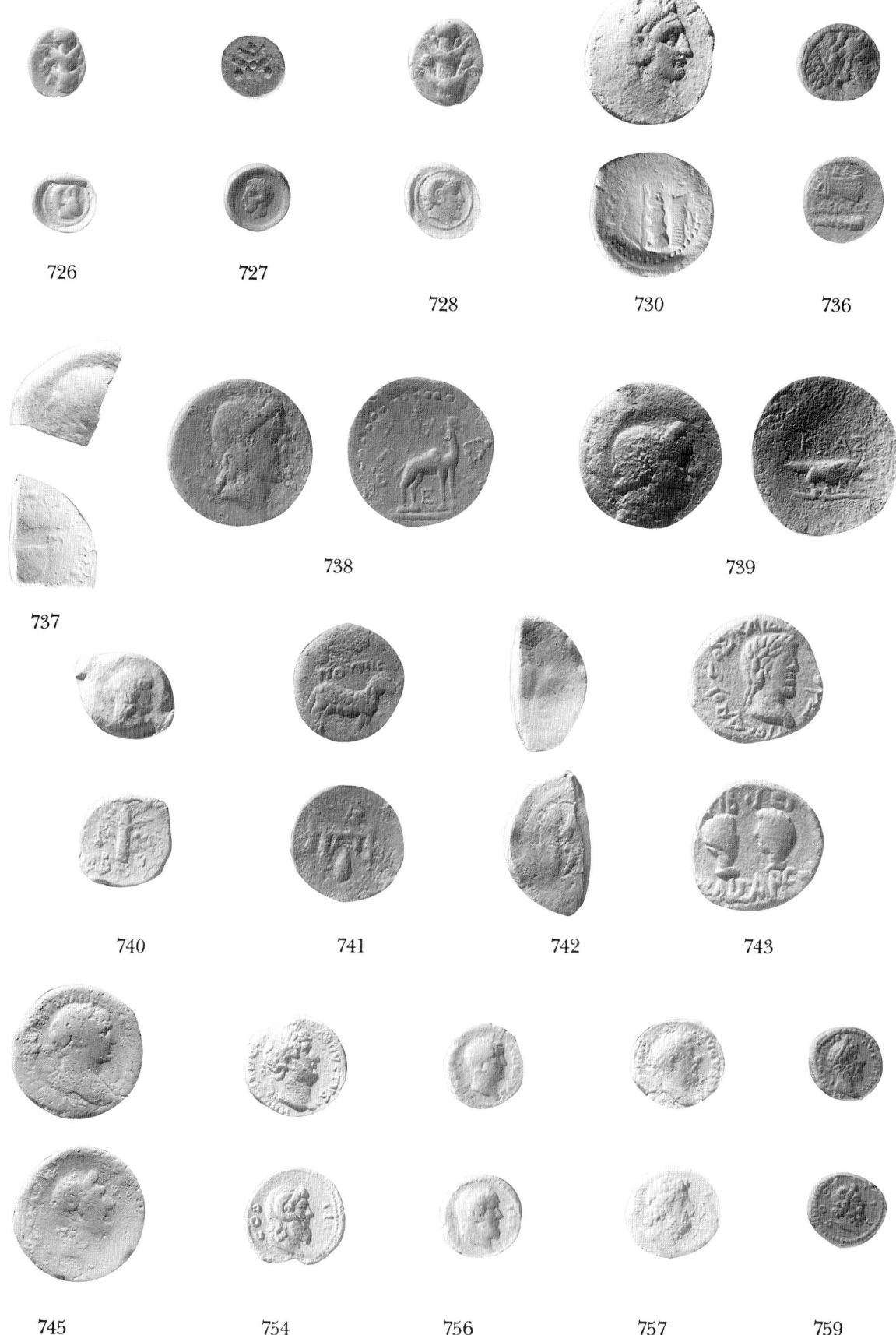

GREEK COINS OUTSIDE CYRENAICA (*760A–773*), ROMAN (*778–795*), LATER (*803, 805*)   PLATE 11

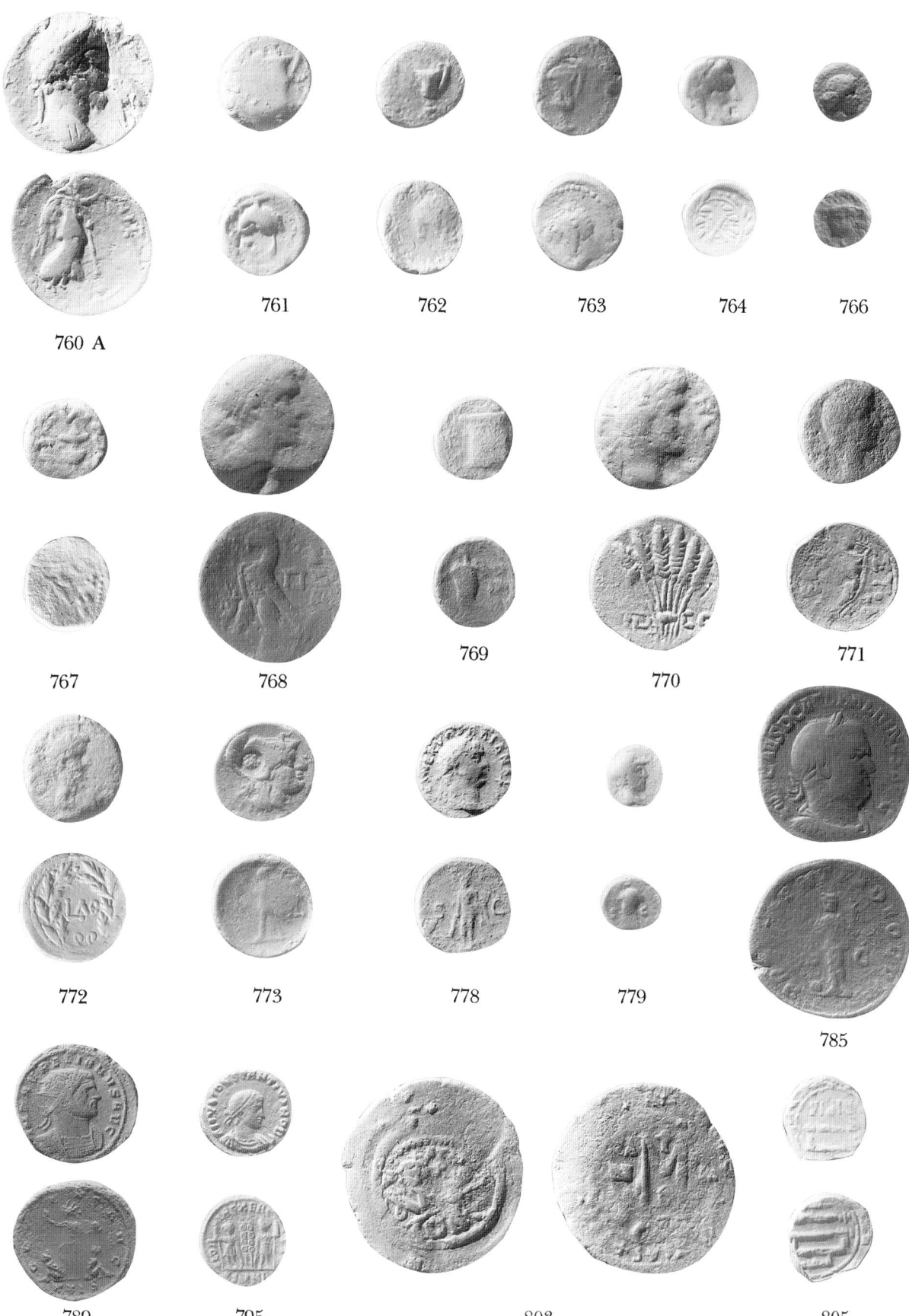

PLATE 12   APPENDIX: UNPUBLISHED FINDS FROM EUESPERIDES

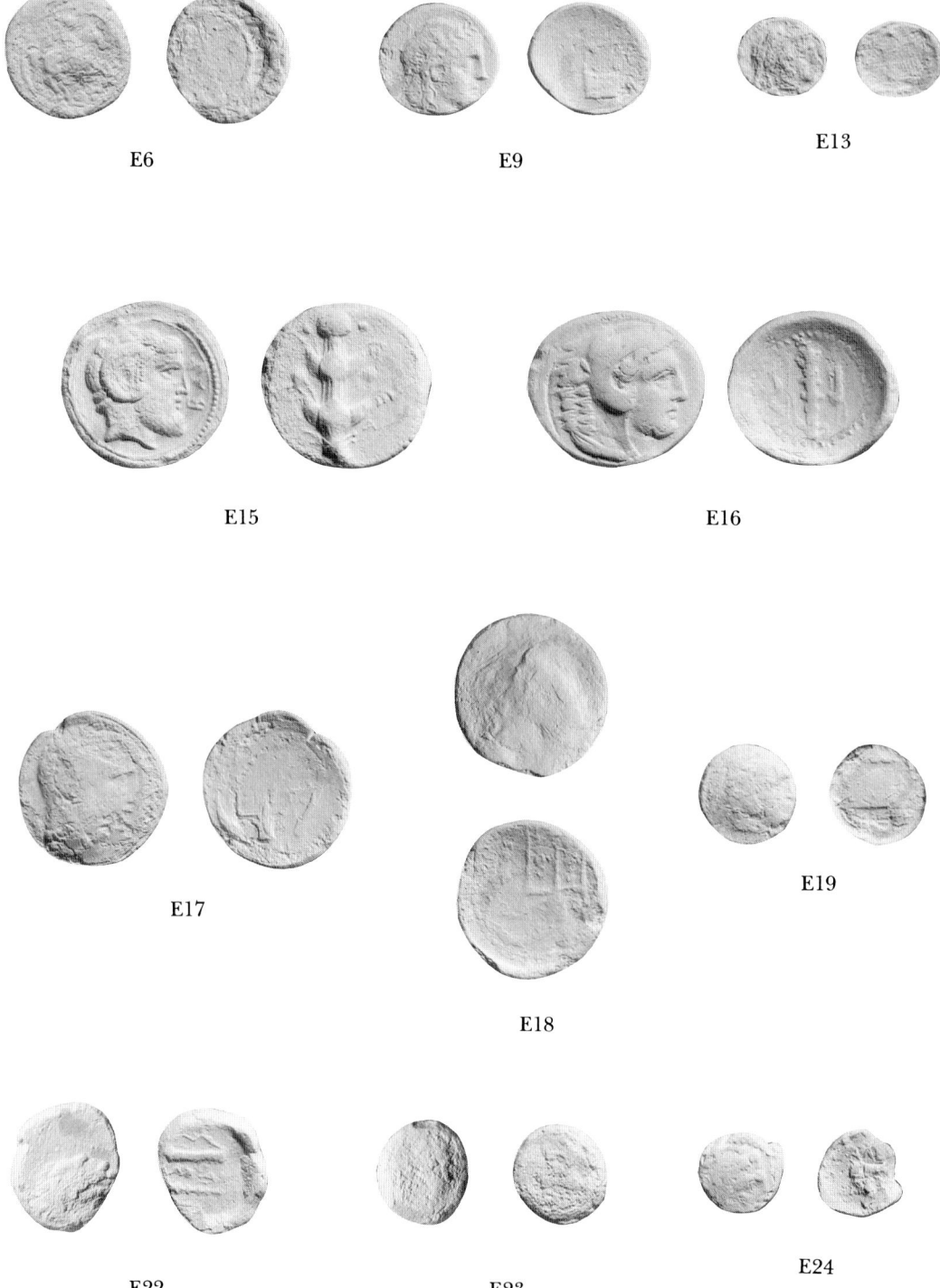

E6   E9   E13

E15   E16

E17   E18   E19

E22   E23   E24

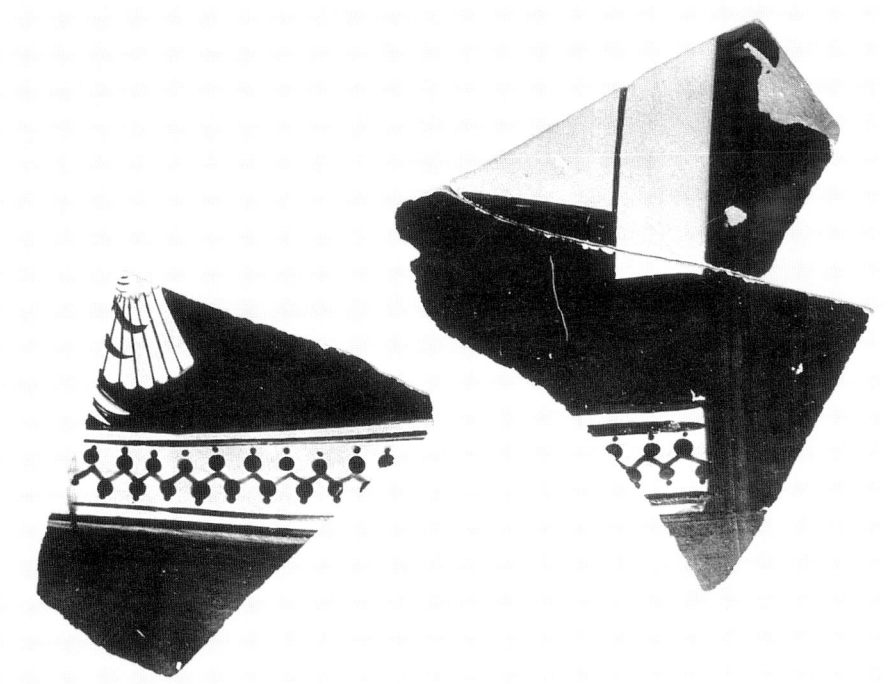

3

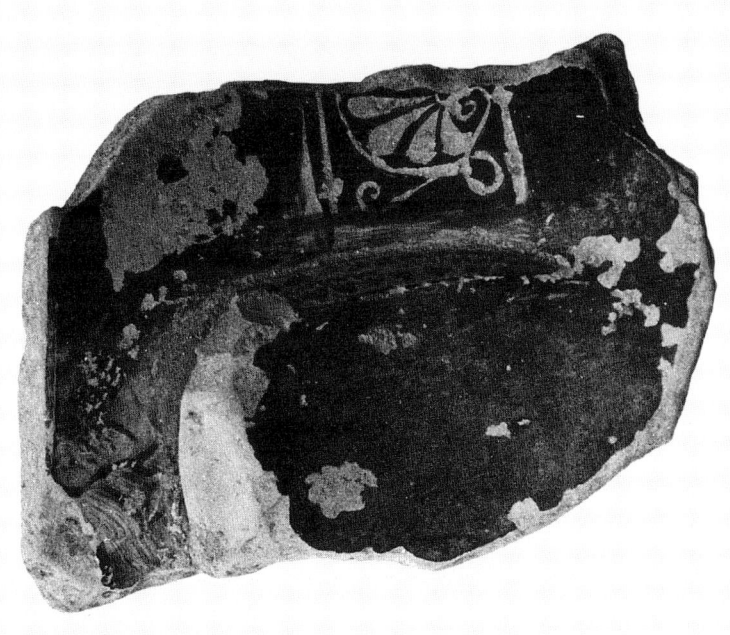

2

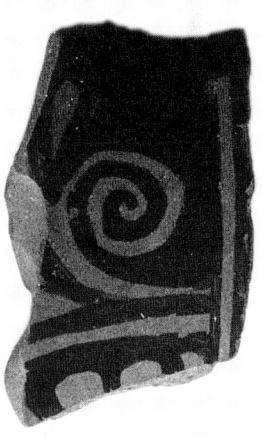

4

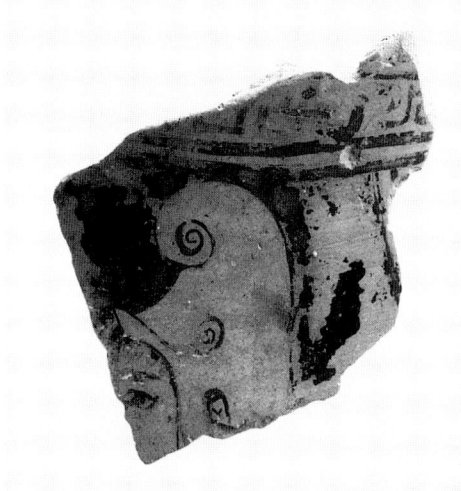

5

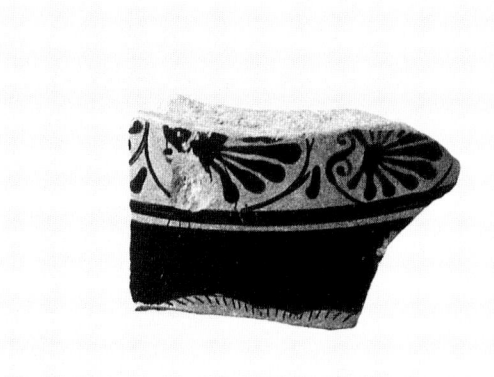

6

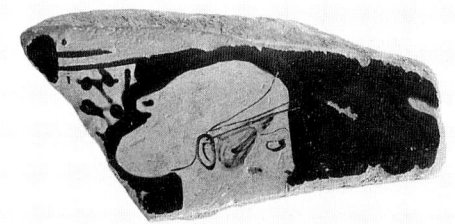

7

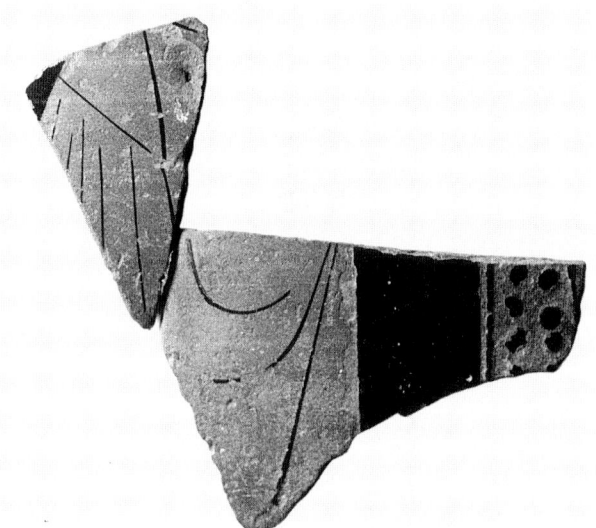

8

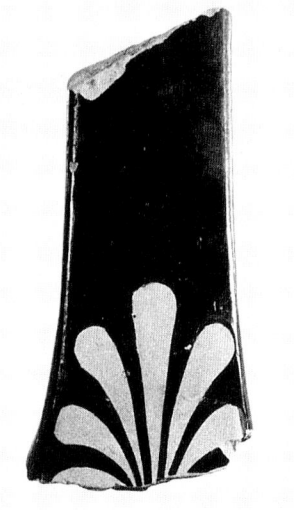

9

1:1

PELIKAI (10–14) PLATE 15

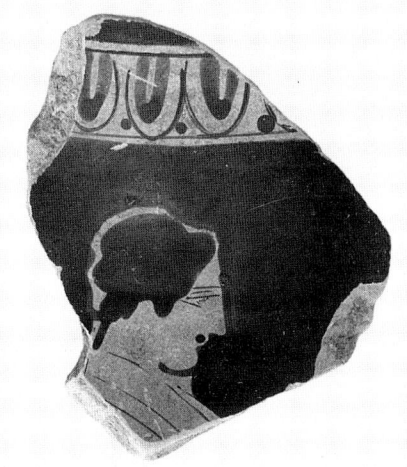

10

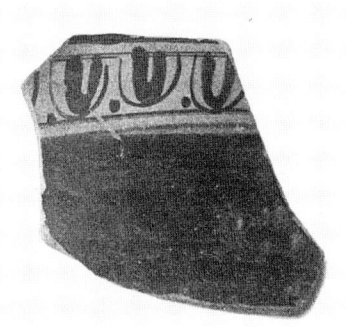

11

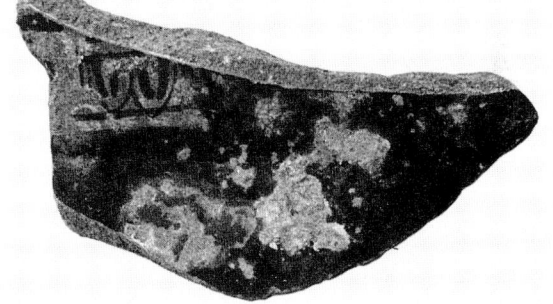

12

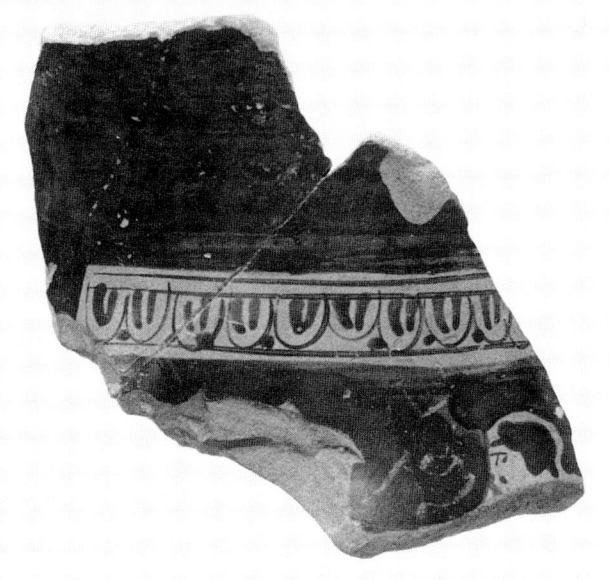

13

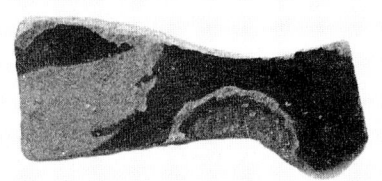

14

1:1

PLATE 16 LEBETES GAMIKOI (15–17)

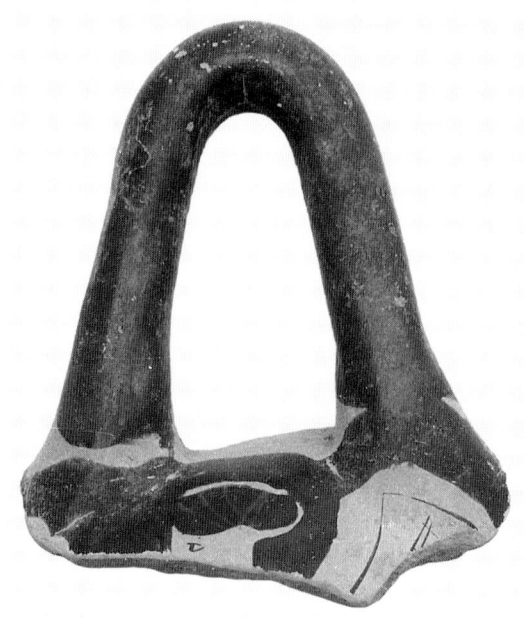

15

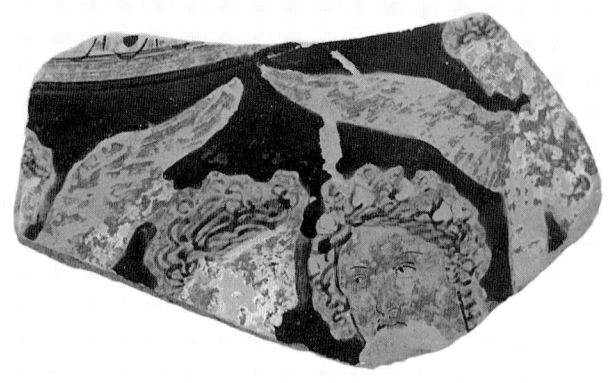

16

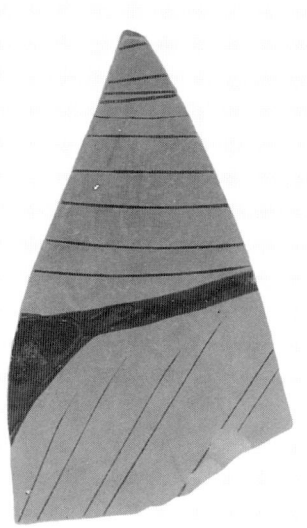

17

1:1

COLUMN-KRATERS OR STAMNOI (*18–20*) PLATE 17

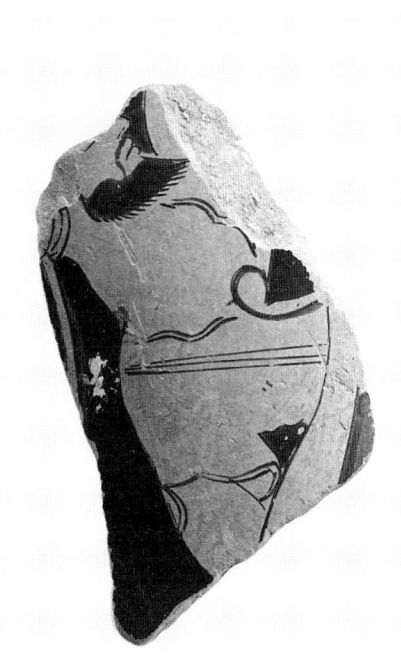

19

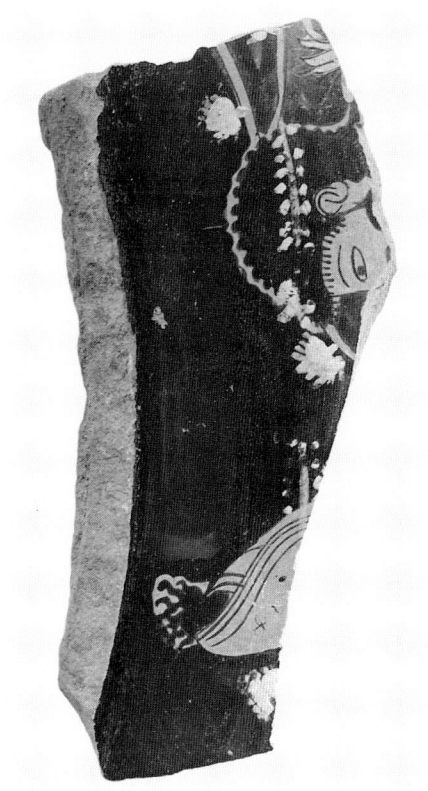

20

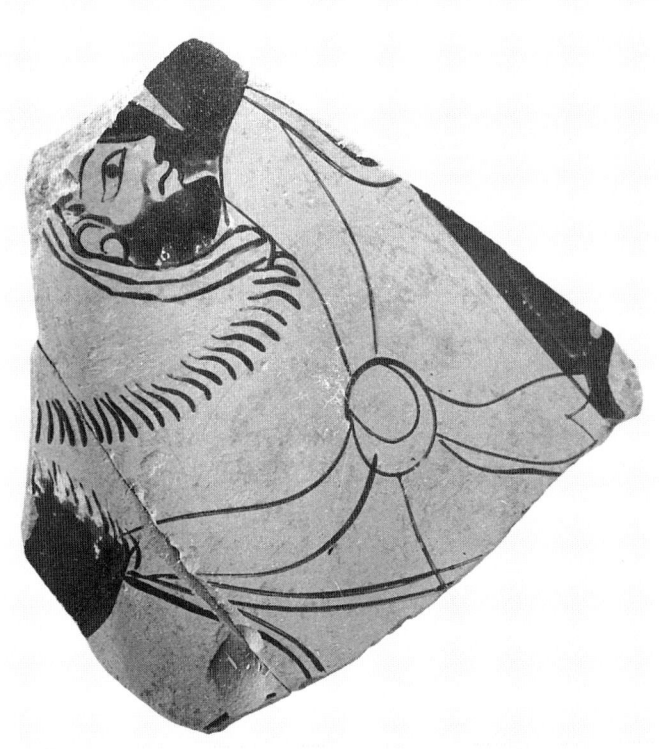

18

PLATE 18 COLUMN-KRATERS OR STAMNOI (21A–23)

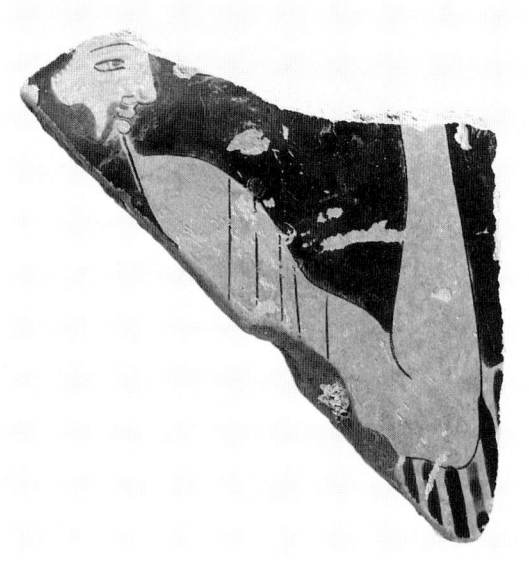

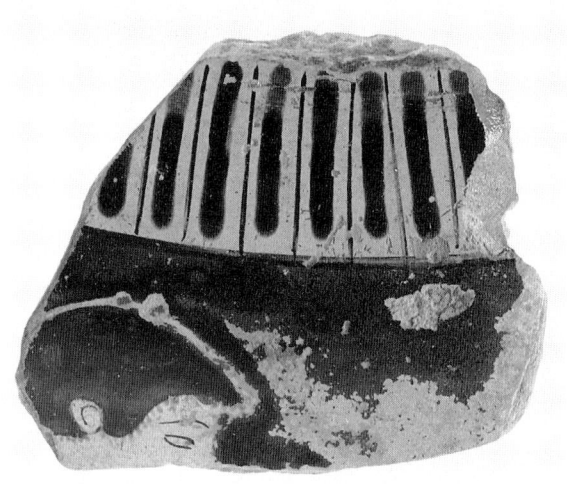

21 a b

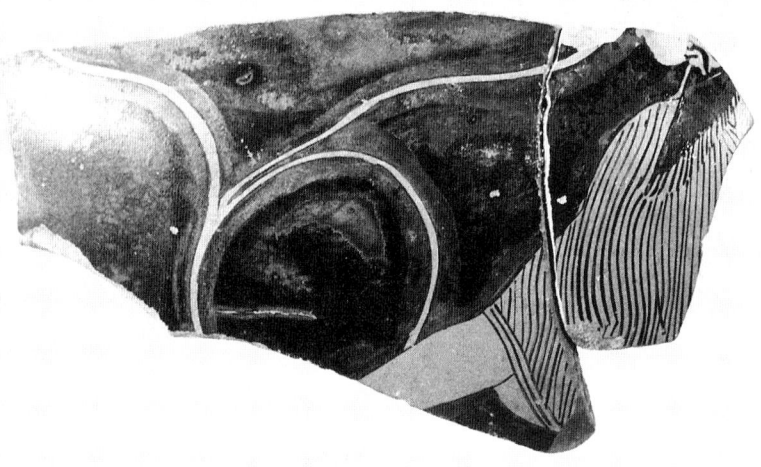

23

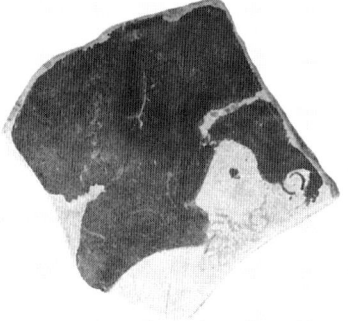

22

1:1

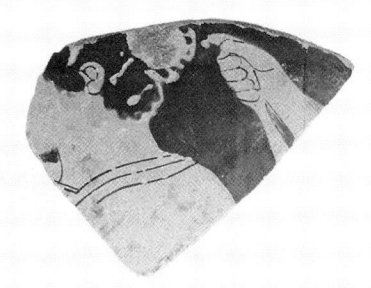

24

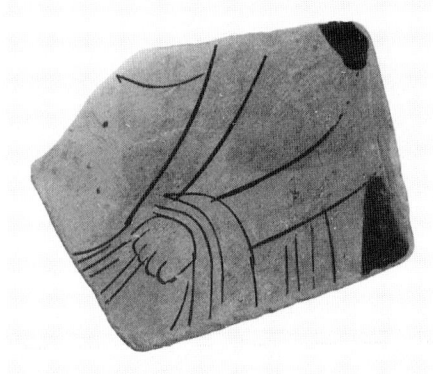

25

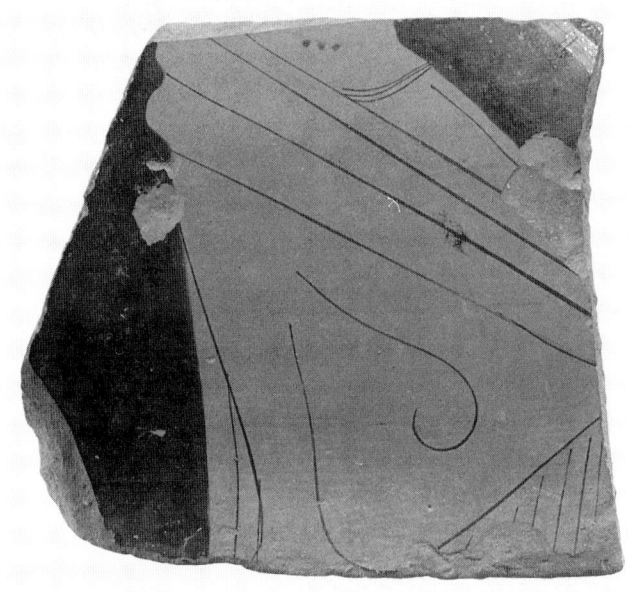

26

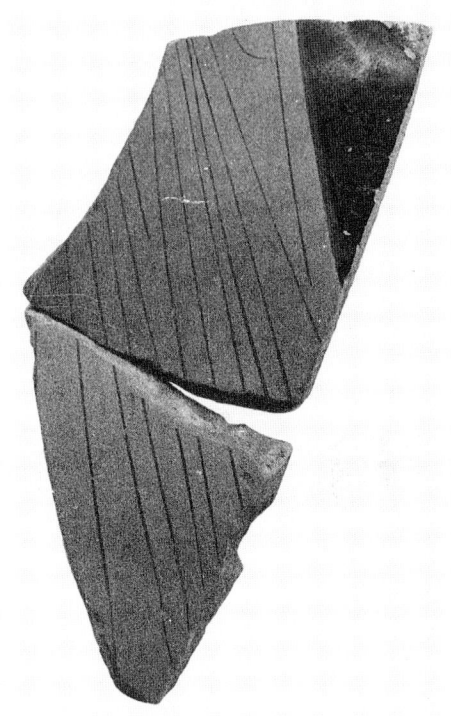

27

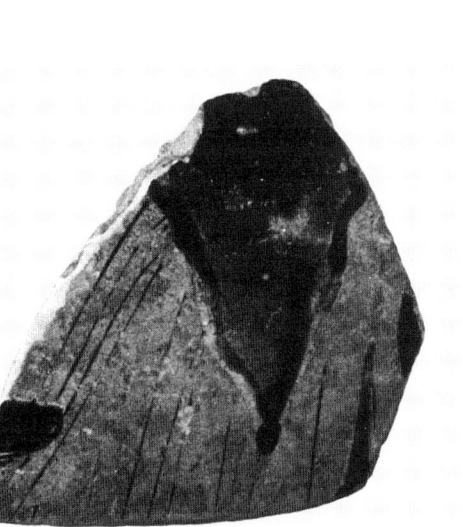

28

1:1

PLATE 20 COLUMN-KRATERS OR STAMNOI (29–33)

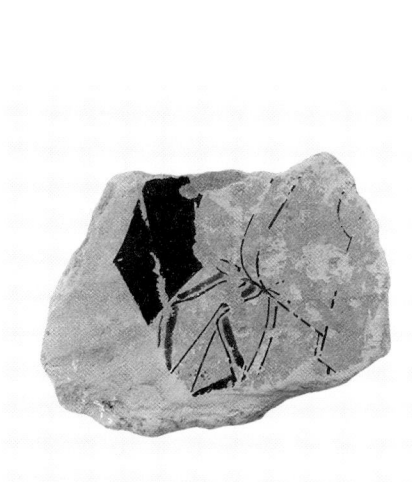

29

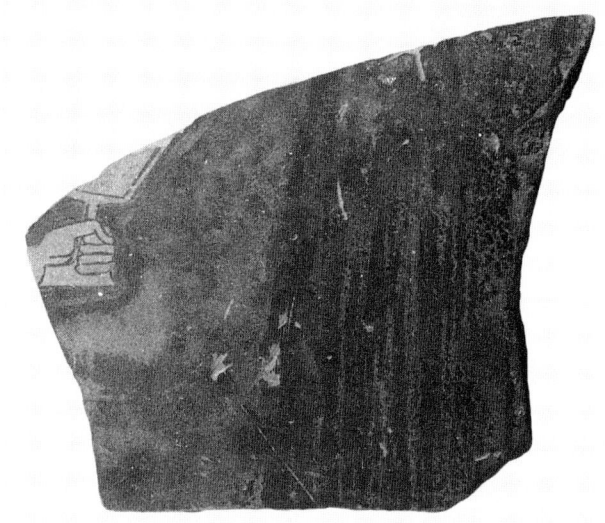

31

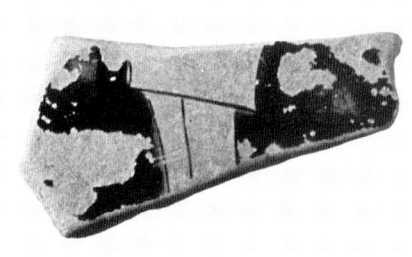

30

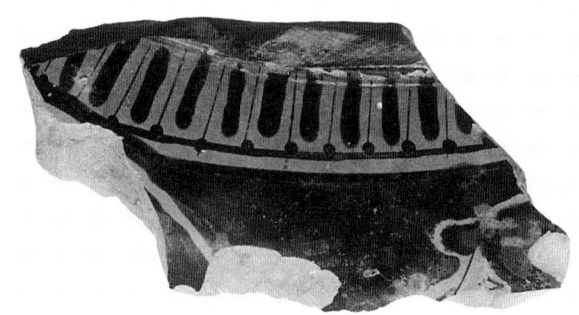

32

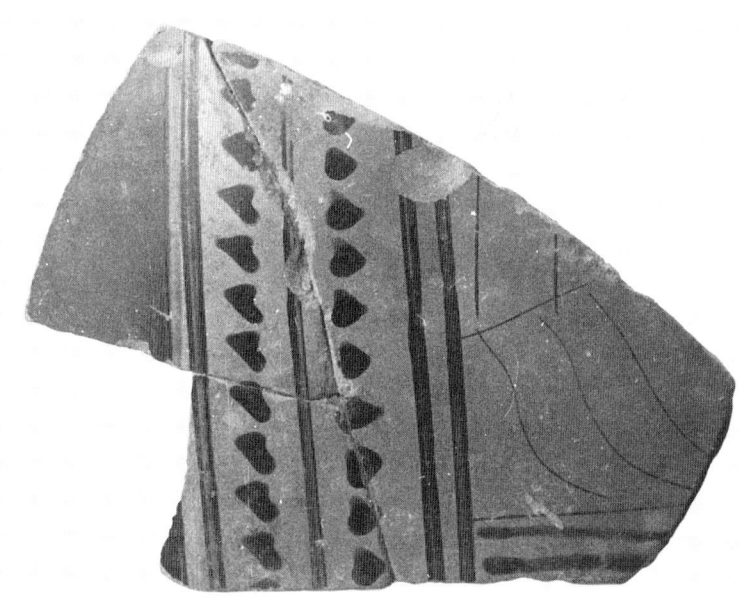

33

1:1

COLUMN-KRATERS (34–36) PLATE 21

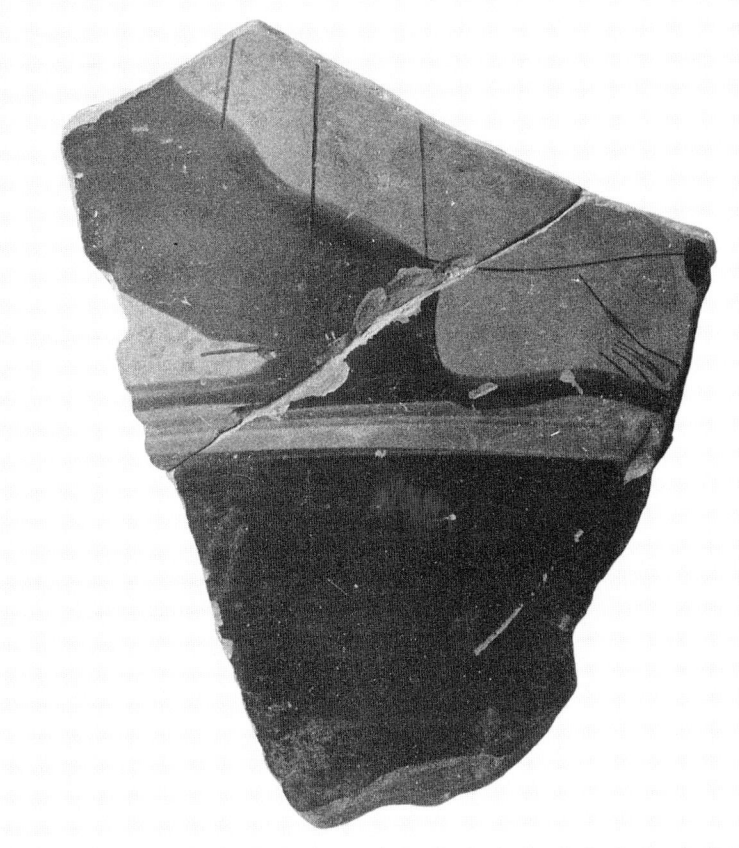

34

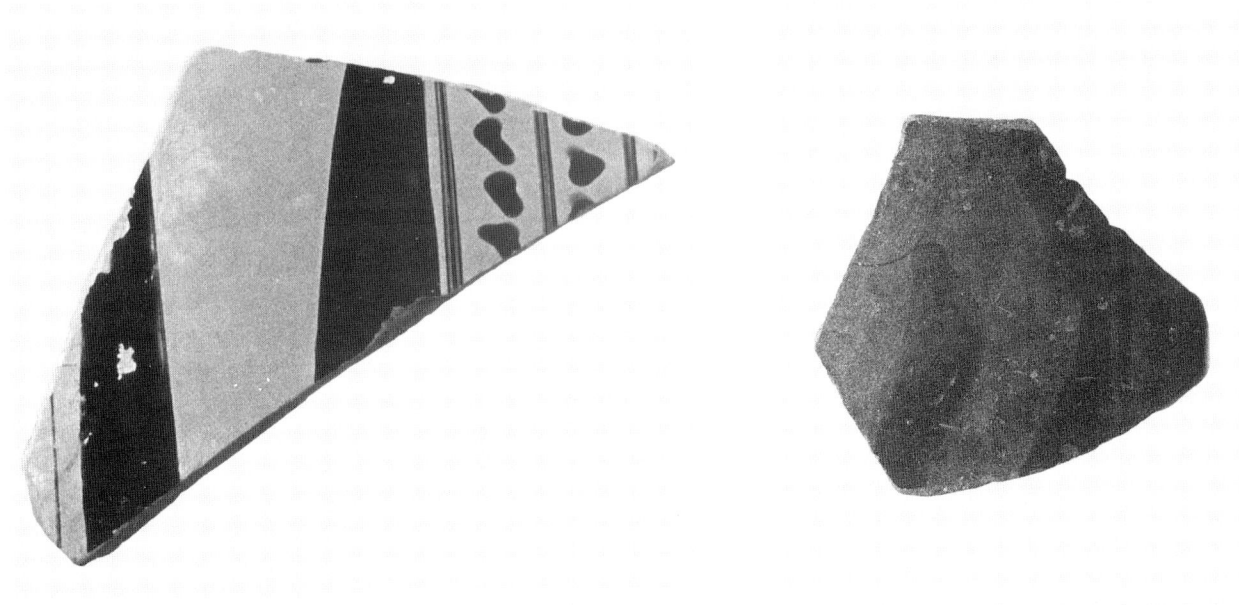

35

36

1:1

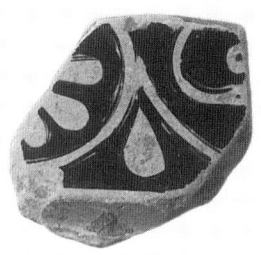

37

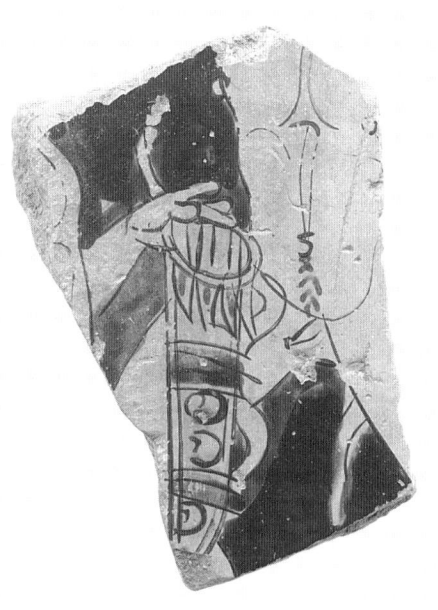

38 a

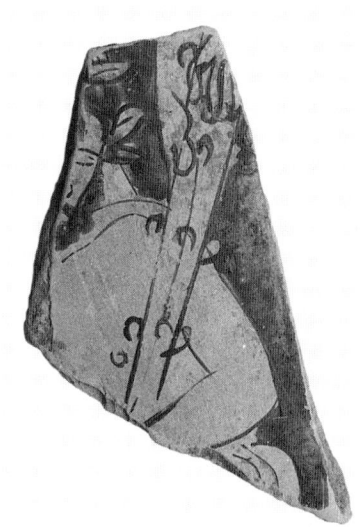

b

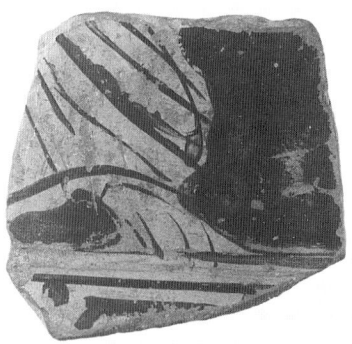

39

1:1

BELL-KRATERS (42–46) PLATE 23

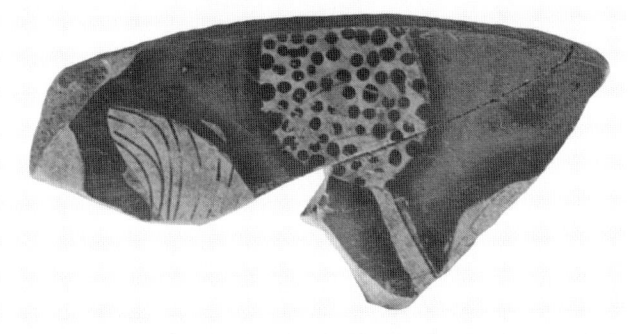

42

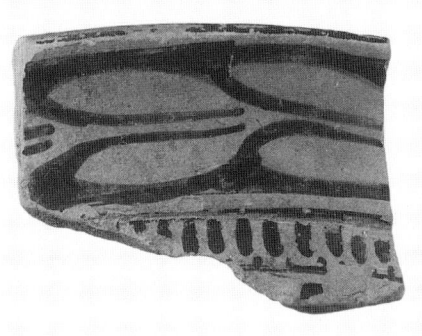

44

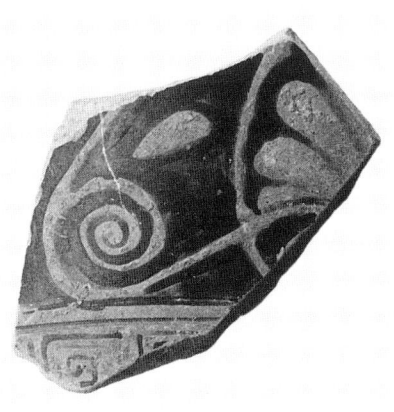

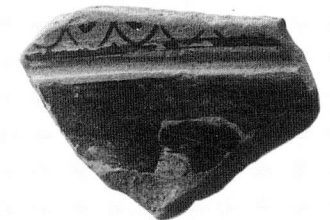

45 46

1:1

PLATE 24   BELL-KRATERS (*47A–E*)

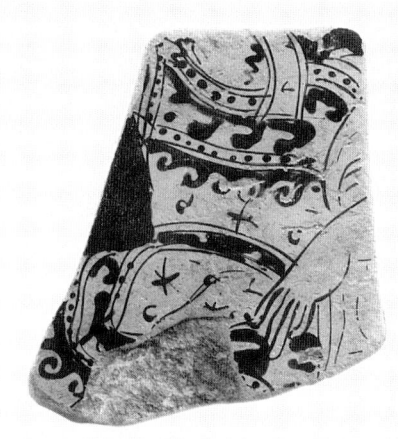

a

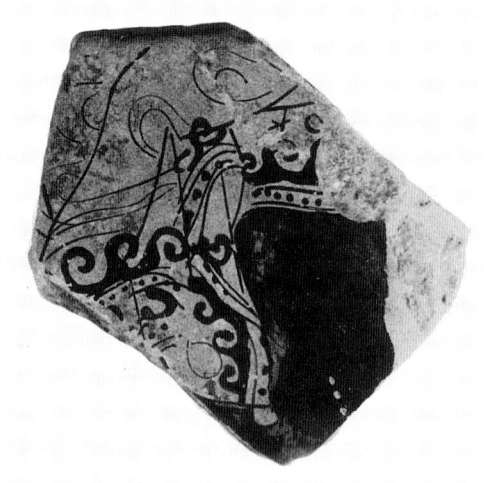

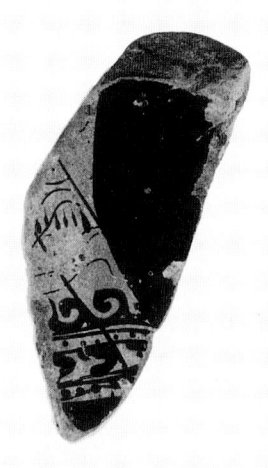

b   c

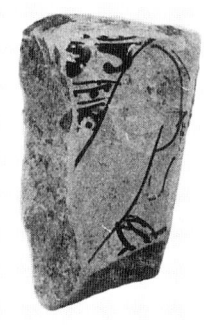

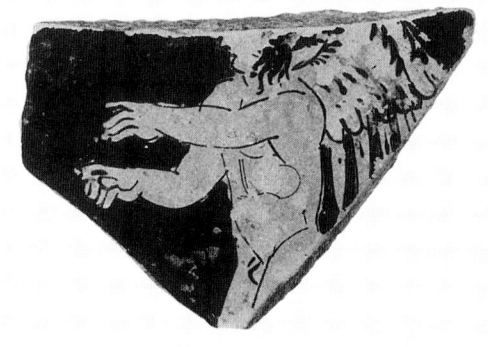

d   e

47

1:1

BELL-KRATER (*48A-G*) PLATE 25

PLATE 26 BELL-KRATERS (49–52)

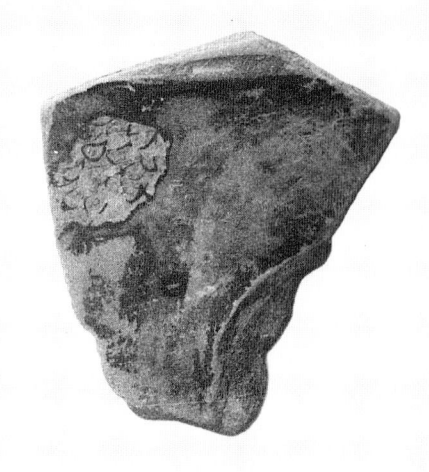

49

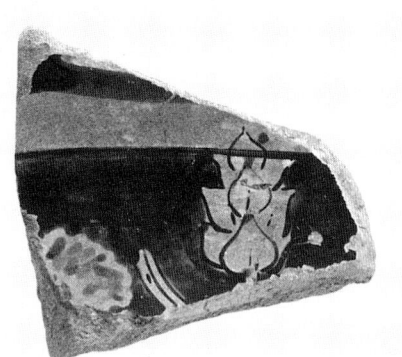

50

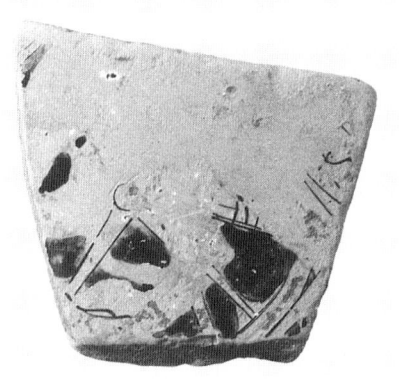

51

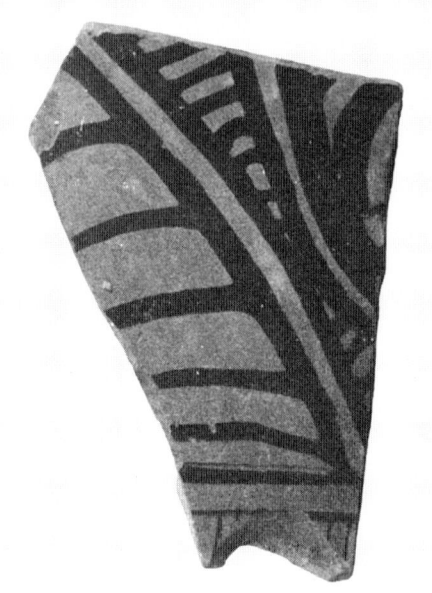

52

1:1

KRATERS (53–58)   PLATE 27

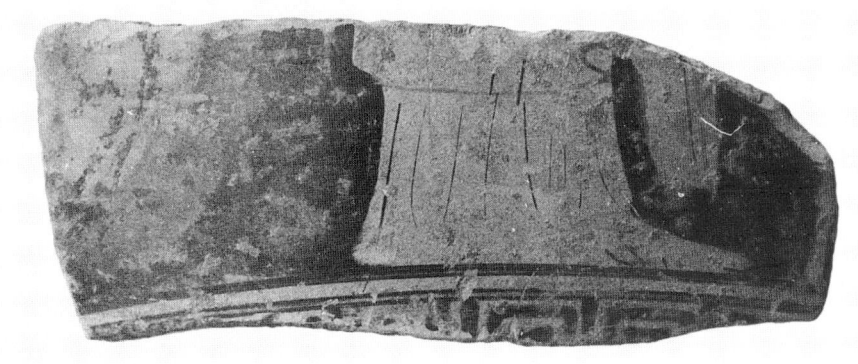

53

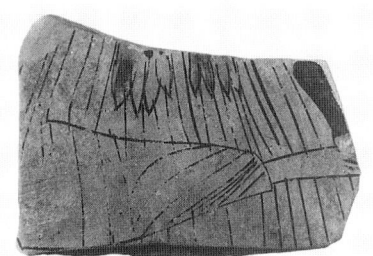

54

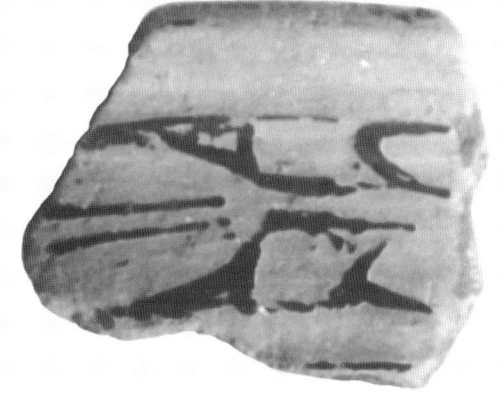

55

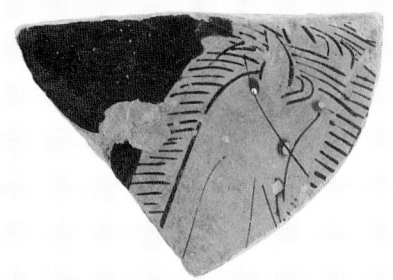

56

57

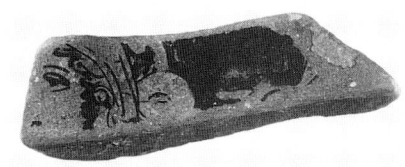

58

1:1

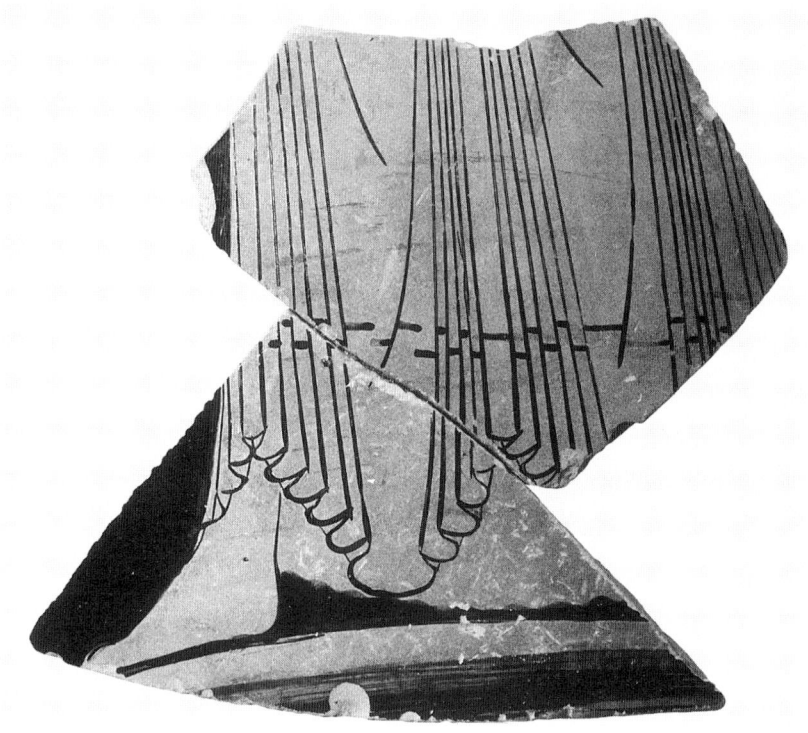

61

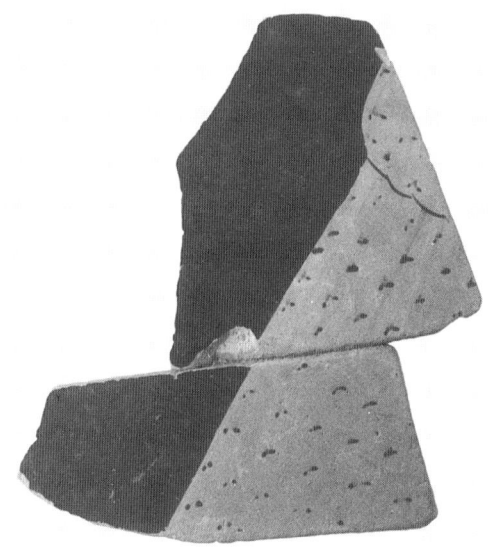

62

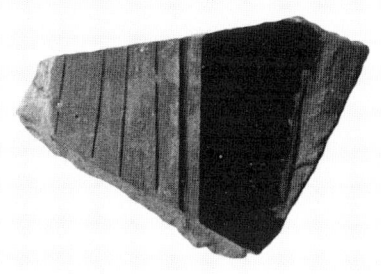

b

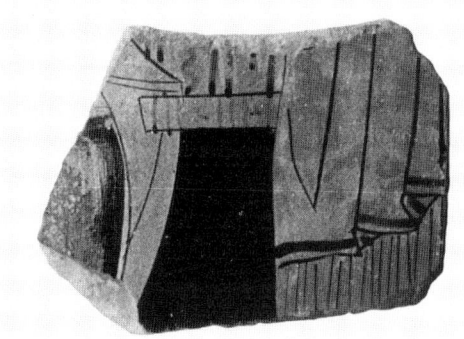

63 a

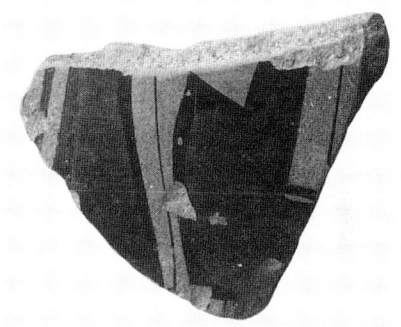

64

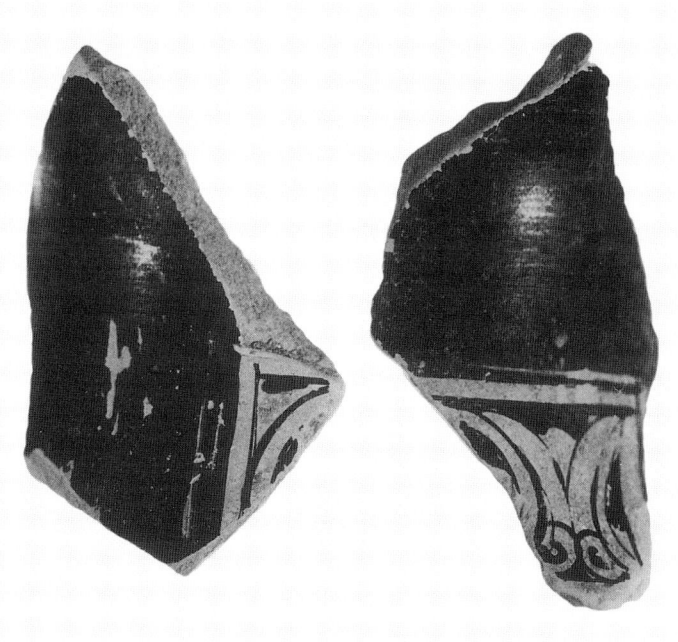

65

PLATE 30   HYDRIAI (66–68)

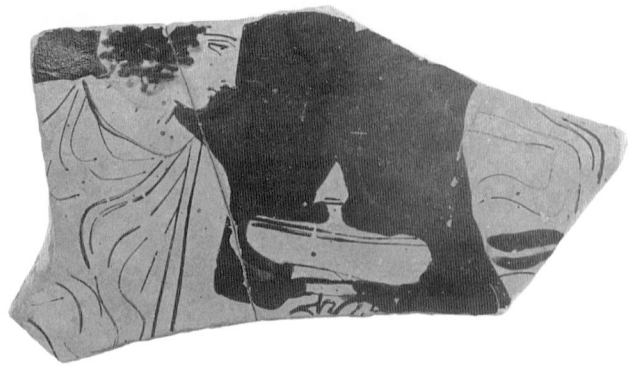

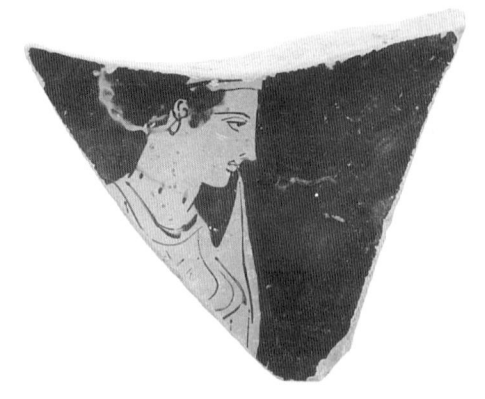

66

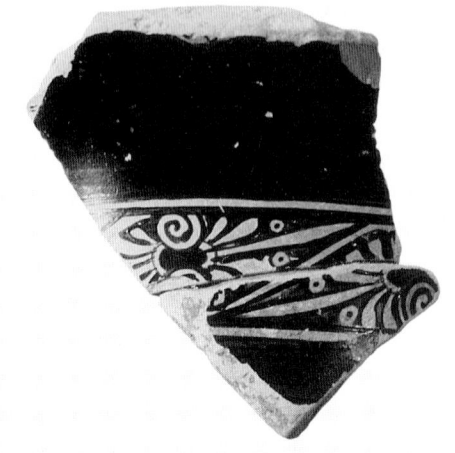

67

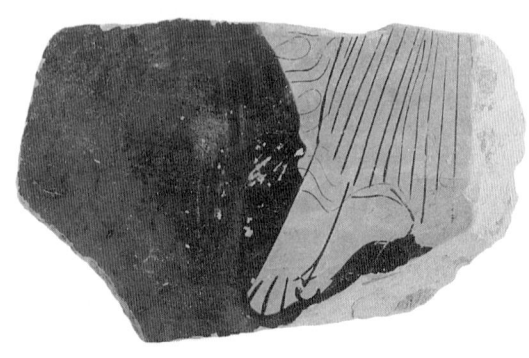

68

1:1

HYDRIAI (69–73) PLATE 31

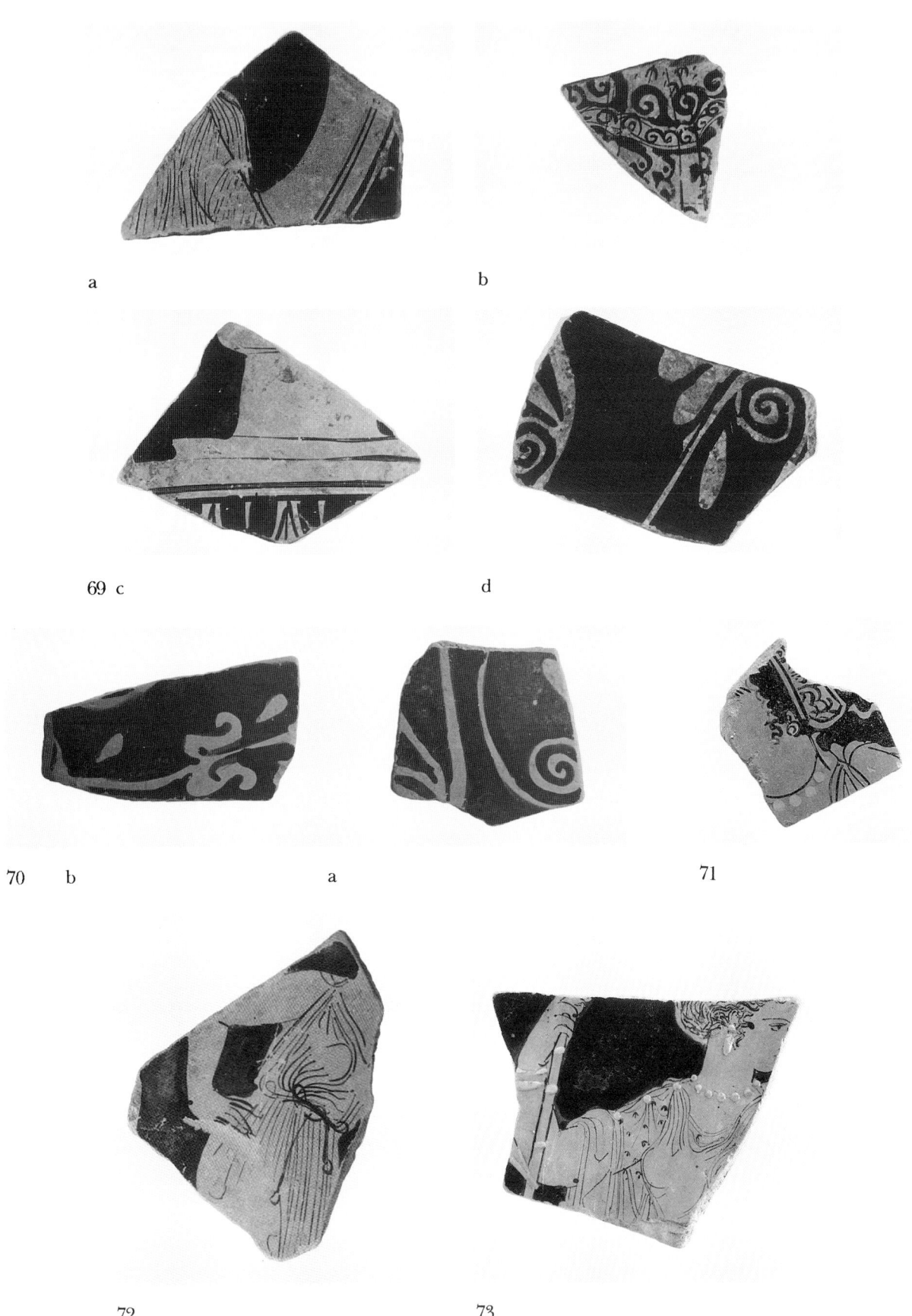

a b

69 c d

70 b a 71

72 73

1:1

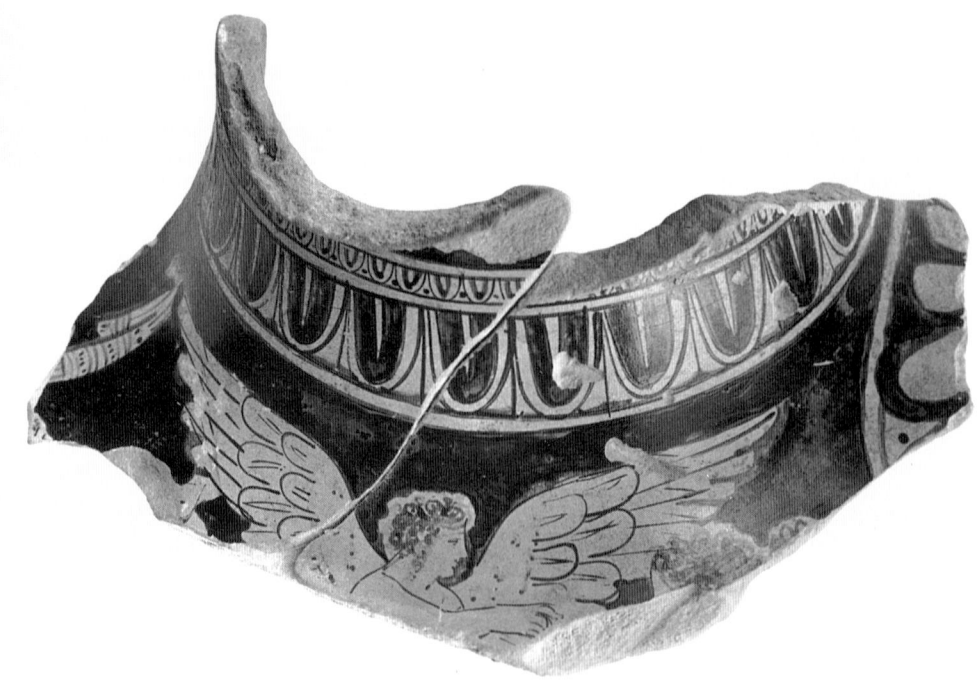

74

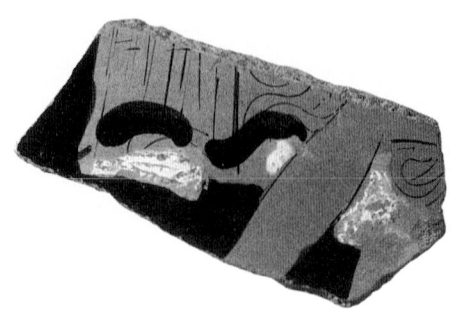

75

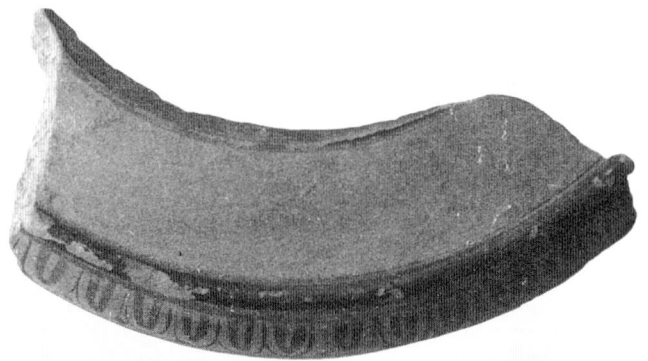

77

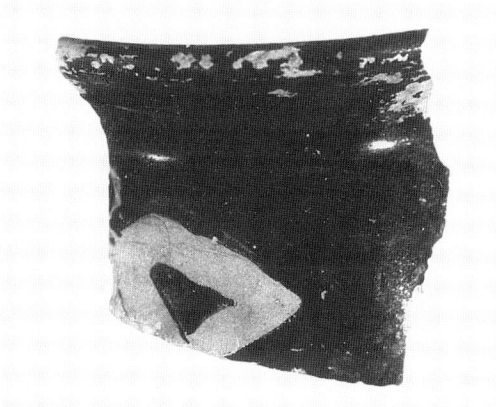

78

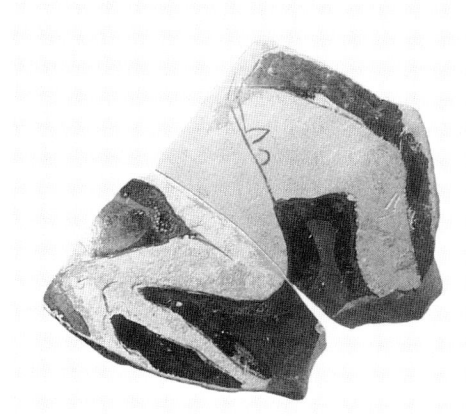
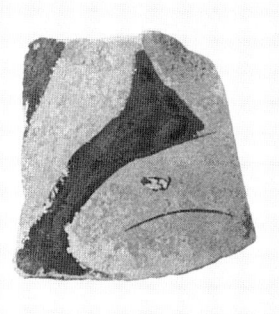

79 a b

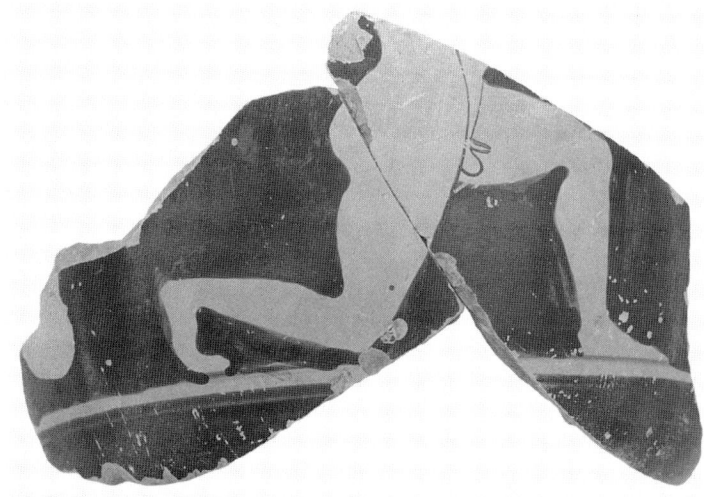
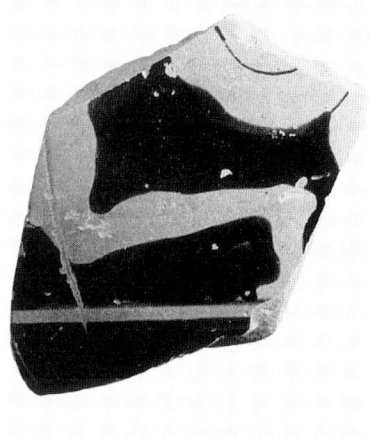

80 a b

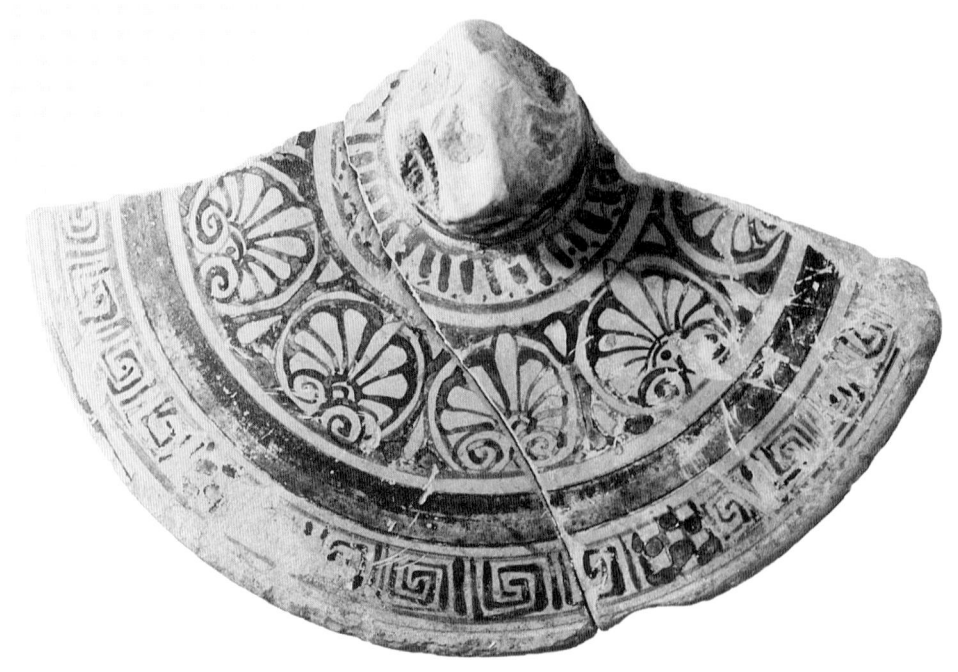

81

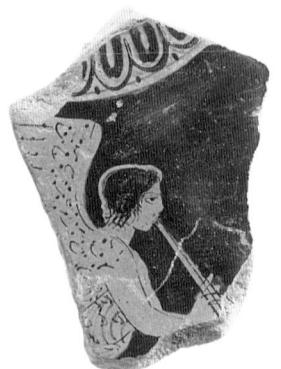

82

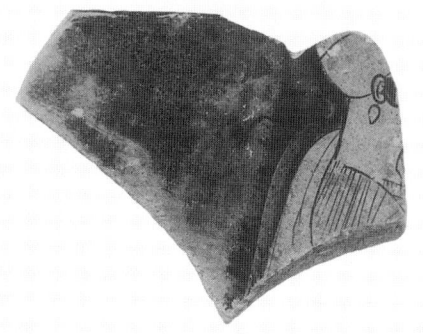

83

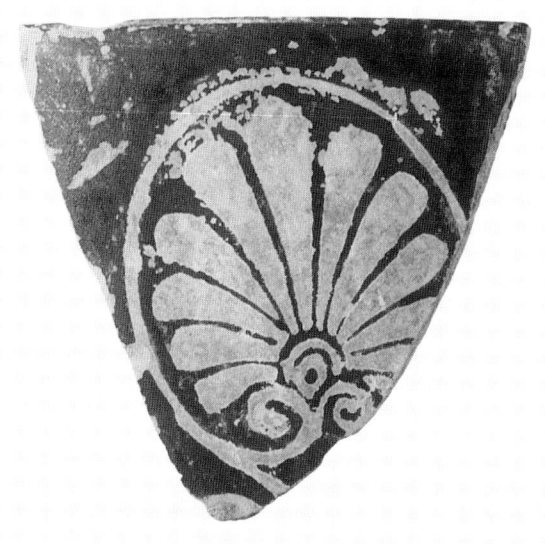

84

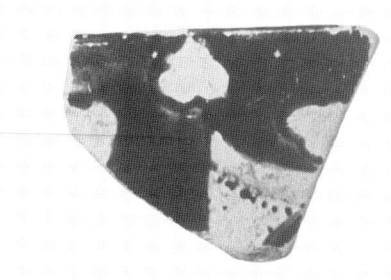

85

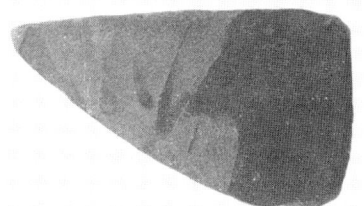

86

PLATE 36 SKYPHOS (87A–M)

3:4

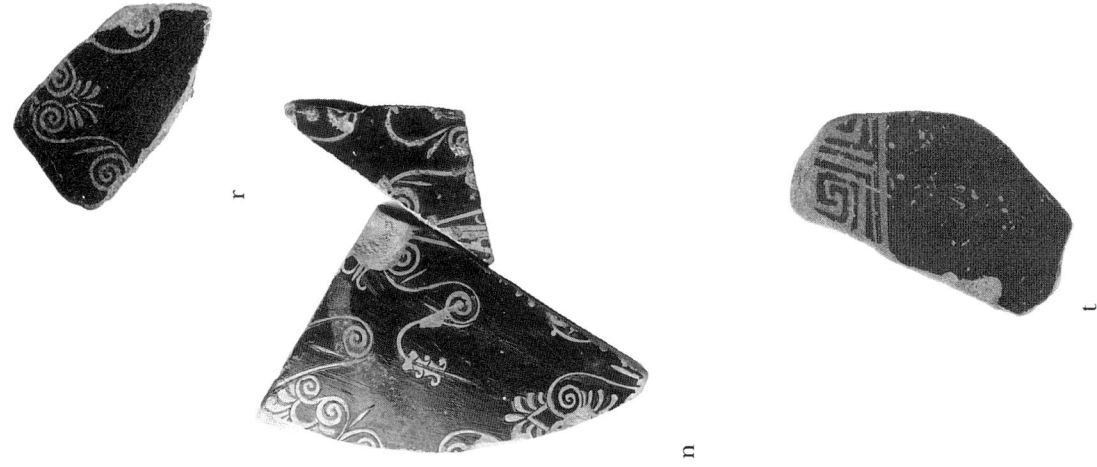
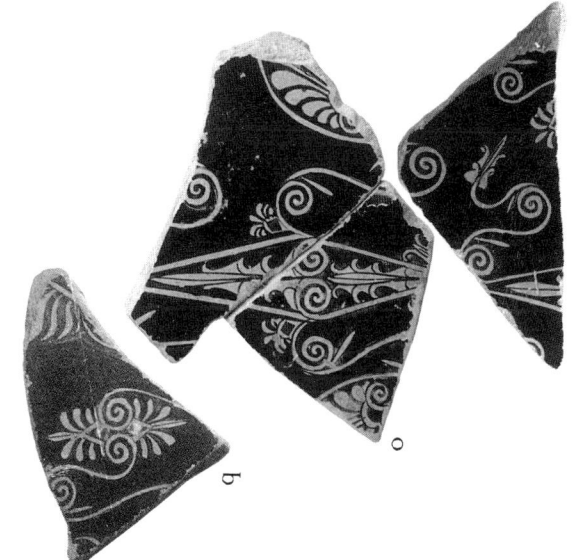
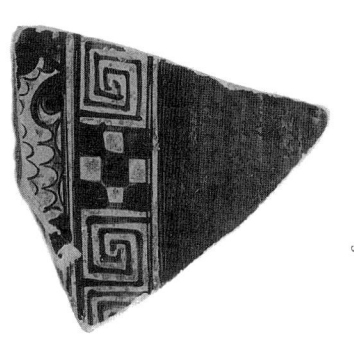

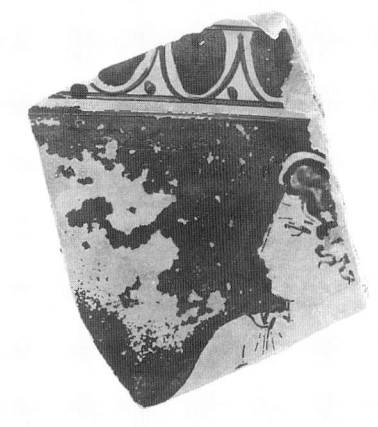

88

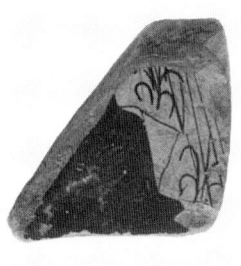

89

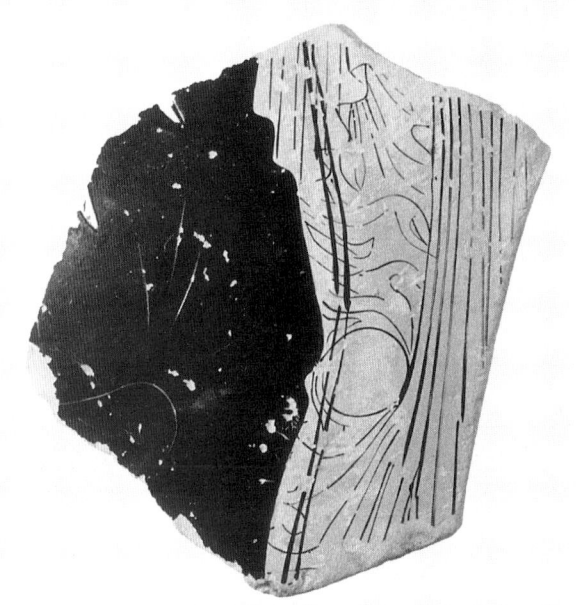

90

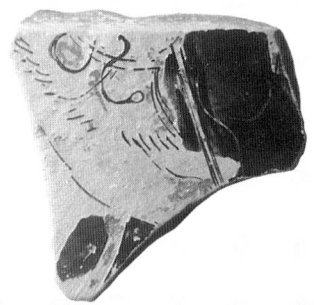

91

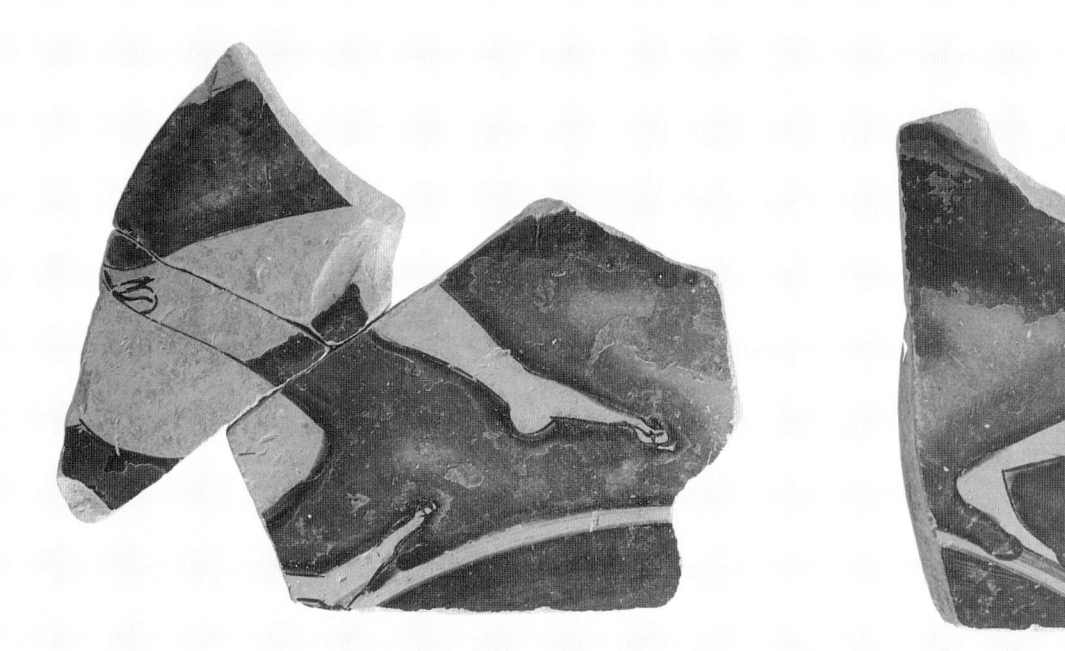

92

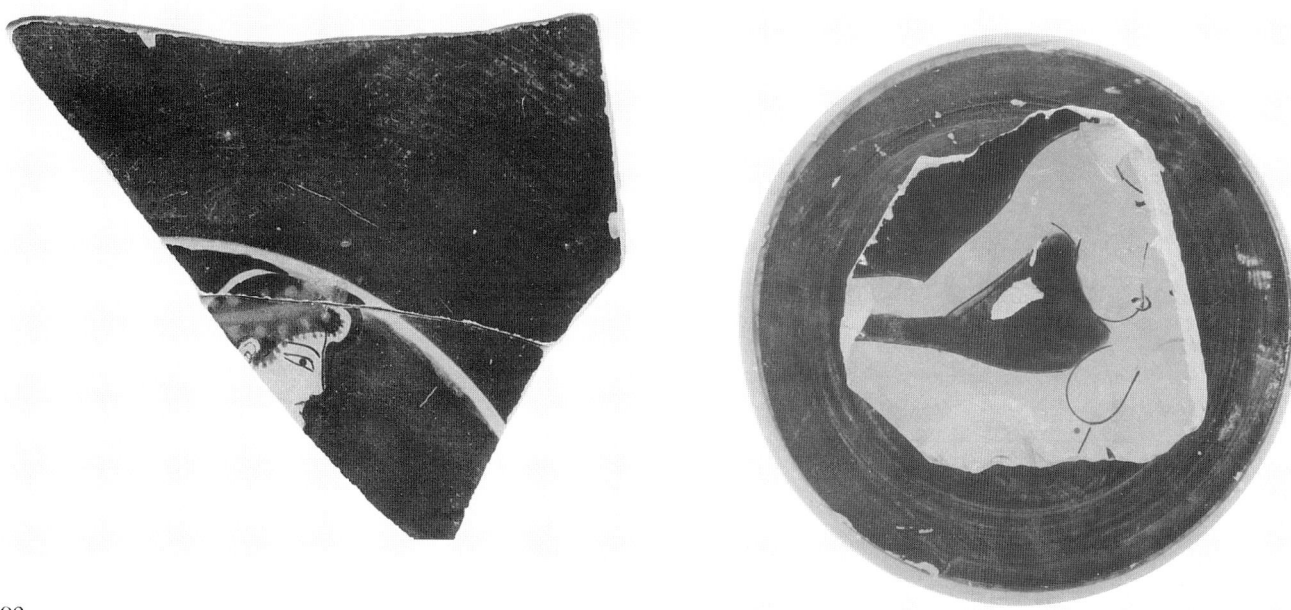

93

94

1:1

PLATE 40   CUPS (95–103)

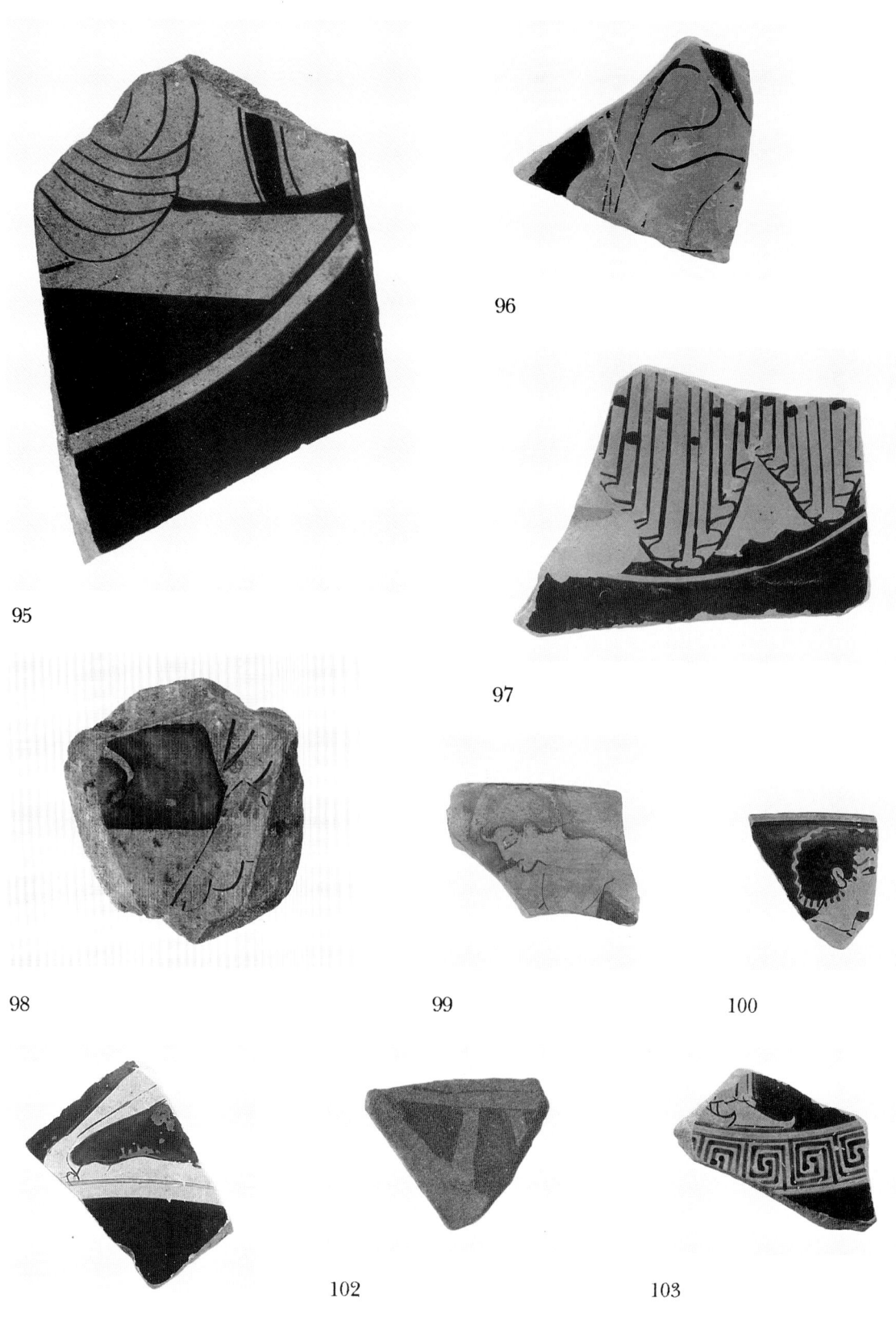

95

96

97

98   99   100

101   102   103

1:1

CUPS OR STEMLESS CUPS (105–107)

PLATE 41

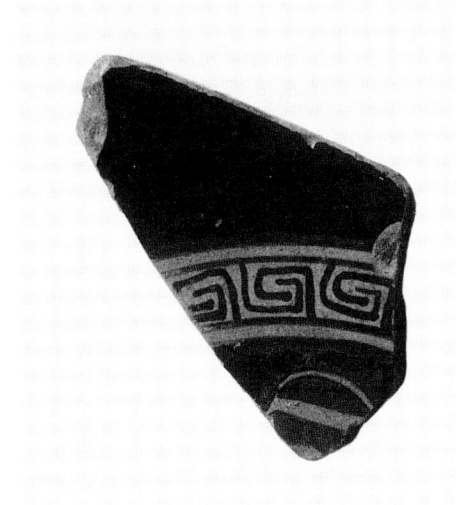

105

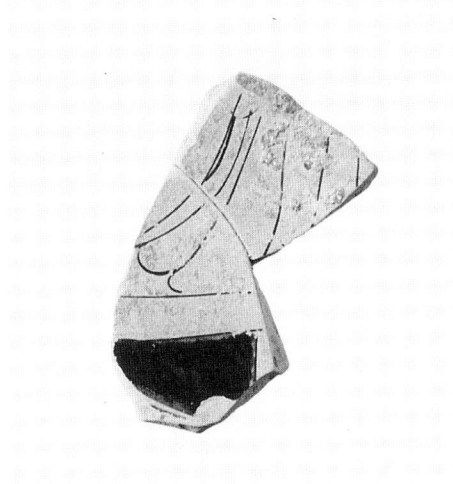

106

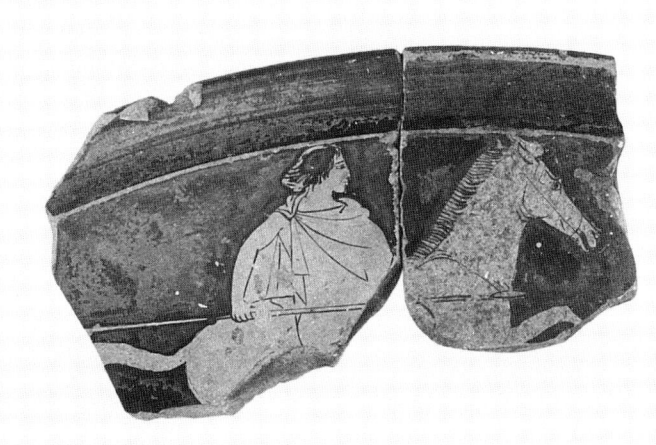

a

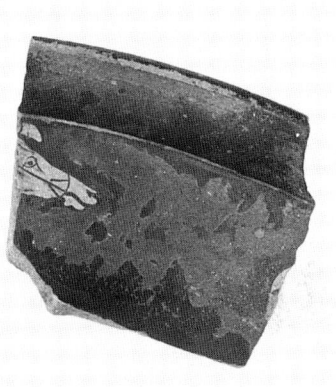

b

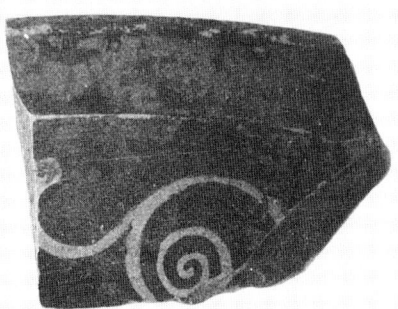

107   c

1:1

PLATE 42 CUPS OR STEMLESS CUPS, AND PLATES (*108–112*)

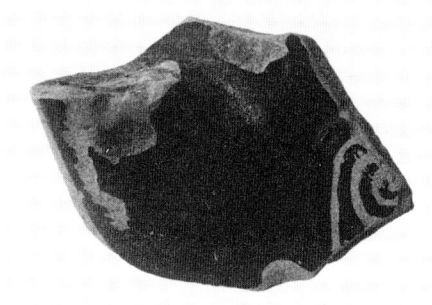

108

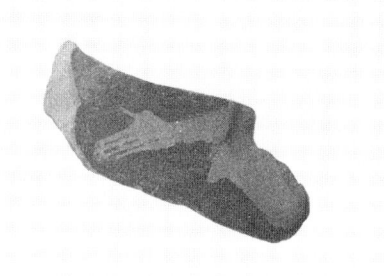

109

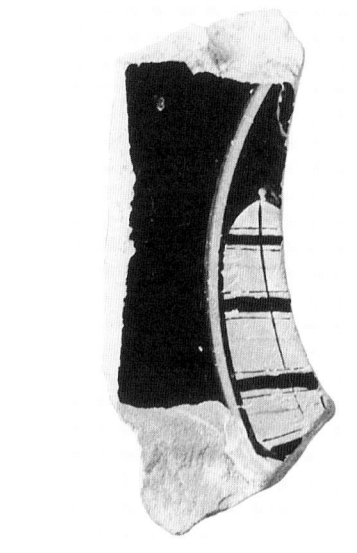

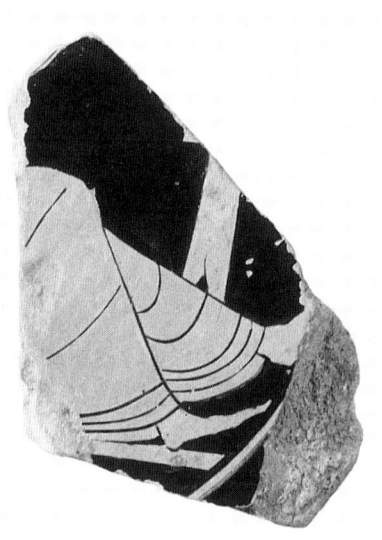

110

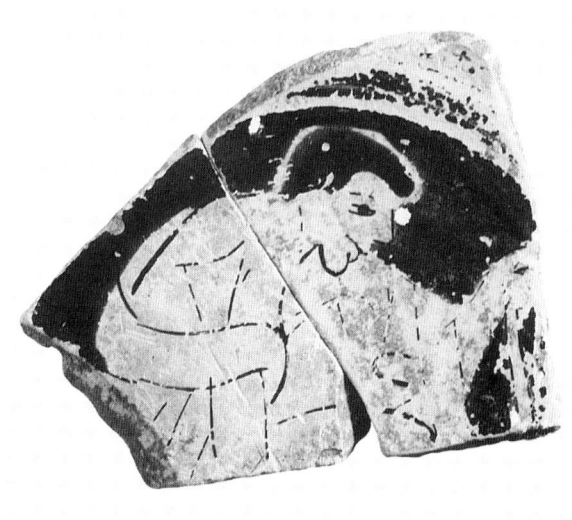

111

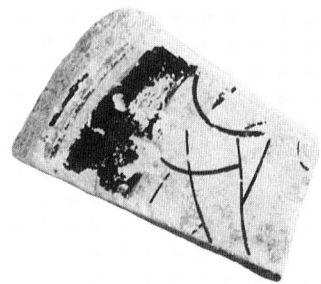

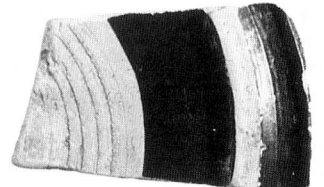

112

1:1

"CLOSED" SHAPES (113–116) PLATE 43

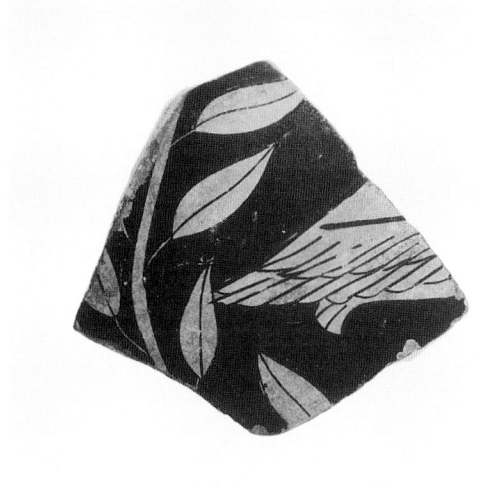

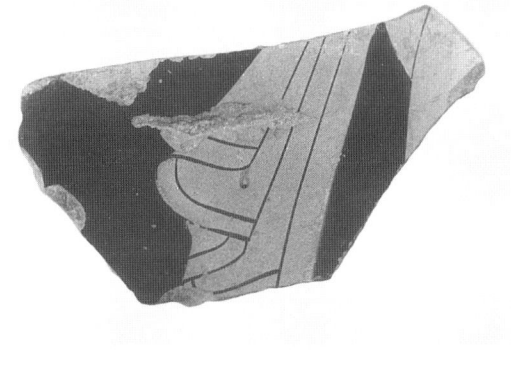

114

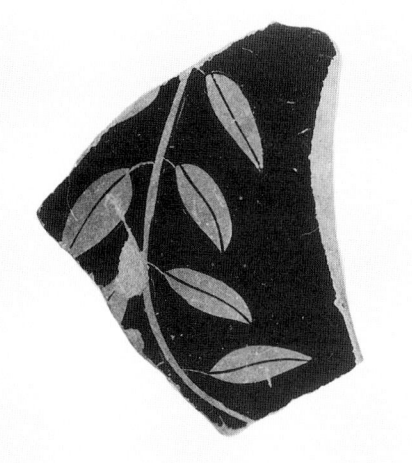

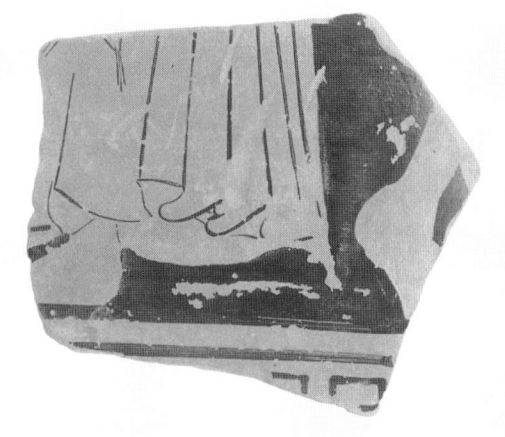

115

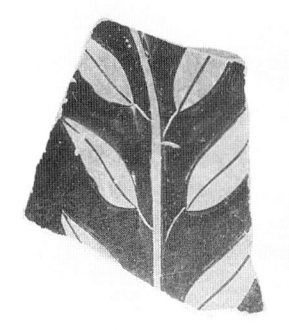

113 a,b,d

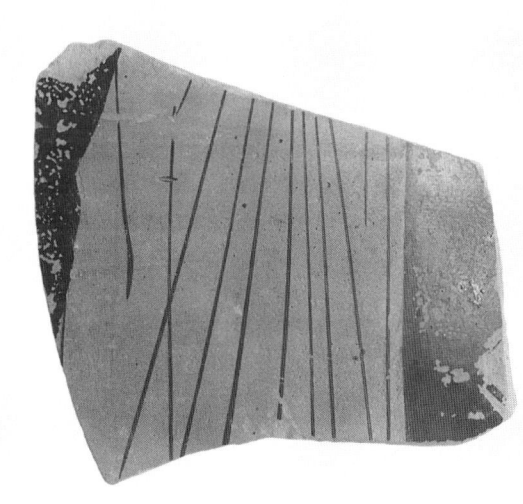

116

1:1

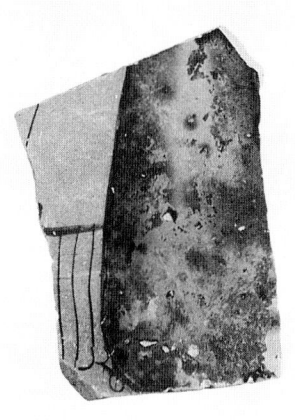

117

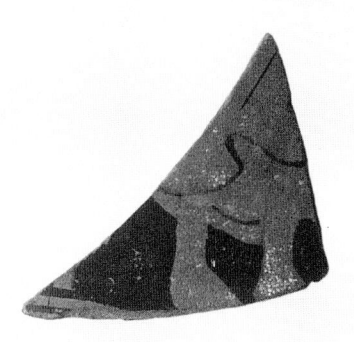

119

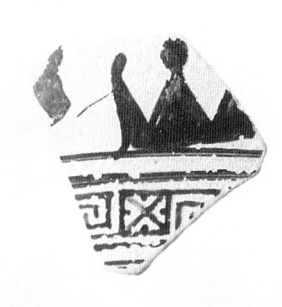

118

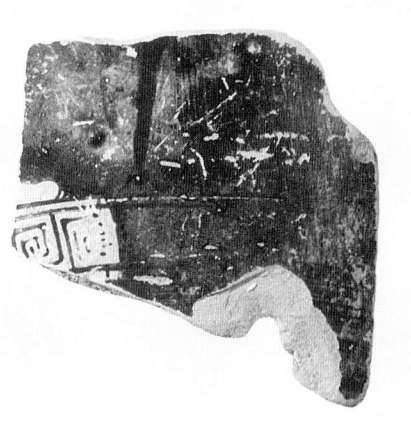

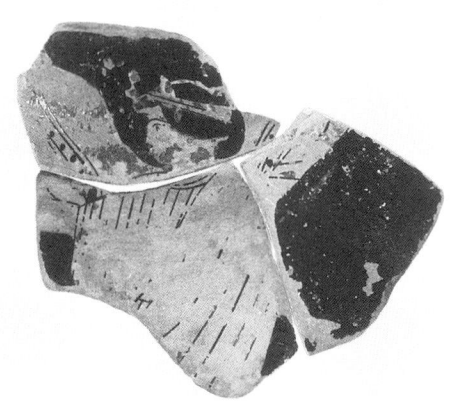

120

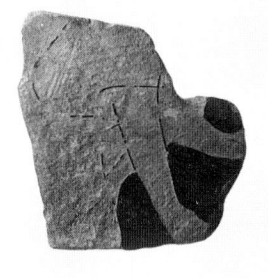

121

"CLOSED" SHAPES (122–124) PLATE 45

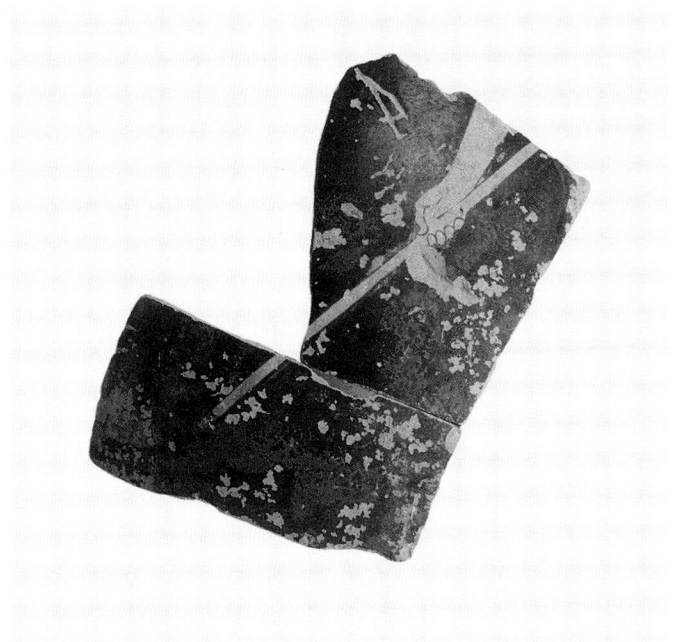

122

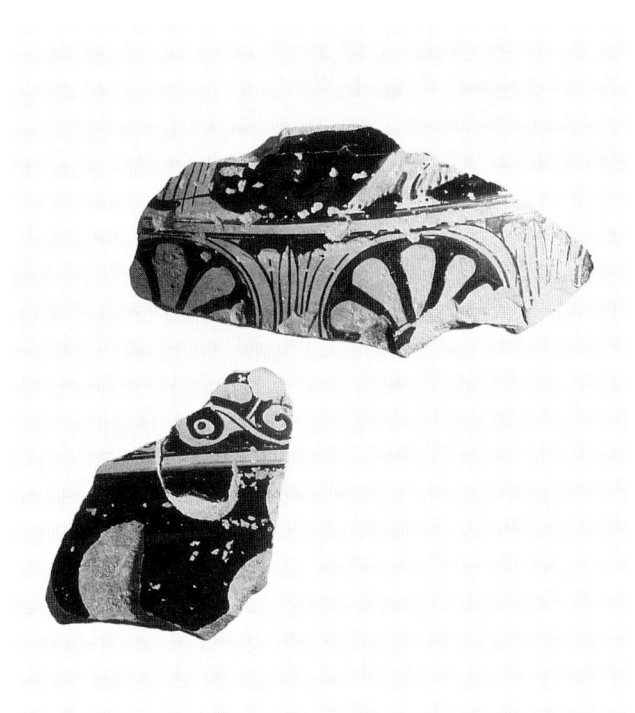

123

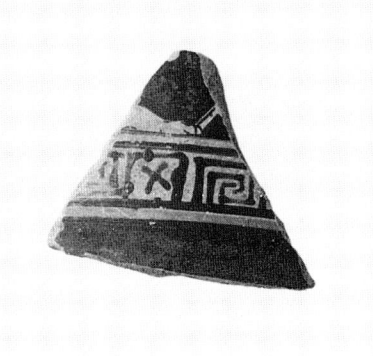

124

3:4

PLATE 46 "CLOSED" SHAPES (*125–129*)

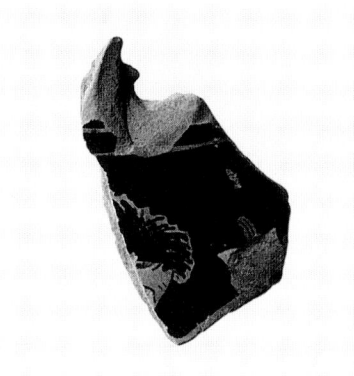

125

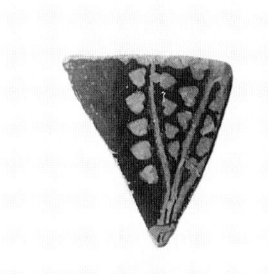

126

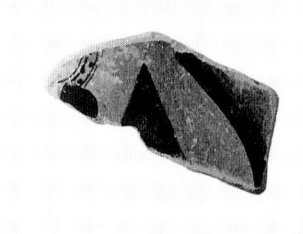

127

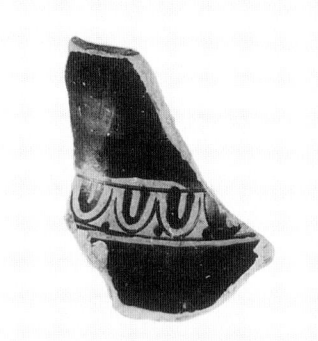

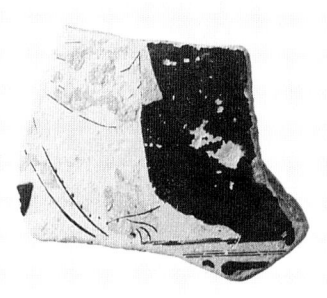

128

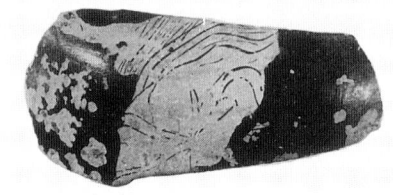

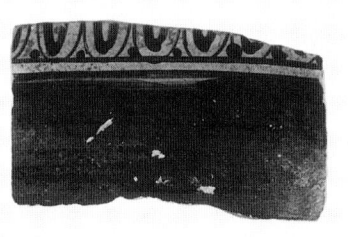

129 b,a,c

3:4

EPINETRA (130–132)

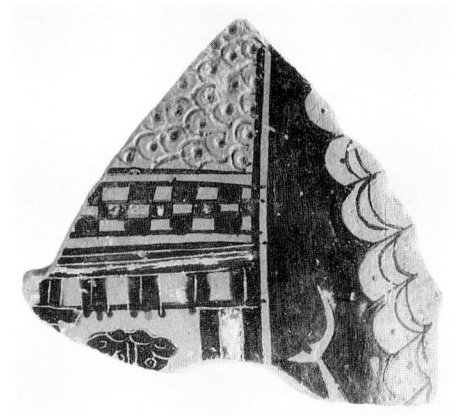

130

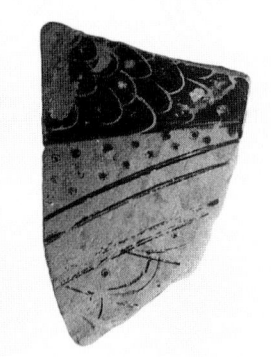

b

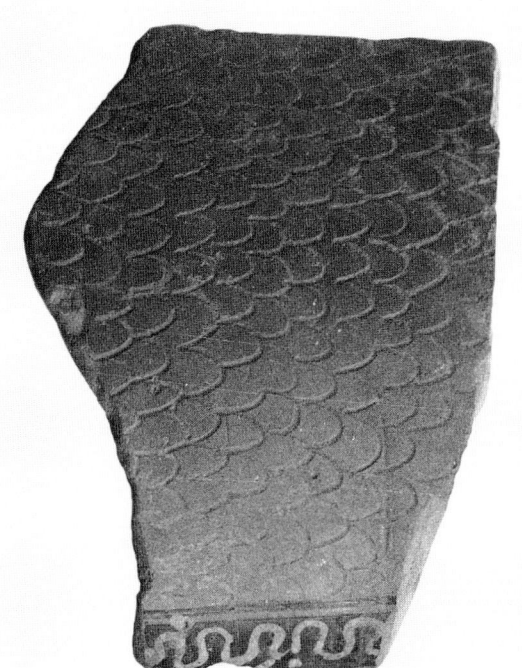

131 a

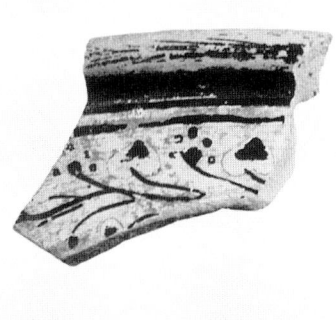

132 b

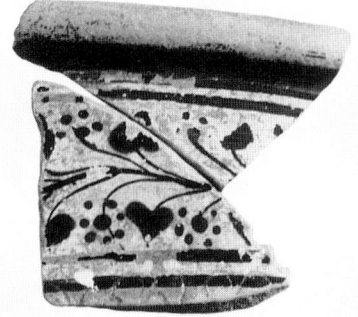

a

1:1

PLATE 48 ALABASTRON, PLASTIC AND RELIEF VASES, AND UNCERTAIN FABRIC (*133–138*)

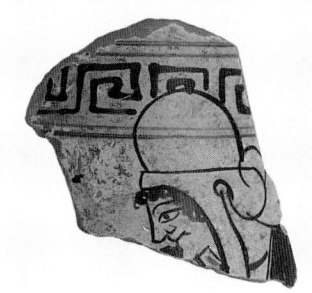

133 a

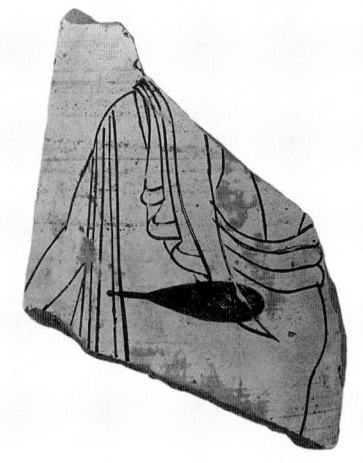

b

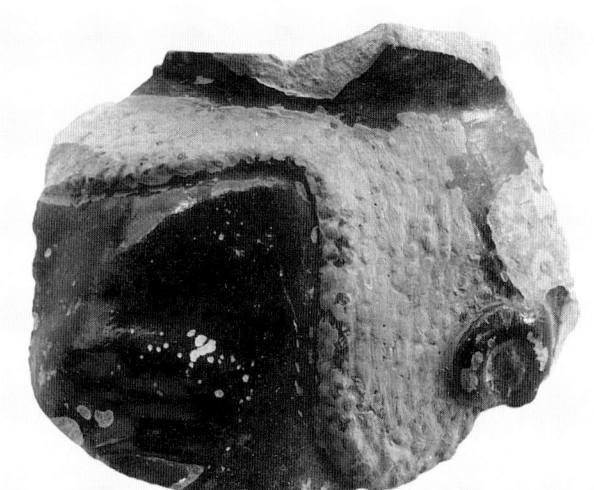

134

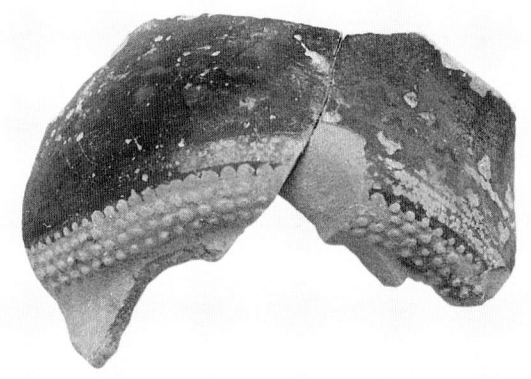

135

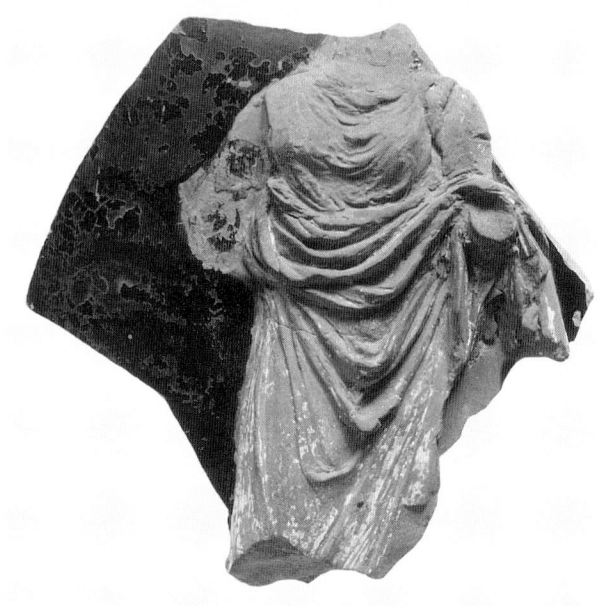

137

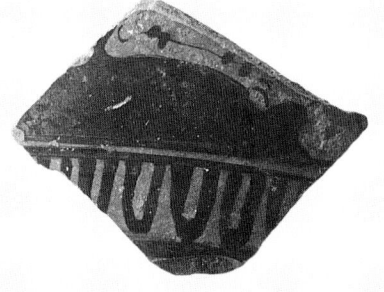

138

1:1

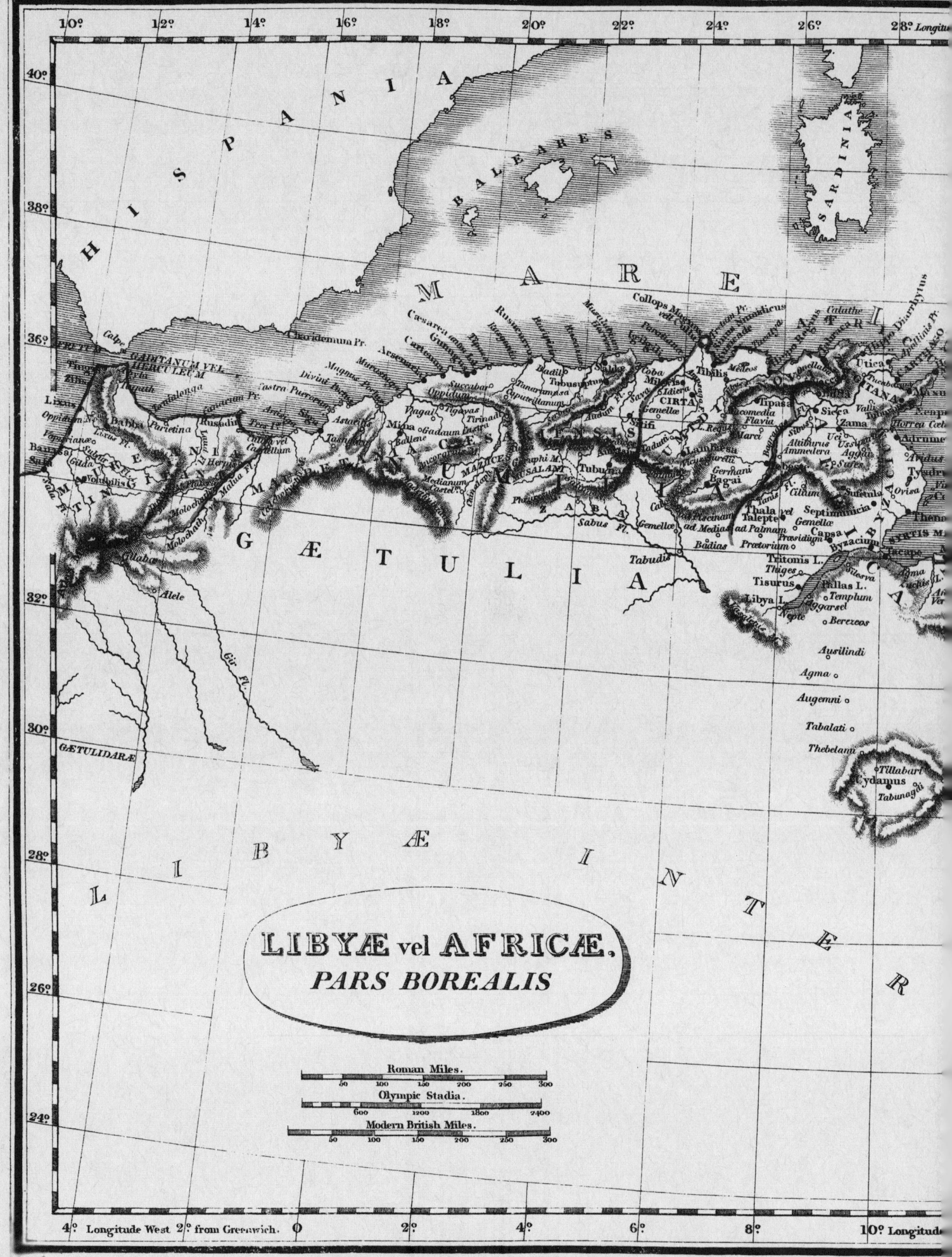